WITHDRAWN

A Global World ?

Re-ordering Political Space

The Shape of the World Course Team

The Open University

John Allen	Senior Lecturer in Economic Geography and Course Team Chair
James Anderson	Senior Lecturer in Geography
Robin Arkle	Graphic Designer, BBC
Melanie Bayley	Editor
Brian Beeley	Senior Lecturer in Geography
Pam Berry	Compositor, TPS
Gail Block	Assistant Producer, BBC
John Blunden	Reader in Geography
Chris Brook	Lecturer in Geography
Margaret Charters	Course Secretary
Allan Cochrane	Senior Lecturer in Urban Studies
Debbie Crouch	Graphic Designer
Stuart Hall	Professor of Sociology
Chris Hamnett	Professor of Urban Geography
Fiona Harris	Editor
Christina Janoszka	Course Manager
Pat Jess	Lecturer in Geography
Jack Leathem	Producer, BBC
Michèle Marsh	Secretary
Doreen Massey	Professor of Geography
Anthony McGrew	Senior Lecturer in Politics
Diane Mole	Graphic Designer
Eleanor Morris	Series Producer, BBC
Ray Munns	Graphic Artist
Judith Rolph	Series Production Assistant, BBC
Philip Sarre	Senior Lecturer in Geography
Paul Smith	Media Librarian
Doreen Warwick	Discipline Secretary
Kathy Wilson	Production Assistant, BBC
Chris Wooldridge	Editor

External Assessor

Nigel Thrift	Professor of Geography, University of Bristol

Consultants

Rick Ball	Tutor Panel
Erlet Cater	Lecturer in Geography, University of Reading
Ray Hall	Senior Lecturer in Geography, University of London
Russell King	Professor of Geography, University of Sussex
Andrew Leyshon	Lecturer in Geography, University of Hull
Matthew Lockwood	Lecturer in Sociology, University of Sussex
Jenny Meegan	Tutor Panel
Richard Meegan	Senior Lecturer in Geography, University of Liverpool
Phil Pinch	Tutor Panel
Gillian Rose	Lecturer in Geography, University of Edinburgh
Steven Yearley	Professor of Sociology, University of Ulster

The Shape of the World: Explorations in Human Geography

Volume 1: Geographical Worlds

Edited by John Allen and Doreen Massey

Volume 2: A Shrinking World? Global Unevenness and Inequality

Edited by John Allen and Chris Hamnett

Volume 3: An Overcrowded World? Population, Resources and the Environment

Edited by Philip Sarre and John Blunden

Volume 4: A Place in the World? Places, Cultures and Globalization

Edited by Doreen Massey and Pat Jess

Volume 5: A Global World? Re-ordering Political Space

Edited by James Anderson, Chris Brook and Allan Cochrane

A Global World ?

Re-ordering Political Space

edited by
James Anderson, Chris Brook and Allan Cochrane

WITHDRAWN

The Open University OXFORD

The five volumes of the series form part of the second-level Open University course D215 *The Shape of the World*. If you wish to study this or any other Open University course, details can be obtained from the Central Enquiry Service, PO Box 200, The Open University, Milton Keynes, MK7 6YZ.

For availability of the video- and audiocassette materials, contact Open University Educational Enterprises Ltd (OUEE), 12 Cofferidge Close, Stony Stratford, Milton Keynes, MK11 1BY.

Oxford University Press, Walton Street, Oxford OX2 6DP
Oxford   New York
Athens   Auckland   Bangkok   Bombay
Calcutta   Cape Town   Dar es Salaam   Delhi
Florence   Hong Kong   Istanbul   Karachi
Kuala Lumpur   Madras   Madrid   Melbourne
Mexico City   Nairobi   Paris   Singapore
Taipei   Tokyo   Toronto
and associated companies in
Berlin   Ibadan

Oxford is a trade mark of Oxford University Press

Published in the United States
by Oxford University Press Inc., New York

Published in association with The Open University

First published 1995

Edited, designed and typeset by The Open University

Printed and bound in Great Britain by
Butler and Tanner Ltd. Frome and London

A catalogue record for this book is available from the British Library

Library of Congress Cataloguing in Publication Data applied for

ISBN 0 19 874193 6 (paper)

ISBN 0 19 874192 8 (cloth)

10121C/d215v5pi1.1

A Global World?
Re-ordering Political Space

Contents

Preface

A Global World? Re-ordering Political Space is the last of five volumes in a new series of human geography teaching texts. The series, entitled *The Shape of the World: Explorations in Human Geography* is designed as an introduction to the principal themes of geographical thought: namely, those of space, place and the environment. The five volumes form the central part of an Open University course, with the same title as that of the series. Each volume, however, is free-standing and can be studied on its own or as part of a wide range of social science courses in universities and colleges.

The series is built around an exploration of many of the key issues which are shaping our world as we move into the twenty-first century and which, above all else, are geographical in character. Each volume in various ways engages with taken-for-granted notions such as those of nature, distance, movement, sustainability, the identity of places and local cultures to put together what may be referred to as the building blocks of our geographical imagination.

In fact, our understanding of the nature of the geographical imagination is one of three shared features which distinguish the five volumes as a series. In developing the contribution that geography can make to our understanding of a changing world and our place within it, each volume has something distinct to offer. A second feature of the volumes is that the majority of chapters include a number of selected readings – extracts drawn from books and articles – which relate closely to the line of argument and which are integral to the discussion as it develops. The relevant readings can be found at the end of the chapter to which they relate and are printed in two columns to distinguish them from the main teaching text. The third shared feature of the volumes is the student-orientated nature of the teaching materials. Each volume is intended as part of an interactive form of study, with activities and summaries built into the flow of the text. These features are intended to help readers to grasp, consider and retain the main ideas and arguments of each chapter. The wide margins – in which you will find highlighted the concepts that are key to the teaching – are also intended for student use, such as making notes and points for reflection.

While each book is self-contained, there are a number of references back (and a small number of references forward) to the other books in the series. For those readers who wish to use the books as an exploration in human geography, you will find the references to chapters in the other volumes printed in bold type. This is particularly relevant to the final chapters of Volumes 2–5 as they form a sequence of chapters designed to highlight the uneven character of global development today. On a related teaching point, we have sometimes referred to the group of less developed and developing countries by the term 'third world', in inverted commas to convey the difficulty of continuing to include the diverse range of countries – which embraces some rapidly industrializing nations – under this conventional category. The 'disappearance' of a second world, with the demise of the Communist bloc, also questions the usefulness of the category and, in one way, simply reaffirms the significance of the world's changing geography.

Finally, it remains only to thank those who have helped to shape this Open University course. The names of those responsible for the production of this course are given in the list of Course Team members on page *ii*. Of those, we would like to extend our thanks to a number in particular. It is fair to say that the course would not have had the shape that it does were it not for the breadth of intellectual scholarship provided by our external assessor, Professor Nigel Thrift. Over a two-year period, Nigel, among other activities, commented and offered constructive advice on every draft chapter discussed by the Course Team – in all, some eighty-plus drafts! The Course Team owe him a major debt. We also owe a special debt to our Tutor Panel – Rick Ball, Jenny Meegan and Phil Pinch – for their ceaseless concern that the teaching materials were precisely that: materials which actually do teach. Our editors at the Open University, Melanie Bayley and Fiona Harris, not only raised the professional standard of the series as a whole with their meticulous editing, they also became involved at an early stage in the Course's life and thus were able to smooth the path of its development. Thanks also to Ray Munns for his cartographic zeal and to Paul Smith, our media librarian, who, as ever, translated our vague descriptions of this or that image into an impressive array of illustrations. The typographic design and initial cover idea were developed by Diane Mole who then relinquished the course to Debbie Crouch; their expertise has transformed our typescripts into this handsome series of volumes. The speed and accuracy with which the multiple drafts were turned round by Margaret Charters and Doreen Warwick also deserves our special thanks. Without their excellent secretarial support, the course would not be in any shape at all.

Lastly, in the collaborative style of work by which Open University courses are produced, the awesome task of co-ordinating the efforts of the Course Team and ensuring that the materials are produced to schedule, falls to the course manager. It is still a source of amazement to us how our course manager, Christina Janoszka, managed this task as if it were no task at all. We owe her probably more than she is aware.

John Allen
on behalf of
The Open University Course Team

Introduction

We live in interesting times. The world is changing before our eyes in ways which are often unexpected, exciting or disturbing. And our own positions within it also seem to be increasingly uncertain and changeable. Earlier volumes in this series have identified some key features associated with the changes we are experiencing – sometimes summarized in notions such as 'time–space compression' and a 'shrinking world'. They have, for example, looked at economic and environmental implications and considered the possibility of a 'borderless world' (see **Allen and Hamnett, 1995**[*]); they have highlighted some of the difficulties of achieving sustainable development, in the context of changing patterns of population growth and migration and the continuing search for natural resources (**Sarre and Blunden, 1995**); and they have shown how the places in which we live can only be understood by locating them within much wider sets of relationships which stretch across the globe (**Massey and Jess, 1995**). Above all, they show the unevenness of global change and the contested nature of its representations (see also **Allen and Massey, 1995**).

This immediately raises the question posed in our title: *A Global World?* Do these changes add up to a world in which all the most important processes operate at a global scale? What do the changes mean for the ways in which everyday life is experienced by different people? What sorts of political re-ordering are likely to take place in response to the major economic and social changes associated with globalization? And what sorts of political movements are likely to be most successful in influencing or challenging the direction of these changes? These questions underlie many of the debates discussed in this volume.

For some people – at least for those who are better off and live in the richer parts of the world – globalization may be experienced as a substantial expansion of opportunities. Many people are enjoying things undreamt of only a generation ago. 'The world', it seems, 'is their oyster', as they take package holidays to the tropics, watch international satellite television and key into the communication networks of the 'global village' and 'information superhighway'. But for many others, probably a majority of the world's population, times are difficult, dangerous and sometimes downright catastrophic. They may know little of the world beyond their own village or neighbourhood, even as their lives and localities are stunted or turned upside down by forces operating beyond their local horizons. Not for them the 'brave new world' of high-tech globe-trotting and jet-setting, more likely the fear or reality of unemployment, starvation or war.

They would understand that the Chinese salutation 'May you live in interesting times' is indeed a curse – it rules out times which are boringly predictable but also safe and secure. Even the fortunate minority currently enjoying the interesting times may wonder how long can it last. As far as they are concerned, many spatial barriers have been lowered or overcome, and it seems that in purely technological terms almost all the world's problems could be solved, despite the forebodings about economic disaster and social breakdown. But the threat of unemployment and redundancy is never far

[*] A reference in emboldened type denotes another volume, or a chapter in another volume, of the series.

away, even for the most apparently successful of business executives, while being an international tourist also seems to be getting more dangerous, in Florida as well as in Egypt. There is little consolation in the questionable assertion that 'everywhere is becoming the same' – if that were the case, why bother to travel anyway? At the same time as spatial barriers are coming down for some people, other barriers are going up, as immigrant workers facing the border controls of 'Fortress Europe' or the work-permit requirements of individual states, can testify.

So is globalization more than a representation, more than an imagery of the powerful which necessarily brings with it the marginalization of the weak? The answers given in this volume are by no means clear-cut or unequivocal. For example, in discussing Islam's global role in Chapter 4, Brian Beeley explores some of the ways in which Islam has been 'constructed' by a world system now dominated by Western (and often ex-colonial) powers. In that sense, perhaps, the world of Islam is defined negatively by what it is not: not developed, not secular, not democratic, not Western. But Beeley also goes on to outline some of the ways in which the various followers of Islam are able to develop alternative visions of the world, with the help of their own cultural and religious understandings. In other words, attempts to marginalize particular groups of people may also encourage them to redefine what is marginal, reasserting the apparently 'marginal' as the main focus of concern in ways which challenge the legitimacy of the 'centre'.

If, as indicated above, globalization is sometimes understood as a homogenizing force, in which 'everywhere becomes the same', politically the re-ordering of space has also been interpreted as heralding a world in which truly global initiatives, even some form of world government, may become possible, perhaps with world policing handled through the United Nations or through 'coalitions' led by the USA. There was talk of a 'new world order' to follow the end of the Cold War and the collapse of the bipolar world defined by conflict between a 'capitalist West' and a 'communist East'. Dreams of 'world government' may seem improbable, but the search is on for political arrangements which go beyond the nation-state, moving towards global solutions. In Chapter 1, Anthony McGrew considers some of the ways in which international regulatory and other regimes have begun to emerge, indicating important elements of continuity as well as highlighting what is distinctive about the new arrangements. In Chapter 3, Chris Brook critically assesses claims that the European Union may be a stepping-stone towards more global forms of government and political accountability.

Yet the more globalizing images of power co-exist alongside others which emphasize uncertainty and 'fragmentation' – the break-up of old orders rather than the construction of new ones. Globalization is happening unevenly in an already uneven world. This can be seen as reproducing and sometimes encouraging counteractions of increasing fragmentation, rather than, or as well as, creating more uniformity. Powerful examples include the break-up of the former Soviet Union; the division of Czechoslovakia into its two component parts; the long agony of the former Yugoslavia as the historical meaning of 'Balkanization' is rediscovered; and even the apparent ungovernability of countries, such as Somalia, split between warring factions at the start of the 1990s. Not only do societies obviously differ to begin with, so too do the various institutions, sectors and groups in any particular society. Pre-existing cultural and political differences offer significant possibilities of fragmentation, as societies respond to the promises and the threats of globalization.

These conflicting trends, of globalization and fragmentation, underlie arguments – critically discussed by James Anderson in Chapter 2 – about whether or not the nation-state is in terminal decline. It is questioned whether it is any longer meaningful to talk of 'national' economies, since the power of nation-states is being eroded by increasingly transnational global forces which appear to cross boundaries with relative impunity. This in turn increases the pressures for more say and influence at sub-state levels where regional cultures and local economic interests may feel threatened by forces that appear increasingly outside the control of even the nation-state. There may also be pressure for local groups to respond by getting together on a wider transnational basis because of some shared concern – cultural, environmental or economic.

And yet, nation-states remain key sources of power and control with little sign of a new global authority emerging. In practice, many of the sub-state challenges 'from below' turn out to be claims for the legitimacy of new, redefined and often smaller nation-states, in what Ignatieff (1993) has called the 'narcissism of minor differences'. At the same time, rather than disappearing into a melting pot of global mixing, states have responded by stretching and overlapping their relations, and by combining with other states and with non-state bodies, to produce increasingly complex and often fluid political arrangements (as discussed in Chapters 1 and 3). States are redefining their roles to fit with a changing world.

The re-ordering of political space is a complex and often confusing process in which the different actors and spaces are constantly being redefined and are redefining themselves. In a sense, geography actively *constitutes* or shapes political arrangements, through processes of uneven development over time. Geography is not merely about the places in which politics happen to occur. This raises immediate issues for the analysis of global political processes, because it undermines attempts to identify (or create) institutions which might be developed in the image of traditional state forms. The search for a single or unitary 'new world order' is likely to be as chimerical as the search for world government has turned out to be.

The extent to which decision-making processes in the emerging world can be democratized and opened to public scrutiny is a question which underlies much of the agonized discussion about the European Union considered by Chris Brook in Chapter 3. Is the European Union a bureaucratic and centralized political expression of economic globalization or does it open up the possibility of democratic involvement in global politics in a European context? In Chapter 5, Steven Yearley looks at another aspect of vital importance to debates about democratization by examining the possibility of transnational political movements and institutions, with specific reference to environmentalism. Environmental politics appear to offer the possibility of linking local concerns and local campaigns to much more global concerns and campaigns. The interrelationships between local and global campaigns suggest that the changing world is one in which new political opportunities may be opening up.

Whatever the eventual verdict, we can note here that 'world orders', old and new, involve economic, cultural and environmental arrangements and movements as much as political institutions. Changes in the structure of the world economy are crucially important. In recent decades, there has been a marked globalization of economic linkages and other interdependencies across different countries and continents, whether seen in terms of the stretching of relations across space, or time–space compression, which brings some places and people closer together (see **Allen and Hamnett, 1995**). Not only is there more international trade, but multinational corporations have become more global in their operations, with different parts of manufacturing processes located in different states. There has also been an explosive growth in foreign investments and round-the-clock financial trading in the 'world cities' of Tokyo, London and New York – 'the keyboards of the world economy' (see, for example, **Leyshon, 1995**). Moreover, these developments have cultural implications, reflected, for instance, in notions of hybrid cultures and in the inadequacy of the viewpoint that 'everywhere is becoming the same' (**Hall, 1995**). Various forms of cultural and communal identity – ethnic, religious, national, some strongly territorial – received widespread emphasis in the 1980s and early 1990s, perhaps reflecting insecurities and tensions associated with accelerated globalization. Transnational cultural movements, such as Islam or what Gilroy (1993) has called the 'black Atlantic' (linking the musical forms of soul, reggae and rap), as much as Hollywood or satellite television, help to define the spaces of emergent but contested world orders.

What are the implications of such changes for political processes? What, for example, is the political significance of cultural reactions to perceived threats of global homogenization? What are the political implications of 'multinationals' perhaps becoming less rooted in particular states, less dependent on their 'home base'? (see **Allen, 1995**). How do we explain the neo-liberal revival of *laissez faire* ideas and the associated wave of 'privatizations' of state-run economic activities which became worldwide phenomena in the 1980s? And have nation-states really lost all control of their 'national' economies? Or, conversely, is the inertia of territorially rooted institutional structures, which were developed to serve a different sort of society, now inhibiting economic globalization, and is this in itself a cause of global disorder?

o   o   o   o   o

This volume is structured in ways which make it possible to identify the changes which are taking place, to raise and help answer questions about the new political spaces which are emerging. It starts by focusing explicitly on debates about the development of new global political arrangements, before considering the position of nation-states within them, and the development of global regions. Formal political structures, however, only tell part of the story, so subsequent chapters focus on the role of cultural and political movements – specifically Islam and environmental movements – both as constitutive elements of political re-ordering and as alternative visions of the global future. The final chapter brings the arguments together, stressing the importance of uneven development in the shaping and representation of global processes in practice and rhetoric.

In Chapter 1, 'World order and political space', Anthony McGrew explores the dynamics of the contemporary global political order, highlighting the ways in which globalization is transforming the conduct of politics. The chapter introduces and critically assesses dominant approaches to the analysis of global politics. McGrew questions what has been called the 'realist' position which maintains that the world political arena is constituted by separate sovereign states, and he suggests instead that it is more useful to interpret global politics in terms which emphasize increasing fluidity and the porosity of political boundaries. With the aid of a series of case studies, the chapter highlights the increasing importance of transnational regulatory arrangements or 'regimes' which link together groups on the basis of shared concerns. They may be intergovernmental or non-governmental in character, but in all cases they are political responses to the uneven nature of time–space compression and the need to manage complex 'webs' of global activity. States no longer respond to global change simply through formal international relations. Instead, they have to adapt their roles by stretching political relations across space to produce overlapping functional regimes, where states share their roles with many other agents. They attempt to maintain influence through involvement in a diverse network of political arrangements (multilateral, transnational and regional) which itself undermines the broader claims to sovereign power often made on their behalf.

The pressures on nation-states 'from above and below', and the ways in which their roles are changing, are dealt with more fully by James Anderson in Chapter 2. The title of the chapter, 'The exaggerated death of the nation-state', reflects the apparent resilience of the state, despite the globalization trends discussed in Chapter 1 and in earlier volumes in this series, and despite related internal pressures from more local or sub-state regional forces. Some commentators argue that the state has outgrown its usefulness, while others comment on its continued robustness and the lack of any effective alternative political arrangement. Anderson considers these various arguments and also new ways of interpreting state systems which acknowledge the possibility of political linkages cutting across traditional boundaries and hierarchies. He draws analogies from the political order of medieval Europe and suggests that these are useful in indicating how, with time–space compression, the ground may be shifting underneath established political arrangements and concepts. But this does not mean that new developments can simply be explained as a 'new medievalism'. On the contrary, Anderson argues that the usefulness of such an historical analogy is strictly limited. More detailed analysis is required, for while territoriality is becoming less important in some policy areas, it is retaining its critical importance in others, and differences between states in different parts of the world are likely to be as significant as their similarities. Anderson notes that globalization has undermined the notion that, in order to be viable, states have to be large, and this has encouraged sub-state or 'micro'-regions to aspire to statehood. He points to cases such as Singapore and Luxembourg to show how size is not essential for success, certainly in economic terms, as long as states are effectively linked into wider networks. It can be argued that the development of global or 'macro'-regions such as the European Union has increased the viability of smaller states and of micro-regional movements by providing an economic and political 'umbrella' within which they can operate more effectively. The chapter confirms the continued importance of the state, but also stresses the changes it is experiencing and the enormous variation of the forms which it can take.

If the position of nation-states is becoming less certain, then perhaps new state forms or (more modestly) new political arrangements are emerging elsewhere, beyond the nation-state. This is the starting point of Chapter 3, 'The drive to global regions?', in which Chris Brook examines the emergence of new macro-regional economic groupings of states, the best developed example of which is probably the European Union. Evidence of macro-regionalism can also be found to a lesser extent in the Americas, but talk of regionalism elsewhere (for example, on the Pacific Rim) is more speculative. The main means of achieving such regional co-operation has been trade liberalization between member states, but a common driving force is the belief that these states, by combining together, will be able to share in an increased economic and political leverage on the world stage, while at the same time strengthening their collective territorial security.

Brook uses the example of the European Union to show that, while there is growing evidence for the emergence of transnational political arrangements, the state system retains a key influence within these. Paradoxically, regional integration may bring into sharper relief the economic and cultural differences within the macro-region, and allowing transnational economic forces to range more freely across quasi 'single markets' may exacerbate the tensions of uneven development. This is likely to make it increasingly difficult for member states to co-operate in a sustained and meaningful way, while pressures against macro-regional integration may also be generated through the ways in which local interests form linkages within and beyond regional groupings. It may be that, instead of reducing territorially based political conflict, the shifting of decision-making from national to supranational agencies has, again paradoxically, helped to generate new forms of political division as well as complicating earlier differences. Uneven development shapes and limits the extent to which the enlargement of macro-regions and the 'deepening' of their integration are possible, while increasing the pressures for more differentiated and unequal regional arrangements.

A key issue is whether regional groupings like the European Union provide a stepping-stone or a barrier to wider global co-operation. It might be argued, for example, that the arrangements underlying macro-regional integration leave less scope for the development of more genuinely global – worldwide – forms of political accommodation, because they reinforce divisions between major global players. But matters may be more complex than that. As Chapter 1 shows, political power is increasingly expressed through a mix of regimes and linkages, multilateral and transnational as well as regional. If one expression of globalization is the stretching of political relations in a wide variety of different ways, then it becomes increasingly important to acknowledge the multifaceted aspects of this expression, and not to conclude that the changes are moving along some predetermined and unilinear route.

The importance of this is highlighted in Chapters 4 and 5 which build on the earlier chapters to consider forms of politics based around culture and the environment, often outside the traditional understanding of formal politics. In Chapter 4, 'Global options: Islamic alternatives', Brian Beeley examines the impact of Islam both as a transnational force within the existing world order and as a source of political and cultural mobilization which appears to exist outside or in opposition to it. The main centres of Islam lie outside the world's core areas of political and economic power, and Islamic states assume a largely subordinate role in a globalization which has been orchestrated by 'Western culture', 'first world' states and big business. Yet while Islam plays a significant role in challenging the present orthodoxies and providing an alternative basis of transnational influence and identity, it cannot simply be placed in a separate category, distinct from 'Western globalization'. In Europe there are substantial Muslim communities whose members have learned to survive (and even to influence) the dominant cultures within which they are situated. At the same time, they have maintained family and cultural linkages across the world to places which help to define their identities, while being firmly located within a set of wider global cultural and political networks which they have themselves helped to create.

Despite the features which make it possible to identify Islam as a global force, in practice identifying a coherent or hegemonic movement is more difficult because of divisions and unevenness across the Islamic world. There are many dimensions to this unevenness. Islam contains many religious and political divisions and different groups which are spread unevenly across the Islamic world. These divisions are aggravated by a state system bequeathed from the colonial era that does little to reflect the cultural identity or diversity of Islam. The huge social and economic divisions across these territories are most clearly exemplified by the contrasting fortunes of oil-rich and oil-poor states, but they are also expressed in dramatically different political regimes and in their different relationships with the West. Given the divisions and differences, it is perhaps unlikely that Islam can provide the basis of a new global order, but it will continue to play an important role in the more differentiated and continuing process of ordering and re-ordering the spaces of global politics.

In Chapter 5 the volume turns to a consideration of 'The transnational politics of the environment', and Steven Yearley looks at another set of developments which undermines traditional ways of understanding and analysing global politics. The global significance of environmental issues is becoming increasingly clear. Yearley notes how this 'globality' is linked to the character of the environmental phenomena themselves: the threat to the environment is essentially 'transnational' and in principle appears little affected by political boundaries. It is marked by increasing global reach and impact because of the scale of pollution and the shrinking world of transport and communication. The extent to which the environment provides a basis for global or transnational politics is one of the issues which underlies the arguments of the chapter.

Environmental groups themselves have increasingly sought to achieve transnational social and political responses to what they perceive as global threats. They have consciously and deliberately set out to link local campaigns and threats to local environments with wider global concerns. Although defending woodland and meadows in the south of England from the encroachments of the road-building lobby may not have the same global significance as defending the Amazonian rainforest from development and degradation, it may nevertheless be seen as part of an informal but potentially powerful network of global 'green' politics, a politics largely independent of government and party politics. Even the more formal aspects of transnational environmental politics fit uneasily with traditional state-focused analysis. Yearley, for example, points to the emergence of world scientific communities producing and assessing evidence of environmental degradation. He notes the growth of environmental pressure groups like Friends of the Earth and Greenpeace, which have developed worldwide organizations and relationships with a multiplicity of non-governmental organizations, to co-ordinate policy responses and influence governments.

But how global is global in this context? Chapter 5 reminds us that environmental impacts are far from uniform. Some environmental processes such as global warming and the depletion of the ozone layer appear genuinely worldwide in significance, but even here there are likely to be differential impacts, spatially and socially. Yearley points out that not only will impacts vary, but the very idea of a common global concern may be contested. A key factor limiting co-operation and progress is the unevenness of the economic development process itself which means that local areas are in global competition for investment and jobs. In 1960 the per capita gross domestic product (GDP) in Latin America was approximately 22 per cent of the average GDP of the 'developed' countries; by 1987 it had dropped to only 12.5 per cent. The figures for Africa, always poorer, dropped from about 7 per cent to 3.5 per cent. Thus, it is hardly surprising that the governments of some 'third world' countries argue that the 'West's' interest in environmental issues has more to do with finding ways of regulating and reducing competition by reducing industrial investment in newly industrializing countries, than with any more noble concerns about the survival of the earth. Concerns about global warming may be seen as a luxury by those whose main worry is to find food to survive from day to day. It is of little surprise that the political response to global environmental issues has been so varied, even patchy.

Finally, in Chapter 6, 'Global worlds and worlds of difference', Allan Cochrane draws on material from the preceding chapters to assess and analyse political responses to, and the shaping of, a globalization marked by unevenness and fragmentation. A key argument running through the volume, and a particular focus for Chapter 6, is the impact of uneven development on attempts to develop a coherent global political response. Transnational social movements will vary in their geographical and social impact. Some transnational groups attempt to advance macro-regional interests like European integration, while others have global aspirations but appeal to some groups more than others. Even global pressure groups like Greenpeace and Friends of the Earth are themselves products of uneven development. They emerged initially in the richer countries of the world in response to global issues which were often seen as shaped and defined by 'first world forces', and later they attempted to build linkages to groups, and even to launch their own campaigns and initiatives, in other parts of a world marked by huge differences in development. Such are the differences in power and interest that, as Cochrane suggests, the search for political movements which are truly global may be a fruitless one.

Chapter 6 also considers the increasing scope for local or place-based politics. Some view the fragmentation inherent in present globalization processes as creating opportunities for more local proactivity. Others suggest that, since control of wealth creation and power is likely to lie outside the local area or region, there is little scope for local politicians to shape events. Much, in fact, depends on the character of local areas themselves. Different places play different roles in the international division of labour: they may be sites of wider economic and political influence, or they may be marked by a high level of external control and economic weakness. Differences in the location and character of areas can influence the effectiveness of local political action. Much also depends on the existing network of interdependencies linking local areas and the dynamics of uneven development. Different groups in the same local area may be tied into contrasting global networks to produce extreme contrasts of rich and poor, making it difficult to generalize on local area opportunities. In essence, the fortunes and opportunities for local politics must be set within wider but uneven global networks which they also help to shape.

Chapter 6 mirrors the volume as a whole in highlighting the complexity of globalizing forces and of political attempts to manage those forces. All the chapters touch on processes of transnationalism, centralization, fragmentation and localization and the ways in which these interact to provide intersecting political possibilities. Throughout, the authors show that traditional state-centric and institutional interpretations cannot easily be applied to changes taking place in the 1990s, though individual states may remain key agents in the developing multicentric arrangements. McGrew quotes Rosenau's observation that 'politics everywhere, it would seem, are related to politics everywhere else' (Rosenau, in Mansbach *et al.*, 1976, p. 22) – the exercise of political power now involves stretching and sharing in ever more complex ways. At the same time, the recast political formations are fluid and uneven, not pointing straightforwardly to the building of a 'new world order', but rather emphasizing the continuing dynamism and instability of political ordering and re-ordering.

○   ○   ○   ○   ○

The series of which this volume is a part starts by highlighting the importance of the 'geographical imagination', and that notion underpins the arguments developed in all the other volumes. Without grasping the significance of the geographical imagination it is impossible to identify the broad direction of the changes taking place in the modern world, while at the same time being able to explore them in their full richness and complexity. It is necessary to acknowledge that different imaginations are in contention as attempts are made to define the world and our positions within it, although it is also important to acknowledge that some representations and some imaginations are more powerful than others. Perhaps nowhere is that more clear than in the discussions of political space and the political re-ordering of the world which are undertaken in the chapters which follow here. Global politics is fundamentally about different ways of 'imagining' the world, with different definitions being developed to reflect and endorse (or challenge and question) emergent forms of political and economic power.

It may always have been the case that the world's political arrangements were 'imagined' or constructed (around 'nation-states', the 'Cold War', or a British Empire on which 'the Sun never set'), and they have certainly been 'global' in some sense for a very long time, even if the globe itself has been defined differently in different historical epochs and in different cultures. For example, the global reach of capitalism has been recognized since at least the nineteenth century, and it has been accompanied by the development of powerful formal and informal empires which have effectively defined the world for those dominated by them. However, it is probably now easier to acknowledge the importance of the geographical imagination at a time when there is no single dominant version or definition of the world – a clear-cut world order – which could simply be taken for granted. We may live in a world dominated by networks of connections and flows which generate and reproduce specific forms of power and control, but how we describe the outcomes of those flows – how we 'map' them or 'imagine' them – is of vital importance in determining how we respond to them and how we understand the world in which we live. It is central to the ways in which we define our own political spaces and how we choose the political commitments we make. By exploring – and metaphorically 'mapping' – some of the imagined geographies of global politics, this volume should also help in informing those choices.

James Anderson, Chris Brook and Allan Cochrane

References

ALLEN, J. (1995) 'Crossing borders: footloose multinationals?', in Allen and Hamnett (eds) (1995).

ALLEN, J. and HAMNETT, C. (EDS) (1995) *A Shrinking World? Global Unevenness and Inequality*, Oxford, Oxford University Press in association with The Open University (Volume 2 in this series).

ALLEN, J. and MASSEY, D. (EDS) (1995) *Geographical Worlds*, Oxford, Oxford University Press in association with The Open University (Volume 1 in this series).

GILROY, P. (1993) *The Black Atlantic: Modernity and Double Consciousness*, London, Verso.

HALL, S. (1995) 'New cultures for old', in Massey and Jess (eds) (1995).

IGNATIEFF, M. (1993) *Blood and Belonging: Journeys into the New Nationalism*, London, BBC/Chatto and Windus.

LEYSHON, B. (1995) 'Annhilating space?: the speed-up of communications', in Allen and Hamnett (eds) (1995).

MANSBACH, R., FERGUSON, Y. and LAMPERT, D. (1976) *The Web of World Politics*, New York, Prentice-Hall.

MASSEY, D. and JESS, P. (EDS) (1995) *A Place in the World? Places, Cultures and Globalization*, Oxford, Oxford University Press in association with The Open University (Volume 4 in this series).

SARRE, P. and BLUNDEN, J. (EDS) (1995) *An Overcrowded World? Population, Resources and the Environment*, Oxford, Oxford University Press in association with The Open University (Volume 3 in this series).

World order and political space

Chapter 1

by Anthony McGrew

1.1 Introduction

On Wednesday 16 January 1991, at 7.38 pm EST (23.38 GMT), a US-led coalition, acting under the authority of the United Nations, launched the largest military campaign in Middle East history since the Second World War, with the aim of liberating Kuwait from Iraqi occupation. The ensuing war dominated media news reports across the globe and, in effect, 'normal politics' almost everywhere was suspended temporarily as the world became a spectator to twenty-first century warfare. If any single historical episode from the early 1990s epitomizes the phenomenon of a 'shrinking world' it is the Gulf crisis. For it exemplifies how, in a densely interconnected world system, local decisions and actions triggered global political repercussions, and how the fate of communities in one region became inextricably linked with the politics of the White House Situation Room and the United Nations Security Council, a continent away.

Four aspects of the Gulf Crisis are worth dwelling on in so far as they symbolize distinctive features of the globalization of contemporary political life. First, advanced communications technology and the reporting of the electronic media transformed the diplomacy of the crisis. Within the allied coalition, the domestic politics of the crisis in each national capital became entwined with international political processes of consensus building and coalition management. As part of a political strategy to mobilize US and international public opinion behind a policy of military response, President Bush construed the Iraqi invasion as the first major threat to the emerging

President Bush addresses the nation at the start of Gulf War hostilities

'new world order'. Saddam Hussein, too, utilized the electronic media, specifically the US news station CNN, to influence Western and Islamic public sentiment. As viewers or spectators, the world's television-gazing public became 'voyeurs' of the unfolding *global politics* of the crisis. The Gulf conflict reflects the globalization of modern political life: the stretching of political processes across the globe; the conduct of 'political action at a distance'; the existence of a truly global political system; and the overlapping 'spaces' of domestic and international political action.

global politics

Second, Operation Desert Storm demonstrated the revolutionary importance of advanced surveillance, command, control and communications technologies not only in the actual conduct of the military operations, but equally as importantly in ensuring that political leaders retained ultimate control over the prosecution of the war. Decision and reaction times were speeded up both for military commanders on the ground as well as for politicians and diplomats in allied capitals. Democratic checks and balances were effectively marginalized as processes of decision making became dominated by the narrowing of response times and the complexities of allied coalition diplomacy. The actual land war came to be measured in hours, not weeks, nor in the traditional military currency of territory conquered (Ó Tuathail, 1993).

Third, the ramifications of the crisis were not confined to the immediate combatants, but rather cascaded through the global political economy. Oil price rises, the economic blockade and Iraq's hostage taking were felt in many disparate communities across the globe from Asia, Africa and Latin America to Eastern Europe.

Fourth, in the West the crisis came to be portrayed almost uniformly in geopolitical terms: as a fundamental challenge to Western strategic interests, including secure oil supplies. Underlying this geopolitical construction of the

Gulf War desert patrol establishing their position with the aid of the global satellite positioning system (GPS)

13

world is a conception of the global system as a single, highly integrated spatial order. Accordingly, the annexation of Kuwait was perceived as a direct threat since it was interpreted as taking place in 'the West's back yard' rather than many thousands of miles away. Political rhetoric and distance-shrinking technologies contributed to an effective annihilation of geographical space, both in material and cognitive terms.

For these four reasons the Gulf Crisis of 1990–1991 stands as powerful evidence of the remarkable intensification of patterns of political globalization in the late twentieth century. It exhibits vividly the implications of a shrinking world for conventional accounts of politics which assume a natural separation of the domestic and the international spheres – the realm of internal politics and external relations respectively. In an era in which world politics is being transformed beyond recognition, conventional accounts of political life no longer seem adequate to account for a complex and confusing 'reality'. A shrinking world implies a world that is being remade, reconfigured or reconstituted. We need therefore to explore as systematically as we can how far, and in what ways, this shrinking world may be restructuring the architecture and the conduct of modern politics. This raises, in turn, a fundamental question concerning processes of globalization and world order: specifically whether globalization is contributing to a transformation or a reconstitution of existing political structures, thus creating new kinds of 'political space' and political arrangements which transcend the nation-state.

The end of the Cold War has brought to a close the bipolar geopolitical order and the superpower rivalry which dominated international politics for almost half a century. The demise of bipolarity therefore undeniably defines an important historical conjuncture. But significant as it is, this shift in the geopolitical order may have distracted our attention from a more profound restructuring of the global order which is associated with processes of globalization. Put simply, the argument is that not only are the key players in world politics changing, but, much more significantly, so too is the very stage upon which the political game itself is played out. A dramatic (even traumatic) reorganization of international political space, propelled by processes of globalization, is said to be unfolding before us (Ruggie, 1993). Globalization, it is argued, appears to be eroding the political foundations of the twentieth-century world order which assumes a world organized into territorially bounded sovereign political communities or 'political spaces' (see **Allen, 1995a**). For the intensification of patterns of global interconnectedness dissolves the boundedness of modern nation-states, as political and other social activities transcend territorial borders, creating new forms of political organization and a 'search for new political spaces ... not limited to the national stage' (Pattie, 1994, p. 1010). In effect, globalization is said to be undermining the dominant pattern of modern political organization which assumes that notions of political space and political community are rooted in, and defined by, the bounded, territorial nation-state. As Ruggie suggests, rather than a world order constituted by 170 (or so) sovereign political spaces, each fixed within the impermeable boundaries of the nation-state, globalization is creating a much more complex architecture of political power and political space (Ruggie, 1993).

It would appear that globalization invites a serious challenge both to the traditional conception of political space, as synonymous with the bounded territorial space of the modern nation-state, and also to conventional conceptions of politics which are constructed around a strict separation of the domestic and the international spheres, 'inside and outside' the state respectively. In evaluating this potential challenge, this chapter seeks a critical examination of the contradictory tendencies evident in contemporary world politics: the persistence of the nation-state juxtaposed with the growing globalization of political and social activity. It is therefore concerned primarily with three interrelated issues:

1   The identification of the significant changes in the form and characteristics of the contemporary global political order.

2   The evaluation of the implications of globalization for traditional conceptions of the 'political' and 'political space'.

3   The definition of the key features of the 'new world order'.

Each of these issues is addressed directly in the subsequent sections of the chapter. Accordingly, we commence with an examination of what may be familiar to many – the geopolitical imagination and its distinctive interpretation of the world order at the century's end.

1.2   Geopolitics and the 'new world order'

The 1991 Gulf War is a powerful reminder of the centrality of the nation-state and military force in world affairs. Historically, war and conflict have been dominant features of world politics such that 'keeping the barracks' staffed remains a universal activity. Indeed, the conventional geopolitical interpretation of world order retains its intellectual primacy over military and diplomatic conceptions of the political world. Consequently, *geopolitics* remains of enduring significance in determining national foreign and defence policies. Even though Operation Desert Storm was justified by reference to international law and the United Nations (UN) Charter, it was largely the geopolitical implications of the annexation of Kuwait which conditioned the Western response. Significantly, although the war demonstrated the annihilation of *space*, through the ability to project military power successfully across vast distances, it simultaneously reinforced the strategic importance of the particularities of *place* within international relations. For Kuwait's vast oil reserves made it strategically important to the West. Military action on a similar scale, for instance, was never countenanced in respect of the territorial integrity of Bosnia, following the break-up of Yugoslavia in the early 1990s.

geopolitics

1.2.1   The geopolitical world order

In the post-Cold War era the question of world order has acquired a special significance, since the end of the East–West struggle has brought with it the demise of superpower rivalry. From 1945 until 1990 world politics was dominated by the global rivalry of the Soviet Union and the USA. The world became a unified strategic arena in which the struggle for ideological and military supremacy permeated every geographical region (see Figure 1.1). As Waltz observes: 'In a bipolar world there are no peripheries. With only two powers capable of acting on a world scale, anything that happens anywhere is

Cold War alliances and alignments
mid-1982

States central to the Western
military system

States with strong economic ties to the
West and shared political traditions

States central to the Eastern
military-economic system

States with ties of convenience to the East

Non-aligned states

Figure 1.1   *The bipolar world (Source: Kidron and Smith, 1983, p. 31, Map 16)*

potentially of concern to both of them' (Waltz, 1979, p. 171). Even the political identity of those states which sought political neutrality was defined in relation to the superpower competition; they became the 'Non-Aligned'. The 'Great Contest' structured world politics for almost five decades and its demise has focused attention on the emergence of a 'new world order'. But what are we to understand by the term 'new world order'?

The phrase 'new world order' was popularized by President Bush in an address to a special Joint Session of Congress on 11 September 1990. In this address, delivered a month after Iraq's annexation of Kuwait, the President clarified his vision for the post-Cold War world:

We stand today at a unique and extraordinary moment ... Out of these troubled times ... a new world order can emerge ... Today, that new world order is struggling to be born, a world quite different from the one we have known, a world where the rule of law supplants the rule of the jungle, a world in which nations recognize their shared responsibility for freedom and justice, a world where the strong respect the weak.

(Bush, 1990)

But these aspirations bear only a tangential relationship to the anarchic geopolitical environment which most foreign policy makers believe constitutes the 'real world'.

Activity 1 Notice how, in the quotation above, George Bush refers to the 'rule of the jungle'. What do you think he is referring to here?

To me his remarks reflect a view of world politics which emphasizes the lack of any world government or authority to police world order. As a result, states or governments have to protect their own interests with the consequence that 'might becomes right'.

Do you think Bush's vision for a 'new world order' is therefore 'realistic' or 'idealistic'? Spend a few minutes identifying the reasons for your own response to this question. Of course, the answer to this question depends critically upon one's assumptions about the nature of world politics. But it is highly likely that you will have viewed Bush's vision as somewhat 'idealistic' in that it seems to go against much of the general commonsense view of how world politics operates – as a struggle for power and national advantage between states. Just reflect on any major current international political event and how it is reported in the media: in the language of national security, conflict, state power, the national interest, and so on. Such language illustrates the dominance of the geopolitical imagination in defining the reality of world politics.

Traditional geopolitical thinking constructs the globe as a single strategic space in which states compete for power and advantage. With no world government or authority to protect them, states are led to acquire power in order to protect themselves against potential external threats. Security and power are thus intimately linked – the more powerful the state the more secure it is believed to be. Security is also conceived primarily in territorial terms – that is, ensuring the territorial integrity of the state. World order is maintained either through a balancing of power amongst the great powers of the day, or by a hegemonic state (dominant state) imposing order through the exertion of coercive power. In this geopolitical construction of the world, states are conceived almost exclusively as territorially bounded power-containers. As such, their external environment is understood in terms of potential threats and dangers. States are judged in relation to their strategic location, their power capabilities and their capacity to disrupt regional or global stability. Traditional geopolitics is therefore essentially concerned with the relationship between space, place, territorial security and state power. This is made explicit in Readings A and B at the end of the chapter.

Activity 2   Turn now to Reading A, 'National Security in the post-Cold War world', by Les Aspin, US Secretary of Defense (1993), and Reading B, 'National security strategy of the United States'. Both extracts are taken from official US government publications.

In reading these extracts take especial note of the language used – 'states', 'threats', 'interests', 'regional balance', 'power equation' – and how world politics is constructed in terms of: threats/stability, allied/friendly, aggression/co-operation.

As the two short readings demonstrate, traditional geopolitical thinking retains a continuing influence upon the perceptions of political leaders and the behaviour of states. Initially, geopolitics became fashionable in the late nineteenth century as space-compressing technologies began to create a sense of 'global closure', the strategic unity of the planet (Kearns, 1993). This was the era of the second wave of European imperial expansionism in which territorial imperatives were justified in terms of the logic of geopolitics. Expansionism was judged necessary in order to enhance the industrial power, social solidarity and national security of the great powers in their struggle for hegemony in Europe. With the aid of new communications and transportation technologies, the European powers were able to project military force across significant distances. As a result, rivals 'moved' closer, whilst the security of raw materials supply and overseas markets was placed in potential jeopardy, particularly in times of war. Consequently, the late nineteenth-century European balance of power system was transformed from a primarily regional into a global struggle for control over distant territories. Globalization, as Modelski reminds us, is a decidedly historical process which, in different periods, has been fuelled by politico-military imperatives and has always been accompanied by tremendous 'arrogance and violence' (Modelski, 1972, p. 49). Geopolitics, from the work of its original founder Ratzel through MacKinder, Mahan and others, rationalized this process of imperial expansion (see Kearns, 1993).

More recently, attention has been focused upon the geoeconomic struggle for industrial supremacy rather than on the struggle between states for political power and military security. Some now consider that geoeconomics – the struggle for national economic or industrial supremacy – has replaced traditional geopolitics. Power, in this geoeconomic world, is measured in terms of global market share rather than military capabilities or acquired territorial space.

What connects this more recent geoeconomic agenda with classical approaches to geopolitical analysis is a set of shared assumptions concerning the nature of the world order and world politics. In essence, both derive from a 'state-centred' or 'realist' conception of international politics.

1.2.2 Globalization and world order: a realist account

The realist account of world order issues from an influential and dominant body of thinking and theorizing within the academic study of international relations: namely *realism*. Whilst realism may not claim to be a completely scientific or objective account of world politics, it does claim to provide a particular representation of (or way of thinking about) international affairs which reflects the way the world is, rather than how the observer might desire it to be. Accordingly, realism remains very much a guiding discourse amongst diplomats, generals and politicians and is deeply embedded in the diplomatic practices of states. In part this is because realism asserts the primacy of the nation-state and in part because it addresses, almost to the exclusion of all else, the issue of the effective management of inter-state or power politics. In so far as it remains a guide to state practices, realism constitutes a privileged and influential interpretation of world politics and the dynamics of world order.

realism

Realism is a sceptical discourse in that it assumes that politics is motivated primarily by a desire for power. As Prince Metternich, one of the great practitioners of *realpolitik*, is rumoured to have remarked on hearing that the Russian Tzar was dead: 'I wonder what his motive could have been' (quoted in Geertz, 1993, p. 26). Realism accepts the primacy of the sovereign territorial nation-state and so is often referred to as 'state-centred'. It assumes a sharp distinction between the domestic and external realms of political action. Accordingly, in many textbooks it is often referred to as the 'billiard-ball model' of international politics since states are represented as having a hard shell separating the inside from the outside (see Figure 1.2).

This separation of the domestic sphere from the international sphere is of crucial significance to realist analysis. Differentiating inside from outside denotes a profound difference in the political constitution of each domain. Whereas the domestic domain is construed as an arena of sovereign political power, in which governments can act with political authority, the international domain is construed as an arena constituted by sovereign states which recognize no superior authority. By definition, there can be no overarching authority within the inter-state system since all states are sovereign within their own territory. The international arena is therefore conceived of as being anarchic in the sense that it is a domain in which: might rather than right dominates; politics involves a struggle for power between states; there are no authoritative mechanisms for enforcing international law or international rules; and order is always contingent upon a balance of power between the most powerful or the coercive power of a hegemonic state. Additionally, since states exert sovereign political power over a defined territory and peoples, their domestic affairs are considered beyond the legitimate jurisdiction of other states and, especially, of international bodies. World order is therefore understood as little more than the international order created by the mutual agreement of sovereign states and, effectively, reflects the interests of the most powerful. Such a conception differs enormously from a much broader vision of world order embracing the global community of humankind. As Bull suggests: 'Order among mankind [*sic*] as a whole is something wider than order among states; something more fundamental and primordial' (Bull, 1977, p. 22).

Although most realists accept that, increasingly, states are enmeshed in ever denser flows of capital, services, ideas, images, crime, pollution, information, knowledge, migrants, arms trade, and so on, they consider that such

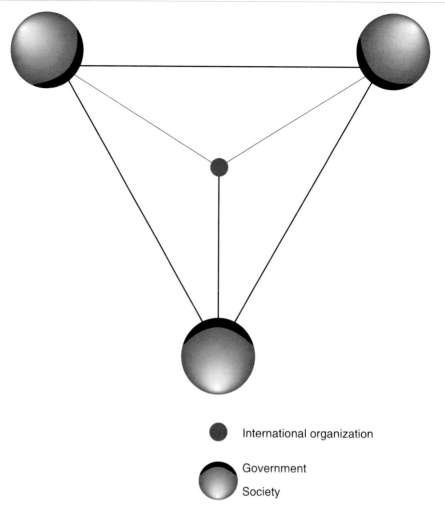

Figure 1.2   *The billiard-ball model of international politics (Source: McGrew, 1992, p. 6, Figure 1.2)*

enmeshment reinforces rather than undermines the existing political organization of humankind into 170 sovereign nation-states. Indeed, Waltz argues that, historically, such flows have always existed, although perhaps not with the same intensity or extent as today (Waltz, 1979). Gilpin, too, argues that this phenomenon of a shrinking world is primarily an expression of the struggle for power and advantage between the great powers of the day. He asserts that each historical phase of globalization has been associated with the hegemony of a liberal power (Gilpin, 1987). Thus, in the post-Second World War era, US hegemony underwrote the stability and security of the non-communist world, thereby fostering the massive expansion of global production and exchange. In comparison, globalization in the late nineteenth century was expressed through Western imperial expansion which, as noted earlier, was a product of European inter-state rivalry. As a French statesman of the time observed: 'to remain a great nation or to become one, you must colonize' (quoted in Joll, 1984, p. 148).

Realists, therefore, take issue with the view that globalization is a permanent fixture of the modern age and is leading to a more interdependent world.

This is a very timely argument since in the post-Cold War era the global system is fragmented into regional blocs and lacks a clear hegemonic power capable of, in Gilpin's words, 'imposing order' (Gilpin, 1987). Moreover, in the absence of a global ideological threat to unite the most powerful capitalist states, and given the resurgence of ethnic, nationalist and protectionist political forces, 'the golden era' of post-war globalization may be reaching its limits.

For realists the 'new world order' is more about continuity than transformation. Whilst the end of the Cold War and the demise of bipolarity are rightly regarded as historic events, they are significant only in so much as they identify the beginnings of a transitional era in international politics: a transition to a new configuration of global power relations in which there are new players, but in the same old 'game', or an old 'game' in the distinctive shell of geoeconomics. Paul Kennedy has described this realist 'game' as the rise and fall of the great powers. This is not to downplay its significance, since it remains of great import whether the future configuration of global power relations is unipolar – effectively, US preponderance; or multipolar – the great powers being the USA, Germany, Japan, Russia and China (see Figure 1.3); or tri-regional – a contest between the European Union (EU), the Pacific region and the North American region.

As the history of the last two centuries has shown, the distribution of power in the international system is an important determinant of international stability and of the prospects for war or peace. However, this realist account of world order assumes that the political organization of the world into bounded, sovereign territorial spaces is somehow frozen in time. It neglects the fact, as Walker comments, that: 'Once upon a time, the world was not as it is' – or even now how realists believe it to be (Walker, 1993, p. 179).

Summary of section 1.2

o The geopolitical imagination constructs the world in terms of a single strategic space in which states compete for power and advantage.

o More recent approaches to geopolitics emphasize the growing significance of geoeconomic factors in defining patterns of world order.

o Underlying the traditional geopolitical analysis of world order is a realist or 'state-centred' account of world politics which emphasizes the primacy of the sovereign territorial nation-state.

o For realists, world order is order amongst states. Moreover, globalization is considered to be contingent upon particular patterns of global power relations and to reinforce the primacy of states in world politics.

o For realists and traditional geopolitical analysts the 'new world order' defines the transition to a new configuration of global power relations.

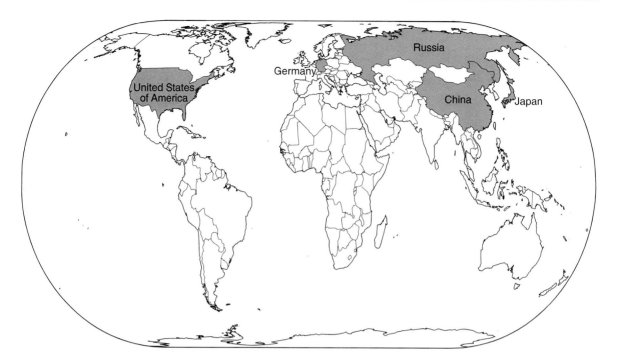

Size	USA	Russia	Japan	Germany[a]	China
Population (1990, in millions)	249.2	147.4	123.51	77.6	1,139.1
(World rank)	(4)	(7)	(8)	(12)	(1)
Territory (sq. km)	9,372,614	17,075,400	377,708	357,039	9,561,000
(World rank)	(4)	(1)	(60)	(61)	(3)
Wealth					
GDP (1992 US$ in billions)	5,446	1,466[b]	3,141	1,486	416
(World rank)	(1)	(4)	(2)	(3)	(10)
GDP/capita (1992 US$)	21,700	4,003[b]	25,430	19,530	370
(World rank)	(9)	(45)	(5)	(13)	(123)
Total industrial output (1987 US$ in billions)	1,495	485[b]	1,156	495	201
(World rank)	(1)	(4)	(2)	(3)	(8)
Total exports (1992 US$ in billions, fob)	393	109.2[b]	280.4	396.7	61.3
% of world total	12.5%	3.6%	7.9%	11.2%	1.4%
(World rank)	(1)	(10)	(3)	(2)	(19)
Military might					
Nuclear arsenals					
ICBMs deployed	2,370	5,575[b]			175
SLBMs deployed	3,840	2,696[b]			
1989 military expenditures (US$ in thousands)	304,000	311,000[b]	28,410	33,600	22,330
(World rank)	(2)	(1)	(6)	(5)	(7)
Personnel (1991, in thousands)	2,241	3,700[b]	247	503	3,903
(World rank)	(3)	(2)	(27)	(14)	(1)

Figure 1.3   *The post-Cold War world: an emerging multipolar system of five great powers (Source: adapted from Short, 1993, p. 59, Figure 3.1; and Kegley and Raymond, 1994, pp. 176–7, Table 8.1)*

Note: ICBMs = intercontinental ballistic missiles; SLBMs = submarine-launched ballistic missiles.

[a] Figures are for the Federal Republic of Germany.

[b] Figures are for the Commonwealth of Independent States.

1.3   Critical geopolitics: a world of connections and flows

Whilst realism may provide a convincing interpretation of the nature and operation of the states system, it may be less helpful in describing the rather messy reality which confronts us every day. As Rosenau observes, a single day's news often provides as many reports of significant events which escape the boundedness of sovereign states, as fit within the traditional realist framework (Rosenau, 1990). For instance, the 'people's revolutions' which spread across Eastern Europe in 1989, and in the process transformed the geopolitical map of the continent, cannot be entirely accounted for within a realist view of the world. Many significant events therefore appear as political 'anomalies' in the realist construction of political life since realism reifies the division of the world into territorially bounded sovereign spaces. It tends to fix such boundaries as permanent, immutable features of the political landscape almost as if they are, in some sense, 'natural' boundaries. As Agnew puts it: 'state territories have been reified as set or fixed units of sovereign space' (Agnew, 1994, p. 59). Yet the history of the states system suggests that the sovereign nation-state is a somewhat contingent and unstable entity.

Since 1648, when the Treaty of Westphalia formalized the division of Europe into sovereign territorial states, the defence of boundaries and the territorial integrity of the state have become central preoccupations of governments everywhere. Wars and conflicts over the demarcation of sovereign territorial boundaries, as events in the Gulf and the former Yugoslavia illustrate, are a prevalent feature of the contemporary states system. But even where boundaries are not subject to disputation they remain subject to state surveillance, regulation and policing. Thus the USA expends huge resources in policing its borders with Mexico to keep out illegal immigrants. The point is that national territorial boundaries may be fixed in a legal sense but they have to be actively enforced to retain their political significance. Similarly, states in their everyday diplomatic and political practices continuously assert and reinvent their claims to sovereign power. Accordingly, the claim to sovereign power has to be distinguished conceptually from the actual substantive possession of such power. Realism, however, accepts almost dogmatically this claim to *sovereignty*, including its associated rigid territorial demarcation of political space, with the consequence that it comes close to being '... little more than an idealized representation of the way physical and political space are presently organized' (Camilleri and Falk, 1992, p. 226). Consequently, rather than '... constructing empirical evidence on the basis of prior assumptions about how conceptual lines are to be drawn through messy appearances, we need to explore further the messy appearances [that is, the political anomalies] for what they may tell us about those prior assumptions' (Walker, 1993, p. 180).

sovereignty

1.3.1   Connections and flows

In the mid-1980s, just prior to a critical Senate debate on the imposition of sanctions against South Africa, several US senators received personal telephone calls from the South African Foreign Minister, a continent away, offering substantive 'clarification' of the implications of their voting behaviour. How are we to characterize this communication: as an unwarranted 'intervention' in the sovereign affairs of the USA or as evidence of the globalization of political activity? During the sterling crisis of September 1992 many 'British' banks expended millions of pounds of their 'British' customers' cash balances in speculating successfully against their own national currency, contributing to its eventual devaluation and the dramatic collapse of the principal foundation of the government's economic 'strategy': membership of the European exchange rate mechanism (ERM). Is the behaviour of these banks to be characterized as an act of economic 'treason' or a sensible financial hedge in the global financial market? These kinds of 'anomalies' arise because there are extensive global flows, connections, activities, interactions, relations, networks and imagined communities which transcend the territorial boundaries of the nation-state.

In almost every domain of social activity, from the economic to the ecological, states have become the sites of global flows and connections. Leyshon, for instance, has noted how the financial revolution of the 1980s established a complex global financial system which is beyond the capacity of any single state, including the most powerful, to regulate effectively (**Leyshon, 1995**). Similarly, in the ecological domain Yearley has described how environmental degradation is at the same time a local, national and transnational phenomenon (**Yearley, 1995**). Even the very places in which we live and our own individual identities are shaped by the intersection of local particularities and global forces (**Hall, 1995**). How then should we conceptualize the political consequences of this world of flows and connections?

critical geopolitics   Attempts to address this question can be found in the growing literature of *critical geopolitics*. Located at the intersection of the study of international relations and political geography, the emerging school of critical geopolitics seeks to make sense of politics in a shrinking world. As Ó Tuathail has stated:

'Critical geopolitics' is a paradoxical promissory declaration. ... On the one hand, it promises the possibility of a new and radically different reconceptualization of the traditional concepts, concerns, and modes of thought that have defined the study of geopolitics for almost a century. 'Critical geopolitics' promises both a new degree of politicization to understandings of geography and a new degree of geographicalization to the study of global politics. It seeks to transgress boundaries and challenge what are held to be essential identities, whether they be imagined communities or inherited philosophical boundaries. On the other hand, the term is an awkward oxymoron, an attempt to force together a word usually associated with the questioning of power with another whose very mode of being has been power and the calculated use of it for reactionary ends. The 'critical' asserts a connection to the new critical social movements that challenge state-centric thinking, yet 'geopolitics' is most often associated with precisely such thinking, with policy prescription for the state.

...

'Critical geopolitics', as I understand it, is a question not an answer, an approach not a theory, which opens up the messy problematic of geography/global politics to rigorous problematization and investigation.

(Ó Tuathail, 1994, pp. 525, 527)

Commencing from a critique of the realist assumptions and world view which define the agenda of traditional geopolitics, the literature of critical geopolitics constructs a very different account of world order: one which is not state-centred and which embraces the interrelated scales of contemporary political life from the local to the global. Three specific arguments flow from this assault on the traditional geopolitical and realist representation of world order:

1   Realism and traditional geopolitics construct an account of world order which claims to reflect the 'real world' as it appears to the objective observer. Yet, as noted above, both Rosenau and Walker suggest that such accounts deny the significance of important political anomalies, ignoring the world of messy appearances (Rosenau, 1990; Walker, 1993). This is because realism is closely associated with the practices of states and 'statesmen'. This privileges it both as an explanatory framework and as 'commonsense' since it reflects the language of power and the powerful. But a moment's consideration of the complexity and ambiguity of world politics suggests a more perplexing 'reality'. As George notes, realism and traditional geopolitics reduce '… a complex, ambiguous, and heterogeneous matrix of existence … to a simplistic, universalized image of the "real" world, which is fundamentally detached from the everyday experience of so much of that world' (George, 1994, p. 11). Accordingly, critical geopolitics questions the arrogant claim of realism to be the truth rather than a partial and particular representation of world order (Dalby, 1992; Ó Tuathail, 1993; Ruggie, 1993). Whilst for much of the post-Second World War era realism has achieved the status of a dominant discourse in accounts of world politics, it is now under attack from the proponents of critical geopolitics and critical international relations theory who question its assumptions and its partial representation of the 'messy appearances' which define contemporary world affairs.

2   Alongside this questioning of the conventional geopolitical imagination is a critique of the territorial conception of political space and the associated boundedness of the sovereign nation-state which dominate much realist thinking about world order. Globalization, it is argued, is bringing about a spatial reorganization of political life in which political space is no longer defined by national territorial boundaries. Politics and political activity no longer, if they ever did, 'stop at the water's edge'.

Activity 3   In Reading C, 'Emerging spatial forms', by John Agnew, located at the end of the chapter, the above two points are expanded upon further, from within the 'critical geopolitics' school. In reading this extract you should take notes on both the arguments and the evidence Agnew deploys in respect of:

(a)   The complexity and messy appearance of world politics.

(b)   The signs of a new spatial organization of political life.

(c)   The critique of conventional geopolitics and realism (that is, mainstream international relations theory).

3   Agnew's conclusion in Reading C relates to a final point in the critical geopolitics literature: the need to broaden our conception of world politics and world order to take account of an emerging global political system and a

'global politics'. As both Agnew and Walker suggest, to understand the politics of a shrinking world requires an abandonment of the vocabulary of realism, the grammar of inside/outside the state (Agnew, 1994; Walker, 1993). Instead, we need to concentrate our intellectual energy on the task of identifying the spatial patterns of power and authority in what, today, is a global political arena: one in which nation-states are conceived of as the sites of flows and connections rather than primarily as containers of political power and action. Globalization brings into question the significance of political boundaries and the conflation of political space with the sovereign territorial nation-state.

1.3.2 Global politics in a shrinking world

Writing several years ago, Rosenau observed that, in the modern era: 'Politics everywhere, it would seem, are related to politics everywhere else ... [N]ow the roots of ... political life can be traced to remote corners of the globe' (Rosenau in Mansbach *et al.*, 1976, p. 22). In identifying the globalization of the political arena as a distinctive feature of contemporary politics, Rosenau directly questions the traditional primacy attached to national territorial boundaries and sovereignty as the organizing parameters of political space and political community. The notion of a shrinking world contains within it the implication that political action and political processes must be conceived of as a social activity with a global dimension.

'Global politics' is a term which captures this 'stretching' across space of political processes; the exercise of political power and political activity associated with a shrinking world. Politics is a social activity which is no longer confined within the territorial boundaries of the nation-state. Today, decisions and actions in one part of the world very rapidly acquire worldwide

A combine harvester sits by the roadside near Strasbourg covered in slogans protesting against the French government's agricultural policy, including the GATT negotiations, 1993

ramifications. In addition, sites of political action or decision become linked through rapid communications and media reporting into complex networks and cascades of decision making and political interaction. A good illustration of this 'stretching' of the political process occurred in 1993 during the culmination of the negotiations of the General Agreement on Tariffs and Trade (GATT) Uruguay trade talks. Representatives of American, French and British farmers developed a common position in opposing the final GATT deal and jointly put political pressure on their respective governments. This involved joint delegations to the US Congress and standing side by side at political demonstrations in Washington, Paris and Brussels.

This kind of political action at a distance is becoming increasingly frequent as processes of globalization bind together the fate of communities across the globe in complex networks of political decision making. This 'stretching' of political processes is a direct political consequence of the intensification of 'time–space compression' – a shrinking world. But a shrinking world for whom? For there remain vast global inequalities in terms of access, resources and political power which ensure that global politics is a distinctly remote activity for the majority of the world's population. Accordingly, global politics is inherently stratified and unevenly experienced across the world.

Associated with this 'stretching' is a 'deepening' in that political 'action at a distance' permeates with greater intensity the social conditions and cognitive worlds of specific places or policy communities. As a consequence, developments at the global level frequently acquire serious local consequences and vice versa. A pertinent illustration of this also arises from the 1993 Uruguay GATT negotiations. In the final GATT agreement Japan was forced to liberalize its rice market with the consequence that traditional patterns of rural political support for the established ruling party, the Liberal Democratic Party (LDP), were severely undermined. This in turn contributed to the sensational defeat in 1993 of the LDP as the 'natural party of government'. Moreover, by allowing the import of cheaper American rice, those rural communities dependent on rice production have been forced to adapt very traditional patterns of social organization to the requirements of global competition. This has entailed significant social dislocation. Globalization in the political domain is therefore evident in the growing enmeshment of local and global issues such that global conditions come to have a pervasive impact upon local life, and vice versa (this issue will be raised again in Chapter 5).

The idea of 'global politics' transcends the traditional distinctions between inside/outside, the domestic/international, as embedded in conventional conceptions of the 'political'. It also highlights the richness and complexity of the interconnections which transcend states and societies in the global system. A specific illustration of this is the way in which Iraq's invasion of Kuwait in 1990 created short-term instabilities in world oil and financial markets which in turn had serious economic consequences for many countries, especially the world's poorest nations, triggering a co-ordinated international response. Moreover, it emphasizes the fluid and decentred nature of the global system. This process of decentring is evident in:

1   The demise of the Cold War. The relative decline of the USA and the collapse of the Soviet Union affirm the end of the superpower era. Accordingly, the notion that, in the last analysis, there are only two centres of power which count in global politics, namely Washington and Moscow, is no longer true. New loci of power, such as Germany and Japan, are emerging,

articulating a marked transformation in the global power structure. Combined with the increasing importance of economic and industrial power, such developments have undermined the conventional picture of international politics as an activity centred upon or contingent on the actions of only two superpowers.

2 Although governments remain powerful actors in the global system, they share the global arena with a vast array of other agencies and organizations. The state is confronted by quasi-supranational institutions, like the European Union, whilst alongside it there exist an enormous number of *international regimes* intergovernmental organizations (IGOs), agencies and *international regimes* which operate across different spatial reaches. Non-state actors or transnational bodies, such as multinational corporations, transnational pressure groups, transnational professional associations, and so on, also participate intensively in global politics. So too do many subnational actors, such as city governments, local authorities, national political parties and national pressure groups, whose activities often spill over into the

Greenpeace disrupts the World Bank Summit in Madrid in 1994

international arena. Accordingly, the global arena is best conceived of as a 'mixed actor system'. This conception challenges the conventional realist characterization of the global political system as primarily 'state-centric'.

3 Technological change combined with economic and political developments have thrust a whole new set of problems on to the global agenda. Pollution, drugs, outer space, human rights and terrorism are amongst an increasing number of transnational policy issues which cut across territorial jurisdictions and existing global political alignments, and which demand international co-operation for their effective resolution. Defence and security issues therefore no longer dominate the global agenda or even the political agendas of national governments.

Within this decentred universe of political activity the mapping of political power and authority becomes an exceedingly difficult task. Unlike realism, which assumes that states are the primary actors in world politics, the global politics perspective suggests a more complex and fluid configuration of political power.

Activity 4 In Reading D, 'The global architecture of power' by Joseph A. Camilleri and Jim Falk, the authors isolate some of the distinctive features of the power structure of global politics. Read this extract now and, in taking notes, concentrate upon the following two questions:

(a) Why do Camilleri and Falk consider this architecture dynamic and unequal?

(b) What do they believe are its implications for sovereignty?

To understand more fully the nature of this 'architecture of power' we shall explore it through both an examination of the growing institutionalization of global politics and, in section 1.4, the political dynamics of three global policy domains or issue areas: telecommunications, international human rights and global security.

1.3.3 Internationalization and transnationalization

In early 1994 the finance and employment ministers of the world's leading capitalist states (known collectively as the G7 or Group of 7), together with their EU counterparts, met in Detroit to discuss the problem of global unemployment. The principal object of this special G7 'summit for jobs' was to review how international co-ordination of national economic strategies might assist job growth across the G7 nations.

This summit had a symbolic importance in bringing jobs to the top of the Western political agenda. Indeed, since 1975 the annual G7 summits have focused their attention increasingly on issues which might previously have been regarded as primarily 'domestic' or welfare issues. In effect, this summitry represents an attempt to manage or 'govern' those aspects of international affairs which escape the control of any single state. With the intensification of patterns of global enmeshment this has meant an increasing focus on questions of economic, ecological and social security, rather than on traditional geopolitics and military security. The G7 summits highlight what has been evident for some time: a growing 'institutionalization' of global politics as governments and their citizens come to terms with a world of flows and transnational connections.

President Clinton addresses the G7 Summit for Jobs, 1994

This kind of institutionalization is not simply a twentieth-century phenomenon. In fact, international mechanisms to 'govern' aspects of global affairs have been in evidence since the early nineteenth century – and long before if one counts the balance of power as such a mechanism. But it was not until the mid-nineteenth century, the era of industrialization, with its rapid exploitation of space-compressing technologies, that distinctive forms of international governance emerged in the form of the international public unions. The International Telegraph Union was the first such international organization, founded in 1865 in order to facilitate international telegraphic communications across Europe. Many others followed in rapid succession such that, by 1914 (as Table 1.1 indicates), significant aspects of global affairs were subject to international regulation by world organizations.

Table 1.1 *World organizations in 1914 (by main area of responsibility and date of founding)*

Fostering industry

Infrastructure

1865	International Telegraph Union
1874	Universal Postal Union
1884	International Railway Congress Association
1890	Central Office of International Railway Transport
1894	Permanent International Association of Navigation Congresses
1905	Diplomatic Conference on International Maritime Law
1906	Universal Radiotelegraph Union
1909	Permanent International Association of Road Congresses

Industrial standards and intellectual property

1875	International Bureau of Weights and Measures
1883	International Union for the Protection of Industrial Property
1886	International Union for the Protection of Literary and Artistic Works
1912	International Bureau of Analytical Chemistry of Human and Animal Food

Trade

1890	International Union for the Publication of Customs Tariffs
1893	Hague Conference on Private International Law
1913	International Bureau of Commercial Statistics

Managing potential social conflicts

Labour

1901	International Labour Office

Agriculture

1879	International Poplar Commission
1901	International Council for the Study of the Sea
1902	International Sugar Union
1905	International Institute of Agriculture

Strengthening states and the state system

Public order and administration

1875	International Penitentiary Commission
1910	International Institute of Administrative Sciences

Managing interstate conflicts

1899	Permanent Court of Arbitration
1907	International Court of Justice

Strengthening society

Human rights

1890	International Bureau Against the Slave Trade

Relief and welfare

1907	Bureau for Information and Enquiries Regarding Relief to Foreigners

Table 1.1 *World organizations in 1914 (by main area of responsibility and date of founding) (continued)*

Health

1900	Commission on Revision of the Nomenclature of the Causes of Death
1907	International Office of Public Hygiene
1912	International Association of Public Baths and Cleanliness

Education and research

1864	International Geodetic Association
1903	International Association of Seismology
1908	International Commission for the Teaching of Mathematics
1909	Central Bureau for the International Map

Source: Murphy, 1994, pp. 47–8

Throughout this formative phase of international organization building, regulatory activity gradually extended beyond the boundaries of Europe to embrace a more global jurisdiction. The expansion of these distinctive forms of international regulation had significant political consequences since:

... in those realms where the Unions contributed to the substantive regulation of the European economy the indirect evidence of their effectiveness is straightforward and compelling. Telegrams, letters and packages flooded the international networks at the end of the nineteenth century. The tonnage of goods – especially of industrial products – shipped along European railways and roads constantly increased. National courts defended foreign holders of copyrights, patents and trademarks. Producers increasingly employed the same standards. The benefits received by Europe's most privileged workers converged. The slave trade waned. Fewer epidemics crossed national frontiers.

(Murphy, 1994, p. 106)

By creating a form of international order conducive to stability and the international expansion of industrial capitalism, the international public unions of the nineteenth century laid the foundations of a more comprehensive, although fragmented, system of global regulation in the late twentieth century.

In the post-Second World War era there has been a phenomenal expansion of such institutions or mechanisms of global and regional 'governance'. Just as the world has experienced massive leaps in flows of trade, foreign direct investment (FDI), financial commodities, tourism, cultural links, migration, hazardous waste, knowledge, crime, narcotics, etc., so it has witnessed the corresponding evolution of global (and regional) institutions or forms of international co-operation to manage, regulate, facilitate or even prevent these burgeoning flows and connections. This is not to argue that such regulation is simply the product, or consequence, of a shrinking world, since, as Murphy (1994) argues, there are strong reasons to believe it may be an important underlying contributory cause. Rather, it is simply to assert that there is a distinct relationship between historical patterns of globalization and historical patterns of global institutionalization.

Some indication of the scale of the transformation in progress since 1945 is evident in the historical statistics shown in Figure 1.4. Whereas in 1955 there were 123 intergovernmental organizations – that is, formal organizations created by two or more governments – by 1986 there were 337, in comparison with only 37 in 1909 (Zacher, 1992). During the period 1946–1975 the number of international treaties in force between governments more than doubled from 6,351 to 14,061, whilst the number of such treaties embracing intergovernmental organizations expanded from 623 to 2,303.

Such evidence suggests that a rapid process involving the 'internationalization' of the state has been underway in the post-war era. But even these figures conceal the explosive growth of transgovernmental communication and interaction – that is, policy networks or communications networks connecting officials in government departments in one state with their opposite numbers in other governments or with an IGO (for example, officials in the British Treasury are in direct contact with their counterparts in the US Treasury

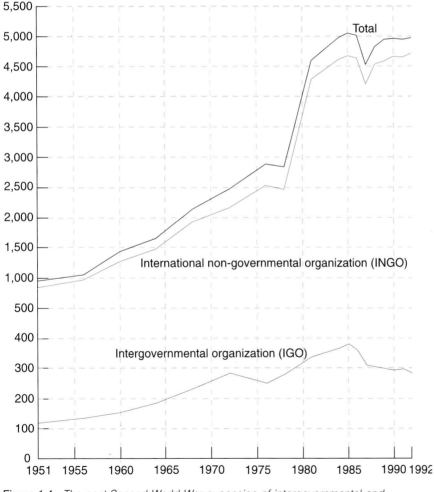

Figure 1.4 *The post-Second World War expansion of intergovernmental and international non-governmental organizations (Source:* Yearbook of International Organizations, *annual, various, Brussels)*

Department and the International Monetary Fund, or IMF). These transgovernmental policy networks are extensive and highly active on a day-to-day basis, facilitated increasingly by electronic communications. As Clarke observes in relation to the UK, foreign policy effectively has become 'external policy' as '… domestic departments are increasingly having to come to operate in the international environment in order to fulfil their responsibilities. Every month some two hundred officials from the Ministry of Agriculture, Fisheries and Food alone are required to travel to Brussels' (Clarke, 1992, p. 95). This creates enormous problems of policy co-ordination such that often the state appears not so much as a single actor on the world stage but as a multiplicity of actors in many different forums. In 1989, for instance, the Departments of Health and Social Security found themselves agreeing to a World Health Organization (WHO) charter on environmental issues, blissfully unaware that it undermined the Department of the Environment's negotiating position within the EU in opposition to tougher environmental standards (Clarke, 1992, p. 165).

If we were to add to this extensive intergovernmental and transgovernmental activity the key international policy-making conferences of the post-war period, the annual G7, EU and IMF summits, the vast array of temporary and informal intergovernmental arrangements, and the many other official summits, an image of extremely intense and overlapping networks of global, regional and multilateral governance would appear. These networks, however, are highly uneven in terms of their spatial reach, functional embrace, jurisdiction, power, and political salience (see Figure 1.5). Nevertheless, a very clear pattern emerges in respect of the internationalization of the institutions, practices and policy-making processes of the modern

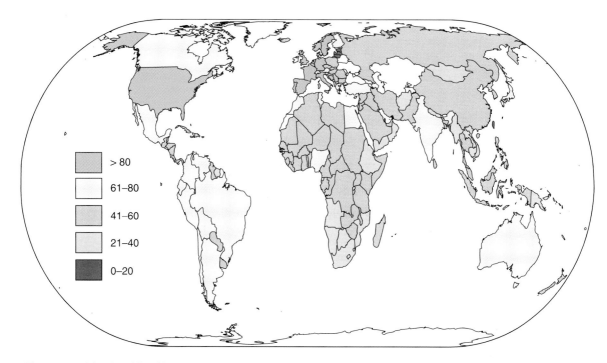

Figure 1.5 *Membership of intergovernmental organizations in 1991 (number of IGO memberships by country)*
(Source: Nierop, 1994, p. 54, Figure 3.4)

nation-state. Government, as the locus of state power and authority, is far from being a monolithic entity, but rather is locked into an array of global, regional and multilateral systems of governance.

But the institutionalization of global politics is not restricted to this internationalization of the state. Alongside the latter can be charted a corresponding transnationalization of domestic (civil) societies or national communities. In almost every sphere of social activity, from the economic to the cultural, there has been a significant institutionalization of transnational relationships – that is, those cutting across national territorial boundaries. Trade flows now account for 20.5 per cent of Western gross domestic product (GDP), as compared to 9.5 per cent in 1960, whilst foreign exchange dealings each day top US $900 billion, and transnational corporations account for 28.6 per cent world GDP (compared to 17.7 per cent in 1960). International communications have increased exponentially, with calls from the USA rising from 199,880 million in 1980 to 685,673 million in 1988 (Wade, 1994). But such crude quantitative measures of these flows disguise the processes of qualitative transformation that are at present underway. For new transnational organizational forms have emerged, organizing people, co-ordinating resources, information and sites of social power across national boundaries for political, cultural, economic, technological or social purposes (Lash and Urry, 1994).

This transnationalization is most conspicuous in relation to the globalization of production, the 'footloose multinationals' (**Allen, 1995b**). But it is also evident in other domains. In 1973, 239 national banks established the SWIFT (Standardized World Inter-Bank and Financial Transactions) system, creating a worldwide framework for standardized and rapid inter-bank communications; by 1989 SWIFT had 1,000 members in 51 states (Ward, 1989, p. 263). In the political domain there exist scores of transnational pressure groups and international non-governmental organizations (INGOs), from Greenpeace to the International Confederation of Trade Unions (ICTU); in the cultural domain there are groups such as the World Muslim Congress; in the social domain there are many organizations such as the International Red Cross, the Catholic Fund for Overseas Development (CAFOD), OXFAM, and so on; and in the scientific domain, professional organizations such as the International Association of Nutritional Sciences and the International Political Science Association. Since the 1950s the growth of such transnational organizations (or INGOs) – that is, non-governmental organizations which have members in more than two nations – has been explosive: from a total of 832 in 1951 to 4,649 in 1986, compared with 176 in 1909 (see Figure 1.4).

Even though such figures may not be entirely accurate they indicate the trend, in most parts of the globe, towards the institutionalization of social, cultural and political relations which transcend national societies. These transnational organizations function to co-ordinate action at a distance, organizing communities of interest across territorial boundaries (see, for instance, the discussion of environmental groups in Chapter 5). Some represent particular transnational communities such as, for example, the Catholic Church, or social movements such as that of ecology or the women's movement. In effect, these are transnational 'imagined communities' which transcend the nation-state. Equally, there are less benign forms of transnational organizations such as terrorist and criminal organizations. In recent years the growth of transnational criminal organizations related to the trade in narcotics and the expanding geographical reach of organized crime (the Triads, Cosa Nostra, etc.) has become a major concern of governments and police forces across the globe. As Williams observes, since '... criminal groups are used to operating outside the rules, norms and laws of domestic jurisdictions they have few qualms about crossing national boundaries illegally ... transnational criminal organizations are transnational organizations par excellence' (Williams, 1994, p. 100).

Whatever the underlying causes of this dramatic internationalization of the state and transnationalization of domestic (civil) societies, there is considerable evidence to suggest that many different domains of global activity are increasingly regulated or governed despite the absence of a world government.

Summary of section 1.3

This section has focused upon the nature of critical geopolitics and the characteristics of global politics. Several points have emerged:

- o   Critical geopolitics arises from an acceptance of the messy reality of a world of connections and flows. It questions the conventional representation of world politics provided by realism and traditional geopolitical analysis.

- o   Critical geopolitics acknowledges that globalization has created a truly global political system, however stratified and uneven.

- o   Global politics is a term which captures the stretching and deepening of political processes across space and time. It describes the politics of a shrinking world.

- o   Global politics is a term which provides a representation of the decentred and fluid nature of world order. It also highlights the growing internationalization of the state and transnationalization of civil society – that is, the institutionalization of global political activity.

1.4   Power, sovereignty and global governance

'We live in a world of international regimes', suggests Young in his analysis of the growing institutionalization of global politics (Young, 1989, p. 11). International regimes, as the phrase implies, are forms of international governance which are distinct from traditional notions of government conceived of in terms of institutionalized sites of sovereign political power. In the contemporary system of sovereign states there is no political authority above the state, no world government. But even in this kind of self-help environment international regimes have developed rapidly, reflecting the intensification of patterns of global and regional enmeshment. International regimes exist to 'manage' common problems, or to regulate distinct aspects of global activity such as telecommunications and the environment. As Young remarks:

International regimes cover a wide spectrum in terms of functional scope, geographical domain, and membership. Functionally, they range from the narrow purview of the polar bear agreement to the broad concerns of the arrangements for Antarctica and outer space. The geographical area covered may be as limited as the highly restricted domain of the regime for fur seals in the North Pacific or as far flung as that of the global regimes for international air transport (the International Civil Aviation Organization/ International Air Transport Association system) or for the control of nuclear testing. With respect to membership, the range runs from two or three members, as in the regime for high-seas fishing established under the International North Pacific Fisheries Convention, to well over a hundred members, as in the nuclear nonproliferation regime. What is most striking, however, is the sheer number of international regimes. Far from being unusual, they are common throughout international society.

(Young, 1989, p. 11)

International regimes can be conceived of as institutional frameworks regulating specific sectors of global or international activity. They are, in effect, arrangements for governing specific activities or domains of international life. In Young's view they represent '... social institutions governing the actions of those involved in specifiable activities or set[s] of activities ... Like other social institutions, regimes may be more or less formally articulated, and they may or may not be accompanied by explicit organizations' (Young, 1989, pp. 12–13). Although international regimes reflect the internationalization of the state, in its attempts to regulate or govern transnational activities and flows, transborder externalities or global common issues, there are also non-governmental transnational regimes which regulate specific private activities. The SWIFT regime, mentioned in section 1.3.3, is one, but Islam, as a global cultural regime (see the discussion in Chapter 4), or the expert International Ethics Committee on AIDS, which is attempting to 'legislate' global ethical standards for AIDS patients, are others. International regimes, in effect, are proto-forms of international governance designed to regulate those aspects of social life which are increasingly affected by, or reliant upon, the growing enmeshment of states and societies in global networks and systems. International regimes therefore represent a political response to the shrinking world, to time–space compression, and arguably can be seen to involve a reconstitution of international political space.

International regimes normally embrace a wide range of political actors, including governments, government departments, sub-national governing authorities and international non-governmental organizations, such as transnational pressure groups or social movements, in their decision-making processes. Although international regimes differ enormously in this respect, they are generally 'mixed actor' systems. Moreover, whilst many regimes have at their core an intergovernmental organization, many are much more fluid arrangements, arising from specific treaties, collective policy problems or transnational communities of interest. Thus, the international security regime in Europe is constructed around complex relationships amongst several institutions, such as the North Atlantic Treaty Organization (NATO), the EU, the Western European Union (WEU) (a collective defence organization of nine West European states formed in 1948) and the Organization for Security and Co-operation in Europe (OSCE) (a grouping of 50 states, all European but including the USA and Canada, whose main function is to foster political stability and military security in Europe). In comparison, the international nuclear non-proliferation regime has no formal international organization at its core, but instead an international treaty combined with rolling international conferences at which key decisions are taken. This is very similar to the Law of the Sea regime governing the exploitation of resources on the sea bed. In addition, international regimes have many different core functions. Some simply engage in monitoring activities, as is the case for many arms control regimes, such as that regulating arms reductions in Europe (the Conventional Forces in Europe Treaty, or CFE), whilst others may take decisions upon international property rights, as in the allocation of radio frequencies, satellite orbits, or sea-bed exploitation. Despite this diversity in forms, functions and constitutions, international regimes nevertheless articulate a system of 'governance without government' in the contemporary world order (Rosenau, 1992, p. 5). The nature of this governance and the corresponding global politics will be explored more fully in respect of three issue areas: global communications, human rights and international security.

By focusing upon these three issue areas a fairly rounded picture should emerge, both of the nature of global politics and the form of the contemporary world order. For the global telecommunications regime illustrates the growing political power of transnational corporations. It also highlights how forms of political regulation are implicated in the very process of time–space compression which is itself at its most visible in the realm of telecommunications. The international human rights regime demonstrates the emergence of a new kind of global politics around 'life issues' and the significance of contemporary transnational social movements in shaping the world order. Finally, the changing nature of the international security regime, following the demise of the Cold War, provokes serious doubts concerning the ability of sovereign states to achieve one of their most cherished objectives – national security – without resort to forms of international co-operation. National security is being redefined and, in the process, sovereign statehood and world order are having to adjust to new realities.

1.4.1 The global telecommunications regime

Telecommunications is one of the technologies most implicated in the time–space compression of the globe. Today's global telecommunications network embraces every nation, although not the majority of the world's population. It reflects, like other global networks, the geography of power and privilege. The person-to-person, or point-to-point, international telephonic or fax service we are used to in the advanced capitalist world, is not available in many parts of the world. For instance, in the small town of Villes de Bravo, west of Mexico City, most of the population rely on communal telephonic services, whilst in other parts of the country even those services are sparse.

The global telecommunications network is one of the most highly regulated sectors of transnational activity. It is 'governed' by the international telecommunications regime, embracing the International Telecommunication Union (ITU) (which in turn embraces a Radiocommunication Sector, the World Radiocommunications Conferences and the International Satellite Organization) and various regional organizations (see Box 1.1).

Box 1.1 Regional telecommunication organizations

'Some of the main intergovernmental regional telecommunications organisations:

- The **Asia-Pacific Telecommunity (APT)**, founded in 1979, is based in Bangkok with 26 member countries.

- In Africa, the **Pan-African Telecommunications Union (PATU)** was established in 1977 based on the desire to have a continental institution co-ordinate the development of telecommunications in Africa.

- The Arab **Telecommunications Permanent Committee** of the Arab League groups the ministers of communications in the Arab-speaking world.

- The **Conference of European Postal and Telecommunications Administrations (CEPT)** began as a consultative group of Western European PTTs [Post, Telegraph and Telephone administrations]; it recently admitted members from Eastern Europe. With structural reform taking place in many countries in the region, CEPT has evolved into a grouping of ministries of communications and regulatory agencies and operators have created their own group.

- The **Inter-American Telecommunications Commission (CITEL)** is a branch of the Organization of American States; all countries in the region except Cuba are members.

- The **Regional Commonwealth for Communications (RCC)** based in Moscow, groups the posts and telecommunications ministries of the Commonwealth of Independent States.'

Source: International Telecommunication Union, 1994, p. 93, Box 5.9

Between them, these organizations provide the mechanisms of international co-ordination which facilitate the smooth operation of the entire system of worldwide telephonic, telegraphic, radio and satellite communication.

Each time we make an international telephone call, or send an international fax, we rely not just on the technical hardware and software of the global communications infrastructure, but also indirectly upon the effective application of the rules and regulations of the international telecommunications regime. Since the formation of the International Telegraphic Union in 1865, international communication has been the subject of intense European and, later, global regulation. Jealous of their national sovereignty, whilst also wishing to protect national military and commercial security, European governments 'policed' vigorously their 'telegraphic ports' in the early days of the telegraphic revolution. The complexity of establishing, on a bilateral basis, rights of passage for telegraphic traffic created serious barriers to an internationally connected network. This in turn created the absurdity of telegrams being decoded at national boundaries, walked through customs where a tariff was imposed, and then literally handed over to the telegraph office on the other side of the customs post (Cowhey, 1990). With the establishment of the ITU regime in 1865, international co-ordination and co-operation facilitated the more familiar practice of uninterrupted flow dependent upon '... an international telegraph regime requiring its members to accept all international messages and to link the wires of the separate national systems into a single network' (Murphy, 1994, pp. 86–7). The advantages of this system meant that by the turn of the century the ITU's European regime had become globalized.

The headquarters of the International Telecommunication Union, Geneva

By the late twentieth century the problems of maintaining an effective global communications network have become much more complex and more highly politicized. The stakes are incredibly high in that the global market for the provision of communication services is huge: an estimated US $550 billion per annum. The implications for national sovereignty are also immense in that, unlike the early days of the telegraph, no state can effectively police or control the transnational flows of electronic mail, images, data, broadcasts, and so on, which cross its boundaries. A particularly interesting case in this regard is the Internet (those linked networks of computer systems which together connect electronically millions of computer users across the globe). For some time the G7 nations have sought to regulate this rather anarchic global network since information placed on the 'net' does not respect national boundaries or national laws. Only co-ordinated international regulation can prevent what many governments consider potential abuses of this global collective good (for example, the transnational distribution of pornography) (see Box 1.2).

Just the sheer scale of telecommunications activity is startling: in 1980 there were 240,000 million international calls made from Germany, but by 1988 the figure was 600,352 million; and for Thailand and China the respective figures are 873 million to 12,646 million, and 1,075 million to 45,030 million (Zacher, 1992; see also Table 1.2). Moreover, as the world's airwaves and satellite orbits have became more crowded, the role of the international telecommunications regime has become increasingly important in allocating international rights to exploit usable frequencies and satellite orbital slots free from undue interference. Without the kind of international regulatory activity undertaken within this regime, the entire system of global communications would become increasingly fragmented and, arguably, increasingly inefficient. Even countries such as Japan, the USA and the UK, which could opt out of aspects of the regime, have not done so because of the overall benefits of international co-ordination in such a crucial commercial sector.

Box 1.2 How big is the Internet?

'In July 1993, there were some 50,000 registered networks on the Internet of which 14,000 are directly interconnected. These networks give access to some 1.8 million computer hosts which are theoretically *reachable*, in the sense that messages can be sent or data retrieved from them by others on the network either directly, or indirectly via electronic mail or gateways. Converting the verified number for hosts into an estimated number of *users* is problematic:

- Unlike telex, videotex or fax, the Internet is dominantly a service rather than a hardware market. Thus estimates have to be based on the number of users rather than the number of terminals sold.

- A host can be an individual workstation, an individual local area network or a gateway to a wide area network. Thus the multiplier could be anywhere between 1 and 100,000.

- For many users, interconnectivity is only theoretical in that they do not make use of the facility. Thus the number of potential users is much higher than the number of actual users.

- The average number of users per host has changed over time. Initially it increased as local area network technology spread during the 1980s. However, this trend is counteracted by a second trend which is that, as the network grows, newcomers are increasingly marginal, and therefore most likely represent smaller networks in terms of users and traffic flow.

For the purposes of estimation, the ITU has assumed that the average number of *users per host* increased during the early 1980s to reach a maximum of 12 per host in 1988, since when it has declined to around 7.5 per host in 1993. This places the estimated number of users in July 1993 at around 13.3 million. In relation to other text communication technologies ... this means that Internet overtook telex in terms of users some time in 1990 and overtook videotex some time in 1992. If growth trends in 1993 continue, then Internet should overtake fax terminals some time during 1994. However, its ultimate growth is probably limited by the global population of Personal Computers which is around 100 million, or less than one fifth of the global installed base of telephones.'

Source: International Telecommunication Union, 1994, p. 47, Box 3.6

The politics of the international telecommunications regime is significant for what it reveals about the balance of state and corporate power in global politics. Until the 1970s the regime operated with little controversy. Since the global financial services revolution and the deregulation of the telecommunications business in the USA and UK, however, the regime has become highly politicized. The basic norms of the regime – standardization of networks, collective decision making over global commons issues (broadcast spectrum and satellite orbital slots), jointly provided services and multilateral co-ordination – remain intact. So too, for the most part, do the regime's rules and decision-making mechanisms. The result has been to ensure that all states have minimal levels of access to the system, particularly satellite-based communications, which a purely market-driven regime would not have provided. The regime has, in some sense, introduced global equity and justice into aspects of its international decision making. Conditioning this approach is the distinctive institutional politics of the regime. This gives 'third world' states, and their national communications monopolies, greater voting power than might be warranted by their economic status, in comparison with the advanced capitalist states and major multinational communications corporations, although most decisions are taken by consensus.

However, as deregulation of the communications sectors in advanced economies has proceeded apace, a transnational coalition of multinational corporations has emerged to press for a more liberal international telecommunications regime. Backed also by a transnational community of finance and banking interests which are reliant upon cheap communications, the pressures for liberalization of the global communications market – to move further away from equity and justice in decision making – remain intense. Yet, as Vogler notes, even the USA, the most resolute proponent of global deregulation, has been prepared to accept '… the principle of planning a fixed satellite services system which allows each nation its own orbital position' (Vogler, 1992, p. 13) in order to avoid the breakdown of the entire regulatory order.

Table 1.2 *The top 20 traffic countries. Countries ranked by outgoing international telephone traffic, 1992, 1983 and 2000*

Country	1992		1983			2000	
	Rank	Outgoing MiTT	Rank	Outgoing MiTT	CAGR 1983–1992	Country	Outgoing MiTT*
USA	1	10,210	1	2,692	16.0%	USA	33,400
Germany	2	4,087	2	1,491	11.9%	China	12,000
UK	3	2,849	3	1,010	12.2%	Hong Kong	10,300
France	4	2,320	4	1,012	9.7%	Germany	10,000
Canada	5	2,260	5	620	20.1%	Japan	8,000
Switzerland	6	1,525	6	608	10.8%	UK	7,200
Italy	7	1,473	8	451	14.1%	Canada	7,200
Japan	8	1,284	15	164	25.7%	France	4,900
Hong Kong	9	1,137	20	95	31.7%	Italy	4,200
Netherlands	10	1,134	7	487	9.8%	Switzerland	3,500
Belgium	11	911	9	327	12.1%	Spain	3,000
Spain	12	804	13	178	18.3%	Mexico	2,900
Austria	13	713	11	250	12.3%	Taiwan, China	2,800
Sweden	14	693	10	282	10.5%	India	2,700
Australia	15	659	16	143	18.5%	Korea (Rep.)	2,400
China	16	635	36	36	37.6%	Australia	2,400
Mexico	17	599	19	102	21.8%	Netherlands	2,400
Denmark	18	425	14	172	10.5%	Belgium	2,300
Saudi Arabia	19	424	12	198	8.9%	Russia	2,000
Taiwan, China	20	367	35	37	29.1%	Austria	1,800
Total of 20 above		32,973		9,873	14.3%		
Share of world		80.6%		82.0%			
World total		40,894		12,042	14.6%		

Note: *Year 2000 data based on 1983–1992 growth rates. China and Hong Kong shown separately to maintain comparability. MiTT: millions of minutes of telecommunication traffic; CAGR: Compound Annual Growth Rate.

Source: International Telecommunication Union/TeleGeography, Inc., 1994, p. 7, Table 2.2

The politics of the regime is therefore effectively shaped by the interplay of a relatively small coalition of governments, corporate interests and technical specialists pressing for greater liberalization and a much larger group of states, and their respective national communications monopolies and technical specialists, desiring to limit, but not necessarily prevent, further liberalization. The result is the complex interaction of international and transnational political forces in which political outcomes are mediated by the institutional dynamics of the regime. Policy outcomes, as Vogler notes, do not simply reflect the underlying structure of power in the telecommunications domain (Vogler, 1992). The fact that the USA, the UK and Japan constitute 60 per cent of the global telecommunications market has not been the overriding force shaping international regulatory outcomes.

The nature of the contemporary telecommunications regime illustrates the dynamic interplay between the domestic and the international domains. Furthermore, it suggests that political space cannot be simply conceived of as coterminous with the boundedness of the territorial nation-state: politics and governance spill across national boundaries, such that there is no simple inside/outside or domestic/external duality. The telecommunications regime represents a kind of functional political space which transcends national territorial boundaries and which articulates a sense of political community, not anchored in a territorial logic, but rather in a transnational community of interests whose commonality resides in their position as provider, consumer or regulator of international telecommunications services.

1.4.2   The international human rights regime

'The defence of human dignity knows no boundaries' observes Emilio Mignone, a famous Argentinian human rights campaigner (quoted in Brysk, 1993, p. 281). This statement captures the essence of the international human rights regime as a global political and legal framework for promoting a universal or cosmopolitan conception of individual rights. It also highlights the potential conflict between a cosmopolitan view of the world, which emphasizes the notion of a proto-'global citizenship' – a universal charter of human rights – and the political organization of the world into sovereign nation-states which vigorously champion the right of non-intervention in their internal affairs. Human rights is one domain in which the clash between sovereign political power and alternative, transnational principles of political community, authority and legitimacy is most acute.

Human rights activists, such as Mignone, vigorously reject the notion of the nation-state as a bounded political space within which political authorities can treat their citizens as they so desire. But sovereignty, by implication, involves not just ultimate power over a defined political community and within a delimited territory, but also a rightful claim by the state to non-intervention in its domestic affairs by external agencies. The very existence of international human rights therefore can be considered (and is by many governments) as an unwarranted intervention in the internal affairs of sovereign states. Yet, curiously, in the post-Second World War era all states have nonetheless acquiesced in the development of a comprehensive international human rights regime.

The contemporary human rights regime consists of overlapping global and regional institutions and conventions. At the global level, human rights are firmly institutionalized in the International Bill of Human Rights, which

The European Court of Human Rights

comprises the UN Declaration of Human Rights of 1948, and the several Conventions on Civil, Political and Economic Rights adopted predominantly in the 1960s and 1970s. These were complemented in the 1980s by the Convention on the Elimination of Discrimination against Women and the Convention on the Rights of the Child. The UN Commission on Human Rights (UNCHR) is responsible for policing this system and bringing to the attention of the UN Security Council persistent abuses. In addition, the International Labour Organization (ILO) polices the area of workers' rights.

Within all the world's global regions there is an equivalent legal structure and machinery. In the case of Europe the European Commission on Human Rights (ECHR), the European Court of Human Rights and the Organization for Security and Co-operation in Europe (OSCE) oversee human rights issues and adjudicate abuses. Beyond Europe, in Africa the Banjul Charter and in the Americas the Organization of American States (OAS) Inter-American Committee on Human Rights have similar functions. But the most significant and arguably most powerful actors in promoting human rights are the multiplicity of international non-governmental organizations such as Amnesty International (AI), the League of Human Rights and the International Commission of Jurists (ICJ).

Since the 1970s '… both the number of human rights NGOs and the level of their activity has increased dramatically' (Donnelly, 1993, p. 14). There are now over 200 US NGOs associated with human rights issues, a similar number in the UK and across Europe, and expanding numbers of such organizations within the 'third world'. The significance of these NGOs is not simply that they monitor and publicize human rights abuses, but that they also campaign on specific causes and, combined, form a global network of human rights organizations.

They also operate transnationally with the consequence that they bypass governments and establish vigorous global or regional networks of activists.

In effect, these human rights NGOs represent a distinctive kind of transnational social movement which in many national contexts is regarded as radical in its espousal of citizen power and the autonomy of civil society against the dictates of the state. A telling illustration of the global role of NGOs in the area of human rights issues concerns the case of Argentina in the 1970s and early 1980s, following the military coup of 1976.

In 1977, during a visit to Argentina, US Secretary of State Cyrus Vance handed to the president of the military junta, a list of 7,500 cases of unexplained 'political disappearances', a list prepared initially by Argentinian human rights activists and forwarded to Washington-based human rights NGOs. (This figure represents only about a quarter of the number of people who are estimated to have 'disappeared' during almost eight years of dictatorship.) These disappearances were one aspect of appalling human rights violations taking place in the country at the time. By mobilizing the machinery of the international human rights regime and global networks of human rights NGOs, Argentinian activists were able to bring world media and political attention to focus on the country's human rights record. Concerted mobilization of international pressure through transnational networks, the UNCHR, OAS and individual governments, involved intense global and regional political activity. Las Madres de Plazo de Mayo (the Mothers of the Plaza de Mayo, or Mothers of the Disappeared; see Fisher, 1989), one of the most well-known human rights groups in Argentina:

> ... visited the United States, Canada and Europe in 1978 ... were delegates to the Catholic Church's Pueblo Conference, the OAS and the United Nations in 1979, testified before the US Congress in the same year, and were nominated for three Nobel Prizes in 1980. When Las Madres toured Europe ... they were received as visiting dignitaries by the Prime Minister of Spain, the French President, and the Pope.
>
> (Brysk, 1993, p. 265)

In turn, this activity focused bilateral and multilateral pressure from the US and European governments on the Argentinian state, including aid cut-offs, 'inspections' from the UN and OAS and other sanctions. External assistance from such diverse sources as the Ford Foundation, the World Council of Churches, Amnesty International, the Norwegian Parliament, Dutch churches, the governments of the USA, France, Sweden, Denmark and Switzerland, and the UN, ensured, too, that the civil liberties and human rights movements in Argentina remained highly active throughout the entire period of the military dictatorship. As a consequence, it is possible to argue that the 'international human rights regime was both an ally and arena for the Argentine human rights movement' (Brysk, 1993, p. 266). In other words, it was in some sense an extension of national political space, a new arena in which the civil rights struggle could be advanced.

However, it would be highly misleading to read from the Argentinian case that the global human rights regime is a powerful deterrent to the violation of human rights. Even international action against Argentina, by itself, did not bring about the termination of human rights abuses. On the contrary, it is quite a weak regime in that its formal organs, such as the UNCHR, have no powers of enforcement. Only in Europe is there a much more well-developed legal enforcement regime. Moreover, since states still claim sovereign immunity there is little that can be done except publicize violators and agitate for bilateral and multilateral action in other forums.

Nevertheless, the political and legal significance of the regime, in qualifying the notion of sovereign political space, should not be underestimated.

As Vincent observes, human rights have not only been incorporated into the national foreign policy postures of many states – the Dutch section of AI drafted the human rights provisions of the Dutch government's 1979 White Paper on foreign policy – but they '... now play a part in the decision about the legitimacy of a state in international society' (Vincent, 1986, p. 13). This is a significant development in the international legal practices of states with respect to what constitutes legitimate sovereign statehood.

In addition, the existence of international human rights makes individuals, not just states or IGOs, the subjects of international law, so creating a notion of 'global citizenship' which transcends the particularities of time and place. This notion of global citizenship, of rights and duties which transcend borders, has gained increased legitimacy in the post-Cold War world. The customary belief that humanitarian intervention to prevent grave violations of human rights or human tragedy is unacceptable, simply because it infringes the principle of national sovereignty, has been diluted progressively by UN-sponsored interventions in Iraq, Somalia and Bosnia. For instance, UN Security Council resolution 688 (5 April 1991), which legitimized the notion of safe havens for Kurds within Iraq, '... broke new ground in the degree to which it involved the Security Council in taking a stand against a state's ill treatment of its own people' (Greenwood, 1993, p. 36). As a consequence, there is a detectable shift of international legal and political opinion and practice against the traditional priority accorded to state sovereignty over humanitarian demands. As the UN Secretary General has stated: 'We are witnessing what is probably an irreversible shift in public attitudes towards the belief that the defence of the oppressed in the name of morality should prevail over frontiers and legal documents' (quoted in Greenwood, 1993, p. 35). But the international machinery for enforcing human rights nevertheless still remains exceedingly weak in relation to the power of most states.

What is important here is the extent to which the traditional notions of sovereign political space and political community are being reconstituted by the nature of the international human rights regime and the activities of transnational social movements in the human rights domain. Of course, the impact of this reconstitution and transnational activity is unevenly experienced across the globe: the human rights regime is barely visible in many parts of the world. Nevertheless, it is indisputable that:

... there is now an area of domestic conduct in regard to human rights ... that is under the scrutiny of international law. This does not issue a general licence for intervention ... But it does expose the internal regimes of all the members of international society to the legitimate appraisal of their peers.

(Vincent, 1986, p. 152)

In this sense states, as well as their citizens, are becoming constituents of a cosmopolitan world community.

1.4.3   Global and regional security regimes

A primary function of the state is to ensure the security of its citizens and its own territorial integrity. Yet the existence of global and regional security regimes imposes significant constraints upon the freedom of action of states in this most essential domain of state power. Indeed, there is a clear tension between the notion of the state as an autonomous actor (that is, having ultimate responsibility for its own survival), equipped with an 'independent' military capability, and its insertion into global and regional security structures which set limits to the kinds of defence and foreign policies (or actions) which governments may pursue.

Until fairly recently the security of all states was shaped decisively by the 'Great Contest' between the USA and the Soviet Union. In this bipolar system the scope for states to initiate an 'independent' foreign and defence policy was considerably restricted. In the post-Cold War world of the 1990s such external constraints have not been eradicated completely, they have merely been reconfigured. The global power structure is today more multipolar, bringing with it a highly complex set of international constraints. Within this more complex structure, the strategic and foreign policy options confronting an individual state are defined by its geographical location and its insertion into global and regional power hierarchies. The tendency has been for increasing emphasis to be placed upon collective defence and this is particularly evident in the post-Cold War European security system.

For the present (at the time of writing), NATO remains the key forum within which Western European defence strategies are formulated and agreed. Its day-to-day functioning has encouraged the creation of strong transgovernmental networks, or communities of interest, between national defence bureaucracies and military forces. Even the ending of the Cold War

NATO headquarters, Brussels

has not undermined its primary functions since it now embraces the former Warsaw Pact members, including Russia, in a Partnership for Peace (P for P) arrangement and the North Atlantic Council for Co-operation (NACC). Both the P for P and the NACC bring together the governing bodies of the Alliance and military and diplomatic representatives from former neutral states like Sweden, and the newly established Eastern European and ex-Soviet states to debate European-wide security matters and to develop military co-operation.

In both the routine conduct of its affairs and in times of international crisis (such as the 1991 Gulf War), NATO provides an institutional mechanism for multilateral decision taking and military co-operation which qualifies very significantly notions of national sovereignty. Its most powerful impact has been in redefining, through multilateral mechanisms of defence policy making and co-ordination, the national defence strategies of its member states, including even the USA. Security is therefore no longer defined primarily in terms of the defence of national territorial boundaries, but rather in terms of collective defence and thereby international security.

The ending of the Cold War, combined with instabilities in Europe, has encouraged further this internationalization or, more accurately, regionalization of security affairs. Existing institutions such as the Western European Union and the Organization for Security and Co-operation in Europe have been given new responsibilities and functions. These have involved the creation of distinctive mechanisms of international consultation and co-ordination which reach deeply into the domestic affairs of member states. Europe, in effect, is witnessing the development of a new structure of collective security – a revised 'Concert of Europe' – which invites a tighter integration of military and security affairs. Collective, rather than national, defence is today a developing reality. It is instructive to note that even traditionally neutral states, such as Sweden, no longer feel able to sustain their military independence and neutral posture. Moreover, given increasing budgetary constraints and the escalating costs of defence hardware, '... in the not too distant future, no European country will be able to mount a unilateral conventional military campaign that can defeat any adversary able to conduct modern military operations' (Zelikow, 1992). Military-industrial factors reinforce the trend towards stronger collective organization of defence functions. As the 'New Concert of Europe' evolves, aspects of state sovereignty and autonomy are being renegotiated and qualified for each state by overlapping security regimes and organizations. As Rotfeld concludes, in Europe the:

> ... formation of a new co-operative security system calls not only for adapting existing procedures and mechanisms to a completely new situation but also, above all, for agreeing new principles of collaboration for those states. It requires a departure from the classical academic interpretation of sovereignty and a new definition of matters which fall within the discretionary internal competencies of states.
>
> (Rotfeld, 1992, p. 582)

Beyond Europe, too, there are similar moves towards the regionalization of security regimes in Asia, Africa and Latin America.

Alongside this regionalization of security is a developing recognition that traditional conceptions of security, which privilege both notions of 'national security' and 'military security', are no longer adequate to capture the full range of potential threats to the welfare and survival of national communities. Thus economic security and environmental security have crept up the agenda of state policy making. In the USA both economic and environmental security figure prominently in contemporary national security strategy. Many of these new threats to security are inherently transnational in character and require multilateral resolution. As Dalby observes, this new security agenda represents a further distinct challenge to traditional conceptions of security, but most particularly: '… the modern political assumptions of territorial strategies for its provision' (Dalby, 1992, p. 504).

It would be absurd to conclude from this discussion that 'national security' is an obsolete concept or practice. Rather, the point is that in the post-Cold War world the interlocking nature of the world military and security order means that national security can no longer effectively be achieved by unilateral, or simply military, means (if it ever could). National security is now intimately connected to the dynamics of regional and global security regimes and is being redefined in respect of vulnerabilities to new transnational (economic and ecological) threats. Even within the sacred domain of security, processes of globalization and regionalization have called '… into question the meaning of the traditional division between "inside" and "outside" on which rests the conceptualization of the sovereign state as a self-contained, territorially bound decisional unit' (Camilleri and Falk, 1992, p. 166).

1.4.4 Regimes, disjunctures and political space

Globalization, as the discussion of regimes indicates, involves the tighter enmeshment of states and societies in global, as well as regional, networks and systems of interaction. Simply in order to fulfil the demands of their citizens, governments, in a highly interconnected world order, become '… increasingly enmeshed in a network of interdependencies and regulatory/collaborative arrangements from which exit is generally not a feasible option' (Zacher, 1992, p. 60). This 'shrinking political world' highlights the growing disjunctures between the actual practices of states and the ideology of sovereign statehood and state power. It also destabilizes the conventional representation of international political space as organized solely into strictly delimited, bounded, exclusive and sovereign territorial units. Both these points demand further scrutiny.

Whilst the discussion of regimes indicates that states remain of continuing importance in global politics, it also suggests that the nature of sovereignty is being recast and reconstituted by complex patterns of global and regional enmeshment. This reconstitution arises from the growing disjunctures between the formal claim of states to sovereign power and the actual practices of states confronted by overlapping global, regional, multilateral and transnational networks and power structures. In the economic, cultural, security, ecological, social and political domains, globalization has stretched social relations across territorial space, dissolving the boundaries between the domestic and the external realms. One of the political consequences of this enmeshment is to compromise the claims of states to have ultimate control over their own destinies. The notion of the sovereign state as 'a national community of fate', which governs itself and determines its own future, sits uneasily alongside the globalization of economic production and exchange, the internationalization of security, the growing authority of international regimes and global institutions, the internationalization of domestic policy and the domestication of international policy. For globalization encourages a growing separation or distancing of sites of political decision taking from the communities, local or national, which are the subjects (intended or unintended) of such decisions. This has profound consequences both for the doctrine of national sovereignty and democratic polities which are constructed upon an assumption that the state has sole jurisdiction within its own territorial boundaries and is directly responsible for ensuring the welfare and security of its citizens. Yet this '... idea is challenged fundamentally by the nature and pattern of global interconnections ... National communities by no means exclusively "programme" the actions, decisions and policies of their governments and the latter by no means simply determine what is right or appropriate for their own citizens alone' (Held, 1991, p. 202).

Although the post-Second World War phase of globalization is often interpreted as signalling the decline of the nation-state, the evidence from the discussion of regimes suggests that, on the contrary, the state remains a robust and powerful actor in the global system. But the disjuncture between the ideology and practices of modern states reveals the beginnings of a re-ordering of sovereign authority and a reconfiguration of international political space. To talk in terms of the end of the nation-state is to misread the contemporary conjuncture (this is discussed further in Chapter 2). Rather, the evidence suggests that global and regional patterns of enmeshment are displacing '... notions of sovereignty as an illimitable, indivisible and exclusive form of public power ... Sovereignty itself has to be conceived today as already divided among a number of agencies – national, regional and international – and limited by the very nature of this plurality' (Held, 1991, p. 222).

Associated with this reconstitution of sovereignty is a re-ordering of international political space. The existence of international regimes, global and regional institutions of governance, and transnational social movements, organizations or communities points to the emergence of new kinds of political space which are not primarily territorially rooted or territorially bounded. Thus in the case of the telecommunications and human rights regimes it is possible to think of political space in functional, rather than territorial, terms. Each of these regimes regulates a specific field of social activity across national territorial space. Moreover, transnational social movements and political organizations reflect the growing significance of attempts to redefine political space and political community in terms which escape the boundedness of the territorial nation-state. Human rights activists, as with the ecology movement, therefore commence from the assumption of global community or global citizenship and the indivisibility of local, national and global political space. Globalization involves a spatial reorganization of political life and activity in which political space is no longer coterminous with sovereign territorial space.

If globalization is responsible for a reconfiguration of international political space it, is also implicated in the reinterpretation and changing meaning attached to the notion of political community. Since the emergence of the modern state the 'good community' has been associated solely with the national community and sovereign territorial space. Sovereignty and nationalism thus fixed the notion of the 'good community' in terms of 'us' versus 'the other', insider/outsider. A world of flows and connections promotes loyalties and allegiances which transcend national boundaries and thus creates the potential for new kinds of transnational 'imagined communities' (discussed further in Chapters 4 and 5). This is evident in respect of new social movements, such as the women's and environmental movements, but also in respect of ethnic and cultural communities which retain a sense of hyphenated identities. On to a global mosaic of national communities globalization is overlaying new kinds and forms of political community which transcend territorial boundaries.

However, it would be foolish to read these developments as prefiguring the emergence of a world society or a global polity in which the nation-state is made powerless. For globalization is a highly uneven process and is associated with the reproduction of global hierarchies of privilege, control and exclusion. It fragments as it integrates so that some regions, states, communities and households are tightly enmeshed in global or regional networks whilst others are completely marginalized. This unevenness characterizes a highly asymmetrical pattern of global power relations. Globalization therefore contributes to global processes of social and political fragmentation and stratification which are most clearly expressed in the contemporary urban settings of today's major world cities. Neither is there any logical reason to assume that a shrinking world is a more harmonious world since, as Bull observes: '... awareness of other societies, even where it is "perfect", does not merely help to remove imagined conflicts of interest or ideology which do not exist; it also reveals conflicts of interest or ideology that do exist' (Bull, 1977, p. 280).

Activity 5 Turn now to Reading E, 'Rethinking sovereignty: some tentative conclusions', by Joseph A. Camilleri. As you read it, think about the following questions:

(a) What are the main trends and countertrends which Camilleri identifies?

(b) What are the implications of globalization for sovereign statehood?

(c) Can you identify in the discussion of the three regimes specific illustrations of what Camilleri refers to as a cosmopolitan ethic or transnational loyalties?

(d) What is his vision of the emerging world order?

(e) How would you classify his theoretical approach in relation to the realist versus critical geopolitics debate, and why?

Camilleri concludes that the contemporary world order is beset with contradictory impulses and therefore appears incredibly 'disordered'. Indeed, as the discussion of global politics and international regimes has demonstrated, globalization is associated simultaneously with the persistence of the nation-state, the emergence of a distinctive form of global politics and governance, and the beginnings of a re-ordering of international political space. It might be argued therefore that the contemporary world order is best described as bifurcated: on the one hand there is the persistence of the states system and on the other hand, a growing plurality of authority structures and overlapping loyalties which represent an emerging global society. Such a bifurcated order embodies many possible future end-states: from an increasingly fragmented and conflictual world to the formation of the world's first global civilization.

Summary of section 1.4

This section has explored the nature of governance in the global political system and the disjunctures between the claims of states to sovereign statehood and the actual practices of states. This has involved:

o Examining the dynamics of international regimes which can be defined as international social institutions governing or regulating specific domains of international or transnational activity.

o Drawing upon the workings of the telecommunications, human rights and global security regimes to highlight the globalization of political activity, the emergence of new kinds of political space and the challenges to sovereign statehood.

o Isolating the growing disjunctures between the actual practices of states and the ideology of the sovereign territorial state and state power brought about by intense patterns of global and regional enmeshment.

o Indicating how globalization is encouraging a reconstitution of sovereignty and a re-ordering of international political space.

o Demonstrating how globalization is transforming the contemporary world order which is best described as bifurcated.

1.5 Conclusion: globalization, world order and political space

This chapter has explored two quite distinct conceptions of world order and political space: that associated with traditional geopolitics and realism alongside that associated with critical geopolitics. It has argued that whilst processes of globalization are transforming the very foundations of world order, by reconstituting sovereign statehood and re-ordering international political space, this project is neither historically inevitable nor yet fully realized. As a result, the contemporary world order is best understood as a *bifurcated world order* in which the inter-state system is juxtaposed with an evolving global society in which politics and political space are being rearticulated.

bifurcated world order

There is much to commend the concept of a bifurcated world order as a description of the 'messy appearances' or 'patterned mess' (to borrow Michael Mann's phrase) which defines global politics at the end of the twentieth century (Mann, 1993, p. 4). But a bifurcated world order is by no means a stable one and its inherent contradictions may well prove the source of its undoing. For, as Camilleri hinted in Reading E, the present conjecture has historical parallels. In particular, the medieval era in Europe, during which modern states and territorial conceptions of sovereign political space were violently forged, has some resonance in contemporary developments. The existence in medieval times of overlapping loyalties and an array of authority structures from the local to the transnational, supranational and national, co-existing alongside an evolving system of territorially defined political communities and sovereign states, has similarities to the pluralistic character of global politics and the bifurcated world order which define the contemporary historical condition. This is not to argue the case of those who suggest that 'back to the future' best describes the present. Rather, it is to suggest that a 'new medievalism' may be a useful, if perhaps historically inaccurate, metaphor for thinking about the present era.

As Bull describes it, the 'new medievalism' represents:

... a modern and secular equivalent of the kind of universal political organization that existed in Western Christendom in the Middle Ages. In that system no ruler or state was sovereign in the sense of being supreme over a given segment of the Christian population; each had to share authority with vassals beneath, and with the Pope and (in Germany and Italy) the Holy Roman Emperor above ... It might ... seem fanciful to imagine ... a modern and secular counterpart of it that embodies its central characteristic: a system of overlapping authority and multiple loyalty.

(Bull, 1977, p. 254)

This is very similar to the kind of world order which has been described in the preceding pages. Moreover, as Bull goes on to remark:

It is familiar that sovereign states today share the stage of world politics with 'other actors' just as in medieval times the state had to share the stage with 'other associations' ... If modern states were to come to share their authority over their actions, and their ability to command their loyalties, on the one hand with regional and world authorities, and on the other hand with sub-state or sub-national authorities, to such an extent that the concept of sovereignty ceased to be applicable, then a neo-medieval form of universal political order might be said to have emerged.

(Bull, 1977, pp. 254–5)

A neo-medieval world order is one in which, like the bifurcated world order of today, political space is not defined solely by the territorial boundaries of the sovereign state. A prime illustration of this neo-medievalism is the European Union which is constituted by overlapping authorities and contested loyalties. In this sense the EU represents a continuous struggle or '... search for new political spaces' and poses rather dramatically the question: where lies '... the proper place for political action and accountability: the nation-state or the international body?' (Pattie, 1994, p. 1010). However, this question, alongside further exploration of the nature of today's 'neo-medieval' world order, is addressed more substantively in succeeding chapters.

References

AGNEW, J. (1994) 'The territorial trap – the geographical assumptions of international relations theory', *Review of International Political Economy*, Vol. 1, No. 1, pp. 53–80.

ALLEN, J. (1995a) 'Global worlds', in Allen, J. and Massey, D. (eds) *Geographical Worlds*, Oxford, Oxford University Press in association with The Open University (Volume 1 in this series).

ALLEN, J. (1995b) 'Crossing borders: footloose multinationals?', in Allen and Hamnett (1995).

ALLEN, J. and HAMNETT, C. (1995) *A Shrinking World? Global Unevenness and Inequality*, Oxford, Oxford University Press in association with The Open University (Volume 2 in this series).

BRYSK, A. (1993) 'From above and below – social movements, the international system, and human rights in Argentina', *Comparative Political Studies*, Vol. 26, No. 3, pp. 259–85.

BULL, H. (1977) *The Anarchical Society*, London, Macmillan.

BUSH, PRESIDENT G. (1990) Address to the Special Joint Session of Congress, 11 September, Washington, DC, United States Information Service.

CAMILLERI, J.A. (1990) 'Rethinking sovereignty in a shrinking, fragmented world', in Walker, R.B.J. and Mendlovitz, S.H. (eds) *Contending Sovereignties: Redefining Political Community*, Boulder, CO, and London, Lynne Rienner Publishers.

CAMILLERI, J.A. and FALK, J. (1992) *The End of Sovereignty: The Politics of a Shrinking and Fragmented World*, Aldershot, Edward Elgar.

CLARKE, M. (1992) *Britain's External Relations*, London, Macmillan.

COWHEY, P.F. (1990) 'The international telecommunications regime', *International Organization*, Vol. 44, No. 2, pp. 169–98.

DALBY, S. (1992) 'Ecopolitical discourse: environmental security and political geography', *Progress in Human Geography*, Vol. 16, No. 4, pp. 503–22.

DONNELLY, J. (1993) *International Human Rights*, Boulder, CO, Westview Press.

FISHER, J. (1989) *Mothers of the Disappeared*, London, Zed Books.

GEERTZ, C. (1993) *Local Knowledge*, London, Fontana Press.

GEORGE, J. (1994) *Discourses of Global Politics – A Critical (Re) Introduction to International Relations*, London, Macmillan.

GILPIN, R. (1987) *The Political Economy of International Relations*, Princeton, NJ, Princeton University Press.

GREENWOOD, C. (1993) 'Is there a right of humanitarian intervention?' *The World Today*, February, pp. 34–40.

HALL, S. (1995) 'New cultures for old', in Massey, D. and Jess, P. (eds) *A Place in the World? Places, Cultures and Globalization*, Oxford, Oxford University Press in association with The Open University (Volume 4 in this series).

HELD, D. (1991) 'Democracy, the nation-state and the global system', in Held, D. (ed.) *Political Theory Today*, Cambridge, Polity Press.

INTERNATIONAL TELECOMMUNICATION UNION (1994) *World Telecommunication Development Report 1994*, Geneva, ITU.

INTERNATIONAL TELECOMMUNICATION UNION (1994) *Direction of Traffic: International Telephone Traffic 1994*, Geneva, ITU.

JOLL, J. (1984) *The Origins of the First World War*, London, Longman.

KEARNS, G. (1993) 'Fin de siècle geopolitics', in Taylor, P.J.S. (ed.) *Political Geography of the Twentieth Century*, London, Belhaven Press.

KEGLEY, C.W. JR. and RAYMOND, G. (1994) *A Multipolar Peace? Great Power Politics in the Twenty-First Century*, New York, St Martin's Press.

KIDRON, M. and SMITH, D. (1983) *The War Atlas: Armed Conflict–Armed Peace: A Pluto Press Project*, London, Pan.

LASH, S. and URRY, J. (1994) *Economies of Signs and Spaces*, London, Sage.

LEYSHON, A. (1995) 'Annihilating space?: the speed-up of communications', in Allen and Hamnett (1995).

MANN, M. (1993) *The Sources of Social Power II*, Cambridge, Cambridge University Press.

MANSBACH, R., FERGUSON, Y. and LAMPERT, D. (1976) *The Web of World Politics*, Englewood Cliffs, NJ, Prentice-Hall.

McGREW, A. (1992) *'Conceptualizing global politics'*, in McGrew and Lewis (eds) (1992).

McGREW, A. and LEWIS, P. (EDS) (1992) *Global Politics*, Cambridge, Polity Press.

MODELSKI, G. (1972) *Principles of World Politics*, New York, Free Press.

MURPHY, C. (1994) *International Organization and Industrial Change*, Cambridge, Polity Press.

NIEROP, T. (1994) *Systems and Regions in Global Politics*, Chichester, John Wiley and Sons.

Ó TUATHAIL, G. (1993) 'The effacement of place? US foreign policy and the spatiality of the Gulf Crisis', *Antipode*, Vol. 25, No. 1, pp. 4–31.

Ó TUATHAIL, G. (1994) '(Dis)placing geopolitics: writing on the maps of global politics', *Environment and Planning D: Society and Space*, Vol. 12, pp. 525–46.

OFFICE OF THE PRESIDENT OF THE UNITED STATES (1991) *National Security Stategy of the United States*, Washington, DC, The White House.

PATTIE, C.J. (1994) 'Forgetting Fukuyama: new spaces of politics', *Environment and Planning D*, Vol. 26, No. 7, pp. 1007–10.

ROSENAU, J. (1990) *Turbulence in World Politics*, London, Harvester Wheatsheaf.

ROSENAU, J. (1992) 'Governance, order and change in world politics', in Rosenau, J. and Czempiel, E-O. (eds) *Governance Without Government*, Cambridge, Cambridge University Press.

ROTFELD, J. (1992) 'European security structures in transition', in *SIPRI Yearbook 1992*, Stockholm, Oxford University Press.

RUGGIE, J. (1993) 'Territoriality and beyond', *International Organization*, Vol. 41, No. 1, pp. 139–74.

SHORT, J.R. (1993) *An Introduction to Political Geography* (2nd edn), London and New York, Routledge.

US DEPARTMENT OF DEFENSE (1993) *The Bottom-Up Review: Forces for a New Era*, Washington, DC, US Department of Defense.

VINCENT, J. (1986) *Human Rights and International Relations*, Cambridge, Cambridge University Press.

VOGLER, J. (1992) 'Regimes and the global commons', in McGrew and Lewis (eds) (1992).

WADE, R. (1994) 'Globalization: evidence and hype', mimeo.

WALKER, R. (1993) *Inside/Outside*, Cambridge, Cambridge University Press.

WALTZ, K. (1979) *Theory of International Politics*, New York, Addison-Wesley.

WARD, B. (1989) 'Telecommunications and the globalization of financial services', *Professional Geographer*, Vol. 41, No. 3, pp. 257–71.

WILLIAMS, P. (1994) 'Transnational criminal organizations and international security', *Survival*, Vol. 36, No. 1, pp. 96–113.

YEARLEY, S. (1995) 'Dirty connections: transnational pollution', in Allen and Hamnett (1995).

YOUNG, O. (1989) *International Regimes*, Ithaca, NY, Cornell University Press.

ZACHER, M. (1992) 'The decaying pillars of the Westphalian temple', in Czempiel, E-O. and Rosenau, J. (eds) *Governance without Government*, Cambridge, Cambridge University Press.

ZELIKOW, P. (1992) 'The New Concert of Europe', *Survival*, Vol. 34, No. 2, pp. 13–30.

Introduction

The Cold War is behind us. The Soviet Union is no longer. The threat that drove our defense decision-making for four and a half decades – that determined our strategy and tactics, our doctrine, the size and shape of our forces, the design of our weapons, and the size of our defense budgets – is gone.

Now that the Cold War is over, the questions we face in the Department of Defense are: How do we structure the armed forces of the United States for the future? How much defense is enough in the post-Cold War era?

Several important events over the past four years underscore the revolutionary nature of recent changes in the international security environment and shed light on this new era and on America's future defense and security requirements.

o   In 1989, the fall of the Berlin Wall and the collapse of communism throughout Eastern Europe precipitated a strategic shift away from containment of the Soviet empire.

o   In 1990, Iraq's brutal invasion of Kuwait signaled a new class of regional dangers facing America – dangers spurred not by a global, empire-building ideological power, but by rogue leaders set on regional domination through military aggression while simultaneously pursuing nuclear, biological, and chemical weapons capabilities. The world's response to Saddam's invasion also demonstrated the potential in the new era for broad-based, collective military action to thwart such tyrants.

o   In 1991, the failed Soviet coup demonstrated the Russian people's desire for democratic change and hastened the collapse of the Soviet Union as a national entity and military foe.

In the aftermath of such epochal events, it has become clear that the framework that guided our security policy during the Cold War is inadequate for the future. We must determine the characteristics of this new era, develop a new strategy, and restructure our armed forces and defense programs accordingly. We cannot, as we did for the past several decades, premise this year's forces, programs, and budgets on incremental shifts from last year's efforts. We must rebuild our defense strategy, forces, and defense programs and budgets from the bottom up.

[…]

An era of new dangers

Most striking in the transition from the Cold War is the shift in the nature of the dangers to our interests … .

The new dangers fall into four broad categories:

o   **Dangers posed by nuclear weapons and other weapons of mass destruction,** including dangers associated with the proliferation of nuclear, biological, and chemical weapons as well as those associated with the large stocks of these weapons that remain in the former Soviet Union.

o   **Regional dangers,** posed primarily by the threat of large-scale aggression by major regional powers with interests antithetical to our own, but also by the potential for smaller, often internal, conflicts based on ethnic or religious animosities, state-sponsored terrorism, and subversion of friendly governments.

o   **Dangers to democracy and reform,** in the former Soviet Union, Eastern Europe, and elsewhere.

o   **Economic dangers** to our national security, which could result if we fail to build a strong, competitive and growing economy.

[…]

Major regional conflicts

During the Cold War, our military planning was dominated by the need to confront numerically superior Soviet forces in Europe, the Far East, and South-west Asia. Now, our focus is on the need to project power into regions important to our interests and to defeat potentially hostile regional powers, such as North Korea and Iraq. Although these powers are unlikely to threaten the United States directly, these countries and others like them have shown that they are willing and able to field forces sufficient to threaten important US interests, friends, and allies. Operation Desert Storm was a powerful demonstration of the need to counter such regional aggression.

[…]

[…] Hence, we must prepare our forces to assist those of our friends and allies in deterring, and ultimately, defeating aggression, should it occur.

[…]

Source: US Department of Defense, 1993, pp. 1–3

Reading B: *'National security strategy of the United States'*

East Asia and the Pacific

East Asia and the Pacific are home to some of the world's most economically and politically dynamic societies. The region also includes some of the last traditional Communist regimes on the face of the globe. Regional hotspots tragically persist on the Korean peninsula and in Cambodia, and there are territorial disputes in which progress is long overdue, including the Soviet Union's continued occupation of Japan's Northern Territories.

In this complex environment, an era of Soviet adventurism is on the ebb, even while its effects linger. This is placing new stresses on Vietnam, Cambodia and North Korea as Soviet military and economic aid declines and Moscow seeks to improve relations with Seoul, Tokyo and other capitals. China is coming to view its neighbors in a new light, and is gradually adjusting to a changing perception of the Soviet threat.

Through a web of bilateral relationships, the United States has pursued throughout the postwar period a policy of engagement in support of the stability and security that are prerequisites to economic and political progress. U.S. power remains welcome in key states in the region, who recognize the pivotal role we continue to play in the regional balance. We remain a key factor of reassurance and stability. By ensuring freedom of the seas through naval and air strength and by offering these capabilities as a counterweight in the region's power equations, we are likely to remain welcome in an era of shifting patterns and possible […] new frictions.

Today's basically healthy conditions cannot be taken for granted. We will continue to be a beacon for democracy and human rights. We will meet our responsibilities in the security field. We will also remain actively engaged in promoting free and expanding markets through Asian Pacific Economic Cooperation, recognizing that economic progress is a major ingredient in Asia's political stability and democratic progress.

[…] [O]ur alliance with Japan remains of enormous strategic importance. Our hope is to see the US–Japan global partnership extend beyond its traditional confines and into fields like refugee relief, non-proliferation and the environment.

On the Korean peninsula, we and the Republic of Korea seek to persuade North Korea of the benefit of confidence-building measures as a first step to lasting peace and reunification. We firmly believe that true stability can only be achieved through direct North–South talks. At the same time, the United States remains committed to the security of the Republic of Korea as it continues to open its economic and political systems. We are increasingly concerned about North Korea's failure to observe its obligations under the Nuclear Non-Proliferation Treaty, and consider this to be the most pressing security issue on the peninsula.

China, like the Soviet Union, poses a complex challenge as it proceeds inexorably toward major systemic change. China's inward focus and struggle to achieve stability will not preclude increasing interaction with its neighbors as trade and technology advance. Consultations and contact with China will be central features of our policy, lest we intensify the isolation that shields repression. Change is inevitable in China,

and our links with China must endure.

[...]

Source: Office of the President of the United States, The White House, 1991, p. 9

Reading C: *John Agnew, 'Emerging spatial forms'*

[...] Over the past 20 years, [...] spatial practices, the ways in which space is produced and used, have changed profoundly. In particular, both territorial states and non-state actors now operate in a world in which state boundaries have become culturally and economically permeable to decisions and flows emanating from networks of power not captured by singularly territorial representations of space (Nye, 1988; Stopford and Strange, 1991).

[...]

[...] The pace of economic transactions has quickened exponentially over the past 20 years (Knox and Agnew, 1994). Wealth is no longer tied very closely to territory. An interesting example of this is how little of the accumulated wealth of Kuwait was accessible to the Iraqi army after its invasion of Kuwait in 1990. Much of it was stashed away in *foreign* assets and bank accounts. [...]

[...]

[...] The signs of a new spatial organization departing from the conventional spatial representation of state territoriality are everywhere. On one scale there is fragmentation or localization; what Eco (1987) calls 'the return of the Middle Ages'. The Soviet Union, which was in part an attempt to weld many regional ethnic groups into one state, has broken up along its ethnic fault lines. The replacement states are trapped between the desire to acquire the accoutrements of statehood (flags, currencies, militaries, etc.) and the need to collaborate economically with one another. In the former Yugoslavia Serbs and Croats fight violently with one another and with the Moslems of Bosnia over national differences that in a multicultural milieu like New York City would not seem of major import. Many

French-speaking Quebecois openly advocate separation from a state, Canada, that has already given them considerable autonomy. In nominally secular India radical Hindus suggest that the country should become more Hindu, initiating a renewal of regional, linguistic and religious enmities. In Africa the territorial states inherited from colonialism have failed to establish national identities that override local and ethnic loyalties, leading to complaints that they are 'failed' or 'quasi' states (Jackson, 1990).

Regions, religions and ethnicity everywhere challenge territorial states as the loci of political identity. In many countries social classes and established ideologies appealing to 'class interests' have lost their value as sources of identity. Increasingly, the links between the places of everyday life in which political commitments are forged and the territorial states that have structured and channelled political activities are under stress. New loyalties everywhere undermine state political monopoly.

On another scale, in the Uruguay Round of the GATT, states are negotiating about opening up trade in services, which would involve them admitting more foreigners and 'foreign' ways of doing business into their territories. Foreigners are already migrating at rates rarely experienced in modern world history. In Europe the dominant political issue of the 1990s is the movement towards a more unified European Community and whether membership should be expanded or political unification deepened. The world's financial service industries are increasingly globalized, operating around the clock without much attention to state boundaries. Many manufacturing industries have branch plant and research facilities scattered across the globe. Even that most sacrosanct of state powers, the power to wage war, is becoming the mercenary activity that Machiavelli decried in his day. The 1990–1 Gulf War, the first major post-Cold War conflict, involved the US in a major exercise in coalition building, cost sharing, and use of the United Nations that smacks more of collective security with the US as its military arm than of unilateral action by a single nation-state.

Why have these apparently contradictory spatial forms of fragmentation and globalization emerged together? The most obvious point is that globalization is not synonymous with homogenization. The globalized world economy is based on the transnational movement of the mobile factors of production: capital, labour and technology. As this movement has occurred at an increasing pace, localities and regions within states have become increasingly vulnerable to economic restructuring. [...] With increasing economic competition and increased capital mobility and the collapse of state socialism, the outcome has been increased uneven development and spatial differentiation rather than homogenization.

[...]

One result has been an evolving redefinition of economic interests from national and sectoral (age group, social class, etc.) divisions to regional and local levels. The struggle for jobs and incomes takes place within a global spatial division of labour that no longer parallels territorial-state boundaries. Another has been that political identities are no longer anchored in singular nation-state identities. For one thing, increasing numbers of people live in what Said (1979, p. 18) has called 'a generalized condition of homelessness': a world in which identities are less clearly bonded to specific national territories. Refugees, migrants and travellers are the most obvious of these homeless. [...] From this perspective, globalization has provided the context for fragmentation. Without the first, reducing expectations of and loosening ties to the state, the second, disturbing and reformulating identities, could not occur.

Of course, the territorial state, especially in Western Europe and North America, has continuing strengths within its borders. National political identities are still strong within many territorial states. Mann's (1984) 'society-defining' state is still not exhausted despite attempts in the 1980s to spread the gospels of economic liberalization and privatization of state-provided services. States are major employers and through their demand for goods and services they are also important economic actors in their own right. The state still provides 'legitimation services' through social spending and potential levers over economic transactions that a fragile position within the world economy has not totally undermined. States, especially the more powerful ones, are not yet pitiful giants. Labour, investments and, sometimes, monetary policies can still have tremendous impacts on retaining and attracting investments (Parboni, 1984; Garrett and Lange, 1991).

At the same time, however, states must now mobilize more actively than in the past to attract and keep capital investment within their borders and open up foreign markets for their producers. Much contemporary economic discussion in the United States is about how best to do this. One group preaches a 'geoeconomic doctrine' in which the US (and 'its' capitalists) is portrayed as in an economic 'war' with Japan (in particular) (see Ó Tuathail, 1993). Another group accepts the advent of transnational capitalism and argues for policies that will encourage investment in the US territorial economy irrespective of its 'national' origin (e.g. Reich, 1991). As Reich puts it, 'Who is Us?' is the question of the day.

Finally, the territorial state has a continuing *normative* appeal. In his classic work *Politics and Vision*, Wolin made the case as follows:

To reject the state [means] denying the central referent of the political, abandoning a whole range of notions and the practices to which they point – citizenship, obligation, general authority. [...]

(Wolin, 1960, p. 417)

However, such a juridical state should not be confused with the absolute sovereign of conventional modern political theory. Territorial states as we have known them are not necessarily the best instruments for Wolin's political life. [...]

The main point in reviewing the continuing strengths of territorial states is to suggest that globalization and fragmentation do not signal their terminal decline; the Final Fall of the territorial state. But at the same time, [...] the world that is in the process of emergence cannot be adequately understood in terms of the fixed territorial spaces of mainstream international relations theory.

Conclusion

By means of three geographical assumptions the territorial state has come to provide the intellectual foundation for [...] mainstream [...] international relations theory [...]. The first assumption, and the one that is most fundamental theoretically, is the reification of state territorial spaces as fixed units of secure sovereign space. The second is the division of the domestic from the foreign. The third geographical assumption is of the territorial state as existing prior to and as a container of society. Each of these assumptions is problematic, and increasingly so. Social, economic and political life cannot be [...] contained within the territorial boundaries of states through the methodological assumption of 'timeless space'. Complex population movements, the growing mobility of capital, increased ecological interdependence, the expanding information economy, and [...] new military technologies challenge the geographical basis of conventional international relations theory.

The critical theoretical issue, therefore, is the historical relationship between territorial states and the broader social and economic structures and geopolitical order (or form of spatial practice) in which these states must operate. It has been the lack of attention in the mainstream literature to this connection that has led into the territorial trap. In idealizing the territorial state we cannot see a world in which its role and meaning change. [...]

References

ECO, U. (1987) *Travels in Hyperreality*, San Diego, CA, Harcourt Brace Jovanovich.

GARRETT, G. and LANGE, P. (1991) 'Political responses to interdependence: what's "left" for the left?', *International Organization*, Vol. 45, pp. 539–64.

JACKSON, R. (1990) *Quasi-states: Sovereignty, International Relations and the Third World*, Cambridge, Cambridge University Press.

KNOX, P. and AGNEW, J. (1994) *The Geography of the World Economy*, London, Arnold.

MANN, M. (1984) 'The autonomous power of the state: its origins, mechanisms and results', *European Journal of Sociology*, Vol. 25, pp. 185–213.

NYE, J. (1988) 'Neorealism and neoliberalism', *World Politics*, Vol. 40, pp. 235–51.

Ó TUATHAIL, G. (1993) 'Japan as threat: geo-economic discourses on the US–Japan relationship in US civil society, 1987–1991', in Williams, C.H. (ed.) *The Political Geography of the New World Order*, London, Belhaven Press.

PARBONI, R. (1984) *The Dollar and its Rivals*, London, Verso.

REICH, R. (1991) *The Work of Nations: Preparing Ourselves for 21st Century Capitalism*, New York, Knopf.

SAID, E. (1979) 'Zionism from the standpoint of its victims', *Social Text*, Vol. 1, pp. 7–58.

STOPFORD, J.M. and STRANGE, S. (1991) *Rival States, Rival Firms: Competition for World Market Shares*, Cambridge, Cambridge University Press.

WOLIN, S.S. (1960) *Politics and Vision: Continuity and Innovation in Western Political Thought*, Boston, MA, Little, Brown.

Source: Agnew, 1994, pp. 72–80

[...]

We find it useful to consider political actors as now interacting within a global *architecture of power*.[1] As with the architecture of a city, the ability to exercise power is shaped by an integrated technical, physical and social environment. Also, as in a city, the exercise of power occurs in a recognizable if complex pattern. In this sense, as with the architecture of most cities, the architecture of power has a design although no single designer. In invoking this description we are seeking to avoid the trap of privileging one particular mechanism or structure of power (the nation-state, military force, the market, ideology, technology) before we begin our analysis. Rather, we are approaching the exercise of power, constraint and control as a systemic phenomenon. From this perspective we may inquire into the current and developing form of the architecture of power and its effects on individuals, institutions (whether corporations, states, or elements of states, markets, ideology), and much more. Each of these both shapes and is shaped by the architecture of power.

In the globally integrated social world of the 1990s, although the actions of corporations and local, national, regional and international government agencies influence, and are in turn influenced by, the development of worldwide systems of technology, the resulting architecture of power has a form which is not simply determined or planned by any individual or single institution. Its form develops dynamically, according to the results of struggles and alliances between the various social and physical components which make up that architecture. At any given time it allows some actors to be more powerful than others, but the power configuration is neither fixed nor immutable, since the shape of the architecture is itself undergoing change. It is within this more complex and integrated architecture of power that states must now act, and it is in relation to its dynamically developing form that the validity of the picture of a world of sovereign states and communities must now be assessed.

The shape of the architecture of power is by no means uniform. [...] There are differences yet there are also many commonalities – in the way workers are controlled, in the technology of production and the direction of its development, in the technology of coercion, in the desire to trade, in the increasingly important intrusion of transnational corporations of various complexions and in the potent dynamics of the global market. Further, [...] there is an evident process of convergence. As trade, finance and production are increasingly transnationalized, the commonalities multiply and spread across the world. Nowhere is this clearer than in Eastern Europe and the [ex] Soviet Union, where extraordinarily rapid changes are now occurring with the explicit aim of restructuring these economies upon market principles, revamping their industrial infrastructure with infusions of Western capital and technology, and fully integrating them into the global market.

From the above vantage point, sovereignty appears not merely as a single idea, constructed out of a series of historically established ideas and past political formations, but as part of a living discourse which is itself the subject of an ongoing contest over how the future is to be shaped. 'Sovereignty' may be invoked as a principle in order to support the continuing importance or expansion of the state, the programme of particular political parties, various ideological or policy positions, and a range of different commercial initiatives. 'Cultural sovereignty', 'economic sovereignty', 'technological sovereignty' and 'national sovereignty' have become widely used terms, appealing in part to the traditional authority and respect vested in the concept, yet modifying and stretching the term to try and paper over the contradictions which now confront its original meaning.

[...]

Note

1 This concept has been used, albeit somewhat differently, in Hill, S. (1989) *The Tragedy of Technology: Human Liberation versus Domination in the Late Twentieth Century*, London, Pluto Press.

Source: Camilleri and Falk, 1992, pp. 115–16

Reading E: Joseph A. Camilleri, 'Rethinking sovereignty: some tentative conclusions' __

The picture that emerges [...] is neither simple nor unidirectional. There are both trends and countertrends. On the one hand, the nation-state remains a highly conspicuous and authoritative entity jealously guarding its territorial boundaries. The centralization of state power goes hand in hand with the internationalization of economic activity. As Heilbroner rightly points out, it is the enlargement of the state apparatus that makes possible the co-ordination and expansion of the productive process [Heilbroner, 1977, pp. 63–78]. The state system constitutes the necessary institutional prop for capital accumulation on a global scale as well as for the system of unequal exchange that underpins the international division of labour.

On the other hand, the state's capacity to articulate and satisfy human needs appears to be in relative decline. There is a widening gap between promise and performance, between the power of the state and the public participation in the exercise of that power, between the state and civil society. The delicate relationship between the public and private realms that is central to the nature and functioning of sovereignty in a domestic context appears to have been seriously impaired. Similarly, national sovereignty in an international context has been greatly eroded by a web of mutually reinforcing dependencies and interdependencies.

The state continues to perform important internal and external functions, but is it truly sovereign? The principle of state sovereignty can now be seen to have emerged and developed under conditions that are fast disappearing. While some states remain relatively strong and others may become relatively stronger, it would seem that states, weak and strong alike, are becoming less able to modify or preserve the complexion of their internal and external environment in line with the autonomously expressed preferences of the communities they claim to represent. Everywhere the cohesion of national societies seems likely to diminish, and so too the mobilizing efficacy of national governments. Historically, state sovereignty may turn out to have been a bridge between national capitalism and world capitalism, a phase in an evolutionary process that is still unfolding.

It is arguable that as time goes on this bridge will prove less and less serviceable either in interpreting or in organizing late twentieth-century experience. The image of a world made up of sovereign states internally supreme over the territory they control and externally unrestrained by outside does not explain the character of the present world, much less permit an appreciation of its possible future. The sovereign state represents one way in which power and authority may be exercised. It is not the only way. The territorial and omnipotent state was the product of the revolutionary changes that swept across Europe in the sixteenth and seventeenth centuries. The religious unity of medieval Europe and the ill-defined political loyalties that it subsumed gave way to a secularized but fragmented system of sovereign states. It may well be that the capitalist reorganization of the world and the contradictions to which it has given rise point to the re-emergence of a cosmopolitan ethic that coexists with and nourishes a bewildering array of local, regional, national and transnational loyalties and institutions. It may be that the contemporary period is one of considerable fluidity, when the most fundamental questions regarding the exercise of power and authority have been thrown back into the crucible of history.

At stake is not only the size of political entities or even the demarcation of their boundaries, but the very meaning of boundaries, the very nature of the political domain. In this transitional phase characterized by shifting allegiances, new forms of identity, and multiple tiers of jurisdiction, we are witnessing the growth of a more complex and more variegated, yet more unified world order than the system of sovereign states. The basic contradiction today is not between state sovereignty and the growing interdependence of states but rather between two forms of interdependence: one that institutionalizes the principle of popular sovereignty and another that negates the principle by clinging to the increasingly illusory notion of state sovereignty. [...] Needless to say, old habits and old ideas will persist even as new ones develop to cope with the emergence of a pluralistic polity that is at once part local, part regional, part national and part transnational. What concrete shape the political map of the world will take in the twenty-first century remains unclear. But both objective conditions (that is, the contradictions we have identified) and the universal revolt of conscience (that is, the impulse for emancipation and legitimacy) already suggest that state sovereignty is unlikely to be the distinguishing principle of political organization.

Reference

HEILBRONER, R.L. (1977) *Civilization in Decline*, Harmondsworth, Penguin Books.

Source: Camilleri, 1990, pp. 38–9

The exaggerated death of the nation-state

by James Anderson

Chapter 2

2.1 Introduction

There is a growing belief that the nation-state has outlived its usefulness. Seen as too small for the big policy issues facing the world, but too big for people's more personal concerns, its decline and death has been widely predicted. The nation-state will, apparently, fragment into small sub-state regions and dissolve into larger supra-state entities more appropriate to contemporary culture and economics. Occupying a central position in the shifting geopolitics of globalization, this key political institution of modern society is apparently being squeezed by a combined pincer movement 'from above' and 'from below': 'Globalization encourages macro-regionalism, which, in turn, encourages micro-regionalism' (Cox, 1992, p. 34), and in between is the nation-state, subject to interacting pressures from without and within.

In Chapter 1 it was suggested that globalization is overlaying the mosaic of nation-states and national communities with other forms of 'political community', for example the environmental movement and the women's movement, which transcend territorial boundaries. As globalization 'shrinks the political world', states and societies are becoming more tightly enmeshed in transnational networks and interactions. It was suggested that globalization is reducing the state's capacity for effective action; that there are growing disjunctures between the ideology of independent, sovereign statehood and the actual practices of contemporary states and of politics more widely defined.

However, it was also argued that globalization is 'far from ... bringing about the decline of the nation-state' and talk of 'the end of the nation-state' is gross exaggeration. For example, the clash of different 'national interests' and nationalisms within and between the states are continuing obstacles to the emergence of an integrated European 'super-state'. But sovereignty is already divided among various 'national, regional and international agencies' and, as Chapter 1 concluded, the European Union (EU) perhaps illustrates a 'new medievalism' of overlapping authorities and contested loyalties between nation-states and other agencies. This global 'macro-region' might be neither an emerging federal 'super-state' nor simply a traditional intergovernmental arrangement of sovereign states. Instead it may be a new type of political organization reminiscent of the political arrangements which existed in medieval Europe before the modern nation-state emerged (Bull, 1977).

The suggestion is that we may now be witnessing a transformation in state sovereignty and territoriality comparable to the 'medieval-to-modern' transition which started in the sixteenth century. That transition was associated with a radical transformation in how people experienced and represented geographical space; with contemporary globalization, it is suggested that we are experiencing a similarly radical change – that, in a sense, the ground is now shifting underneath established political institutions, practices and concepts. Changes in territorial statehood may be directly linked to the contemporary 'shrinking of the world' and 'time–space compression' (**Leyshon, 1995**) which Harvey (1989) argues is the greatest transformation in geographical space since the Renaissance ushered in the modern era.

It is pointed out, for instance, that it is now increasingly difficult to find one fixed viewpoint or perspective from which to make sense of territorial sovereignty and distinguish between 'foreign' and 'domestic' affairs. A telling example points to the worldwide, rather than merely European, nature of the political change and to possible links with economic globalization:

This is the world in which IBM is Japan's largest computer exporter, and Sony is the largest exporter of television sets from the United States ... the world in which ... a Japanese concern assembling typewriters in ... Tennessee, brings an antidumping case before the U.S. International Trade Commission ... against ... an American firm that imports typewriters into the United States from its offshore facilities in Singapore and Indonesia.

(Ruggie, 1993, p. 172)

It is not just that the state borders are becoming porous – in varying degrees they have always been. Whereas previous historical transformations have been represented as 'the world turned upside down', the appropriate metaphor now might be 'the world turned inside out and outside in'. Yet in some ways the modern nation-state, with its sovereignty defined by familiar territorial boundaries, seems as firmly rooted as ever: tax-collectors stop at the border, immigrants are stopped at the same border and transnational (or, more strictly speaking, trans-state) linkages can still be arbitrarily snapped off by independent state powers.

Clearly the evidence is contradictory and the issues complex. We are living in the middle of some exciting changes, and you are not alone if you find them perplexing. They involve a great diversity of states and societies, and uneven developments across a broad historical time sweep. But do they add up to a fundamental re-ordering of political space in which states and nations, territoriality and sovereignty are losing their importance? What are the dominant tendencies and how do they relate to globalization? What counter-tendencies might be working in opposite or different directions? And what are the connections between the pressures on the state 'from above and below', 'from without and within'?

Even if transnationalism, 'macro-regions' and 'micro-regions' are all becoming more important politically, does it necessarily follow that the nation-state is in terminal decline? Maybe questions about the 'life' and 'death' of the nation-state are misleading – could a simplistic choice between just two alternatives be obscuring the possibility that something else is happening? Is it, perhaps, a case of the state and territoriality being reshaped as states adapt to a changing world – some new qualitative changes not captured by the idea of 'decline'? Rumours of their death may be 'greatly exaggerated', as Mark Twain wrote about reports of his own death.

To begin to answer these questions, even to decide what the right questions are, we have to generalize (but hopefully not over-generalize) about the implications of global developments for *modern* – alias *territorial*, alias *sovereign*, alias *nation*-states. In section 2.2 we differentiate between these elements, for it was only with the 'medieval-to-modern' transition that they came to be packaged together. We need to outline how and why this happened, in order to get an historical perspective on a possible 'new medievalism', and, more generally, to appreciate that long-established arrangements are neither 'natural' nor unchangeable: what was packaged can be unpackaged and the 'death' of one element would not necessarily mean the 'death' of all of them. This is what is often assumed in tales foretelling the death of nation-states and nationalisms. An often justified distaste for their more undesirable,

indeed obnoxious, manifestations can lead to wishful thinking about their demise rather than accurate prediction. The difference between what *is* and what *ought to be* can become confused, and we need to distinguish the analysis of actual tendencies from the future we might like to see.

Sections 2.3 and 2.4 address the question of how globalization 'encourages macro-regionalism, which, in turn, encourages micro-regionalism'. Does it only happen in this order or can globalization directly encourage micro-regionalism; and how are states affected by these connected pressures? Section 2.3 outlines two debates – one about the relationship between the state and 'transnational' capitalism, the other about an alleged disjuncture between the territorial fixity of states and the relative geographical fluidity of today's world economy. Section 2.4 discusses how processes of globalization and Europeanization often exacerbate fragmentation tendencies and divisions within states – does the consequently increased importance of micro-regional politics threaten the state with internal dismemberment from below?

As we shall see in section 2.5, the greatest regional threats in some nation-states are nationalisms. They are sub-state nationalisms which, far from being 'anti-state' in principle, typically want new states for themselves; nevertheless they demonstrate very clearly how existing economic and cultural divisions and conflicts within states can be exacerbated by external forces. On the other hand, these conflicts also indicate the continuing power of existing states and state nationalisms; and some of the weaknesses of the sub-state nationalisms point to the political impact of uneven development within their own regions. With globalization continuing to generate uneven development, we shall see that there are grounds for thinking that nationalisms and nation-states are a long way from 'dying'. But this is far from the whole story, and in section 2.6 we come back to directly address what is perhaps the 'right' question: not the 'death' of states, but whether we are witnessing the emergence of 'new medieval' territorialities in Europe, and what this might mean for states in other parts of the world.

Thus the chapter deals with how economic, cultural and political processes interact in the context of uneven globalization. Its overall objective is to demonstrate some of the ways in which space and geography are integral to some of the political processes re-shaping our world.

2.2 States – territorial, sovereign, national

Because we generally experience territoriality, sovereignty, nationalism and states as all tightly packaged together, it is not easy to think of the different elements separately; but territorial, sovereign *nation-states* are in fact very recent arrivals in human history. For instance, nations are far from being 'natural', or essential and timeless features of human society, despite what some nationalists would have us believe as they trace their nation's ancestry to mythical heroes, gods, or (if all else fails) 'a lost tribe of Israel'. Nations are human constructions and a distinctly modern form of 'imagined community'.

nation-state

Box 2.1 Imagined political communities

'... the nation ... is an imagined political community – and imagined as both inherently limited and sovereign.

'imagined community'

It is *imagined* because the members of even the smallest nation will never know most of their fellow-members, meet them, or even hear them, yet in the minds of each lives the image of the communion ... In fact, all communities larger than primordial villages of face-to-face contact ... are imagined. Communities are to be distinguished, not by their falsity/genuineness, but by the style in which they are imagined ...

The nation is imagined as *limited* because even the largest of them ... has finite, if elastic boundaries, beyond which lie other nations. No nation imagines itself coterminous with mankind [*sic*]. The most messianic nationalists do not dream of a day when all members of the human race will join their nation in the way that it was possible, in certain epochs, for, say, Christians to dream of a wholly Christian planet.

It is imagined as *sovereign* ... nations dream of being free ... The gauge and emblem of this freedom is the sovereign state.

Finally, it is imagined as a *community*, because, regardless of the actual inequality and exploitation that may prevail in each, the nation is always conceived as a deep, horizontal comradeship. Ultimately it is this fraternity that makes it possible, over the past two centuries, for so many millions of people, not so much to kill, as willingly to die for such limited imaginings.'

Source: Anderson, 1983, pp. 6–7

What was 'imagined' and recently created may be 'unimagined', demolished, superseded or overlain by other imaginings, other creations. To show that fundamental change is conceivable, we need to outline the emergence of the sovereign nation-state ideal and how its unrealizability in many geographical situations feeds hopes of its death.

2.2.1 From medieval to modern

Nation-states and nationalism are now so firmly stamped on the world map, so imprinted in our identities, that often they really do seem 'natural'. But they were unimagined and unimaginable in medieval times. They did not exist even as aspirations. Antiquity provided no 'models'.

Different types of state have existed for thousands of years, but for most of that time 'nations' were unheard of. In medieval Europe, for example, people identified with communities and political units which were generally much smaller (and in some cases much larger) than the supposedly 'natural' nation or present-day states: their parish or diocese, manor, guild or city, whilst many were subjects of city-states, duchies or principalities. These small units were often part of a complex hierarchy of political or cultural entities, such as the Church of Rome, the Hanseatic League, or the dynastic Habsburg Empire ... The smaller units ... generally did not encompass all the members of a particular cultural group, and the larger ones ... generally encompassed a multiplicity of cultures and linguistic communities ... However, contrary to nationalist myth, this lack of geographical fit between political organization and cultural group did not worry those who experienced it. On the contrary, it was as 'natural' to them as nations and nationalisms are to us today.

(Anderson, 1986, pp. 115–16)

sovereignty Political *sovereignty* in medieval Europe was shared between a wide variety of secular and religious institutions and different levels of authority – feudal knights and barons, kings and princes, guilds and cities, bishops, abbots, the papacy – rather than being based on territory *per se* as in modern times. Indeed the territories of medieval European states were often discontinuous, with ill-defined and fluid frontier zones rather than precise or fixed borders. Then the term 'nation' meant something very different and *non*-political, generally referring simply to people born in the same locality. Furthermore, the different levels of overlapping sovereignty typically constituted *nested* hierarchies, for example parish, bishopric, archbishopric for spiritual matters; manor, lordship, barony, duchy, kingdom for secular matters. People were members of higher-level collectivities not directly but only by virtue of their membership of lower-level bodies.

The rise of the modern state, and what distinguished it from medieval predecessors, centred on the removal or displacement of these complex nested hierarchies and the development of state sovereignty as absolute and territoriality undivided authority within a precisely delimited *territory*. Initially this sovereignty was monopolized by 'absolute' monarchs: England's Henry VIII, who put down revolts in the English regions, 'nationalized' the Church in/of England and expelled papal authority, is a prime example. The inhabitants of the kingdom were now directly the subjects of the king and no one else. Later on, territorial sovereignty was 'democratized' as something to be exercised by 'the nation'. Individuals deemed to belong to the nation belonged directly 'in their own right', rather than through membership of lower-level bodies, and the 'territorial' state became also the 'nation' state.

Modern states, nations and nationalisms are all territorial in that they explicitly claim, and are based on, particular geographical territories, as distinct from merely occupying geographical space, which is true of all social organisations.

(Anderson, 1986, p. 117)

Nationalism defines people primarily in terms of belonging to a particular nation and territory, rather than by, for example, status or class. Nationalism is a cultural as well as political phenomenon; and each nationalism typically finds its unifying symbols, sense of identity, and criteria of 'belonging' in the particular history and geography of its territory. They emphasize *uniqueness*, and, indeed, each nationalism is unique in important respects for each one is shaped by its own particular territorial setting. They are *internally unifying*: they play down the divisions and conflicts of, for instance, class and gender within the 'imagined community', partly by 'externalizing' the sources of its problems. However, in doing so they are *externally divisive* with respect to people defined as 'other' (**Rose, 1995**), and hence they create or exacerbate divisions between different peoples and territories.

nationalism

Historically, the modern state, territorial sovereignty, and nationalism developed more or less together; and the nationalist ideal is that the two territorial entities, nations and states, should coincide geographically in *nation-states*. According to nationalist doctrine, the territory of the nation and that of the state should be one and the same: to each nation its own state, each state the expression of a single nation, a happy coincidence of cultural community and political sovereignty. As a political doctrine, nationalism links historically and culturally defined territorial communities, called nations, to political statehood, either as a reality or as an aspiration. According to Sack (1986, p. 46), 'the anchoring of society to place in the nation-state ... [developed into] ... one of the clearest expressions of mythical-magical consciousness of place in the twentieth century'.

Thus the long 'medieval-to-modern' transition involved a 'territorialization' of politics, with a sharpening of differences at the borders of states and of nations between 'internal' and 'external', 'belonging' and 'not belonging', 'us' and 'them'. The nested hierarchies and different levels of authority in medieval Europe – the vertically segmented, overlapping sovereignties defined in terms of functional obligations as well as in loosely territorial terms – gave way to sovereignty delimited only and much more precisely by territory. In effect the multilevel medieval authorities were collapsed to one all-important level, that of the sovereign territorial state, as power within the territory was centralized and outside powers were excluded. Formal sovereignty over everything secular and spiritual was 'bundled' together into territorial state 'parcels'.

This has had a whole range of related consequences for the ways in which we have traditionally thought about and represented the state and politics. But the traditional representations were always inadequate, and now they are becoming even more inappropriate. This should become clearer as we discuss contemporary developments and particularly in section 2.6 where we discuss the partial, but accelerating, 'unbundling' of sovereignty.

Firstly, *the* state – territorial, sovereign, national – is often idealized as timeless and unchanging, whereas *states* (plural) come in all shapes and sizes and can develop into a wide variety of different forms. Secondly, the idealization has helped to foster the 'life or death' debate where the 'realism' school in international relations seems to think the nation-state will live for ever, and 'idealist' or 'functionalist' school go to an opposite (and mirror image) extreme – they think, or try to proceed as if, it is already dead or dying. Thirdly, we are all to some extent victims of the 'territorial trap' (Agnew, 1994): we still tend to think that 'state' delimits 'society' and that 'societies' are simply the populations 'contained' within states, and (like nations) are synonymous with them, for example 'French society' or 'Indonesian society'. Transnational terms, such as 'European society' or 'Islamic society' are used less often; and 'Irish society' often refers only to the 26-county Republic, excluding the Northern Irish and forgetting about the Irish diaspora in Britain, North America, Australasia and elsewhere. Fourthly, many people, especially those in large and powerful states, often over-generalize about human society on the basis of 'their own society', giving their particular (for example British, French or North American) views a phoney 'universality'. Fashionable ideas about 'the death of the state', for instance, often reflect the fact that powerful states are now subject to some of the same external pressures that have long been the lot of weak ones. By contrast, people in weak colonial or post-colonial states with a history of 'outside interference' are less likely to equate limited sovereignty with 'the decline', never mind the 'death', of the state as such; and they are also much less likely to see a sharp division between the 'internal' and 'external'.

A fifth consequence is that the traditional internal/external or 'domestic/foreign' dichotomy has led to a debilitating intellectual division (particularly within large states) between political theories focused on internal rule, and a supposedly separate realm of 'inter*national* relations'. Despite its name, the latter has often been preoccupied with states (not nations) as the only important actors in the so-called inter*national* arena (largely ignoring non-state transnational networks and actors such as multinational corporations). The collapse of formal sovereignty to only one level has usually meant that levels 'above' and 'below' the state remained relatively undifferentiated and unexplored (Walker, 1993, p. 131). 'Above' was widely seen as just an anarchical collection of competing states (a very impoverished view as you will appreciate from Chapter 1); while levels 'below' were usually ignored in 'political theories' preoccupied with 'national' (that is, state) politics. Lower levels were treated mainly as particular sidelines, such as 'local government' or 'federal systems', or became a focus of attention only when states faced powerful regional groups defined as being 'troublesome'.

Furthermore, when other levels are discussed, as in debates about the state's 'life or death', there is often an assumption that any serious threat or replacement can only come from state-like bodies – the state 'writ large', as in a federal United States of Europe for example, or 'writ small', as in separate regional governments. The only real change is a change of geographical scale; and there is a failure to recognize that political processes and institutions at different levels are qualitatively, not just quantitatively, different (Walker, 1993, pp. 133–4). This is sometimes called the 'Gulliver' fallacy (after the two societies which Gulliver met in his travels – one of giants, the other of midgets, but both exact replicas of human society).

Along with some of the other conceptual inadequacies, it is rooted in a way of thinking which sees geographical space as 'absolute' rather than 'relative'.

Box 2.2 Absolute and relative space

The '*absolute*' conception of space is exemplified in Euclid's geometry and Newton's physics, and, despite our actual experience of geographical space, it is usually in operation when space is simply taken for granted. It sees space as homogeneous and unchanging. In Euclidean geometry the shortest distance between two points is always the same straight line, to be measured in standard units of distance such as miles or kilometres. In contrast, the '*relative*' conception sees space as variable, changing and changeable, a necessarily relative phenomenon bound up with the flow of time. As in Einstein's physics, things exist in a world of four dimensions – the time dimension as well as the three dimensions of space – a world of 'time–space' (see also **Leyshon, 1995, pp. 17–19**). This is also the world we live in. You will be well aware that in the actual social space we inhabit, the shortest distance between two places is very rarely a straight line (as it would be in Euclid's absolute space). The distances that matter to us often follow non-straight line routes and are measured in time or money rather than in standard miles or kilometres; and these socially defined distances vary relative to a wide range of factors including who is travelling, and how, where and when they are travelling. A lack of knowledge, or of a passport or visa, can make travel impossible. And this is, of course, the space within which political (like all social) processes occur – a highly variable geographical space which is produced historically by human society (rather than being simply given by 'nature'); very much 'relative' rather than 'absolute'.

The 'absolute' conception, always inadequate, is seriously counter-productive if we want to understand how the 'ground' of 'time–space' is now shifting under established political arrangements.

[margin notes:] absolute space

relative space

Traditional 'absolute' views of space and 'one-level' thinking fixated on the state are completely inappropriate for assessing contemporary political transformations. We have to deal with multilevel and multifaceted political processes which span global regulatory regimes, macro-regions, micro-regions, 'world cities' and localities, as well as states. Whether or not we are seeing a 'new medievalism' requires new thinking.

Activity 1 This is the appropriate point to study Reading A, 'Pre-modern to modern territoriality' by John Gerard Ruggie, which you will find at the end of this chapter. This reading emphasizes that the 'territorially defined, territorially fixed, and mutually exclusive state formations' which first appeared in the modern era are 'a peculiar and historically unique configuration of territorial space' (Ruggie, 1993). As you will see, there is perhaps a warning for us today in the lack of vision of Francis I, the sixteenth-century French king, who, in his division of France, failed to see the 'pre-modern to modern' spatial transformation. Ruggie's outline of pre-modern territorialities is suggestive of some contemporary possibilities. Note for instance the points about fluidity, movement and *non*-exclusive territoriality which are relevant to the discussion in later sections of this chapter.

2.2.2   Death foretold and celebrated

Tales foretelling the death of states reflect traditional misconceptions about space and politics. They also, however, reflect justifiable objections to nation-states and nationalisms, and an awareness of increasing tensions between state politics and the global political economy.

Death may be wished because the nation-state ideal is often unrealizable due to people of different nationalities being geographically intermingled. Attempts to make the ideal a reality have produced, and continue to produce, much human misery. Far from the ideal of nation and state coinciding geographically, there are often glaring disparities in their distributions. State-building and nation-building both developed unevenly and sometimes in conflict with each other. Thus in some states (and Britain, as we shall see in section 2.5, is a spectacularly good example) 'nation-building' by the state to create a single (for example British or Spanish) nation is far from complete, partly because non-state and opposing nationalisms such as those found in Wales, Scotland and Ireland or in Catalonia and the Basque Country in Spain, have their own separate aspirations to independent statehood. State oppression of 'national minorities', local armed responses against states, and violent or non-violent conflict between different national groups within states, are all expressions of the ideal's unrealizability. Considering the widespread and often appalling problems associated with national and territorial sovereignty, there would indeed be good reasons for celebrating its death.

Nationalism has been implicated in some of the twentieth century's worst atrocities – the massacre of a million Armenians in Turkey in 1915, the murder of six million Jews and other 'minorities' in Nazi Germany, or the more recent 'ethnic cleansing' in the disintegrating former state of Yugoslavia. Sub-state national conflicts are essentially about national sovereignty defined in traditional territorial terms. However, in situations where people with conflicting national allegiances are intermingled in the same territory – as in Israel/Palestine, Northern Ireland/the North of Ireland or, with even more complexity, in former Yugoslavia – conflicts so defined are likely to lead to problems of political deadlock or violence, or both – hence the attractions of re-defining sovereignty and territoriality.

Examples of such problems are widespread: Sudan divided by a civil war between the Muslim North and the Christian South; India contending with Sikh separatists and Hindu fundamentalists; Indonesia suppressing East Timor; separatism in the French-speaking province of Quebec fuelling Anglophone reaction in western Canada (with both threatening the Canadian federation), and, within the province of Quebec, the Cree Indian nation has its own rival agenda. The federation that was Czechoslovakia split in two; and Belgium may divide into French- and Flemish-speaking regions. Many states appear to be 'in trouble' because nationalism is on the increase – people want new nation-states. Is this merely the nation-state's 'final fling', its 'death agony' literally and figuratively, or is the nationalist upsurge a general counter-tendency actually fuelled by uneven globalization, with 'fragmentation' being the opposite side of the same coin? We discuss this further in section 2.5.

Many commentators, however, celebrate the coming demise of nation-states for reasons other than the suffering engendered by nationalist conflicts. They focus on general developments such as the leaching of some economic powers away from states to global markets, the consequent weakening of the states' external effectiveness and the simultaneous diminishing of their internal authority. The nation-state can be a confining straitjacket – narrow and parochial. The delimitation of sovereignty simply (or even mainly) in territorial terms clearly does not do justice to the complexity and fluidity of our interdependent world. Major world problems such as environmental degradation cannot be solved state by state, and it sometimes seems that the nation-state continues to exist because of institutional inertia, rather than the needs of contemporary society. From a functionalist viewpoint, nationalism often seems to be an historical anachronism, well past its 'sell-by date', though some of the ills blamed on nation-states and nationalism may be due to other more basic causes such as economic inequalities and crises.

Yet it is mainly because of continuing 'national' problems that hopes are invested in an end of territorially based sovereignty and a transition to 'new medieval' or 'post-modern' forms of inclusive rather than exclusive territoriality. Sovereignty, rather than being monopolized by states, would again be shared between different institutions at different levels, some based on macro- or micro-regional bounded space, others defined more in 'non-territorial' or functional terms, similar to Papal authority in medieval England before Henry VIII territorialized spiritual as well as secular sovereignty. Thus some people, for example Kearney (1988), hoped that the combination of European citizenship and regionalism in a federal 'Europe of the Regions' would help solve the national conflict in Northern Ireland: that the traditional concept of state sovereignty that lies at the centre of the conflict between Irish and British national allegiances would be replaced by a new territoriality which could include both.

'new medievalism'

Before looking at the pressures on states 'from above' and 'from below', it should be noted that the emergence of 'new medieval' territorialities does not require anything as clear-cut or decisive as 'the death of the nation-state'. On the contrary, a return to 'overlapping or segmented authority' is most likely where the changes are more partial and ambiguous, undermining but not relocating sovereignty as presently understood.

Summary of section 2.2

o   Territorial sovereignty in nation-states provides an important key to modern as distinct from medieval politics; by the same token, the 'unbundling' of territoriality could be a key to the contemporary spatial re-organization of politics and states.

o   The 'bundling' of sovereignty into territorial state 'parcels' has fostered misconceptions about geographical space and has led to various representations of states and politics which are increasingly inadequate and inappropriate.

o   There are increasing problems with nation-states and nationalisms, but they may sometimes get the blame for other, deeper problems, and we need to beware of indulging in wishful thinking rather than analysing actual tendencies.

2.3   Dissolution 'from above'?

Focusing on the latest phase of globalization brings out common threads in the very diverse experiences of different states, for instance the general trend of their increased 'vulnerability' to global markets. Chapter 1 has already indicated some of the pressures on states 'from above'; here we look briefly at two debates which further our objectives of relating political to economic change and showing how geography is integral to the future of states. The first debate focuses on historical periodizations and previous phases of globalization. It suggests that very substantial variations in the economic role of states are possible without this necessarily involving state 'decline'. The second, related, debate is about the changing position of states in the global economy. This focuses on contemporary tensions and alleged disjunctures between the spatial organization of politics and economics.

Geographers may be gratified when other social scientists incorporate space into their theories (rather than treating it as an optional extra which can be ignored) but, as we shall see, exclusively geographical arguments can also sometimes be faulty.

2.3.1   Capitalism, 'national' and 'transnational'

Capitalism has always been international in scope, but in recent decades there has been a shift from an *international* towards a *transnational* or global economy, a distinction that is discussed in **Allen (1995)**. It now makes less sense to see national economies as the basic 'building-blocks' of the world economy, as if the world economy is just the sum total of all the economies contained within states.

Broadly speaking, we can distinguish three or four periods of capitalist development since the early nineteenth century, each characterized by very different relationships between states and economies. Up to the 1870s, Britain dominated and policed an international economy of liberal capitalism in which states had a relatively weak and indirect economic role, and national economies were comparatively 'open' to investment and sales by outside (mainly British) interests. By contrast, from the 1880s to the Second World War no single state dominated or policed the world system; imperialist and inter-state rivalries intensified; with the growth of protectionism and of import substitution in 'third world' states, national economies became more 'closed'. In this period states became more centrally involved in economic activities through close partnerships with private capitalist firms, or directly as the owners of state enterprises, most fully in Stalin's 'state capitalist' Russia. In the period following the Second World War, the main changes were that the USA assumed a world leadership role; and a more managed, integrated and successful world economy was established, though, as Agnew (1994, p. 67) notes, this system came under increasing strain in the late 1960s.

For our purposes there is a case for distinguishing a fourth period starting in the early 1970s. Despite war-time changes, direct state involvement in economic enterprises had remained at relatively high levels (for example, Britain's main industrial nationalizations occurred in the post-war period), and many national economies remained relatively 'closed' to outside sellers and investors. Radical change in these areas only came with the ending of the long post-war boom and the re-appearance in the early 1970s of serious depressions in the world economy. Then, for example, large corporations increasingly internationalized their investments and production in an effort to restore falling profitability, and, as a general result, 'national economies' again became more 'open'. Economic liberalization and 'privatization' became 'the order of the day', often literally so, as a USA-dominated International Monetary Fund and World Bank forced many 'third world' states to withdraw from productive activity and from attempting to regulate international trade and investment flows. By the late 1980s even the most state-regulated economies – the former Russian-dominated communist bloc and China – were replacing controls over capital flows with enticements for capital to flow in their direction. Economic production and finance, as well as trade, are now increasingly organized and integrated on a transnational or global basis (**Allen and Hamnett, eds, 1995**).

These changes have undoubtedly weakened the control which states can exercise over economic activities within their territories. But does this equal 'state decline' as some, for example Harris (1986), suggest? The debate can be posed in terms of two opposing tendencies, both of which reflect fundamental features of capitalism. One is a tendency towards *national* or *state capitalism* and the various forms of economic and political integration within states. This reflects the competitive nature of the world economy, the fixity of productive capital (for example, factories) rooted in particular locations, and the need for political support in even the most *laissez-faire* or market-regulated economy: where the competition is international, even global, state support can make all the difference. The opposing tendency is towards *transnational capitalism* and the integration of economic activities across different states. This second tendency reflects the expansionist nature of competitive capitalism which has always spilled over state frontiers in search of markets, raw materials and cheaper labour, and it especially reflects the relative fluidity or lack of spatial fixity of some aspects of the world economy, most notably speculative finance capital which has grown enormously in recent times (see **Leyshon, 1995**).

state capitalism

transnational capitalism

The different periods of capitalist development can be seen in terms of one or other tendency becoming more dominant. Thus transnationalism was more dominant in the mid-nineteenth century than in the period after 1880; in the 1980s developments such as the collapse of Stalin's legacy in Russia, and the worldwide resurgence of liberal arguments against state interference, marked a decisive shift away from state capitalism and back towards transnationalism. The fact that we have to go back over 100 years to find another period when capitalism was as transnational is one measure of the historically important nature of recent changes (comparisons with medieval sovereignty is another). But, of course, this does not mean that the state is in terminal decline, any more than states 'died' in the mid-nineteenth century.

transnationalism There are a number of arguments against such over-statements. The dominance of one tendency – towards *transnationalism* – does *not* mean that the other tendency – towards state capitalism – has simply disappeared. As we saw, the latter reflects the spatial fixity of productive capital and its need for state support. These continue despite the speculative fluidity of much contemporary investment or liberalism's 'pro-market, anti-state' ideology. It is more fruitful to see the two tendencies as continuing to interact and it is quite conceivable that the balance between them will oscillate in the future.

States may have lost some economic power, but, contrary to liberal ideology, they continue to have new and crucial roles. For example, Stopford and Strange (1991) argue that:

Growing interdependence now means that the rivalry between states and the rivalry between firms for a secure place in the world economy has become much fiercer ... As a result, firms have become more involved with governments and governments have come to realize their increased dependence on the scarce resources controlled by firms.

(Stopford and Strange, 1991, p. 1)

Japan's internationalization of its productive and financial capital following the crises in the early 1970s is particularly revealing. The Japanese state played a crucial role in re-orienting the economy away from heavy industry towards electronics, cars and other consumer durables for world markets, and it orchestrated the spread of Japanese capital mainly to the USA, Britain and mainland South East Asia (Kossis, 1992).

With recurring crises, there is still covert protectionism and 'managed' rather than genuinely 'free' trade in many instances. The increase in mutual direct foreign investment makes a *general* reversal to protectionism in larger global trade blocs unlikely for the foreseeable future (though it may occur for particular commodities or industries). However, rather than dissolving inter-state rivalries and getting rid of conflicts, economic globalization is tending to reproduce them in more complex forms. For example, the presence of Japanese car plants inside the EU has occasioned some virulent anti-Japanese prejudice and racism, particularly in France where competing French car manufacturers have demanded tough protectionist measures. But because much of Japan's European investments are concentrated in Britain, many British workers and businesses have a direct stake, for example a job or a customer, in Japanese-owned plants. What might once have been a relatively straightforward conflict involving two countries becomes a conflict involving at least three states and the EU.

2.3.2   Global economics, state politics

The second, related, debate is about whether politics should be seen as
spatially fixed in, or largely confined to, particular territorial states, whereas
economic processes are seen as much more fluid and transnational. There is
something in this argument, but, again, we need to beware of misleading
over-statement.

The basic argument is that the world economy and territorial states used to
be in harmony with one another, but the displacement of state capitalism by
transnationalism has brought about a disjuncture between the 'two systems'
(Harris, 1986). Cox (1992) claims that there is a clash between 'the principle
of interdependence and the territorial principle': the former is seen as
geared to global finance and competition, to be 'non-territorial' and
'unconstrained by territorial boundaries'; the latter, in contrast, is territorially
constrained, 'state-based [and] grounded ultimately in military-political
power'.

Activity 3   Do you find it helpful to see contemporary global change in terms of a
'clash' between two systems or two principles? Note down some advantages and
some disadvantages of analysing global change in this way before reading on. For
'advantages' you could think of the inability of governments to control speculative
finance flows; while for 'disadvantages' bear in mind what you have just read about
the interdependence of 'firms and governments', and what you have already studied
in Chapter 1 about global politics transcending state borders and territoriality.

It is important to stress that economic power usually depends on 'military-
political' power. Self-regulating economies independent of politics are a myth
but this is often forgotten: for example, nineteenth-century British capitalism
could not have flourished without the Royal Navy. Military force, or more
often simply the threat of force, has always been needed to enforce the rules
of supposedly 'free markets', even the economic sanctions of the IMF and
World Bank have ultimately rested on state power, especially that of the USA.
According to Cox (1992, p. 36), 'Globalization in the late twentieth century
also depends upon the military-territorial power of an enforcer'.

The dichotomy between 'territorial' politics and 'non-territorial' economics
has an attractive simplicity, but it is a false dichotomy. Instead of separate
systems, there continues to be a close, although significantly altered,
interdependence between firms and states. Geographical space is central to
the dichotomy, but the geographical arguments are misconceived. On the
one hand, economic activities occur in particular territories and we have
already seen that some parts of the economy are far from being 'footloose
and fancy-free'. 'Fixed' capital has 'fixed' locations. Even large
globe-spanning multinational corporations generally have headquarters in a
'home' state on which they especially depend, though increasingly they also
depend on other states (as in the case cited by Ruggie in Reading A about
the Japanese company assembling typewriters in Tennessee). These
companies may show little loyalty to any state but it is nevertheless more
fruitful to see territoriality with respect to economic processes as becoming
more complex, rather than seeing these processes as 'non-territorial'. On the
other hand, while state sovereignty may be territorial, state power is not
necessarily confined to the state territory, as the whole history of imperialism
demonstrates. Globalization in its past and present phases is a directly

GOT ANY CHANGE TO SPARE, MR ARAB?

'I'D RATHER NOT GET INVOLVED'

'... SO YOU SEE, THE ENTIRE FUTURE OF THE INTERNATIONAL FINANCIAL SYSTEM HINGES ON YOUR CAPACITY FOR QUICK RECOVERY AND VAST ECONOMIC GROWTH.'

political process, not just an economic one (see Chapter 1; **Allen, 1995**). Politics as well as economics spills over state boundaries, as we saw in the example of economic liberalization being literally 'the order of the day' from the IMF and World Bank to some 'third world' states.

Avoiding the misconceived dichotomy is politically important. Writing-off state power could be taken to mean that effective power is now mostly 'top-down' from higher, 'global' levels, and that the possibility of more 'local' forces being effective is virtually ruled out. Writing from a conservative perspective, John Gray (*The Guardian*, 4 January 1994) sees the neo-liberal ideology of globalization via world markets as leaving national and local cultures and interests very vulnerable. Other states, such as France and Japan, have provided more of a 'bulwark' for their respective countries and industries than has the British state. Gray suggests that the 'rhetoric of globalization' provides governments with excuses for the shortcomings of their own policies, as they opportunistically feign 'powerlessness' in the face of the all-important world market (see the edited version of Gray's article opposite).

While neo-liberal ideology suggests that the state is becoming unimportant, the reality as practised by avowedly neo-liberal politicians has, in fact, provided graphic evidence to the contrary. Neo-liberal governments departed completely from their own script on key issues. For example, economic recovery in the 1980s depended on government intervention, especially in the USA where soaring federal budget deficits (US debt grew from 19 per cent of GDP in 1979 to 30 per cent in 1989) due to increased arms expenditure provided the crucial boost to the USA and other Western economies (conversely it also pushed up world interest rates and caused the 'debt crisis' in the 'third world'). This intervention from an ostensibly neo-liberal administration has been dubbed a triumph for 'John Maynard Reagan' and his 'military Keynesianism' (though Keynesians might object that their hero would have been appalled by the waste involved in arms expenditure). More spectacularly, it was only massive state funding of the banking system in response to the 'Black Monday' stock market crash in

Against the world

John Gray

The idea that we live in a global marketplace has become one of the dominant cliches of British political discourse in the nineties. Events such as the creation of the Single European Market and the successful conclusion of the Gatt agreement seem to support the conviction that Britain is caught up in an inexorable movement toward global economic convergence that national policies are powerless to affect.

If distinctive national cultures and local and regional communities continue to exist, they will do so on the terms imposed upon them by global market forces. They can expect no shelter from government, since the principal function of government, on this dominant view, is to make the workforce, in Britain and elsewhere, more responsive to the demands of the world market.

There can then be no national policies – on employment or welfare, say – which aim to conserve a particular way of life, or express an ideal of community. Such ways of life and ideals of community will survive, if at all, as aspects of private life, not as items on the agenda of public policy.

The agenda of public policy is dictated by the world market. If cherished forms of social life are swept away by the gale of market competition, as hypermarkets and warehouse shopping hollow out the centres of cities and complete their destruction as human settlements, there is nothing that public policy can hope to do about this. For Britain must pay its way in the global marketplace, and we cannot afford to be nostalgic about our inherited forms of common life. We have, in fact, no alternative to accepting whatever forms of social life are thrown up by the market, as its incessant changes revolutionise our lives in ways undreamt of in the philosophies of Lenin or Mao.

There has always been, especially in America, a school of market fundamentalism, or capitalist utopianism, which sees communities and distinctive cultures as barbarous relics not worth preserving when they come into conflict with the imperatives of the market. The surprising and ironical development in the eighties was the conquest of British Conservatism by this libertarian view, with its explicit denial, or repudiation, of the human need for rootedness in a common environment.

The truth in the older Conservative philosophy was insight that human beings are fragile creatures who need the support of shared meanings and practices. The task of government, on this old Tory view, was to temper economic change so that its dislocations did not evoke the truly atavistic movements that have recurrently swept continental Europe.

The conviction of the libertarian new right was that such caution about the workings of market institutions was unnecessary, since, left to their own devices, they will generate new communities to replace the ones they have undone. Resistance to the forces of globalisation was denounced as in any case futile, since all modern societies were bent on convergence on a single economic form – liberal capitalism.

[...]

[...] [T]he rhetoric of globalisation serves to restrict public perception of the range of policy options that is actually open to us. It is probably only because French political culture has been staunchly resistant to talk of globalisation that European film makers have managed to avoid domination by an American entertainment industry in which films are merely one leisure commodity among others. It is only because Japanese policymakers have resisted American-inspired demands for the abandonment of lifetime job security that Japan has been able to weather its worst post-war recession with unemployment of under 3 per cent. In both cases, a strong political culture has asserted itself successfully against the supposedly irresistible forces of globalisation.

The danger of the rhetoric of globalisation is that it reduces the scope of democratic political life to marginal adjustments in the management of market institutions. [...]

Source: *The Guardian*, 4 January 1994, p. 18

October 1987, with monetarists becoming Keynesians overnight, that prevented a 1930s-style slump. While the virtually instantaneous, worldwide nature of the 1987 crisis dramatically illustrates the globalization of finance (**Leyshon, 1995, pp. 36–41**), the resolution of that crisis bears eloquent testimony to the continuing importance of states.

Summary of section 2.3

o   There have been a number of major historic shifts in the relationships between states and the world economy. Recent changes, particularly since the 1970s, have weakened the control that states can exercise over economic activities within their territories.

o   Rather than talk of the state 'declining' (much less 'dying') it is more fruitful to think of the state/world economy relationship undergoing a qualitative transformation. States continue to play a crucial, though altered, economic role.

o   Representations of these changes are politically important because of their implications for the effectiveness, or otherwise, of state and other local forces as against more global ones. Neo-liberal accounts of globalization are coloured by 'pro-market, anti-state' ideology.

o   Geographical conceptions are central in some debates about these changes; not least where the geography is misconceived, as in misleading dichotomies between state politics – 'territorial', spatially fixed and constrained – and economic activities – supposedly 'non-territorial', fluid and 'footloose'.

2.4   Dismemberment 'from below'?

Might there perhaps be more of a threat to states from the indirect effects of globalization fuelling internal fragmentation 'from below'? Globalization is an inherently uneven process, impacting on an already uneven world; so too is European integration. Both can create or exacerbate internal divisions and stimulate the growth of micro-regional politics. So how do pressures 'from above' encourage pressures 'from below'?

2.4.1   Globalization and fragmentation

Globalization's fragmenting impact 'from below' can be seen in terms of its effects on the central institutions of the state and on its regional and local components.

Cox (1992) argues that with globalization:

Power within the state becomes concentrated in those agencies in close touch with the global economy – the offices of presidents and prime ministers, treasuries, central banks. The agencies that are more closely identified with domestic clients – ministries of industries, labour ministries, etc. – become subordinated.

(Cox, 1992, pp. 30–1)

The implication is that the agencies most directly involved with maintaining the internal cohesion of the state are being seriously weakened. However, this tendency is at least partly countered by the general population's close identification with those parts of the state that are least 'internationalized' – for example, the agencies for health, education, social security and regional policy, rather than with, for instance, central banks. The potentially harmful effects of internationalization on the legitimacy of the state thus tend to be minimized.

The idea that economic globalization is concentrating power in a few 'internationalized' parts of the central state also needs to be heavily qualified because politics at *micro-regional* and more local levels are generally gaining in importance. Quite apart from what particular state governments may decree – for example some decentralization of power as part of democratization in Spain or Brazil, or more central dictation and resistance to devolution as in Britain – the relative importance of the 'local state' has been increasing in recent decades. This is partly a consequence of the latest wave of globalization: state institutions and social groups in the regions and localities are becoming more directly linked to international institutions and processes (for example, some local authorities now have their own offices in Brussels). They have also had to increase their international links more generally as they compete in trying to attract external investment and multinational branch plants: '… attractive sites for new investment are increasingly those supplying skilled workers and efficient infrastructures' (Stopford and Strange, 1991, p. 1). The local state can play a key role in providing the necessary conditions for private profit-making; it can be the crucial factor in the competition for external investment.

micro-regions

Activity 4   Can you think of examples, perhaps in your own area, of regional or local authorities becoming 'international operators'? And what changes have there been in relations with central government?

Do these developments constitute a threat to the nation-state and, if so, in what ways?

A nation-state may indeed be threatened where the 'local state' is a large and economically powerful region in a 'federalized' state, or to a 'national' region such as Wales or Catalonia where cultural distinctiveness provides a basis for separatist or autonomous movements, as described in section 2.5 below. More generally, the central institutions of the state may experience a relative loss of power 'downwards' to regions, cities and localities, and they may be bypassed altogether as local authorities forge their own international links. However, these developments are best seen as changes in the internal form of the state, rather than its 'decline'. The local state is part of the nation-state, not a separate rival. It is qualitatively different, not simply the state 'writ small' as in the 'Gulliver' fallacy described in section 2.2.1 above. The extent of local autonomy varies widely from state to state, but only within strictly defined and centrally imposed limits, and if serious conflicts of interest arise, the central authorities generally have the upper hand. They can overcome local resistance by centralizing some local functions and powers; by dissolving recalcitrant local institutions (as when Margaret Thatcher's government abolished the Greater London Council); and by fragmenting local government into a local state which includes various unelected bodies removed from local democratic control such as Urban Development Corporations or education boards.

The latter developments have often simply been seen in terms of 'centralization' but it may be more appropriate to see them as part of wider changes that have helped to restructure local political arrangements. In the case of Britain, the direction of change since the late 1970s has certainly been heavily orchestrated by central governments eager to undermine the powers and legitimacy of elected local governments. Major reforms have fundamentally altered the ways in which social housing, education and the social services are delivered at local level, and the funding of local government services has been substantially restructured, with an increased emphasis on the allocation of income from the centre rather than raising it from local taxes. But another way of looking at the changes highlights a different, parallel move towards the 'fragmentation' of local states and the increased involvement of business representatives and business-led approaches, rather than a simple process of 'centralization'. There has been a dramatic growth of locally based political institutions, encouraged both by central government reforms and the initiatives of local government (see, for example, Cochrane, 1993). But these institutions, which range from hospital trusts to housing associations, from training and enterprise councils and local enterprise companies to a wide range of public–private partnerships, have tended to be unelected, with boards made up of people appointed from above and often drawn from the business community. In some respects, it could be argued that this has helped to generate local political activity and even to encourage conflicts with central government over some issues. In other respects, however, it has clearly reduced the possibilities of effective rivalry with central government. Political restructuring cannot be reduced to the simple arithmetic of a 'zero-sum' game in which gains at one level of institutional politics automatically mean losses at another: 'more local' does not necessarily mean 'less central' or vice versa.

2.4.2 Regionalization in Europe

Generally speaking, contemporary globalization is stimulating local and regional politics, but the internal consequences of pressures 'from above' are

regionalism

clearer in the specific case of the European Union. *Regionalism* is being directly encouraged by the EU's central supranational institutions – the European Commission, the European Parliament and the Committee of the Regions. The main objective of this European integration is the creation of a

macro-region

European *macro-region* – political and cultural as well as economic – through the creation of direct micro-region-to-micro-region linkages across state borders. There is also the more political, if less acknowledged, objective of countering or bypassing state governments who can be obstacles to integration, as will be further discussed in Chapter 3. The Commission has encouraged the growth of regional representation in order to enhance its own powers *vis-à-vis* intergovernmentalism and the controlling states, as well as improving social and economic cohesion between micro-regions.

Thus in the early 1990s the Commission proposed that the Committee of the Regions should act as the 'upper house' of the European Parliament. This proposal was later watered down by the Council of Ministers representing the member states, and the Committee was given only a consultative role in narrowly defined 'regional' matters. Nevertheless, Commission officials believe that its role will be progressively enhanced because regionalism is increasingly important 'on the ground', and because the Committee provides a political platform for a growing number of important regional politicians from 'federalized' states such as Germany and Spain (Anderson and Goodman, 1995).

In alliance with the regions, the Commission has devised regional development policies which could potentially undercut existing state authority and legitimize regional movements. Since the late 1980s it has argued that inter-regional disparities are becoming more important than inter-state disparities: inter-regional inequalities have been shown to be accelerating at an alarming rate which cannot be explained in terms of trends at the state level. Furthermore, the Commission sees European integration as itself a major cause of the growth in regional disparities, and this increases the onus on it to take countervailing measures. One result has been a strategy of more 'fine-grained' integration, focused on regions rather than states.

The EU also encourages regionalism more diffusely, but perhaps more powerfully, through the Single European Market (SEM). The SEM is encouraging regions to seek more political autonomy as integration 'regionalizes' what (at least until recently) could be described as 'national' economies. With 'national' economic management weakening, partly because of modifications to sovereignty, development strategies and groupings at sub-state regional levels have become more significant, and greater political autonomy has increasingly been perceived as desirable, even necessary. Unsurprisingly, it is the more prosperous and politically autonomous regions – on the continent rather than in Britain – that have taken the lead in forging new inter-regional groupings. For example, Catalonia, Lombardy, Baden-Württemberg and Rhone-Alps – the so-called 'four motors' – have formed an association which spans the borders of Spain, Italy, Germany and France. Wales has links with the grouping, and the more 'peripheral' regions of the EU are also forging their own associations. Regional pressure groups, such as the campaigns for Scottish and Welsh Assemblies and, in England, a northern Assembly, have argued that regional autonomy is urgently required to prevent further peripheralization as a result of increased competition from the stronger 'core' economies in the SEM. Elected regional bodies are established features of political life in four of the five largest EU states – Germany, France, Spain and Italy – and in several of the smaller ones, Britain and the Irish Republic being notable exceptions.

However, a federal 'Europe of the Regions' is not about to replace the present 'Europe of States' as some have suggested. The growth of regionalism does not necessarily mean that states are 'declining'. It would make no sense, for instance, to say that the federal German state is 'in trouble' because of its strongly developed regional politics, or that, conversely, the Irish and British states are the only EU states not 'in decline'. On the contrary, it is widely argued that the latter are 'in trouble' because they are over-centralized. What we can say, though, is that qualitatively new forms of territoriality and sovereignty may be emerging in the European Union. This is discussed further in section 2.6 below.

Summary of section 2.4

o   Contemporary globalization and European integration are changing the relationships and relative powers of central and local parts of the state, generally in favour of the latter.

o   The changes are best seen as changes to the internal form of states rather than being indicative of states in 'decline'.

o   The internal pressures on states 'from below' are organically linked to those 'from above', rather than being separate from them.

Activity 5   People generally learn more 'by doing' than simply by reading, so as a 'DIY summary', take the three brief summary statements above and jot down some points or examples from section 2.4 which you could use in support of each statement. For instance, support for the third statement includes the point about the supra-state European Commission encouraging sub-state regionalism within member states. This is just one example for one of the statements. You will be able to think of others and to jog your memory you can always skim back over the section.

2.5   Nations against states

Many of the states most obviously 'in trouble' (section 2.2.2 above) face internal opposition from regionally based nationalist movements. Examples of such states include Canada, India, Belgium and former Yugoslavia; examples of nationalist movements include those in the Basque Country, Ireland, Scotland or Wales. Such nationalist movements are generally more powerful that the 'mere' regionalism of areas like Baden-Württemberg or northern England. They have a base in culturally and politically distinctive 'national minorities' which are often long-established (and sometimes called 'historic nations'). As we saw in section 2.2, culture is often of central importance in 'imagining' a distinctive 'national community' and, in the face of recent globalization, it becomes something to be defended. Cultural globalization is now widely perceived to be obliterating local distinctiveness and 'making everywhere the same' **(Allen, 1995; Hall, 1995)**.

However, by definition, nationalist movements are struggling to achieve their own nation-state, or to join another state (as, for example, in the case of the Irish nationalist minority in Northern Ireland), rather than threatening the nation-state in principle. In practice, however, they threaten, erode or weaken particular states. They exemplify geography's centrality in political processes. They demonstrate very clearly how globalization and macro-regionalism can deepen pre-existing cultural and regional divisions within states and encourage those sub-state forces that want to 'fragment' existing territorial structures. They also point to the political impact of uneven development within their 'own' regions, with micro-regional forces in turn being undermined by more local divisions.

2.5.1   Nationalism and uneven development

Nationalism itself is an aspect of uneven development: it can be understood as an outcome of uneven cultural and economic processes between and within states. This perspective highlights the problems of the modern state as a territorial institution, and helps explain how pre-existing regional and cultural differences can be made politically significant.

In *The Break Up of Britain* Tom Nairn (1977) suggests that the impetus for nationalism and aspirations to separate statehood arose as a response to *uneven development*. He criticizes the dominant nineteenth-century view that world progress spread out from the most advanced countries, such as Britain and France, in a benign process where it was simply a matter of time before the less advanced parts of the world received the benefits. Instead he sees the diffusion of progress as highly uneven and contradictory. In some cases the dominance and competition of the advanced countries wrecked technologically less advanced countries and hence weaker societies; and sometimes particular territories and societies were held back by their pre-existing political links with areas that were even more backward. In all cases the less advanced parts of the world faced the problem of how to compete successfully with the advanced countries that had already got a 'head start' on them. According to Nairn's theory the nation-state and nationalism were part of the solution to that problem.

uneven development

Where a viable state already existed, for example in Spain or Japan, nationalism helped to mobilize forces for development; where many small political units had to be combined, for example to create Germany or Italy, it helped to mobilize the forces for unification; where a regional grouping wanted to separate from a larger state in order to form its own state or achieve substantial political autonomy, for example in Ireland or Catalonia, nationalism justified and mobilized the forces for separation.

Furthermore, there were at least three quite different ways in which movements for *national separatism* reflected uneven development. Either they emerged in relatively poor or economically 'under-developed' regions, demanding their own separate regional government or political independence, in order to protect themselves from, and 'catch up' with, the more advanced and dominating regions of the state (the case of Ireland and Irish nationalism in relation to Britain in the late eighteenth and nineteenth centuries); or, alternatively, as in the case of nineteenth-century Catalan separatism in Spain, the sub-state nationalism was the response of relatively advantaged or 'over-developed' areas which felt 'held back' by an archaic or corrupt central state and by being in political union with more backward regions. Early (though not contemporary) Basque separatism represents a third, and less usual, case. The Basque Country in the 1890s was Spain's industrial power-house but Basque nationalism emerged as a reaction *against* industrialization and against full integration with Spain which it saw as *too* 'progressive', a reaction largely explained by the fact that Basque nationalism's early support came from the urban lower middle class who were squeezed between the industrialists and the new working class, and from traditional social elites such as the clergy who were being displaced (Anderson, 1990).

national separatism

Thus, uneven development, interpreted not just in economic terms but also in cultural and political terms, provides a very useful framework for looking at different types of sub-state nationalism and other political regionalisms. For example, the rise of the northern leagues in Italy in the early 1990s, with their resentments against corrupt government in Rome and having to subsidize the Italian south, is, like nineteenth-century Catalan separatism, an example of a relatively prosperous region seeing itself as being 'held back' by an inefficient state and more backward regions. If uneven development *is* a basic cause of nationalism, nationalism's continued future seems to be guaranteed as globalization continues to re-produce uneven development.

To exemplify the politics of uneven development, and also the need for historical and geographical specificity when using such general concepts, we need to look no further than the ramshackle and lop-sided United Kingdom of Great Britain and Northern Ireland. It is a spectacular example of the incompleteness of nation-building, the failure to meet the nation-state ideal, and the resulting regional and national differences available to contemporary nationalist movements. As its cumbersome title suggests, it falls well short of the ideal where the boundaries of state and nation coincide. The United Kingdom of Great Britain and Northern Ireland encompasses distinct Scottish, Welsh, Irish and English identities imperfectly bound together by a wider but incomplete sense of 'Britishness'. England, with over 80 per cent of the total British population, is very much the political 'centre' (though there is increasingly a case for confining that term to the south-east of England). Scotland, Wales and Northern Ireland are politically its 'peripheries', and the need to claim 'unitedness' in the title hints, perhaps, at the incomplete unification of a multinational state in which the three 'peripheries' differ markedly not just from the 'centre' but from each other.

The different territories do not even have fully standardized state statistics: Northern Ireland is often dealt with separately from Britain, and Scotland from England and Wales. Even their designations lack uniformity and general agreement – not only are images and representations of place socially constructed (see **Massey, 1995a,b**), they are also socially contested. Some Scottish and Welsh nationalists object to their countries being referred to as 'regions'; Northern Ireland is sometimes officially alluded to as 'Ulster', but Irish nationalists object that 'Ulster' properly refers to the historic nine-county province, three counties of which are now in the Irish Republic. For the same reason there are objections to referring to Northern Ireland as 'the province', and calling Great Britain 'mainland Britain' can also cause annoyance because it implies that Northern Ireland is part of Britain (when actually it is part of the United Kingdom of Great Britain and Northern Ireland). On the other hand, nationalists annoy Unionists by refusing to use the official designation 'Northern Ireland', substituting 'North of Ireland' or 'the Six Counties'. Neutral terms are not readily available, although Northern Ireland's second city is sometimes referred to as 'Derry/Londonderry', ironically shortened to 'Stroke City'. The verbal minefield reflecting national conflicts would be familiar in similar situations such as the Basque Country.

Northern Ireland has always had its own separate civil service, education system, judiciary, and to some extent its own laws. Under the Prevention of Terrorism Act, Northern Irish people have been sent there from Britain in a form of 'internal exile'. Northern Ireland sends MPs to the London parliament but from 1921 to 1972 it also had its own parliament; in 1974 this was replaced by 'direct rule', in effect rule by a British colonial governor. Wales, by contrast, is a 'principality'; and Scotland, like England, is a 'kingdom' which has retained many of the trappings of a separate state, for example its own state Presbyterian 'Church of Scotland', its own legal and education systems, and its own Trades Union Congress which developed separately from the British TUC in London. Whereas England is administered by the specific departments of state – Education, Employment, Environment, etc. – the 'peripheries' are administered via their 'own' sections of *central* government – the Scottish Office, the Welsh Office and the Northern Ireland Office. The Scottish Office was established in 1886; in contrast the Welsh Office, like the Welsh TUC, was set up in response to nationalist pressure after 1960.

The *ad hoc* character of Britain reflects its different histories. The English kingdom developed from its south-east 'core' region between the tenth and fifteenth centuries, by which time it was a strongly unified state by contemporary European standards. However, it was only in the late sixteenth century that the absolutist Tudor monarchy began to exert political control over the whole of Ireland and even then Ireland retained separate political institutions and its designation as a separate 'kingdom', whereas Wales was fully integrated into the 'kingdom' of England in 1536. In contrast to the military conquests of Ireland and Wales, the Scottish and English crowns were voluntarily joined in 1603 when James VI of Scotland inherited the English throne from Elizabeth I and in addition became James I of England. It was by Acts of the English and Scottish parliaments that the two kingdoms were united as 'Great Britain' in 1707, with a single parliament at Westminster when the one in Edinburgh was dissolved. The next episode in the creation of a unified state – the United Kingdom of Great Britain and Ireland – came with the Act of Union in 1800 and the abolition of the formally independent Irish Parliament following the military defeat in 1798 of Ireland's first nationalist uprising.

There were also major differences in how the three 'peripheries' developed economically, again particularly marked in the Irish case. Scotland and Wales (or at least Central Scotland and South Wales), along with north-eastern Ulster around Belfast, shared fully in the economic benefits and political 'glories' of the Industrial Revolution and the British Empire, whereas much of Ireland, including much of Ulster, did not. This uneven development, combined with a legacy of political, religious and cultural discrimination (for example, the percentage of Ireland's population using the Irish language declined from about 50 per cent to 10 per cent after the union with Britain), resulted in the partitioning of Ireland in 1921, with 26 of its 32 counties breaking away in the first fissuring since 1801. Ulster Unionists had opposed demands for Irish 'Home Rule' since the 1880s, and now Britain's official title became the 'United Kingdom of Great Britain and *Northern* Ireland'. The latter comprised only six of Ulster's nine counties in order to give it a more substantial built-in Protestant majority of roughly a million Protestants to half a million Catholics.

So Britain exemplifies very clearly how uneven development provides fertile ground for sub-state nationalisms. However, nationalisms have not always been active, much less successful, and we need to know why. We need to analyse how and why pre-existing regional differences gain (and lose) political significance.

2.5.2 Sub-state nationalist resurgence

Despite the obviously incomplete unification of Britain, and of other states such as Canada, Spain or Belgium, the resurgence of sub-state nationalisms in the 1960s and 1970s came as a surprise and requires explanation. Britain, far from appearing vulnerable, had seemed to be a particularly successful case of political integration. Northern Ireland did have a separate political culture and its own parliament, but its problems seemed safely locked up there: the main issues of Irish 'Home Rule' had long seemed settled. It was widely believed that modern democratic government and a developed economy had made political separatism a thing of the past. Furthermore, with the extreme nationalism of the Nazis still fresh in people's memory, nationalism in general was widely seen as a dangerous anachronism. The world was becoming too interdependent for people's loyalties to be confined to historic national states, never mind smaller regions within them. The future lay not with smaller political units and the territorial fragmentation of existing states, but with their amalgamation into larger supra-state bodies such as the European Common Market, and some even saw the United Nations as the embryo of world government.

In this 'brave new world' the weak sub-state nationalisms that did exist were widely seen as quaint aberrations (as when in 1952 some Scots stole back the Stone of Scone which Edward I of England had taken away to Westminster Abbey as long ago as 1297). They were easily dismissed as irrelevancies which lacked any serious electoral support, anachronisms certainly but in the 1950s not particularly dangerous ones. Even the IRA lacked popular support and its sporadic military attacks along the Northern Ireland border fizzled out in the early 1960s.

Yet to the surprise of pundits and politicians alike, it was at just this point in history that sub-state nationalisms re-emerged as a serious political force in a variety of first world regions, for example Corsica, Brittany, Flanders, Wallonia, the Basque Country, Catalonia and Galicia, as shown in Figure 2.1. Some of them achieved dramatic increases in support and influence and developed political characteristics which had previously been absent or insignificant.

Within less than two decades the fragmentation of the multinational British state was being discussed as a serious possibility. The extent of the resurgence is reflected in the electoral statistics. For example, both the Scottish National Party (SNP) and, in Wales, Plaid Cymru (PC) had almost ceased to exist in the 1940s and 1950s. In the 1951 General Election PC put up just four candidates who averaged only 6 per cent of the vote, while the SNP had only two candidates and they got only about 10 per cent of the vote in the two constituencies. By contrast, in 1974 the SNP stood 71 candidates. Its percentage share of the total vote in Scotland in the 1945 General Election had been only 1.3 per cent, yet it rose to over 30 per cent in October 1974 (only 6 percentage points behind Labour) and the party won 11 seats. In Wales, Plaid Cymru's share of the vote rose from 1.1 per cent in 1945 to over 19 per cent in 1970. In both cases support has fallen back somewhat, but it remains at much higher levels than before the resurgence, and the main Britain-wide parties have been forced to accept at least part of the nationalists' agendas.

United Kingdom
1 Scotland
2 Wales
3 Northern Ireland

Belgium
4 Flanders
5 Wallonia

France
6 Brittany
7 Alsace
8 Corsica
9 Occitanie

Spain
10 Catalonia
11 Basque Country
12 Galicia
13 Andalusia

Italy
14 Fruili
15 South Tyrol
16 Sardinia

The Netherlands
17 Friesland

Figure 2.1 *Regional nationalist resurgence in Western Europe*

The best-known analysis – indeed advocacy – of nationalism's potential for breaking up Britain is Nairn's *The Break Up of Britain* (1977). Along with others, Nairn saw the disintegration of the British state as both inevitable and desirable because, he argued, its archaic pre-industrial character was now a major obstacle to social and economic progress. Britain had not undergone a full and effective modernizing revolution such as France experienced in the 1790s. The landed gentry and aristocracy retained political power long after the Industrial Revolution, and the internationally oriented financial interests of the City of London still predominate politically over British-based manufacturing interests. In addition, the British state is peculiarly archaic in its lack of a written constitution, its reliance on monarchical legitimation, its treatment of the population as 'subjects' of the monarch rather than as 'citizens' with rights, and its lack of genuine democracy, all of which, Nairn argued, rendered it unable to halt long-term economic and political decline.

This perspective has been criticized for, among other things, treating the French case as the norm and Britain as therefore a deviant case; for failing to appreciate that some of the 'archaic' features of the British state are inventions of the late nineteenth century; and, above all, for wishfully overstating the power of sub-state nationalism and underestimating the state's resilience. There are a variety of reasons why Britain has (so far) withstood the threats 'from below', and the threat from Irish nationalism illustrates some of them.

Firstly, most people accept the state's claim to have a monopoly on the legitimate use of institutionalized lethal force. Others who use armed force are 'terrorists', and this is recognized by other states in international law. Although the British state has been under international pressure to solve the conflict in Northern Ireland, help from other states for the sub-state nationalism generally stops well short of help for its military element. Secondly, the incompleteness or looseness of Britain's integration, particularly evident in the case of Northern Ireland, could be a source of strength for the state rather than a weakness. Certainly it facilitated a policy of 'Ulsterization' – isolating the problem from the rest of the state – and the state has been successful in largely containing the conflict within Northern Ireland. Thirdly, and turning to the weaknesses of sub-state nationalism, there are typical divisions both over ends and means. The opposition to the territorial status quo is split over whether or not physical force should be used, and there are also divisions over how much and what sort of political re-organization is thought necessary or practical – some want a united Ireland, others would settle for a lot less. Fourthly, there is opposition to the sub-state nationalism not just from the central state but also, or even mainly, from within the region itself. Nation-building by the state may have been incomplete but British nationalism has penetrated all of Britain's regions; in Northern Ireland it takes the form of Ulster unionism though this is now increasingly at variance with the nationalism of Britain itself.

Thus the micro-regional challenge 'from below' may itself be countered and weakened by challenges from 'further below'. If the state's cohesion is threatened by uneven development, sub-state nationalisms can similarly suffer from more localized unevenness within their own regions. The important cultural variations and divisions of language within Wales, where the Welsh language is an important element in Welsh nationalism is an example of this (see Figure 2.2).

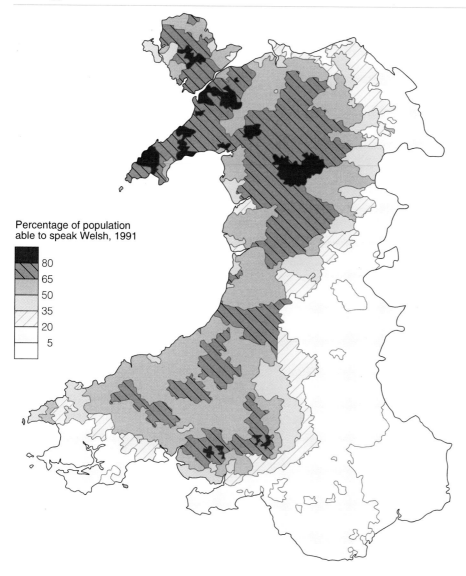

Percentage of population
able to speak Welsh, 1991

	80
	65
	50
	35
	20
	5

Figure 2.2   Welsh speakers in Wales, 1991 (Source: Aitchinson and Carter, 1994)

Another example is the uneven and intermingled geographical distribution of religious groupings in Northern Ireland where there is a strong, though far from total, correlation between membership of the Catholic Church and adherence to Irish nationalism (see Figure 2.3).

The Scottish nationalist claim that North Sea oil was 'Scotland's oil' was countered by the claim that really it belonged to the Shetlands; the hydro-electric power of northern Quebec is a 'bargaining chip' for the Quebec nationalists, but what of counter-claims from the Cree nation for whom northern Quebec is a much longer-established ancestral home? A sub-state nationalism may have to contend not only with the central state but also with conflicts of culture, territory and class in its own area. The overall result may be continuing problems for the central state which fall well short of the sub-state nationalism achieving its aims.

Catholic percentage

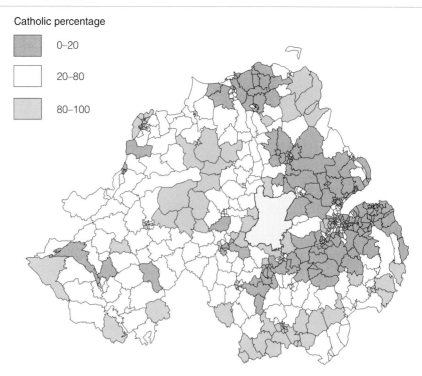

0–20

20–80

80–100

Figure 2.3 *Northern Ireland: Catholic percentage in each electoral ward, 1991 (Source: based on data from the 1991 Census of Population)*

Turning to explanations of the resurgence of nationalism, while there are particular reasons in each specific country, region and sub-state nationalist movements, the widespread nature of the resurgence, and its timing, require some general explanation. Does 'globalization' provide it? We need to look at economic, military, political and cultural factors.

Economic factors include the decline of regional economies and once-prosperous industrial areas, and increased penetration by multinational companies, as happened in Scotland, Wales and Northern Ireland in the 1960s and 1970s. Not only were economic matters increasingly seen as under the control of 'external interests' – the parent companies of branch plants – but the displacement or weakening of local industrial and commercial elites disrupted traditional political processes and channels of integration with the 'central' state. Politically, many of the resurgent nationalists in the first world gained encouragement from anti-colonial struggles in the 'third world', and there was a general strengthening of 'anti-imperialist' and left-wing elements in the revived nationalisms of the 1960s. Many consciously adopted the rhetoric and, in some cases, the armed guerrilla strategies of liberation movements in countries such as Algeria and Vietnam. They noted that many new and small states which had been colonies now had a seat at the UN. Being part of medium-sized states (such as Britain, France or Spain) was perceived as a decreasing asset as the relative standing of these states declined, sometimes because of the loss of empires.

More generally, with the growth of military or economic supra-state institutions, including the European Common Market, there was an historic increase in the relative viability of small states or would-be states. Ideas about *state viability* were transformed. In the nineteenth century – the main period of nation-state building in Western Europe and North America – the dominant idea was that a state had to be of a certain minimum size to sustain its own basic industries, independent armed forces and so forth. Now, in contrast, such objectives were called into question, or seen as unachievable even by quite large states, because of changes which were global in character. The 'Cold War' and nuclear weapons meant that (for perhaps the first time in history) the size of a state ceased to bear a close relationship to military security for all but a few superpowers. Being in a 'security alliance' such as NATO was more important. People in tiny Luxembourg could feel just as secure (or insecure) as their French neighbours who paid for an 'independent nuclear deterrent' (though, as we shall see, this argument is weaker in those parts of the 'third world' that lack the protection of international security regimes). Similarly, economic globalization undermined the idea, still current up to the mid-twentieth century, that a viable state was one with a home market large enough to sustain modern industry. Independent 'national economies' as the essential 'building-blocks' of capitalism lost plausibility. 'Big' may have been 'beautiful' in the nineteenth century, but now when small states such as Singapore are among the most successful economically, or when average per capita income in Luxembourg is about twice that in Britain, the desirability of size *per se* is greatly reduced.

state (size) viability

Supra-state institutions such as the EU now give small states advantages previously available only to larger states. In so-called 'national' regions likes Wales or Scotland this can mean encouragement for sub-state nationalism. Thus the SNP now makes its demands for independence from Britain within an explicitly European framework as shown by its slogan, 'Scotland in Europe, Make it Happen'. Similarly, Plaid Cymru has called for 'full self-government for Wales within the EU'; and both parties (in sharp contrast to British nationalists) have identified strongly with the trend towards regional devolution in mainland Europe.

Global changes in the sphere of culture are also increasingly important to sub-state nationalism. This is both because the changes are widespread and noticeable by the general public (through the media, fashion, entertainment and 'consumerism' in general) and, because local or regional cultures and traditions are generally important supports for nationalists, not surprisingly they react when they feel their own cultural base is threatened. The general arrival of television, the increased impact of 'global culture' (sometimes seen as 'Americanization'), and the widespread belief that globalization brings cultural homogeneity, have all helped to stimulate attempts to defend and revive more local and indigenous cultures (see also **Jess and Massey, 1995**). The threat of cultural terminal decline, as in the case of some languages, has lent such 'revivals' a new urgency.

The increased speed of change, often combined with economic problems, has increased social tensions and insecurity, and one response has been to look for 'security' in a stronger sense of communal or group identity. There has been a marked increase in concern with questions of group identity – ethnic, religious, regional and national – over recent decades, perhaps reflecting insecurities associated with accelerated globalization.

More directly related to questions of state, nationalism and independent or autonomous state institutions can increasingly be seen as offering at least some protection for regional and national cultures threatened by globalization. Even if it were accepted that states are now generally less effective as 'bulwarks' against external pressures, especially in economic matters, sub-state nationalists could still argue convincingly that they are better than nothing, especially in relation to cultural threat. Perhaps the only thing worse than having a nation-state is not having a state at all.

A 'now or never' urgency about halting cultural decline or, in some cases, cultural disappearance, and a related cultural stimulus to sub-state nationalism, are worldwide phenomena, and may prove to be less important among Europeans than in the 'third world' and for so-called 'ethnic groups'. Worldwide there is no comparison between the number of distinct cultural groups and the number of states (or even potential states): there are, for instance, over 5,000 separate languages but only about 170 separate states. Ethnic groups such as the Maoris in New Zealand, the Yanomami in Amazonia and the North American 'Indian tribes' have learned the language of 'nation' and 'nationalism' to further their political rights in the contemporary world. This is reflected in the entirely reasonable demand that they be known by their proper names rather than the pejorative names by which we, through their enemies and detractors, have often come to know them (even the word 'ethnic' in English had pejorative connotations of 'heathen'). For example, they demand a switch from Eskimo ('Eaters of Raw Meat') to Inuit ('the People'); Mohawk ('Man Eater') to Kaniengehaga ('People of the Place of Flint'); Apache ('Enemy') to Dine ('the People'); Comanche ('Enemy') to Numinu ('the People'); Huron ('Unkept') to Wendat ('Islanders'). Cultural groups are under threat the world over, and while states such as Canada and the USA may not respond reasonably, they are at least secure and wealthy enough to grant autonomous 'national rights' to such groups. The same cannot be said for the many insecure 'third world' states (as will be gauged from Reading C).

In very general terms, the latest wave of globalization helps to explain the widespread increase in the importance of sub-state nationalisms since the 1960s, though there is perhaps a danger of globalization (like uneven development) being used as a 'catch-all' factor which 'explains everything and nothing'. Some of the problems attributed to globalization might, more properly, be attributed to a period of capitalist crises and worldwide economic instability, though the two are hard to disentangle because accelerated globalization is happening in just such a period.

Summary of section 2.5

o 'Globalization' and 'uneven development' are helpful as general conceptual frameworks, but not if used as substitutes for more detailed historical and geographical analyses.

o Even if nationalism and the nation-state are a cause of serious problems, it seems to be wishful (and not very helpful) thinking to see national states as historical anachronisms.

o   If we accept that nationalism is generated and re-generated by uneven development, it is likely to persist for the foreseeable future, though perhaps in altered forms.

o   Existing nation-states are unlikely to 'commit suicide'; their greatest threat of dismemberment 'from below' comes from separatist movements which are fighting for nation-state status, encouraged by the fact that small states are now more viable.

o   While uneven development weakens the cohesion of nation-states it also weakens regionally based opposition.

2.6   New territorialities?

Pressures on the state 'from above' and 'from below', but the absence of anything as decisive as 'the death of nation-state', or any clear relocation of its sovereignty to macro-regional or micro-regional levels of government, suggests the possibility that a 'new medievalism' is emerging and that territorial sovereignty is being partly 'unbundled'. But if so, older political forms continue to exist, both in Europe and beyond it.

2.6.1   'New medievalism', 'unbundling' territoriality

Bull (1977) speculated that a 'new medievalism' might arise because of, among other things, a growth of transnational corporations and networks (see Chapter 1), a 'regional integration of states' as in the EU, or 'a disintegration of states' because of sub-state nationalist and regionalist pressures 'from below'.

Box 2.3 A 'new medievalism'

'... a modern and secular equivalent of the kind of universal political organisation that existed in western Christendom in the Middle Ages ... [where] ... no ruler or state was sovereign in the sense of being supreme over a given territory and given segment of the Christian population; each had to share authority with vassals beneath, and with the Pope and (in Germany and Italy) the Holy Roman Emperor above ...

All authority in mediaeval Christendom was thought to derive ultimately from God and the political system was basically theocratic ... but it is not fanciful to imagine that there might develop a modern and secular counterpart of it that embodies its central characteristic: a system of overlapping authority and multiple loyalty ...

If modern states were to come to share their authority over their citizens, and their ability to command their loyalties, on the one hand with regional and world authorities, and on the other hand with sub-state or sub-national authorities, to such an extent that the concept of sovereignty ceased to be applicable, then a neo-mediaeval form of universal political order might be said to have emerged ...

'new medievalism'

We might imagine that the political loyalties of the inhabitants of, say, Glasgow, were so uncertain as between the authorities in Edinburgh, London, Brussels and New York that the government of the United Kingdom could not be assumed to enjoy any kind of primacy over the others, such as it possesses now. If such a state of affairs prevailed all over the globe, this is what we may call, for want of a better term, a neo-mediaeval order ...

If we are looking for evidence that European integration is bringing a qualitative change in the states system, it is more profitable to look not to the imagined end-product of this process, a European super-state which is simply a nation-state writ large, but at the process in an intermediate stage. It is possible that the process of integration might arrive at the stage where, while one could not speak of a European state, there was real doubt both in theory and in reality as to whether sovereignty lay with the national governments or with the organs of the 'community' ...

As in the case of the integration of states, the disintegration of states would be theoretically important only if it were to remain transfixed in an intermediate stage ... We cannot ignore this possibility, any more than that we can dismiss the possibility that sovereignty will be undermined by regional supranational institutions ... Wales, the United Kingdom and the European Community could each have some world political status while none laid claim to exclusive sovereignty.'

Source: Bull, 1977, pp. 254–5, 264–7

The crucial point here is that a return to 'overlapping authority and multiple loyalty' does not involve anything as clear-cut as the replacement of states by scale replicas – either macro-regional or micro-regional (see the 'Gulliver' fallacy in section 2.2.1). On the contrary, it would happen where the pressures 'from above and 'from below' achieved more partial and ambiguous changes, diffusing but not clearly relocating sovereignty as it is presently understood.

The debate around the future of European integration has been mostly about whether it will (or should) result in a federal 'United States of Europe' or revert to being an inter-governmental arrangement of independent states. But maybe 'the future' has already arrived, maybe 'this is it', neither a continuation of the modern system of sovereign states, nor a federal state in embryo, but something quite different from both, an 'intermediate' form which is distinct in its own right rather than merely 'transitional'.

Furthermore, there are other contemporary developments that suggest a 'new medievalism': the emergence of newly important world 'actors' such as 'global cities', for instance (see **Hamnett, 1995**), and the recent growth of transterritorial, functionally defined networks are just two. As Strange (1994) points out, states may be losing some of their autonomy, not because power has been 'lost upwards' to other political institutions such as the EU, but because it has 'gone sideways' to economic institutions and global market forces, and, in some respects, has 'gone nowhere' as economics have outrun politics, and political control is simply lost.

'unbundling' territoriality

All these developments are consistent with the idea that the ground is shifting underneath established arrangements and that *territoriality is being partially 'unbundled'*. If the 'pre-modern-to-modern' transition can be seen in terms of sovereignty over everything being 'bundled' into territorial state 'parcels' (section 2.2.1), then an 'unbundling' of territoriality may be the key to understanding the contemporary spatial reorganizations of politics and states, what Ruggie (1993) describes as a 'modern to postmodern' transition. The medieval to modern transformation of politics was bound up with what Harvey (1989, p. 242) calls 'a radical reconstruction of views of space and time'. For example, medieval painters saw their subjects from different sides and angles rather than from a single, fixed viewpoint, but later paintings differed radically, following the Renaissance invention of perspective from a single fixed point. For Ruggie there is an analogous and related transformation of political space which:

> ... came to be defined *as it appeared from a single fixed viewpoint*. The concept of sovereignty was merely the doctrinal counterpart of the application of single-point perspectival forms to the spatial organization of politics.
>
> *(Ruggie, 1993, p. 159)*

Conversely, the present 'unbundling' of territorial sovereignty can be interpreted as a reversion to multiple perspectives, and this 'reconstruction of views of space' has been anticipated by cubist painters who again show things from different sides and angles.

Activity 6 Turn now to Reading B by John Gerard Ruggie, 'The "unbundling" of territoriality'. Here Ruggie discusses 'unbundling' and a 'multiperspectival' European Union, where 'the process of unbundling territoriality has gone further than anywhere else' and the 'singular sovereignty' of independent statehood is being complicated by multiple and overlapping sovereignties.

Note the points about the 'transformative potential of global ecology' (which is followed up in Chapter 5) and about a 'non-territorial space-of-flows' existing alongside but not as a 'direct challenge' to the more conventional 'space-of-places'.

2.6.2   New and not so new

The idea that globalization requires further 'unbundling' is very persuasive. But these processes are selective and uneven, and the emerging political reality is likely to be a messy mixture of old and new or hybrid forms, with 'territorial', 'transterritorial' and 'functional' forms of association and authority co-existing and interacting. The overall results could be much more complex than 'medievalism'. Firstly, because of accelerated globalization, it is increasingly important to differentiate between various aspects of state power (see section 2.3 above). Territoriality is becoming less important in some fields such as financial investment; however in other fields, such as policing, the modern nation-state with its sovereignty defined by (often the same old) territorial boundaries seems as firmly rooted as ever; and in some aspects of social policy state powers are even increasing. Secondly, the outcomes will differ between states, and particularly across different parts of the world as is emphasized in Reading C.

Activity 7 Now turn to Reading C by Michael Mann, 'Nation-states in Europe and other continents'. Mann argues forcefully that nation-states in Europe and other continents are 'diversifying, developing, not dying'. Note that he both confirms and qualifies some of the points already made in this chapter; and he argues that 'Europe is not the world's future' (an argument which will be underlined by Chapter 4 on Islamic alternatives).

The multiple perspectives of the medieval and cubist paintings contrast with the single, fixed viewpoint of the other painting

Lady Teaching a Child to Read, *Netscher. The National Gallery, London*

House of Peers. Henry VIII. Commons Attending. *The Mansell Collection, London*

Musical Instrument / The Lamp, *K. Malevich. Stedelijk Museum, Amsterdam*

Although a new form, the EU is still territorially based and, in many respects, 'singular sovereignty' remains dominant, whether exercised by the member states (for example when deciding education policies) or by the EU as a political collective (for example when negotiating about world trade). Mann in Reading C refers to 'Fortress Europe', and, from the viewpoint of an intending immigrant, the EU can display exactly the same unfriendly singularity as a conventional territorial state. On the other hand, his argument that the EU's 'democratic deficit' is at least partly due to the diffuse nature and lack of 'singularity' in its decision-making structures, particularly the powerlessness of its central parliament, lends support to the idea that the EU is what Ruggie in Reading B calls a postmodern 'multiperspectival polity'. But this also points to some of the limitations of drawing historical analogies with the very different politics of medieval times.

Ideas of 'new medieval' and 'postmodern' territorialities are very useful in signalling the possibility of a radical shift in the underlying 'time–space' of politics and in highlighting multiple levels and overlaps of authority. However, the medieval analogy has serious inadequacies which are themselves revealing in that they indicate or arise from the greater complexity of the contemporary world. Three differences from the medieval era are particularly important: the experience of democracy, the lack of 'universalism' and the relative absence of ordered hierarchies.

The territorial sovereignty now being 'unbundled' is no longer the sovereignty of monarchs or of a small landowning elite who, in medieval Europe, could treat political territories as their landed estates. In modern democracies where sovereignty belongs to 'the people' or 'the nation', at least in theory if not always in practice, it is *our* sovereignty which is being 'unbundled'. Thus democracy, as presently constituted, tends to be undermined by the 'unbundling' of territoriality. This, not surprisingly, generates popular resistance and democratic opposition, as seen, for example, in the difficulties which several EU states experienced when holding referenda to get popular acceptance of closer European union. Contemporary rulers might well think that political life was simpler for the autocratic ruling classes of medieval Christendom whose nested and non-democratic hierarchies were apparently legitimized by God.

One democratic response to territorial 'unbundling' in the EU is simply to oppose it by, for example, voting against the transfer of further powers to EU institutions. Another, quite different, response is to accept it but to work towards reducing the EU's 'democratic deficit' by strengthening its central institutions, particularly the European Parliament. This, of course, implies ongoing tensions between democratic accountability either via states or directly through EU institutions, with federalization continuing to be 'arrested' in some 'intermediate stage' which would be consistent with Bull's 'new medievalism'. If so, new forms of democracy and new means of accountability may be needed, but here the 'medieval model' is unhelpful to say the least.

The second important difference is that the contemporary world lacks the sort of 'universalism' which stemmed from the theocratic, unifying political system of medieval Christendom. Bull, as we saw, stressed that to qualify as a 'new medievalism' the new political order would have to be 'universal', 'all over the globe'. However, as Mann in Reading C makes very clear, state forms and political developments are extremely uneven across the different continents. It could be argued that this global diversity rules out a secular reincarnation of the 'universality' which cemented medieval Europe. Indeed, contemporary Europe, never mind the world as a whole, could be said to lack a modern equivalent of the unifying 'world view' or 'moral order' which combined all aspects of life – economic, social, cultural, ideological – and held sway over most of medieval Europe.

Global uneveness now matters in a way it did not then. In contrast to medieval times, we now have 'one world', not a series of more or less sealed 'worlds' – 'The Old World', 'The New World', 'Christian', 'Islamic', 'Chinese', 'Aztec' and so on – each of which constituted itself as '*the* world', more or less completely separated from, and sometimes in complete ignorance of, the others. In cultural and ideological terms these are still in many respects 'local worlds' (see **Meegan, 1995**), but now, after some five hundred years of 'time–space compression', they are all part of one interdependent and interacting global system. To put it another way, while the world has been integrated into a capitalist global economy, this has not been matched by anything approaching the cultural and ideological homogeneity of medieval Europe. As well as making for greater complexity, this integration of 'separate worlds' economically but not culturally may also make for more political instability. As the geopolitical theorist Halford Mackinder predicted of political globalization in 1904:

Every explosion of social forces, instead of being dissipated in a surrounding circuit of unknown space and barbaric chaos [sic], will be sharply re-echoed from the far side of the globe, and weak elements in the political and economic organism of the world will be shattered in consequence.

(Mackinder, 1904, p. 421)

The third important difference from the medieval era is the relative absence of ordered hierarchies. Sovereignty in medieval Europe, as we saw in section 2.2.1, was typically divided between different institutions and levels which constituted *nested* hierarchies (for example, manor, lordship ... kingdom) and people were members of higher collectivities by virtue of their membership of lower-level bodies. Now, in contrast, typical hierarchies are *not nested* – people are often *directly* members of international networks, not via national bodies; small local groups increasingly deal *directly* with transnational institutions, not via larger intermediaries; regional groups and institutions deal *directly* with their counterparts in other nation-states without the respective nation-states necessarily having any involvement. Hierarchies may still exist, but not in the medieval 'chain of command' sense, and this 'escape' from nested hierarchies implies more complex and varied relations between the different levels of political power.

2.7   Conclusion: 'a world of adventure playgrounds'?

The world in which states now operate is, in some respects, more complex than it was in the medieval era or for much of the modern period. The nation-state, once born, is continuing to exist rather than being tidily removed to clear the ground for new political forms. Instead, its powers and roles are changing and it is interacting with a plethora of other, different kinds of political institutions, organizations, associations and networks. Contemporary globalization is overlaying the mosaic of nation-states and national communities with other forms of political community and non-political market relations. With the partial 'unbundling' of territoriality, a mixture of old and new forms and processes are now operating at and between different levels, 'above', 'below' and including the nation-state. Contrary to some conventional 'one-level' thinking, the state is not the only important 'actor' on the international stage and it does not enjoy sole authority within its own territory.

The contemporary world, however, is not like a 'ladder' (or even a set of ladders) where the links between different levels are unilinear and processes go up or down in an orderly fashion from one rung to the next. The central state does not mediate all links between higher and lower levels or between external and internal forces. This never was the case, but it is even less true today. Not only are there now more 'rungs' but, qualitatively, they are more

The metaphor of the 'adventure playground', where movement can take place in many directions and between many levels, captures the mixture of political forms and processes in the contemporary world much better than the 'ladder' metaphor

heterogeneous; and direct movements between higher and lower levels, missing out or bypassing 'intermediate rungs', are now a defining characteristic of contemporary life. A complex set of climbing frames, slides, swings and ropes, complete with weak or broken parts – an often dangerous 'adventure playground' in which adults play serious games and sometimes behave like spoilt kids – might be nearer the mark! The metaphor of an 'adventure playground', with its mixture of constructions, multiple levels and encouragement of movement – upwards, downwards, sideways, diagonally, directly from high to low, or low to high – captures the contemporary mixture of forms and processes much better than the 'ladder' metaphor. And given the continued existence of 'separate worlds' within the global system, perhaps we should be thinking of 'a world of adventure playgrounds' in the plural.

In this world the state may remain a central, indeed even the single most important, political institution, but it is only one political construction among many. We saw that recent changes, particularly since the 1970s, have weakened the control which states can exercise over economic activities within their territories, but some other state powers, particularly in areas of social and environmental policy, are still growing. We saw that internal pressures on the state 'from below' are linked to external pressures 'from above', very obviously but by no means only in the European Union (which is discussed in the next chapter). We also saw that these pressures, whether of 'globalization' or 'Europeanization', involve economic, cultural and political processes often inextricably linked together; and that geography is integral to how these processes are re-shaping our world.

The partial 'unbundling' of territoriality means that territory is losing some of its importance as a basis of sovereignty and political rule. But this does not mean that geographical space is becoming unimportant, or that territorially based sovereignty is ending, or that states are 'in decline'. It makes much more sense to see the changes as qualitative transformations. Rather than seeing *the* nation-state in the singular, we need to appreciate that states (in the plural) have assumed, and will continue to assume, a wide variety of forms as they adapt to changing historical and geographical circumstances. Rumours of the nation-state's 'death' are indeed 'exaggerated'. 'The state is dead, long live its different forms!'

Allegations of imminent 'death' are not only incorrect, they could actually prevent us from seeing the much more interesting things that are happening. The contemporary wave of globalization and 'time–space compression' is rendering geographical space increasingly complex, variable and 'relative'. We saw that conventional representations of states and politics which are based on 'absolute' space are increasingly detached from reality: the sharp dichotomy between 'domestic' and 'foreign' affairs, for example, or the 'Gulliver' fallacy of seeing the only real pressure on existing states as coming from larger or smaller 'scale replicas'. The ground is shifting underneath such conceptions, just as the 'stage' is shifting under the political 'actors'. Political re-structuring cannot be reduced to the simple arithmetic of a 'zero-sum game' in which gains at one level of institutional politics automatically mean losses at another: power may seep away from states to global markets rather than to other political institutions, and, in any case, there is not a fixed 'amount of power' to be allocated and reallocated. Despite the problems of historical analogy, ideas of 'new medieval' and 'postmodern' territorialities are useful in signalling the possibility of radical transformations, not just to states and the other 'actors', but to the time-space of the stage on which they have to operate.

References

AGNEW, J. (1994) 'The territorial trap: the geographical assumptions of International Relations theory', *Review of International Political Economy*, Vol. 1, No. 1, pp. 53–80.

AITCHISON, J. and CARTER, H. (1994) *A Geography of the Welsh Language, 1961–1991*, Cardiff, University of Wales.

ALLEN, J. (1995) 'Global worlds', in Allen and Massey (eds) (1995).

ALLEN, J. and HAMNETT, C. (1995) 'Uneven worlds', in Allen and Hamnett (eds) (1995).

ALLEN, J. and HAMNETT, C. (EDS) (1995) *A Shrinking World? Global Unevenness and Inequality*, Oxford, Oxford University Press in asssociation with The Open University (Volume 2 in this series).

ALLEN, J. and MASSEY, D. (EDS) (1995) *Geographical Worlds*, Oxford, Oxford University Press in asssociation with The Open University (Volume 1 in this series).

ANDERSON, B. (1983) *Imagined Communities*, London, Verso (1991 edition).

ANDERSON, J. (1986) 'Nationalism and geography', in Anderson, J. (ed.) *The Rise of the Modern State*, Brighton, Harvester.

ANDERSON, J. (1990) 'Separation and devolution: the Basques in Spain', in Chisholm, M. and Smith, D. (eds) *Shared Space, Divided Space: Essays on Conflict and Territorial Organization*, London, Unwin Hyman.

ANDERSON, J. and GOODMAN, J. (1995) 'Euro-regionalism and national conflict: the EU, the UK, Ireland North and South', in Shirlow, P. (ed.) *Development Ireland*, Dublin, Pluto (forthcoming).

BULL, H. (1977) *The Anarchical Society*, London, Macmillan.

COCHRANE, A.D. (1993) *Whatever Happened to Local Government?*, Buckingham, Open University Press.

COX, R.W. (1992) 'Global Perestroika', in Miliband, R. and Panitch, L. (eds) *Socialist Register*, London, Merlin Press.

GRAY, J. (1994) 'Against the world', *The Guardian*, 4 January.

HALL, S. (1995) 'New cultures for old', in Massey and Jess (eds) (1995).

HAMNETT, C. (1995) 'Controlling space: global cities', in Allen and Hamnett (eds) (1995).

HARRIS, N. (1986) *The End of the Third World: Newly Industrializing Countries and the Decline of an Ideology*, Harmondsworth, Penguin.

HARVEY, D. (1989) *The Condition of Postmodernity*, Oxford, Basil Blackwell.

JESS, P. and MASSEY, D. (1995) 'The contestation of place', in Massey and Jess (eds) (1995).

KEARNEY, R. (1988) Introduction: 'Thinking otherwise', in Kearney, R. (ed.) *Across the Frontiers*, Dublin, Wolfhound Press.

KOSSIS, C. (1992) 'A miracle without end? Japanese capitalism and the world economy', *International Socialism*, No. 54, Spring 1992, pp. 105–32.

LEYSHON, A. (1995) 'Annihilating space?: the speed-up of communications', in Allen and Hamnett (eds) (1995).

MACKINDER, H. (1904) 'The geographical pivot of history', *Geographical Journal*, Vol. 23, pp. 421–37.

MANN, M. (1993) 'Nation-states in Europe and other continents: diversifying, developing, not dying', *Dædalus: Journal of the American Academy of Arts and Sciences*, Summer. (Issued in the *Proceedings of the American Academy of Arts and Sciences*, Vol. 122, No. 3, pp. 115–40.)

MASSEY, D. (1995a) 'Imagining the world', in Allen and Massey (eds) (1995).

MASSEY, D. (1995b) 'The conceptualization of space', in Massey and Jess (eds) (1995).

MASSEY, D. and JESS, P. (eds) (1995) *A Place in the World? Places, Cultures and Globalization*, Oxford, Oxford University Press in asssociation with The Open University (Volume 4 in this series).

MEEGAN, R. (1995) 'Local worlds', in Allen and Massey (eds) (1995).

NAIRN, T. (1977) *The Break-up of Britain: Crisis and Neo-nationalism*, London, New Left Books.

ROSE, G. (1995) 'Place and identity: a sense of place', in Massey and Jess (eds) (1995).

RUGGIE, J.G. (1993) 'Territoriality and beyond: problematizing modernity in international relations', *International Organization*, Vol. 47, No. 1, pp. 139–74.

SACK, R. (1986) *Human Territoriality: Its Theory and History*, Cambridge, Cambridge University Press.

STOPFORD, J. and STRANGE, S. (1991) *Rival States, Rival Firms: Competition for World Market Shares*, Cambridge, Cambridge University Press.

STRANGE, S. (1994) 'The Power Gap: the member states and the world economy', in Brouwer, F., Lintner, V. and Newman, M. (eds) *Economic Policy Making and the European Union*, Conference proceedings, London European Research Centre, University of North London, 14 April, Federal Trust.

WALKER, R.B.J. (1993) *Inside/Outside: International Relations as Political Theory*, Cambridge, Cambridge University Press.

There are at least three ways in which prior or other systems of rule have differed [...] from the modern territorial state.

First, systems of rule need not be territorial at all. That is to say, the basis on which the human species is socially individuated and individuals, in turn, are bound together into collectivities can take (and historically has taken) forms other than territoriality. For example, anthropologists quaintly used to characterize as 'primitive government' those systems of rule wherein the spatial extension was demarcated on the basis of kinship. Moreover, they held that a critical stage in societal evolution was precisely the shift from consanguinity to contiguity as the relevant spatial parameter. To be sure, territory was *occupied* in kin-based systems, but it did not *define* them.

Second, systems of rule need not be territorially fixed. Owen Lattimore's work on nomadic property rights is of relevance here. Writing of Mongol tribes, Lattimore (1940 and 1962) pointed out that no single pasture would have had much value for them because it soon would have become exhausted. Hence, driven by what Lattimore called the 'sovereign importance of movement', the tribes wandered, herding their livestock. But, they did not wander haphazardly; 'They laid claim to definite pastures and to the control of routes of migration between these pastures.' Accordingly, 'the right to move prevailed over the right to camp. Ownership meant, in effect, the title to a cycle of migration'. The cycle was tribally owned and administered by the prince.

Third, even where systems of rule are territorial, and even where territoriality is relatively fixed, the prevailing concept of territory need not entail mutual exclusion. The archetype of nonexclusive territorial rule, of course, is medieval Europe, with its 'patchwork of overlapping and incomplete rights of government' (Strayer and Munro, 1959) which were 'inextricably superimposed and tangled' and in which 'different juridical instances were geographically interwoven and stratified, and plural allegiances, asymmetrical suzerainties and anomalous enclaves abounded' (Anderson, 1974). The difference between the medieval and modern worlds is striking in this respect.

Briefly put, the spatial extension of the medieval system of rule was structured by a nonexclusive form of territoriality, in which authority was both personalized and parcelized within and across territorial formations and for which inclusive bases of legitimation prevailed. The notion of firm boundary lines between the major territorial formations did not take hold until the thirteenth century: prior to that date there were only 'frontiers', or large zones of transition. The medieval ruling class was mobile in a manner not dreamed of since, able to assume governance from one end of the continent to the other without hesitation or difficulty because 'public territories formed a continuum with private estates' (Anderson, 1974). [...]

[In contrast] the modern [...] variant of structuring territorial space is the familiar world of territorially disjoint, mutually exclusive, functionally similar, sovereign states.

The chief characteristic of the modern system of territorial rule is the consolidation of all parcelized and personalized authority into one public realm. This consolidation entailed two fundamental spatial demarcations: between public and private realms and between internal and external realms. The public sphere was constituted by the monopolization on the part of central authorities of the legitimate use of force. Internally, this monopolization was expressed through the progressive imposition of what was called the 'king's peace' or the sole right of the king's authority to enforce the law [...]. Externally, the monopolization of the legitimate use of force was expressed in the sovereign right to make war [...]. Finally, the inclusive bases of legitimation that had prevailed in the medieval world, articulated in divine and natural law, yielded to the doctrine of sovereignty. [...]

To summarize, politics is about rule. And, the distinctive feature of the modern system of rule is that it has differentiated its subject collectivity into territorially defined, fixed, and mutually exclusive enclaves of legitimate dominion. As such, it appears to be unique in human history. [...]

The [medieval-to-modern] transformation in the spatial organization of politics was so profound – literally mind-boggling – that contemporaries had great difficulty grasping its full implications for many years to come. Mattingly (1964), for example, recounts the efforts of Francis I as late as 1547 to reform the apparatus of the French state by fixing the number of *secretaires d'Etat* at four. Rather than separating their duties according to the logical distinction, by modern standards, between domestic and foreign relations,

each of the four was assigned one quadrant of France *and* the relations with all contiguous and outlying states.

References

ANDERSON, P. (1974) *Lineages of the Absolutist State*, London, New Left Books.

LATTIMORE, O. (1940) *Inner Asian Frontiers of China*, London, Oxford University Press.

LATTIMORE, O. (1962) *Studies in Frontier History*, London, Oxford University Press.

MATTINGLY, G. (1964) *Renaissance Diplomacy*, Baltimore, Penguin Books.

STRAYER, J.R. and MUNRO, D.C. (1959) *The Middle Ages*, New York, Appleton-Century-Crofts.

Source: Ruggie, 1993, pp. 149–51, 159–60

Reading B: John Gerard Ruggie, 'The "unbundling" of territoriality'

[...] Having established [absolute and mutually exclusive territoriality] what means were left to the new territorial rulers for dealing with problems [...] that could not be reduced to territorial solution?

This issue arose in connection with common spaces, such as contiguous and transborder waterways as well as the oceans: how does one possess something one does not own? And, still more problematic, how does one exclude others from it? Inland waterways could be split down the middle and typically were, though often not until other and more violent means had been exhausted. Ocean space beyond defendable coastal areas posed a more substantial problem. Spain and Portugal tried a bilateral deal whereby Spain claimed a monopoly of western ocean trade routes to the Far East and Portugal the eastern, but they failed to make their deal stick. [...]

The really serious problem arose not in the commons, however, but right in the heart of the mutually exclusive territorial state formations: no space was left within

which to anchor even so basic a task as the conduct of diplomatic representation without fear of relentless disturbance, arbitrary interference, and severed lines of communication.

In medieval Europe, the right of embassy was a method of formal and privileged communication that could be admitted or denied depending upon the social status and roles of the parties involved and the business at hand. Ambassadors had specific missions, for which they enjoyed specific immunities. For a variety of misdeeds and crimes, however, ambassadors were tried and sentenced by the prince to whom they were accredited, as though they were a subject of that prince. This solution ceased to be acceptable, however, once the right of embassy became sign of sovereign recognition and ambassadors were in place permanently. The short-term response was to grant more and more specific immunities to resident ambassadors as the situation demanded. During the century or so of religious strife, however, that option too came to be undermined by, among other factors, the so-called embassy chapel question.

As the term implies, this had to do with the services celebrated in an ambassador's chapel, at which compatriots were welcome, when the religions of the home and host sovereigns differed. For example, Edward VI insisted that the new English prayer book be used in all his embassies; Charles V would tolerate no such heresy at his court. It was not uncommon for diplomatic relations to be broken over the issue. [...] Rather than contemplate the heresy of a Protestant service at a Catholic court and vice versa, it proved easier to pretend that the service was not taking place in the host country at all but on the soil of the homeland of the ambassador. And so it gradually became with other dimensions of the activities and precincts of embassy. A fictitious space, designated 'extraterritoriality' was invented. Mattingly (1964) has put the paradox well: 'By arrogating to themselves supreme power over men's consciences, the new states had achieved absolute sovereignty. Having done so, they found they could only communicate with one another by tolerating within themselves little islands of alien sovereignty' [...] [w]hat we might call an 'unbundling' of territoriality [...] Various types of functional regimes, common markets, political communities, and the like constitute additional forms whereby territoriality has become unbundled. [...]

[...]

The preceding analysis suggests that the unbundling of territoriality is a productive venue for the exploration of contemporary international transformation [...] The terrain of unbundled territoriality [...] is the place wherein a rearticulation of international political space would be occurring today.

Take first the EC, in which the process of unbundling territoriality has gone further than anywhere else [...] it may constitute the first 'multiperspectival polity' to emerge since the advent of the modern era. That is to say, it is increasingly difficult to visualize the conduct of international politics among community members, and to a considerable measure even domestic politics, as though it took place from a starting point of twelve

separate, single, fixed viewpoints. Nor can models of strategic interaction do justice to this particular feature of the EC, since the collectivity of members as a singularity, in addition to the central institutional apparatus of the EC, has become party to the strategic interaction game. To put it differently, the constitutive processes whereby each of the twelve defines its own identity [...] increasingly endogenize the existence of the other eleven [...] There is no indication, however, that this reimagining will result in a federal state of Europe – which would merely replicate on a larger scale the typical modern political form.

The concept of multiperspectival institutional forms offers a lens through which to view other possible instances of international transformation today. Consider the global system of transnationalized microeconomic links. Perhaps the best way to describe it, when seen from our vantage point, is that these links have created a nonterritorial 'region' in the world economy – a decentered yet integrated space-of-flows, operating in real time, which exists alongside the spaces-of-places that we call national economies. These conventional spaces-of-places continue to engage in external economic relations with one another, which we continue to call trade, foreign investment, and the like, and which are more or less effectively mediated by the state. In the nonterritorial global economic region, however, the conventional distinctions between internal and external once again are exceedingly problematic, and any given state is but one constraint in corporate global strategic calculations. This is the world in which IBM is Japan's largest computer exporter, and Sony is the largest exporter of television sets from the United States. It is the world in which Brothers Industries, a Japanese concern assembling typewriters in Bartlett, Tennessee, brings an antidumping case before the U.S. International Trade Commission against Smith Corona, an American firm that imports typewriters in the United States from its offshore facilities in Singapore and Indonesia. [...] This nonterritorial global economic region is a world, in short, that is premised on what Lattimore described as the 'sovereign importance of movement', not of place. The long-term significance of this region, much like that of the medieval trade fairs, may reside in its novel behavioural and institutional forms and in the novel space-time constructs that these forms embody, not in any direct challenge that it poses as a potential substitute for the existing system of rule.

Consider also the transformative potential of global ecology. The human environment is of central importance for future planetary politics from many perspectives. Central among them is its potential to comprise a new and very different [...] set of spatial, metaphysical and doctrinal constructs through which the visualization of collective existence on the planet is shaped. This [...] would differ in form from modern territoriality and its accoutrements insofar as the underlying structural premise of ecology is holism and mutual dependence of parts [...] The concept of international custodianship is an obvious candidate for closer scrutiny. Under it, no other agency competes with or attempts to substitute for the state, but the state itself acts in a

manner that expresses not merely its own interests and preferences but also its role as the embodiment and enforcer of community norms – a multiperspectival role, in short, somewhat in the manner of medieval rulers vis-à-vis cosmopolitan bodies of religion and law. [...]

[...]

It is truly astonishing that the concept of territoriality has been so little studied by students of international politics; its neglect is akin to never looking at the ground that one is walking on. I have argued that disjoint, mutually exclusive, and fixed territoriality most distinctively defines modernity in international politics and that changes in few other factors can so powerfully transform the modern international polity. [...]

References

LATTIMORE, O. (1962) *Studies in Frontier History*, London, Oxford University Press.

MATTINGLY, G. (1964) *Renaissance Diplomacy*, Baltimore, Penguin Books.

Source: Ruggie, 1993, pp. 164–5, 171–4

Reading C: Michael Mann, 'Nation-states in Europe and other continents'

Many believe we have now reached the old age of the nation-state. Since 1945, they say, its sovereignty has been outreached by transnational power networks, especially those of global capitalism and postmodern culture [...] In the historic heartland of modern society, the supranational European Community (EC) seems to lend especial credence to the argument that national-political sovereignty is fragmenting. Here, the actual death of the nation-state has sometimes been announced – though perhaps a graceful retirement would be more apt life-cycle metaphor for such a view. [...]

It is true that the EC [...] is developing new political forms, somewhat reminiscent of much older political forms [...] But [...] Western European weakenings of the nation-state are slight, *ad hoc*, uneven and unique. In parts of the less developed world, would-be

nation-states are also faltering, but for different, essentially 'premodern' reasons. Across most of the globe, nation-states are still maturing, or they are at least trying to do so. Europe is not the world's future. The states of the world are many and they remain varied, both in their present structures and in terms of their life-cycle trajectories. The few that are near death are not old but are still in their cots.

[...]

In the last twenty-five years, we have seen neoliberal and transnational reversals of some nation-state powers. Yet some of its other powers are still growing. Over this same recent period, states have increasingly regulated the intimate private spheres of the life cycle and the family. State regulation of relations between men and women, family violence, the care of children, abortion, and personal habits that used to be considered private, such as smoking, is still growing. State policies for consumer protection and the environment continue to proliferate, and feminists and 'green' activists demand still more state intervention [...]

The nation-state is thus not in any *general* decline, *anywhere*. In some ways, it is still maturing.

[...]

[...] Europe is not moving toward a single state or even toward a federal state. Different political arrangements for three main types of state function may be distinguished. First, for most economic policy, sovereignty is divided between the EC and the nation-states, though not according to clear, 'federal' or 'confederal' constitutional principles. Second, in other civilian policy areas, sovereignty remains largely, though not entirely, in the hands of the nation-state. Third, in defence and foreign policy, very little effective sovereignty is located anywhere. Overall sovereignty is now divided and messy [...] The EC itself has no single seat or place of sovereignty for what it does control. In democracies, this resides in an elected executive and in a sovereign parliament. Europe is far short of either. [...]

[...]

Indeed, it may be headed back to political arrangements resembling, though in far denser forms, those of earlier feudal times. Like then, Europe has no single locus of sovereignty. It has different political institutions regulating different functions in its EC core, and it contains Powers of greatly differing strengths [...]

[...]

[...] European nation-states are neither dying nor retiring; they have merely shifted functions, and they may continue to do so in the future.

The American and Japanese states

[...] In contrast to Europe, [the other two dominant 'global regions'] are still dominated by single nation-states, who have given no hint of retirement, let alone of death. The Americas are dominated by the United States. The continent's other states are varied and most live with threats to their security from neighbours and dissidents from

within. They are in this respect typical emerging nation-states, with fairly secure territorial scope, fairly stable, large state administrations but contested and volatile political regimes. However, as dependent economies, they also lack the degree of economic sovereignty possessed by most European states of the nineteenth century. Now the US hegemony helps to police the continent.

The United States is itself a nation-state, though never such a right little, tight little nation-state as the European type. The United States has had more ethnic diversity and a weaker, more federal government, reducing national homogenization and centralization. Yet, it is a virtual continent. Its size, ecological variety, and historic isolation have ensured that its economy has remained more self-sufficient than its rivals. [...] Its capitalism is more nationally owned than is the capitalism of any European country. Despite the growth of Japanese investment, the largest single foreign investor remains, as it has always been, Europe's offshore island, Britain. We can find a faint echo of the European Common Market in the free-trade agreements between the United States, Mexico and Canada, but none of the parties are under any illusions as to who is the dominant partner.

[...]

The second region, East Asia and much of the Pacific, is also a varied region dominated economically, though not yet politically, by a single Power, Japan. Japan is the least economically self-sufficient of the three regional Superpowers and is the most isolated from the others. Its state, though formally small, tightly co-ordinates its national capitalism, especially through the patron–client relations of its single ruling party, the Liberal Democratic Party, and through its dominant economic Ministry of International Trade and Industry (MITI). The ownership of its capitalism remains overwhelmingly Japanese. Foreign raiders have found takeovers and subsequent management extremely difficult to accomplish. All of this is reinforced by dense and cohesive social and familial relations of a type unique in the advanced capitalist world.

Like Europe, Japan has not been a 'full state' since 1945, lacking control of its defence and foreign policy. But the size of the American army stationed in Japan, just over 50,000, is small. Though the Constitution restricts military spending to 2 percent of the GNP, the size of that GNP has become so large that Japan now has the fourth largest armed forces in the world. Though the Japanese remain divided and cautious about their rising power, and though Japanese foreign policy remains weak, Japan is objectively a Great Power once again. Most Japanese are quite nationalistic and share a racial myth of common descent – though their actually varied physiognomies derive from many East Asian stocks. Abroad, Japanese 'internationalism' is tinged with economic imperialism, with a tendency to impose particularly exploititive labour relations in the less developed countries of its own Asian-Pacific region [Woodiwiss, 1992].

[...]

So European talk of the death of the nation-state should sound odd in the other two main capitalist regions. The new Euro-institutions are probably not a pattern for the future. It is difficult to see why the United States or Japan should enter into major sovereignty-pooling or sovereignty-shedding with other states or political agencies. They will continue to negotiate with their neighbours and with Europe as single Great Powers.

States in the less developed world

The less developed world presents different and more varied state problems. Most states date their birth or rebirth from after 1945, when decolonization imposed an ostensibly similar nation-state form on all countries, despite massive differences in the real infrastructural capacities of states and civil societies. The UN Charter and the Cold War tended to freeze these often artificial political arrangements. But this short era is now over. States must depend on their own, sometimes limited, power capacities. Few possess the infrastructures and mobilization capacities of true nation-states. [...] Along with the former communist states, many face severe internal dissidence, sometimes combined with threats from their neighbours to their national security. [...]

But state scenarios in the less developed world are also very varied. At one extreme, mostly in Africa, we find collapsing [...] states whose regimes are unable to penetrate their territories to provide even minimal social order – let alone to pursue the development goals required by the new global culture of instant gratification. In their ineffectual violence, the warlords of Somalia, Liberia or Zaire resemble the vast majority of political regimes throughout premodern history. They are not monsters but reflections of our own past – though armed with automatic weapons and Swiss safe deposits. Their problem is not postmodernism, but the absence of a genuinely diffused modernism in their civil societies. This problem lessens as we proceed through the rest of Africa and the less developed South Asian countries, then to Latin American, the former Soviet and the more advanced South Asian countries, and finally to the most successful East European and East Asian countries. By the time we reach Hungary, the Czech lands, South Korea, Singapore, or Taiwan, we encounter civil societies with solid economic and cultural infrastructures, effective state penetration of territories, and political battles over political and social citizenship that are undeniably 'modern', in the sense that they resemble the recent history of Western Europe, North America and Japan (though East European countries also have their own distinctive political battles). In between the Somalian and South Korean poles, a multitude of semieffective states are coping with uneven modernity – unevenly developed or enclave capitalisms, religious or ethnic identities sometimes dividing, sometimes strengthening them, bulging militaries keeping order and oppressing, bulging state administrations sponsoring development and dispensing corruption. Some of the problems of such regimes are indeed distinctively postmodern – they are subverted by the global reach of capitalism and the global culture of instant consumer gratification. But their basic political problem is that formally modern political institutions cannot compensate for the weakness of the other modernizing prerequisite: an evenly diffused civil society. They confront a crisis of modernity, not of postmodernity. [...]

Source: Mann, 1993, pp. 115–16, 118–19, 121–9, 132–7

The drive to global regions?

by Chris Brook

Chapter 3

3.1 Introduction

Nation-states are continuously searching for new ways to achieve some measure of wider political advantage while containing threats to their integrity and identity. In the last chapter, James Anderson reflected on the uncertainties of the future of nation-states and how they appear threatened by forces linking globalization with internal fragmentation. Before that, in Chapter 1, Anthony McGrew showed how states and other agencies have developed a multiplicity of political arrangements (multilateral, regional, transnational) in response to a globalization which is inherently uneven. Indeed, the arrangements themselves become part of such globalization as states *stretch relations across space* in attempts to extend or safeguard their interests. One element in this jockeying for position, and something which has received considerable attention during the latter half of the twentieth century, has been the promotion of new regional groupings of states. From a realist viewpoint, such arrangements provide opportunities to extend state influence. However, the groupings may themselves develop as political units to threaten the sovereignty of member states. At the same time, the power of member states *and* regional groupings may be undermined by internal differences and divisions and by wider connections and dependences which do not map out in clear territorial terms. While there have been intense pressures on some states to get together on a regional or quasi-regional basis, there have been equally powerful pressures fragmenting such arrangements and making it difficult for states to co-operate in a sustained and meaningful way. Both sets of pressures – to integrate and to fragment – are linked to webs of global connections that trace unevenly across, as well as between, nation-states.

relations stretched across space

These conflicting pressures are well illustrated by the development of the European Union (EU), formerly the European Community (EC), in the early 1990s. 1991 saw the signing of the Treaty of Maastricht. It built on the apparent success of the Single European Act (which defined 1992 as the year when formal barriers to movement between member states would be phased out) and was intended to further EU integration with plans for a single currency and central bank. However, the process of Treaty ratification was a long drawn-out affair and there was continuing uncertainty over whether member states could deliver the necessary support. A further test came in September 1992 when global financial markets, whipped up by media speculation, put intense pressure on weaker member state currencies, which were linked together through the Exchange Rate Mechanism (ERM). On 'Black Wednesday' the pressure finally told and both the lira and sterling were suspended from the Mechanism. One year later, more speculative pressure forced the virtual abandonment of the ERM just at a time when a political end to the ratification process was in sight. Political success in engineering plans for closer state-to-state union appeared overwhelmed by global financial markets which operated *transnationally* as well as *internationally*.

The counter-pressures undermining further European integration are, then, considerable, and link together forces of globalization with local differences through uneven development. The ERM was broken because world financial markets were not convinced that the exchange rate bands adequately reflected the unevenness of development across the EU and the national economic concerns to which this gave rise. Markets were also unconvinced of the collective political will among member states to support weaker currencies like the lira and sterling. While globalization has increased pressures on member states to get together to maintain international position and influence, that same complex of forces is also frustrating attempts to increase integration because of differences and inequalities within the EU and the way those differences link unevenly into the world economic system.

Co-operation between states to form wider regional economic groupings – *economic regionalism* – is not unique to the EU. Other groups of states, from different starting-points and facing slightly different circumstances, have attempted regional economic arrangements (Figure 3.1 and Box 3.1), which can take a variety of forms (Figure 3.2). This chapter examines the recent development of such regional economic units and their impact on a world

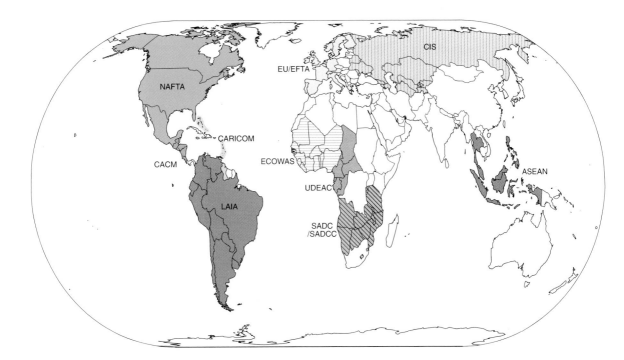

Trading blocs

NAFTA
North American Free Trade Association

CARICOM
Caribbean Community

CACM
Central American Common Market

LAIA
Latin American Integration Association.
(Includes Mexico. There are also
sub-groupings of LAIA members –
see Box 3.1 below)

EU/EFTA
European Union/European Free
Trade Association. (The European
Union and EFTA countries have a
free-trade agreement)

CIS
Commonwealth of Independent States

ECOWAS
Economic Community of West Africa

UDEAC
Central African Customs and Economic Union

ASEAN
Association of South East Asian Nations

SADC/SADCC
South African Development Community
(formerly Southern African Development
Co-ordination Conference)

Figure 3.1 The main regional economic groupings (as at January 1995) (Source: adapted from Evans, 1995, p. 41)

pressured by a globalization that is uneven and fragmented. Often such arrangements appear to be undermined by the very globalization they seek to influence. Although the primary vehicle in these arrangements tends to be economic – trade liberalization between member states, co-operation in areas of economic policy – the ambition is political and designed to further, or at least to underpin, the interests of nation-states. Some commentators argue that we may be witnessing the early stages of a division of the world into vast **global regions** pan-regions or *global regions* centring on Europe, North America and East Asia (see **Allen, 1995a**). However, given the sheer variety of wider political arrangements discussed in Chapter 1 of this volume, and the varied forms of regional arrangements themselves, we are unlikely to see perfectly compact regions with sharp divisions of interest. Instead, spheres of influence are likely to interpenetrate as individual states and their groupings develop a range of contacts/collaborations in response to diverse global interests and pressures. In summary, one would expect regional blocs *to complicate and differentiate further the very globalization process to which they are responding.*

Box 3.1 Regional economic groupings (as at January 1995)

Groupings include:

Europe and Asia

European Union (EU): developed out of the European Economic Community (EEC) and the European Community (EC). First established in 1957 with membership rising from six to fifteen states. A 'Single Market' from 1992 with tentative plans for economic and monetary union.

European Free Trade Association (EFTA): outside the EU but linked to it by a free-trade agreement. Many of the original signatories, including the UK, are now part of the EU. Norway, Switzerland and Iceland remain outside.

Commonwealth of Independent States (CIS): established in 1994 and comprises 15 former Soviet republics. Only a framework agreement at the time of writing in 1995, but with the aim of some form of economic (re)integration between members.

Association of South East Asian Nations (ASEAN): founded in 1967 with plans to establish a free-trade area (AFTA – Asian Free Trade Area) between the six member states (Brunei, Indonesia, Malaysia, the Philippines, Singapore and Thailand) by 2000.

Americas

North American Free Trade Agreement (NAFTA): agreed in 1993 with plans to eliminate most restrictions on trade and investment flows between member states (the USA, Canada and Mexico). This followed the Canada–US Free Trade Agreement (CUSTA) initiated in 1989 with all tariff barriers between the two states due to be phased out by 1998.

Central American Common Market (CACM): established in 1960, bringing together five small Central American states. Broke down during the 1970s but now resusitated. A common external tariff was agreed in 1986.

Caribbean Common Market (CARICOM): established in 1973. Aims to promote economic integration between many of the small Caribbean island economies.

Latin American Integration Association (LAIA): established in 1980, replacing the Latin American Free Trade Association (LAFTA), and includes 10 South American states and Mexico. Aims to promote economic co-operation and to facilitate trade agreements between member states. The Andean Pact and Mercosur arrangements (see below) involve regional sub-groupings of LAIA members.

Andean Pact: established in 1969 with plans for a common market between member states (Bolivia, Colombia, Ecuador, Peru and Venezuela).

Mercosur: established in 1991 by the governments of Argentina, Brazil, Paraguay and Uruguay. Plans to create a 'southern cone' common market.

Africa

Central African Customs and Economic Union (UDEAC): set up in 1964 with six member states; plans to develop into a customs union. Little progress to date: major barriers to trade between members remain.

Economic Community of West Africa (ECOWAS): set up in 1975 with the intention of reducing barriers to trade between 16 West African states, and eventually to establish a common market. To date there has been little progress and plans for greater liberalization of trade between member states have stalled.

Southern African Development Community (SADC): established in 1980 (formerly the Southern African Development Co-ordination Conference, or SADCC) and comprising 10 states. Aims to promote economic co-operation between member states while the SADC Treaty in 1992 stressed the need for economic integration between members.

The chapter is divided into seven sections covering different aspects of the apparent spread of regional economic groupings of states. As you read through we would like you to think about how these regional arrangements are linked to wider processes of *uneven development*. Think about their differing political and economic character and their different internal geographies. Think also about whether the promotion of three core groupings – in Europe, North America and East Asia – would result in less or more unevenness and inequality: are such arrangements encouraging a 'one world globalization', or are they carving the world into bigger, selfish units

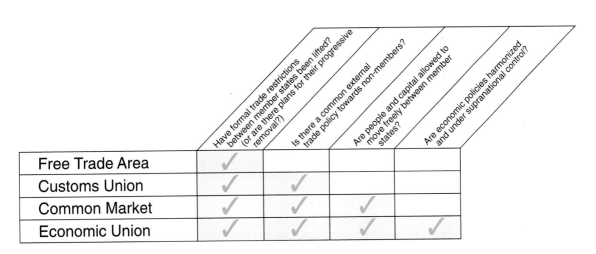

Figure 3.2 Types of regional economic integration (Source: adapted from Dicken, 1992, p. 160, Figure 6.5)

where interests are more jealously guarded and divisions less easy to break down? Most of the discussion focuses on the European Union and, in terms of detail, we would like you to consider the following questions while working through the chapter:

o   What influences underlie the formation and development of post-Second World War regional economic groupings? (Sections 3.2, 3.3 and 3.4.1–3.4.2.)

o   Why is sustained co-operation between states so difficult? (Section 3.4.3.)

o   How can we explain the character of regional integration? (Section 3.5.)

o   Will regional groupings expand or break up? (Section 3.6.)

o   Do regional blocs provide a stepping-stone or barrier to global co-operation? (Sections 3.7 and 3.8.)

3.2   Nothing new?

The use of trade and 'trading regions' as a spearhead to wider political advantage is not a recent phenomenon. In the sixteenth, seventeenth and eighteenth centuries, major European powers such as Britain, France and Spain acquired colonial territories throughout the world guaranteeing their merchants rights to trade within them while restricting competition from merchants from rival powers. During this period no one empire dominated and there was pressure to protect trade routes and colonies in the drive to wealth accumulation and enhanced global status. In the nineteenth century the pressures were rather different. Britain assumed the role of world economic and political leader and there was sufficient confidence in the capacity of its merchants to press for a greater liberalization of world trade. Indeed, a general link is sometimes made between hegemonic power and promotion of free-trade doctrine, with a dominant state wishing to open up world markets which it feels confident that its industries could exploit.

In the first half of the twentieth century, colonial trading practices remained very much in evidence, but came under increasing pressure as colonial territories sought independence and some began to question a pattern of trade in which they had acted in a largely subordinate role, as suppliers of raw materials and as general markets. The break-up was also promoted by the rising power of the Soviet Union and the USA. The Soviets pressed for change through the United Nations (UN) and its agencies and through support of independence movements. An increasingly powerful USA also supported independence and a move away from colonial trade empires, but also saw in a less discriminatory trading system opportunities for US businesses to expand and to extend their own influence. Once again we find a link between a rising superpower and attempts to liberalize trade and fragment earlier regionalizations to its advantage, reflected in the active US government promotion of post-Second World War global institutions such as the International Monetary Fund (IMF), the World Bank and the General Agreement on Tariffs and Trade (GATT).

The situation in Europe was rather different. The Second World War was followed by the Cold War and division of the continent into capitalist West and state-socialist East, dominated by the USA and Soviet Union respectively.

This split, and the legacy of two devastating wars, had a galvanizing effect on both sides of the divide. In Central and Eastern Europe the Soviet Union fashioned the Council for Mutual Economic Assistance (CMEA) to act as a buffer to Western influence. Here state economies were integrated through planned industrial growth rather than through trade *per se*. In Western Europe the tools for regional political co-operation were business, investment and trade. Here the wish to rebuild relations, and US concern to strengthen the region to counter the perceived Soviet threat, brought a series of initiatives including the Marshall Plan (1947) and the establishment of the European Coal and Steel Community (ECSC) (1951). In turn, the success of the ECSC was an important factor underlying agreement to set up the European Economic Community (EEC) under the Treaty of Rome in 1957.

The development of politically inspired 'trading blocs' is, then, nothing new. However, regional arrangements in the latter part of the twentieth century have had to develop and adapt in a climate of intense global economic and political competition and upheaval. In particular, there is pressure on states to develop a variety of international and other links in an attempt to bolster influence and manage global change to their shared advantage. There is also pressure on *neighbouring* states to co-operate, both because of transport and communications advantages and due to concern for regional strategic issues. It should be stressed, though, that proximity is no guarantee of successful co-operation, nor does distance necessarily restrict opportunities. Indeed, agreements on trade and economic co-operation are sometimes used to underpin political and other links between far-flung states. In the 1970s the former CMEA grouping was enlarged to include Cuba (1972) and Vietnam (1979) to support their central planning systems and the expansion of Soviet influence. In 1985 a free-trade agreement was signed between the USA and Israel, giving formal economic expression to their 'special relationship'.

3.3   Is economic regionalism spreading?

This is a difficult question and an answer will depend not only on where you look for evidence, but also on how you interpret and use that evidence. Regional economic integration across Europe continues to grow, though not without counter-pressure to fragment. Elsewhere, in North and South America in particular, there are developing economic groupings of states, but talk of full economic regionalism is more speculative.

The European Union is the most striking example of contemporary regional integration. It is striking not only in the level of integration achieved but also in the size and diversity of membership. Since its establishment as the European Economic Community in 1957, membership has grown from six to fifteen states (Figure 3.3). At the same time, the activities of member states have been increasingly tied, first through the Treaty of Rome and then through the Single European Act and, more speculatively, the Treaty of Maastricht with plans for monetary union (see section 3.1). Restrictions on the movement of goods, people and money between member states have been progressively removed (though many technical and other barriers remain – see section 3.7.1), and this has necessitated both the standardization of trading practices and development of common policies where agreement can be reached. The Union's particular character comes in

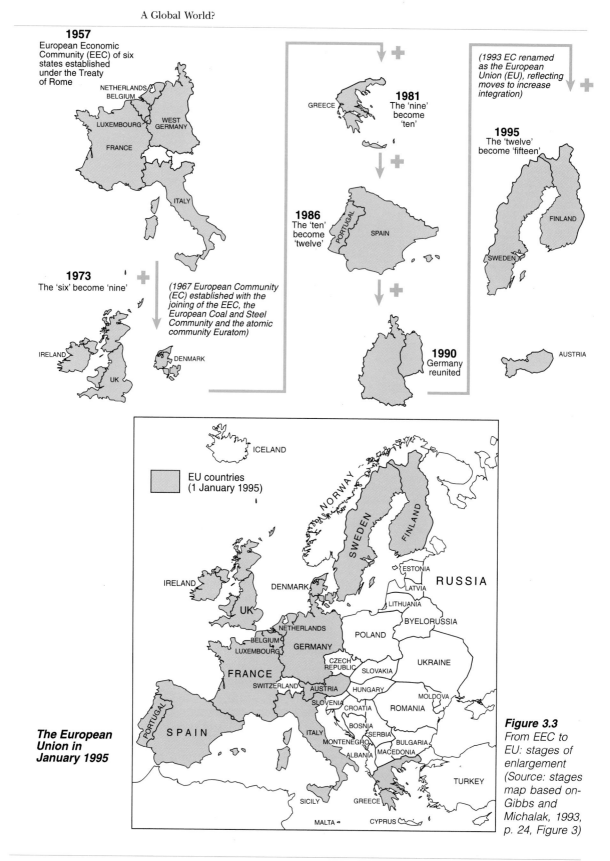

1957
European Economic
Community (EEC) of six
states established
under the Treaty
of Rome

NETHERLANDS
BELGIUM
LUXEMBOURG
WEST GERMANY
FRANCE
ITALY

1973
The 'six' become 'nine'

IRELAND
UK
DENMARK

*(1967 European Community
(EC) established with the
joining of the EEC, the
European Coal and Steel
Community and the atomic
community Euratom)*

1981
The 'nine'
become
'ten'

GREECE

1986
The 'ten'
become
'twelve'

PORTUGAL
SPAIN

1990
Germany
reunited

*(1993 EC renamed
as the European
Union (EU), reflecting
moves to increase
integration)*

1995
The 'twelve'
become 'fifteen'

FINLAND
SWEDEN
AUSTRIA

**The European
Union in
January 1995**

EU countries
(1 January 1995)

ICELAND
NORWAY
SWEDEN
FINLAND
ESTONIA
RUSSIA
LATVIA
LITHUANIA
BYELORUSSIA
IRELAND
DENMARK
UK
NETHERLANDS
BELGIUM
LUXEMBOURG
GERMANY
POLAND
CZECH REPUBLIC
SLOVAKIA
UKRAINE
FRANCE
SWITZERLAND
AUSTRIA
HUNGARY
MOLDOVA
SLOVENIA
CROATIA
ROMANIA
PORTUGAL
SPAIN
ITALY
BOSNIA
SERBIA
MONTENEGRO
BULGARIA
ALBANIA
MACEDONIA
TURKEY
SICILY
GREECE
MALTA
CYPRUS

*Figure 3.3
From EEC to
EU: stages of
enlargement
(Source: stages
map based on-
Gibbs and
Michalak, 1993,
p. 24, Figure 3)*

the way member states have approached these issues with co-operation developing on a largely voluntary basis and through a process of bargaining and concession. Trade between member states has also grown dramatically and by the early 1990s accounted for some 60 per cent of all EU (12) trade (Table 3.1). Nor does regionalism stop at the EU boundary – the 1994 European Economic Area (EEA) agreement established a free-trade area linking EU with EFTA states. In addition, EU trade preferences extend to the former CMEA countries of Central and Eastern Europe under the Europe Agreements as well as to southern Mediterranean states and former colonial territories of France and Britain.

Table 3.1 *Changing patterns of EU (12)* trade (figures in billion US dollars)*

	1980	1986	1989	1992
Total EU (12) trade	1,518	1,578	2,300	2,981
Intraregional	769	897	1,355	1,777
(Percentage)	51%	57%	59%	60%
With rest of world	749	681	955	1,204
(Percentage)	49%	43%	41%	40%

* EU (12) refers to the 12 member states prior to enlargement in January 1995: that is, it excludes Austria, Finland and Sweden. All figures cover the same 12 states.

Sources: Schott, 1991, Tables 1A and 1B; GATT, 1993, Table A10

Activity 1 Turn now to Reading A, 'The European Community and Central Europe', by Richard Gibb and Wieslaw Michalak, which you will find at the end of the chapter. This provides a short introduction to some of the contemporary issues facing Europe, particularly the future relations between the EU and Central and Eastern Europe. As you read through make a note of:

o   stumbling-blocks that make it difficult to integrate East with West; and

o   issues that are bringing the two Europes closer together.

Also give some initial thought to notions of 'deepening' and enlargement. Which should the EU prioritize? You probably have your own views on this. This issue will be taken up in section 3.6.

Note: given that there are two further Readings in section 3.3, you may wish to skim read at this point and return to Activity 1 when you come to section 3.6.

In a recent book charting the development of international regionalism, Gibb and Michalak link the comparative success of regionalism in Western Europe to a resurgence of interest in regionalism in other parts of the world (Gibb and Michalak, 1994). But they also make clear that the circumstances shaping West European integration have been, and are, rather different to those found elsewhere. Indeed, it would be dangerous to assume that other regional arrangements can and will follow the EU model for development.

In the Americas evidence of regionalism is increasing, but is still difficult to assess. In North America a free-trade agreement was signed in 1988 between the USA and Canada (CUSTA) and extended in selective form to include Mexico through the North America Free Trade Agreement (NAFTA) of 1993.

Agreement was in large part due to the existing high, but uneven, level of linkage between these economies. US transnational companies (TNCs) have strong representation in both Canada and Mexico and, in 1992, over three-quarters of Canadian and Mexican trade was with their powerful neighbour (see Figure 3.4). In contrast, only one-fifth of US trade was with Canada and Mexico, reflecting the importance of US global interests and openness of the US market to penetration.

Activity 2 Have a look at the trade statistics in Figure 3.4. Make a quick calculation of what proportion of Mexico's total exports went to other North American economies. What are the comparable figures for the USA and Canada? What do these figures tell us about the dependence of these economies on the NAFTA grouping?

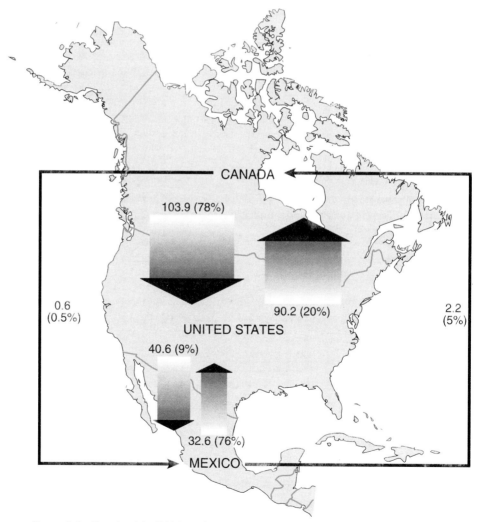

Figure 3.4 *Ties that bind? Value of intra-North American exports, 1992, US $ billion. (Figures in parentheses show these exports as a percentage of the originating country's total exports. Note the uneven level of linkage/dependence) (Source:* The Economist, *13 November 1993, p. 26)*

The position in Central and South America is more ambiguous. There are a number of regional arrangements (see Figure 3.1 again), but, with the possible exception of the Mercosur group, they appear of limited significance in themselves. There is also the question of whether we are witnessing the early stages of a pan-Americas bloc dominated by the USA.

Activity 3   At this point you should look at Reading B, 'The USA and Latin America at the end of the Columbian age: how America "cut the Atlantic apron strings"', by Robert E. Ford and Valerie M. Hudson. This considers the possibility of a new Western hemispheric bloc with the old strategic North Atlantic ties giving way to a core area that is more North–South in orientation, and with more emphasis on cultural and demographic forces. As you read through, think about the role that culture might play in the changing patterns of regional allegiance and influence. Also, what benefits might stem from the creation of a wider Americas bloc? And, as significant, what of the disbenefits? Who would be the winners and who the losers? Section 3.4 will take this up further.

Ford and Hudson appear 'upbeat' on what they call a 'hemispheric zone of co-operation'. But how real is this prospect? Co-operation between North and South remains uneven and any further enlargement is unlikely to mirror EU experience. Unlike the EU, the NAFTA is dominated by a single state, the USA, and any enlargement to the south is likely to be dictated by US interests. Whalley argues that: 'it is the smaller countries who in the main are seeking safe-haven trade arrangements with the United States, driven in part by fears of a collapse in multilateral trade and of future increases in US trade barriers' (Whalley, 1992, p. 139). In consequence, the USA is in a strong position to dictate terms on 'rules of origin', 'local content' and so on. In such an unequal partnership it may be difficult for economic integration to move beyond the initial stages of trade liberalization. Within the NAFTA group, Mexican wage levels and labour productivity are substantially lower than in the USA and Canada, and the burden of adjustment is likely to fall most on unskilled labour in the US/Canadian and Mexican-owned business. If the NAFTA group was enlarged the US government would be fearful of further job losses to low-wage economies in Central and Southern America, while US partners would fear a loss of autonomy and sovereignty. There would also be further threats to indigenous cultures and the environment (this will be discussed further in section 3.4.3 below).

Regionalism elsewhere is much less certain, though this does not necessarily mean that what is going on elsewhere is somehow less important. Indeed, the reverse may be true. There is some talk of the emergence of a new regional bloc linking the Pacific Rim countries of Eastern Asia/Australasia, but evidence remains inconclusive. Figures from Schott (1991) show that trade within this grouping (excluding China) remained low compared to their total trade throughout the 1980s, rising from 33 per cent in 1980 to 37 per cent in 1989. Analysis by Frankel (1991) suggests that a 'Yen region' may be developing on a *de facto* basis, with rising Japanese influence over the region's financial and currency markets. Although substantial Japanese business interests continue outside the region, there is also heavy investment in South East Asia. Elsewhere, the spectacular growth of 'tiger' economies like South Korea, Taiwan and Hong Kong was based initially on export success outside the Pacific region, though regional networks are also gaining in importance – particularly through Hong Kong to China in the lead up to 1997 when the colony is due to be transferred to Chinese jurisdiction. The same is true of a new wave of potentially more substantial development centred on Malaysia, Thailand, Indonesia and, of course, China. The 1991 ASEAN (Association of South East Asian Nations) agreement envisaged a free-trade area between the first three of these countries (plus Brunei, the Philippines and Singapore) by 2005, but trade linkages between member states remain comparatively weak while foreign direct investment in these countries has come increasingly from Japan. To the south, Australia and New Zealand have their own free-trade agreement, but attempts to encourage a wider regionalization of trade with ASEAN countries have not met with conspicuous success.

In China the large pool of low-cost labour has been a spur to inward investment, with many labour-intensive manufacturing operations transferring from South East Asia to southern provinces of China, particularly Guangdong (Tam, 1993). China's re-emergence is further assisted by social and business networks linked to the global dispersal of Chinese peoples over many centuries (see **Allen, 1995b**). Although links between China and South East Asia are developing fast, relations with Japan have been held back by the legacy of ill-treatment by the occupying Japanese forces during the Second World War. If a global region is developing in Eastern Asia, it can only be in outline; the detail is marked by uneven relations between Asian states and punctuated by complex global networks.

Activity 4 Turn this time to Reading C, 'The politics of emerging Pacific co-operation', by Donald Crone. This examines the development of co-operative arrangements across the Pacific Basin and considers the scope for regional bloc formation. As you read it make a note of the different organizations that have been set up and their varying character, membership, organizational make-up and reasons for development.

Crone shows how the increasing density of these Pacific organizations and their overlapping domains reflect a regional environment marked as much by competition as co-operation. Although Crone argues that an 'organizational framework' for co-operation is now in place, power relations remain fluid and regional links unsettled. The US influence within the Pacific has become more dispersed, while Japan's and China's political roles within the region remain unclear. At the same time, cultural and historical differences between East Asian states remain significant sources of suspicion and potential misunderstanding.

In other areas of the developing world, in Africa for example, there have been varied attempts to develop regional economic groupings. The main intention has been to divert trade and build up regional links, to counter the impact of the advanced industrialized world. Many such arrangements have been set up (some are shown in Figure 3.1), but have often been too fragile to have much impact (Langhammer, 1992).

The overall picture to emerge is one of great diversity/variety. The EU remains the most developed regional economic bloc, and it is questionable whether other attempts at regional bloc formation will lead to quite the same level of integration and political linkage, or that those involved will wish to develop closer links in quite the same way.

Summary of section 3.3

o Regionalism has progressed furthest in Western Europe where 15 states are now members of the European Union and a free-trade area extends to remaining EFTA states. Within the EU, restrictions on the movement of goods, people and money have been progressively removed, but other barriers remain and moves to monetary union remain uncertain. Regional co-operation does not stop at the EU border, but uncertainty remains on the level of integration possible with states of Central and Eastern Europe.

o In North America the success of regionalism remains difficult to weigh. The development of the NAFTA provides the USA with the policy option of promoting trade and influence on a more focused regional basis, while smaller states may look to the USA for safe-haven trade arrangements. On the other hand, the past success of the USA is seen by many as built on global interests and the support of multilateral free trade. Talk of a pan-American free-trade area must be tempered by the realities of uneven development.

o Among states of the west Pacific Rim, support for regionalism is much less clear. The growth of these economies is tied in large part to export success outside the west Pacific, though regional networks are also increasing in importance, led by Japan and (increasingly) China. Some organizational structures exist but relations are marked as much by competition as by co-operation.

o Elsewhere, in Africa, in Central and South America, attempts to form regional groupings have been constrained by the weakness of the states involved and the pressures of the global economy.

3.4 Are there general influences at work?

It is clear, then, that the development and spread of regional economic blocs have been influenced by a complex of historical and geographical factors. However, while the specific combination and character of factors leading to each regional grouping is particular to that case, it is also worth seeking to identify common pressures and counter-pressures underlying such arrangements.

3.4.1 Economic forces

Conventional economic arguments for regional economic integration focus on the opportunities afforded by larger barrier-free markets. The formation of a free-trade area or customs union is associated with giving local firms increased opportunities for growth and competition on the international stage. An underlying argument has been that larger markets provide the chance to increase *economies of scale* by allowing fixed production costs to be spread over a larger output level so that the firm can lower the cost of each additional unit. Furthermore, the larger internal market can fuel competition as firms from the different member states jostle for position, forcing businesses to increase efficiency or go under.

economies of scale

trade diversion
trade creation

Some assessments of integration distinguish between *trade diversion* and *trade creation* (after Viner, 1950). In Viner's view, if the reason for the trade bloc was largely protectionist and resulted in higher cost goods from internal sources replacing lower cost goods from outside sources, this would amount to 'trade diversion', which is considered damaging for world trade, and in the longer term perhaps harmful for the trade bloc itself. This, though, discounts the impact of reducing barriers within the trade bloc. A possible effect here is for increased competition across the area to produce some rationalization of industry on the basis of competitive advantage. More efficient industries within the bloc will be well placed to expand into the wider internal market as higher cost industry is run down. This would be viewed as 'trade creation', with member states starting to import from one another things that their own industries would have earlier produced at higher cost.

These kinds of arguments and analyses appear less easy to sustain in the business conditions of the 1990s. The preceding ideas are linked to various assumptions: for example, that all firms are nationally based and enter outside markets through traded exports, and that global investment flows are restricted. Economic realities are more complicated. Transnational firms are exploiting global opportunities in uneven development at an increasing rate, while their activities are linked in increasingly complex ways (**Allen, 1995a**). The acceleration of transport and communications systems has brought a further stimulus (**Leyshon, 1995**). Huge investment transfers are now made between international corporate divisions and through banking and finance houses, which are less easy to monitor and control as they cross political space. A regional grouping may have more counter-leverage than a single national economy in its dealings with international capital, given the size of market opportunities. However, given the level of global interpenetration of political spaces, all political units – regional blocs included – find it necessary to develop, and be part of, complex wider arrangements of governance, both multilateral *and* transnational.

In one sense both regionalism and the development of transnational firms stem from a similar broad concern that benefits can be gained from integrating activities across a group of states. However, whereas transnational activity seeks to integrate individual interests located in different political spaces, regional bloc formation involves the integration of whole political spaces. Sometimes these two sets of forces bring mutual benefit, but there is often a conflict of interest. It can be argued, for example, that regional bloc formation provides the conditions in which a firm with plants located across member states can make more effective use of resources to increase competitiveness. Indeed, it is sometimes suggested that European firms have lost out to those from the USA and Japan because they lacked, prior to 1992, a large integrated home market in which to develop. However, such conditions may add to the problems of uneven development by giving firms greater freedom to merge and rationalize on a regional bloc basis and to externalize control over local activities further. This may in turn lead to a build-up of local social and political pressures that undermine further regional integration.

Additional complications are caused by different (competing) interests *within* a regional bloc. What may be referred to as an 'EU multinational' will be controlled from countries such as Germany, France or the UK and may be viewed as of strategic national concern and prestige. In such circumstances competition within the regional bloc may lead to friction between member states who wish to safeguard their own interests.

Finally, it is often argued that the development of a trade bloc, or increased integration of that bloc, is itself likely to attract new transnational plant and investment; that a larger, more integrated market will have increased appeal to foreign direct investment. However, the particular circumstances of the case are also important. Panic (1991) has argued that the Single Market is unlikely to encourage many new firms to enter the EU and invest in new plants because most foreign businesses capable of competing are already represented. Furthermore, the planned reduction in trade distortions across the EU may produce a greater rationalization of foreign-owned activities with cut-backs in investment and jobs.

3.4.2   Strategic and security issues

Strategic and security considerations are usually of critical importance in the development of regional economic blocs. Although such blocs are created ostensibly to obtain economic and trading advantages, national political interests and objectives are never far below the surface. One influential argument used in support of regional integration is that it provides security for weaker nations against outside economic and political threat. The mushrooming of schemes to develop free-trade areas and customs unions in Africa and Central and South America during the 1960s was designed to reduce dependence on advanced industrial countries and build greater regional security and status. In most cases, however, these ambitious plans came to nothing and have converted into loose non-binding trading arrangements. In North America the NAFTA agreement concluded in 1993 allowed Canadian and Mexican interests to increase access to the US market while guarding against any future fragmentation of world trade and other uncertainties. It has also allowed the USA to safeguard its 'backyard', using economic co-operation as a spearhead. It is possible that such 'safe haven-orientated arrangements' will expand as countries of Central and South America seek stronger links with NAFTA (Whalley, 1992).

In the case of EU development, wider strategic and security considerations have been of particular importance. Here the perceived threat of the Soviet bloc was an important factor in early moves to establish a regional grouping in post-Second World War Western Europe. The development of strong trading links was seen as facilitating co-operation and common fronts in other areas of policy, including foreign policy. A common front was viewed by the USA and its allies as essential to stemming the advance of communism and Soviet expansionism. There was also the need to overcome the traditional rivalry between France and Germany and to restore economic fortunes in the area after two devastating wars.

A frequently heard argument used to promote regional integration is that it can increase a state's 'say in the world'. It is seen as a way of maintaining, even increasing, a country's political as well as economic muscle. This factor was influential in the UK government's decision to seek entry to the European Community both in 1968 and 1973. The EC provided, it seemed, an opportunity to increase political leverage and influence in world affairs, influence which had been lost both through economic decline and strategically with the loss of empire. At a different level, European regional integration is seen as increasing the viability of small states, by giving them a political as well as a market status which they would lack if isolated – an argument also used by regional separatist movements like the Scottish National Party to make the case for a 'Europe of the regions' (see Chapter 2).

There are dangers, though, in assuming that security and strategic interests can always be satisfied through regional integration of territories. While national and military security may be bolstered in this way, other security threats, to the economy and the environment, have a more uneven transnational impact and demand a more varied response – multilateral as well as regional, transgovernmental as well as intergovernmental (see Chapter 1, section 1.4.3). Previous sections of this chapter (3.1 and 3.4.1) have shown how complex economic issues have become. On the environment there is concern not just about the spill-over of pollution to neighbouring states and localities, but also about the increasing globalization of the environmental threat (see Chapter 5).

3.4.3 The pressures against

There are, then, some significant pressures on nation-states to get together; that is, to increase or safeguard influence by combining their strengths. But there are other pressures which make it difficult to co-operate in a meaningful way, or to deepen existing bloc integration. Many of these counter-pressures are characterized by 'difference' – the wish to safeguard cultural traditions and particular ways of doing things. This is underlined by government concern not to cede national sovereignty, the right of nations to manage their own affairs. Many differences and identities are jealously guarded by nation-states, though this is compromised by the increasing level of global interdependence.

It is not hard to find illustrations. Differences between EU states have had a crucial impact on the way the bloc has developed and on the level of meaningful agreement. The final plans for the 1992 Single Market were a watered-down version of the original proposal, with, for example, the UK and Ireland insisting that 'islands' should be treated differently when it came to reforming border controls, and, in response, it was agreed that some border checks could remain to guard against terrorism, drug smuggling, rabies and immigration from non-EU countries. In 1994, terms of EU entry for Austria were threatened for a time by a dispute over the likely build-up of heavy lorry traffic crossing its borders from north to south; here the pressure came from Austria's strategic location within the European transport system.

Nation-states are rarely homogeneous units and there is often considerable cultural and economic diversity across a territory. Many states are amalgams of culturally and economically quite distinct regions, with strong calls for more say over local affairs. Any integration of economies is likely to add to these tensions by further 'externalizing' some of the decision-making processes (for example, from Westminster to Brussels), and exacerbating local economic and social problems by opening the market to increased transnational competition and uneven development. Recession can further fuel these problems. Across the EU, regional disparities remain stubbornly high (Figure 3.5 provides an illustration) and continue to threaten Union cohesion. In response, the EU has attempted to redistribute resources to poorer groups and areas through so-called 'Structural Funds'. To date (at the time of writing in 1995), these programmes appear insufficiently financed or focused to have a significant impact on disparities.

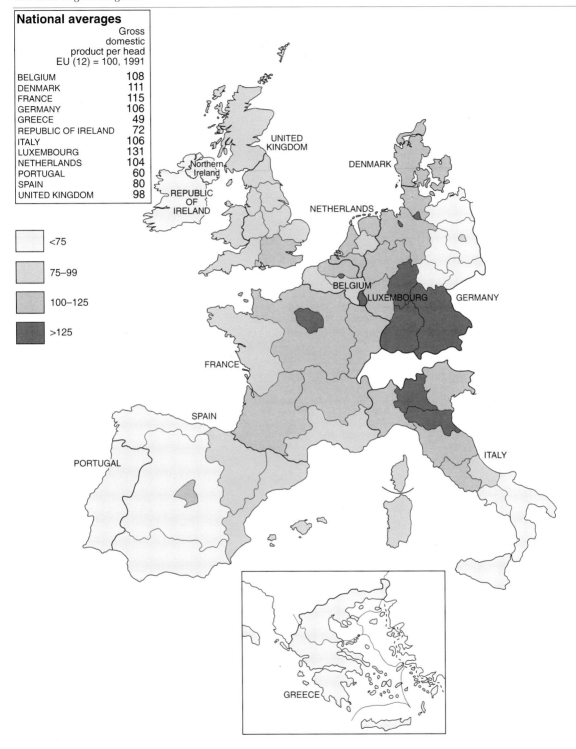

National averages	
Gross domestic product per head EU (12) = 100, 1991	
BELGIUM	108
DENMARK	111
FRANCE	115
GERMANY	106
GREECE	49
REPUBLIC OF IRELAND	72
ITALY	106
LUXEMBOURG	131
NETHERLANDS	104
PORTUGAL	60
SPAIN	80
UNITED KINGDOM	98

<75

75–99

100–125

>125

Figure 3.5 An uneven union – regional disparities in gross domestic product (GDP), 1991
(Source: based on Regional Trends, 1994, p. 35)

Note: variations in GDP per capita are expressed as an index with EU (12) average 100. Areas with highest values were Hamburg (209), Ile de France (Paris: 172) and Brussels (171). Lowest values were found in the five regions of the former East Germany (all below 36) and in Greece (all four regions had values below 55). Across the UK values ranged from 117 (south-east) to 74 (Northern Ireland).

Activity 5 The product of uneven development can be viewed at different levels of abstraction – local, regional, national, etc. Examine the map in Figure 3.5 which shows how GDP per capita varied across the EU (12) in 1991. Look first at the overall figures for each member state – see the inset table, top left-hand corner. Which were the richest and which the poorest states according to this measure?

Now turn to the map itself. Which member states appear to have greatest unevenness across their territories? In some cases the sub-state divisions are pretty broad so you might ask yourself what might be the effect of mapping GDP per capita using smaller area units. Would you be more likely to see inequalities accentuated or reduced? Do not spend too much time on this activity. The important thing to note is that inequality and unevenness are not just issues at regional bloc level, but also for the member states themselves.

In North America the development of the NAFTA has brought fears that hard fought-for local interests and ways of life could be threatened. Within the USA and Canada there is concern that the drift of less skilled jobs to Mexico will accelerate, while many in Mexico fear a further rise in US-based control as local firms become more exposed to northern business interests. In US car manufacturing and agriculture regions there has been particular sensitivity to potential job loss, and special 'local content' deals (which attempt to define how much of the product's inputs are to be supplied locally) and protection for 'vulnerable crops' have been arranged. There were also fears that increased competition to attract jobs would drive down environmental standards as well as wages in more deprived areas, with the notorious 'maquiladora' export-processing zone (an essentially customs-free area with few environmental restrictions) along Mexico's border with the USA cited as illustration (see George in **Yearley, 1995**). In addition, North American integration is likely to increase pressure on indigenous local cultures. In January 1994, Mayan groups living in the southern Mexican state of Chiapas staged a revolt against impending land reform and increased social pressures, resulting in loss of life. It is difficult not to make links between industrialization under liberalized trading conditions and further break-up of minority cultures.

Eat your NAFTA

The Economist *used this cartoon to portray a NAFTA agreement difficult to sell to US voters and politicians*

Nor can these differences be isolated from the outside world. The particular character of an area will be reflected in its uneven web of wider connections. Nation-states have developed a multiplicity of bilateral and multilateral contacts to match their wider interests. This contact is not simply state to state. For instance, national governments are in constant contact with business and other transnational activities over investment, media issues, and so on. Similarly, local differences within states are reflected in their distinctive web of dependences that trace unevenly across countries and globally. Bloc integration brings pressure to rethink, even redraw, these contacts and linkages, and this may be resisted by interests outside as well as inside the bloc. The UK's negotiations for membership of the EC in the early 1970s were lobbied by many Commonwealth states and their interests, concerned at the potential loss of long-standing markets to their strategic industries. During the 1993 NAFTA negotiations European and Japanese car makers were concerned that 'local content' restrictions would limit their penetration of the North American market. In that year a high-profile dispute over the sale of Ontario-built Honda cars to the USA brought together Canadian and Japanese interests to revise the method of local content measurement.

Activity 6 When you pick up a newspaper and read about the EU, NAFTA or some other regional grouping, think about how the issues and debates might illustrate ideas in this section. For instance, you may find examples of concerns which appear to be drawing member states, or specific groups within those states, closer together; or you may find examples of divisions and differences which limit the level of meaningful co-operation/agreement. Also think about the wider global context of these issues. In what ways are transnational or international forces involved? How do these issues link together specific places/social groups inside and outside the regional bloc?

Summary of section 3.4

o Traditional economic arguments based on notions of trade creation/diversion and economies of scale are less easy to sustain given the increasing impact of transnational economic forces. Benefits of regional integration may accrue to home-based and foreign transnational interests and the overall economic gains for global regions are difficult to assess.

o Strategic and security considerations can have a critical influence in promoting regional groupings. Regional blocs provide a perceived safe haven against common external threat as well as scope for states to join forces to extend their international interests. But security threats, to the environment and the economy, are less easy to address through regional arrangements because of their increasing transnational and global impacts.

o Social, economic and cultural differences at state and sub-state level can make it difficult to co-operate in a meaningful way. Uneven development across the regional bloc may be exacerbated through integration initiatives, while decision-making may become more remote. Pressures against integration will often link local interests inside and outside the grouping.

3.5 Framing the process of regional integration

In sections 3.2 and 3.3 we stressed that the development of regional blocs like the EU and NAFTA must be set within their historical contexts. In section 3.4 it was argued that there may also be wider (general) influences behind such changes. What is needed, though, is a framework, or an overarching set of ideas, within which to study such processes. Various frameworks have been adopted in attempts to explain/interpret the process of regional bloc integration; the most discussed are *intergovernmentalism, functionalism* and *transnationalism*. The focus here is on Europe and the EU, but such ideas may have wider application if other regional blocs become established.

3.5.1 Intergovernmentalism

intergovernmentalism   The *intergovernmentalist* school adapts an essentially *realist* position, seeing national governments as the central actors of these regional arrangements. The approach plays down the impact of independent supranational interests and institutions as well as transnational forces.

Those supporting this interpretation would argue that regional integration of states is likely to be accompanied by a *strengthening of national governments*. In the case of the EU, the Council of Ministers, which is intergovernmental in structure (made up of representatives from the governments of member states), has been seen as playing an increasingly influential role in its dealing with the Commission, the central agency of the Union (see Box 3.2). Council activities are supplemented by intergovernmental Technical Councils which focus on specific policy sectors and are attended by the relevant member government ministers. There is also a large number of support and advisory committees, headed by the Committee of Permanent Representatives (COREPER), and all strongly intergovernmental in structure. Such organization appears to reflect a Union dominated by 'national interests' as defined by member governments.

Box 3.2 The institutions of the European Union [detail relates to the early 1990s]

'THE COMMISSION. This is responsible for proposing Union policy and legislation, and then it implements decisions when they are taken by the Council; it also supervises the day-to-day execution of EU policy, and manages the CAP [Common Agricultural Policy].

The executive tasks of the Commission are spread among civil servants in 23 Directorates-General, each dealing with a different area of responsibility, such as energy or agriculture.

The Commission has the reputation of being an open bureaucracy, and its officials, mainly based in Brussels, are the main target for pressure group activity; this is, after all, where the proposals are drafted. Britain has two Commissioners (one dealing with competition policy, one for [transport]), and groups operating in these fields may occasionally meet with them.

THE EUROPEAN PARLIAMENT. The United Kingdom has 81 MEPs [Members of the European Parliament] who travel to Strasbourg for plenary sessions of the Parliament.

The Parliament delivers a formal opinion on most proposals before the Council reaches a decision; much of its work is done in specialist committees which meet in Brussels before the plenary sessions take place.

Pressure groups lobby MEPs, particularly those sitting on the appropriate committee, but as the Parliament has often been portrayed as little more than a talking-shop they concentrate their usually limited resources on the Commission where power resides.

THE COUNCIL OF MINISTERS. Based in Brussels, where it has its secretariat, the Council takes the final decision on matters of policy. It meets behind closed doors, but a powerful group might arrange for telegrams to arrive on a day when it is in session.

THE COURT OF JUSTICE. This rules on the interpretation and application of Union laws, and well-resourced groups will monitor its decisions in their field of activity.

THE ECONOMIC AND SOCIAL COMMITTEE. The UK has 24 members on this advisory body which is often asked to give an opinion.

It comprises representatives of employers, employees and consumers across the Union, and leading groups such as the TUC [Trades Union Congress] and the CBI [Confederation of British Industry] have nominees on the Committee; a third of the 189 members are representatives of firms, so that it is important to the business world.'

Source: Watts, 1993, p. 116, Box 3

Note: European Union has been substituted for European Community throughout this extract.

The increasing importance of European Council or 'Summit' meetings appears to reinforce the intergovernmentalist position. These meetings were formally established in 1974 and were written into the 1985 Single European Act (SEA) which defined 1992 as the completion date for the 'internal market'. Often summits have been able to break through the log-jam of EU business and to obtain agreement and advance key initiatives.

Intergovernmentalism has also proved important in the way the EU Council meetings take decisions. In the Treaty of Rome it was envisaged that there would be majority voting on all issues, but this proved unsustainable. A French boycott of EU institutions in the mid-1960s ended with the so-called 'Luxembourg Compromise', requiring unanimous voting in areas of 'vital national interest', but leaving member governments to define what these interests were. At the time of writing, majority voting is used mainly in relation to internal market legislation under the 1985 Single European Act, and it remains unclear how far it can be extended to new areas under the Maastricht Treaty.

There is, then, considerable evidence to support the view that national governments continue as the key actors in EU decision-making. Attempts at formal integration do not appear to be matched by a transfer of loyalties and sustained political integration.

3.5.2 Functionalism

functionalism

The *functionalist* school views the process of integration rather differently. The argument here is that sustained economic co-operation across the grouping will produce new joint interests as well as commercial links which in turn can feed through to new political arrangements drawing those states together. This might be achieved through common interests *spilling over* into demands for a transfer of powers from nation-state to supranational levels. At the same time, it is suggested that economic integration will gradually undermine the authority of the nation-state, and in time lead to a transfer of loyalties by politicians and other élites to supranational institutions. Early co-operation in less sensitive areas such as trade and competitions policy might in turn lead to pressure for joint action in more politically charged areas such as the harmonization of tax affairs and the development of a common currency.

low politics
high politics

This process has been variously labelled as moving from *low politics* to *high politics*, or from more technical to political spheres. Such distinctions are not altogether satisfactory, though. There is no clear dividing line between these spheres and even technical areas, like the development of common transport or mergers policy, can take on a wider political significance. Just as important, perceptions on what is a 'low' or 'high' political issue may vary between member states and a central authority like the EU Commission. An effective illustration is provided by Webb: 'Averaging out the axle weights of lorries to a Community norm might appear to the Commission to be an essentially technical procedure, to the British it implies an assault on its rural environment, to the French it puts at stake the interests of its leading lorry producer' (Webb, 1977, p. 17).

The experiences of post-Second World War supranational development in Western Europe have placed a number of question marks over functionalist arguments. First, functionalism assumes that it is possible to overcome national political sensitivities by focusing on specific social or economic projects that appeal to Union-wide interests, and then allowing their impact to be felt in other areas. However, the presence of the welfare state and the deep involvement by West European governments in a whole range of everyday issues, has meant that, in practice, it has been difficult to find areas that do not in some way bring government reaction and fuel political controversy. The relative success of the European Coal and Steel Community, established by France, Germany and the Benelux countries in 1951, suggested that it might be possible to use particular sectors (here coal and steel) to spearhead an incremental integration. But the circumstances at that time were quite peculiar, with a heightened concern to maintain peace in Western Europe by placing the development of heavy industry in the hands of a wider authority. Such common interest and political will cannot necessarily be transferred to other time periods, other sectors, or other regional groupings.

The experience of the Common Agricultural Policy (CAP) paints a rather different picture. The CAP was established under the Treaty of Rome in 1957 to safeguard agricultural interests within the original six member states in the face of increasing international competition. At this time there was sufficient economic growth among the six to resource a programme of farm guarantees. However, high spending became increasingly difficult to justify when the economic climate worsened, and the policy was further undermined by EU enlargement to include less prosperous economies – Ireland, Greece, Spain, Portugal – with relatively large agricultural communities. So while a supranational action may be acceptable in more prosperous times, it is less easy to sustain for a more heterogeneous grouping and in periods of economic downturn.

At the heart of functionalist arguments is what has been termed 'the Community method'. In the case of the EU this centres on the perceived relationship between Council and Commission where the Commission is expected to develop a sense of group interest and to formulate common policy, while the Council should accept the Commission as the legitimate agency for collective national government interests. The accumulation of a web of cross-EU interests was expected to bring a progressive transfer of loyalties by influential groups from national to Union institutions. Such expectations are backed by the Treaties of Rome and Maastricht which provide the legal as well as psychological pressure for co-operation.

3.5.3 Transnationalism

There is, though, a third position which argues that functionalism and intergovernmentalism provide rather polarized interpretations of what is a much more complex process. Here it is stressed that the world is much more multi-centred than a focus on nation-state and inter-state arrangements would have us think. *Transnationalism* has a rather different starting-point, with *transnationalism* stress given to the rapid rise of forces that are outside the control of any one state, and cross territorial boundaries with relative impunity (see the discussion of critical geopolitics in Chapter 1, section 1.3). Included here are the global flows of investment and speculative finance, the spread of media images, ideas and knowledge and widening impact of pollution (see **Allen and Hamnett, 1995**). These forces are associated with, or have given rise to, a multiplicity of transnational organizations ranging from global banking systems and business corporations through to global environmental pressure groups and new cultural and religious movements.

The relations between transnational forces and regional economic integration are complex, even ambiguous. Since these forces are outside the control of a single state, there is pressure on states to get together to manage these influences to their mutual advantage or to safeguard existing interests. At the same time, transnational impact across territories is uneven and this can frustrate and undermine meaningful international agreement. Through the late 1980s and early 1990s, EU member states attempted to gain wider competitive advantage through the Single Market initiative. But shifts in investment and transnational activity under liberalized trading conditions exacerbated the problems of uneven development (see, for example, Dunford and Perrons, 1994). This placed further pressures on EU cohesion and increased the stumbling-blocks to full Economic and Monetary Union. Similar ambiguities can arise over environmental pressures. In 1993 final ratification of the NAFTA was threatened when environmental groups obtained a ruling from US officials that an Environmental Impact Statement should be prepared. The decision was later overturned but stoked uncertainty over the ability of the NAFTA to carry through planned environmental safeguards under conditions of heightened competition for transnational investment and jobs.

Not all transnational pressures are at odds with regional bloc formation. Some transnational groupings develop precisely in response to regional integration and may reinforce that process; that is, they appear to support functionalist arguments though their impact is often uneven. Many of the transnational interest groups with a presence in Brussels are Euro groups linking together economic and social interests across the Union; employers' groups, trade union groups, groups representing sectors such as agriculture, banking and insurance (see, for example, Greenwood *et al.*, 1992). Sometimes the shared concern links together similar kinds of places rather than particular social groups. For example, the Association of Traditional Industrial Regions in Europe argues for more assistance to older industrial areas against a background of increased pressure for funds from the less developed Mediterranean areas.

Global transnational interests have also had to respond to regional bloc formation. Many high-profile companies have permanent representation in Brussels, and collective TNC lobbying has developed in some sectors. Collective action has been long established in pharmaceuticals where EU and non-EU based companies like Glaxo, Ciba Geigy and Smith Kline Beecham have found it necessary to form general interest groups in response to a range of national and EU regulations. Sometimes representation links nation-state with transnational interests. One particularly influential Brussels group is the American Chamber of Commerce which represents large numbers of US organizations, including many powerful TNCs.

These varied transnational pressure and interest groups weave complex patterns of interdependence and fragmentation across the EU and globally. This is in contrast to the clearer vertical divisions and continuing national separation espoused by intergovernmentalism, and the perceived trend to supranational convergence under functionalism. Under transnationalism the dominant image is of power being chipped away from national governments without accumulating at supranational level. Instead, power becomes more diffuse and uncentred, channelled through a multiplicity of global political arrangements.

3.5.4 Which framework works best?

It may be a mistake to adopt a single framework to study the process of regional economic integration. Evidence from EU development suggests that the relative significance of these different frameworks may change over time. For instance, Webb (1977) has argued that functionalism and the 'Community method' appear to fit best with developments in the 1950s and early 1960s when there was a small and relatively close-knit group of six states, with a limited set of mutually acceptable objectives, in a general climate of increasing group prosperity, and where globalization pressures were less intense. In contrast, the period of the late 1960s and early 1970s was characterized by increasing intergovernmentalism, with the growing significance of 'summits' and their formalization as European Councils. At that time more apparent emphasis was given to the 'national interest', which was given force by the 'unanimous voting' arrangements under the so-called Luxembourg Compromise (see section 3.5.1). More recently, in the 1980s and early 1990s, there appear to be strong reasons for adopting a framework which reflects the growing presence of global forces that act (unevenly) across and not just between territorial units. In section 1.5 of Chapter 1, Anthony McGrew refers to the transitional nature of a world 'bifurcated' between a persisting state system and a more multicentred system of cross-cutting loyalties and networks. The EU and other regional arrangements sit uneasily within this transitional world, *responding to globalization but weakened because of it, and further complicating its pattern.*

Summary of section 3.5

o   Three frameworks are often used to examine regional bloc development. *Intergovernmentalism* stresses the role of national government in regional economic arrangements and plays down the impact of independent supranational interests. *Functionalism* stresses the spilling over of economic co-operation into pressure for supranational political action. *Transnationalism* highlights forces acting across political boundaries to chip away power from territorial units, national and supranational, and to produce a more multicentred global society.

o   There is debate over the relative significance of these frameworks; evidence points to the growing impact of transnational forces on the state system.

3.6   To enlarge or deepen?

There are continuing pressures on regional blocs to extend influence and safeguard interests, and one possible option is to *enlarge* their geographical extent through increased membership. Many of the international and transnational pressures that lead states to form groupings in the first place (see section 3.3) can also fuel interest in selective enlargement of those groupings. But extending membership is likely to mean an increase in the diversity of interests (locally and in the variety of wider connections) as well

regional bloc enlargement

deepening integration

as in the number of states. This in turn may make it more difficult to consolidate existing arrangements between member states and to *deepen integration* generally (see Box 3.3). Issues of enlargement and deepening are of potential relevance to all regional groupings. Indeed, one can speculate whether we are likely to see major regional blocs expanding until they meet and, together, contain most of the world's land mass. Or whether those same blocs will break apart long before that point is reached, undermined by the increasing diversity and unevenness across their territories, exacerbated by global transnational forces.

Box 3.3

Before moving on, turn briefly to the initial section of Reading A where Gibb and Michalak elaborate on notions of 'enlargement' and 'deepening' as well as introducing a third notion, that of 'widening'. They associate deepening with increasing co-ordination and consolidation within the *existing* scope of regional arrangements, while an extension of bloc co-operation to *other* policy areas is referred to as widening. In section 3.6 we use deepening in a more general way, to cover all forms of regional bloc integration whether through developing existing arrangements or extending co-operation to other areas. You should also note that many authors use widening to mean enlargement, so if you read further on the subject you will need to check how these terms are defined.

The debate about whether to enlarge or deepen has been given particular prominence in the European Union where the existing level of regional integration is comparatively high and remaining national interests are jealously guarded. In North America and East Asia, regional arrangements have yet to reach the intensity where such issues and their interrelations are as keenly debated. In one sense, what is happening in North America and East Asia is very different with, for example, arrangements dominated by single states (the USA and Japan respectively) and tied to different geographies and histories. Readings B and C provide illustration of this. Yet, whatever the path followed by regional arrangements, issues of enlargement and deepening will never be far from the agenda.

In this section the focus is on the EU, but the case is designed to show the complexity of these issues and that 'enlarging' and 'deepening' are often interconnected as options – one often has implications for the other, though the impact for both will be selective and uneven. For the EU the issue is further complicated by the break-up of the former state socialist bloc in Eastern Europe and concern at how best to assist the peaceful development of these countries as fledgling Western democracies.

3.6.1 Pressures for enlargement

Pressures to enlarge a regional grouping may come from a variety of sources and bring together interests outside and inside the bloc. The pressures on non-member states to join may be considerable, particularly if those states have strong existing ties with that bloc. Take the case of EU enlargement to include Austria, Finland and Sweden in January 1995. Here a key argument used in national referendum campaigns was the importance of pre-existing trade with the EU and a wish to have more influence over the rules governing that trade. Second, a regional bloc's perceived status and leverage can be a significant attraction to governments of neighbouring states. It is argued that EU membership would provide states in Central Europe, particularly newly formed small states like the Czech Republic, Slovakia and Slovenia, with increased economic and political viability, as well as supporting their development as democracies. For prospective members like Malta and Cyprus there is the economic draw of being tied to a much more prosperous grouping with a policy framework for redistributing wealth to 'less advantaged regions'.

But not all states, or groups within states, see their futures within regional blocs. In 1972, and again in 1994, the Norwegian people voted against EU membership, choosing independence from Brussels rather than the supposed trade advantages of economic integration. Switzerland, with its history of non-alignment, has decided against EU membership and views independence as an asset to its international and transnational dealings. The underlying message is clear. *Regional integration can undermine certain national interests and their wider networks of interdependence just as transnational forces undermine regional integration.*

Support for enlargement from within a regional bloc will also be uneven. In the late 1980s and early 1990s, successive UK Conservative governments were perhaps most vocal in making the case for a wider EU, but with strong support from groups in countries like Denmark. Here a number of arguments were used. In the case of former EFTA countries like Sweden, Austria and Finland, there was the attraction of a group of stable democracies with high GDP per capita, making them potential net contributors to the EU Budget. On Eastern Europe, views were much less clear. There has been concern to assist new democracies and to have some say over environmental and security problems that could also threaten existing EU states. But many have argued that integration is only possible when certain economic as well as social conditions are met. Finally, many of those (such as the UK) favouring enlargement also favour a looser, less integrated EU which is seen as a likely product of increased membership.

Activity 7 Look again at Reading A and at the section entitled 'Central Europe and the EC'. How do Gibb and Michalak assess the pressures for further enlargement to include Central Europe?

3.6.2 Pressures for deepening

Pressures for further integration can also be considerable. In the case of the EU, it should be noted that the process of regional integration across Western Europe has been going on, at a varying pace, since the 1950s. Developments like the signing of the Treaty of Rome in 1957 and the Single European Act in 1985 not only brought deepening in themselves, but, as Nugent (1992) and others have noted, have also increased pressure for yet more deepening. Under the 1985 Act the immediate objective was to obtain barrier-free movement for goods, services, capital and people by 1992. But this development introduced other pressures: pressures for a strong 'social dimension' to safeguard workers' rights under more liberalized trade conditions, and pressures for a common currency within which Union business could operate more effectively. Such pressures provide some support for the functionalist arguments about spill-over effects and how greater involvement in one area can bring calls for more co-operation in others.

Economic deepening has also produced pressures for closer political involvement between EU member states, and for greater democracy at EU level. There has been concern in some quarters that the Union's importance as a market and economic power has not been matched by an ability to influence international events politically. This was highlighted by the lack of a clear EU voice on the Gulf War of 1991 and then on the civil war in Bosnia. On the issue of democracy, it has long been held that the EU institutions, while growing in perceived importance, were not democratically accountable – the so-called *democratic deficit*. The directly elected forum is the European Parliament but it lacks formal powers. Under both the Single European Act and Maastricht Treaty a limited increase in these powers was agreed, but there are few signs that elected representatives are starting to debate issues more along EU than national political lines.

There has also been pressure for deepening from other quarters. The tensions underlying the resolution of the Uruguay round of world trade (GATT) talks in the early 1990s, and the increasing tide of international competition, brought a heightened concern to safeguard EU markets against 'unfair' trade practices and to monitor cases of environmental degradation. In the fields of terrorism and drug trafficking there have been increasing calls for Union-wide action since border controls were cut as part of the Single European Act. Such activities are themselves developing global networks and it is becoming more difficult to police these developments on a national basis.

Finally, the reunification of Germany was, in the early 1990s, used as another argument for further deepening. When reunification took place in 1990 there was concern expressed by some, notably in France, that integration was crucial to tie Germany to the rest of the Union. The argument was that, if the pace slackened, a combined Germany might refocus its interests to look east rather than west. To some former West Germans, reunification brought a change of mood towards the EU, with increasing concern that the spiralling cost of assisting poorer EU states meant less help to the old East Germany. This only brings counter-pressure for more deepening from those fearful of Germany's imperial past.

Common currency? The ECU, or European Currency Unit, is viewed by the Commission as a symbol of economic integration and is at the heart of plans for a single currency. It is the EU's accounting measure and in 1994 was worth about 80 pence

3.6.3 Is widening compatible with deepening?

Evidence suggests that enlargement and deepening are not necessarily in conflict (see Nugent, 1992). Indeed, pressures for enlargement have inevitably brought counter-pressures for selective deepening and vice versa, and there often appears scope for trade-off between the two. Euro-enthusiasts have been concerned that increasing membership should not be allowed to slow down the process of deepening, while any enlargement is viewed by many Euro-sceptics as a useful foil limiting the pace of programme implementation and perhaps offering opportunities for a looser, more diverse arrangement.

In fact, there has been a tendency for past EU enlargements to be preceded by efforts to integrate the Union further. In 1973 enlargement from six to nine member states (including the UK) was accompanied by ambitious but ill-fated plans for monetary union by 1980. The accession of Spain and Portugal in 1986 was preceded by provisional agreement, in December 1985, to the Single European Act which defined 1992 as the year when internal trade barriers would be phased out. More recently, in 1994, the invitation to Austria, Finland, Sweden and Norway to join the Union was made conditional on EU voting changes, which in effect made it less easy for small groups of member states to veto new Union legislation.

3.6.4 Geographical diversity and uneven integration

How likely, then, is the prospect of a sustained 'deepening' of an enlarged European Union in the context of continuing uneven development? Compared to the original six states, the present Union of fifteen represents a much more diverse and unequal grouping. In particular, southern enlargement to include Greece in 1981 and Spain and Portugal in 1986 led to a significant increase of national and regional inequalities. In turn, such unevenness is tied to diverse networks of global connections, making it difficult to respond on a territorial basis, even at the EU level.

The Commission has attempted to reduce unevenness in various ways. Its own redistribution programmes (through the European Agricultural Guarantee and Guidance Fund, the European Social Fund and the European Regional Development Fund) are designed to assist cohesion by spreading some of the wealth and investment to less advantaged groups and areas. But the scale and impact of these programmes remains limited, as does the shared political will that supports them. In 1988 an *ad hoc* committee of the EC (the Dooge Committee) drew attention to the level of differentiation possible under the existing legislation and since then the Commission has made more ready reference to 'flexibility of take-up', with varied timetables, transitional arrangements and special temporary deals. In the event, some states were able to move more quickly in the implementation of the Single Market and in preparing for the more speculative economic and monetary union promised by Maastricht.

Recognition of the significance of diversity across the Union is also reflected in the growing acceptance by Brussels of the notion of *subsidiarity*. Though its precise interpretation remains unclear, the general argument is that measures should only be taken at Union level where effective decisions are not possible at national level or below. Subsidiarity was made an important element of the Maastricht Treaty, and was designed, in part, to make Economic and Monetary Union more acceptable to member states and

Dover's Eastern Docks and the Single Market. The introduction of the Single European Market from January 1993 meant the end of formal customs barriers and the scrapping of 'green' and 'red' signs. But the elimination of frontier checks on people has proved more difficult. For example, Britain and Ireland have argued that 'islands' should be treated differently when border controls are reformed. Terrorism, drug trafficking and the treatment of refugees have raised major issues and the EU has had to work through intergovernmental co-operation rather than through general Treaty agreement. In 1990 the Schengen Agreement was signed by a number of core EU states, including France and Germany, and came into effect in 1995. It allows nationals the right to move freely across these states, adding a further measure of 'variable geometry' to EU development (Laffan, 1992)

electorates. It also acknowledges the fact that needs and interests do vary significantly between and within nation-states and that the Union may not be able to retain the confidence of citizens of the EU without some level of decentralized decision-making.

If further enlargement occurs, the EU is likely to become more uneven, both internally and in its wider connectedness. The pressure to accommodate a wider, more diverse set of activities and their global connections is likely to lead to an integration which is more differentiated as groups within the Union follow different paths. In other words, enlargement will increase the pressure for political arrangements which, while generating more interdependence, will also have an uneven impact. At the same time, any new supranational initiatives are likely to complicate further the pattern of winners and losers across the EU. During the 1970s and 1980s, and again in 1994, various calls were made to acknowledge *differentiated integration* using notions of a 'two-speed Europe', a 'Europe à la carte', and a 'Europe of concentric circles'. Further enlargement is likely to revitalize such interest.

differentiated (regional) integration

Summary of section 3.6

o Regional blocs are in a continual process of development and change, with pressure to vary membership and the level of regional integration. EU development has been marked both by enlargement and increased (though uneven) integration, reflecting pressures from inside and outside the bloc and tied to different longer-term visions of Europe.

o A key debate for the EU has been whether to prioritize enlargement or deepening. The forces underlying this debate are complex and interconnected, and it is difficult to view enlargement and deepening as separate options. Pressures to enlarge the EU have brought counter-pressures to deepen and vice versa.

o Successive phases of enlargement and deepening have increased pressures for political arrangements to acknowledge uneven development.

3.7   Are regional blocs protectionist?

The development of a single free-trade area across North America and a Single Market across Western Europe has created two vast economic groupings, each with over 300 million consumers. What is less clear is how far these developments help or hinder the expansion of world trade and the breaking down of wider international barriers. Viner's (1950) distinction between 'trade creation' and 'trade diversion' (see section 3.4.1) reminds us that the development of global regions facilitates liberalization of trade between member states *and* may afford protection from outside competition. For the EU, internal trade has grown significantly, but at the same time the Union has been prepared to restrict access to home markets where imports are viewed as posing a threat to local industry and jobs. Here the sentiment has been that the Single Market must advantage, and certainly not damage, EU-based activities, particularly in so-called 'strategic industries'. In consequence, the development of the Single Market has produced fears both inside and outside the Union of a 'fortress Europe' mentality. In the case of NAFTA it is difficult to make early judgements on whether the 1993 agreement will assist or complicate attempts to liberalize world trade.

regional bloc protectionism

At first sight, protectionism appears a more realistic option at supranational than national level. A global region, by definition, will contain more of the world than a single nation with the apparent advantage of a larger internal market and more diversified industrial structure – and therefore more opportunities to develop significant scale economies and build up industrial strength behind trade barriers. A bout of world protectionism will, it is argued, have less impact on those in trade blocs like the EU or NAFTA than on those in a single state.

However, *it is not possible to draw boundaries around nation-states or groups of states and look within those areas for security and well-being.* While regional blocs may provide new possibilities, they cannot provide assurance of security. We live in an increasingly interdependent world, where corporate integration, investment flows, media networks, cultural connections and environmental forces cross political frontiers with relative freedom. Protectionism may produce benefits for specific groups, but is unlikely to provide long-term solutions.

3.7.1 The GATT (WTO) and regional protectionism

The General Agreement on Tariffs and Trade (GATT) was established in 1947. It is a multilateral arrangement freely entered into, and designed to allow the progressive reduction of barriers to international trade. It was signed originally by 23 states but now has more than 100 members, and any country can apply to join. In 1995 the GATT was revamped as the World Trade Organization (WTO) incorporating bodies on intellectual property rights and services. Underlying the GATT are two principles: *non-discrimination* and *reciprocity*. Under the former, signatories are expected to extend to all other GATT countries any trade advantages that they have introduced. The second principle, reciprocity, recognizes that states are unlikely to reduce tariffs automatically. Negotiations within the GATT proceed on the basis of reciprocal reductions using the non-discrimination principle as an objective.

The only real exception to the principle of non-discrimination is found in Article XXIV which permits the development of Free Trade Areas and Customs Unions (look back to Figure 3.2), as long as there is a total (100 per cent) dismantling of trade barriers between members of the regional grouping. Bhagwati (1992) and others have questioned why the GATT rules should allow regionalism at all. He argues that the GATT may have decided this in the expectation that complete liberalization of trade between members will give a regional bloc a 'quasi-national' status which could be conceived of as a stepping-stone to multilateral free trade.

In reality, reductions in trade barriers within a bloc are unlikely, by themselves, to bring a full liberalization of internal trade. January 1993 saw the formal completion of the EU's Single Market, but there remained many technical and other barriers to trade, tied to health regulations, national production standards and the threat of anti-dumping action. National governments also continue to give selective support, direct or veiled, to strategic industries to provide advantageous trading conditions.

A long-debated issue is whether regional bloc formation will assist or hinder the development of the GATT's objectives of global trade liberalization. That is, will such regionalization help to integrate or fragment world trade? This is an under-researched area and many question-marks remain. Bhagwati (1992) has given thought to some of the assertions made about regionalism – that it is a quicker, and more efficient route to trade liberalization – and concludes that these assumptions are difficult to justify. For instance, it is not easy to accept that regionalism provides a quick route to global trade integration given the experience of the Single Market and the EU's reported involvement in slowing progress of the Uruguay Round of the GATT (1978–1993). Furthermore, the trade-offs made by member states in negotiating regional economic integration means that there may be less scope for wider agreement. Any attempt to reduce common external barriers could call into question the finely balanced package of arrangements already agreed within a regional bloc.

Such assessments make the assumption that trade liberalization is itself a good thing. More trade may indeed mean economic growth; final agreement to the Uruguay Round of the GATT in 1993 has been estimated to generate £180 billion of new trade-related income by 2002. But, even if true, benefits will be unevenly spread and there will be additional pressure on local cultures and the environment. Regional blocs introduce a further 'layer' of interests when it comes to assessing the beneficiaries of global trade liberalization.

Box 3.4 Tariffication and the European film industry

The term 'tariffication' was used in the Uruguay Round of the GATT to focus on hidden barriers to trade liberalization. Many of these barriers were associated with national regulations and the support of local traditions and interests. The view of the GATT was that these 'differences' restricted trade and should be counted as a tariff and where possible cut. This brought the GATT and local culture into direct conflict. One of the final obstacles to the Uruguay Round was a French tax on foreign films which raised US $350 million in 1992 and supported the production of up to 150 French films. There were strong arguments on both sides, reflected in a clash of words between leading film directors/producers. While Martin Scorsese argued that restrictions on US films could 'not guarantee a rise in creativity ... or even a rise of interest on the part of local (European) audiences' and Steven Spielberg was concerned that film makers were being restricted from a 'global public', a group of European directors, including Bernardo Bertolucci and Stephen Frears, contended that, without support, US film and television would swamp local activity and culture (as reported in *The Times*, 14 December 1993, p. 11). *Barriers to trade are bound up with different ways of life (and a different importance attached to things) and cannot simply be reduced to what is or is not 'competitive'.* Issues of market penetration and cultural diversity may be linked (**Allen, 1995b**).

3.7.2 Will regional protectionism increase?

This is a tough question and the answer anyway is unlikely to be a clear 'yes' or 'no'. It will depend on the changing global economic climate, whether growth or downturn. Emmerij argues that, in the context of Europe, there are a number of reasons why protectionism, overt or latent, is likely to continue or perhaps increase:

First of all, there is the adjustment burden ... which will be shifted to developing countries. Second, there are the changes in Central and Eastern Europe, bringing in their wake growing competition with the Third World countries. Third, there is the growing preoccupation about the environment,

... which may very well see the erection of 'green protectionism' and 'green conditionality'. Fourth, there are the pyramids of preferences, the reciprocity deals and the anti-dumping procedures.

(Emmerij, 1990, p. 250)

One can also point to two more general factors that could bring protectionist pressures. First, we may be moving towards an era shorn of superpower influence. If this is the case, then a more collective world leadership will be required but competition between a larger 'top table' of states and state groupings may increase uncertainties and add to pressures for protectionism. While it may be in a superpower's interest to pursue trade liberalization policies, with the power to promote actively such objectives, it is much more difficult to predict winners and losers from a loosening of trade barriers in a multipolar world.

There are dangers, though, in simply abstracting from earlier perceived links between hegemony and trade. While economic and other forces have become more global and diverse, attempts to develop state-like formations to manage these relationships have proved rather less successful. If relations between territorial units can no longer effectively influence the pattern of uneven development, and who gains what, it is possible that regional groups could turn in on themselves in an attempt to limit this uncertainty. Such action might be self-defeating and force retaliation, fragmentation and a reduction in global economic growth.

French farmers from the Girande département, south-west France, marking the GATT agreement on 15 December 1993 with a bottle of 'Grand Cru GATT'. A week earlier the wine had been served up by irate farmers at a Paris news conference with the boast that it was 'produced anywhere, is rich in pesticides and drunk by anybody' (The Times, 8 December 1993, p. 10)

Summary of section 3.7

o It remains unclear whether regional bloc formation assists or hinders trade liberalization at a global level. The GATT permits the development of economic regionalism and there appears to be an expectation that such blocs will obtain a 'quasi national' status to provide a stepping-stone to free trade. In practice, regional blocs have remained multicentred and internal barriers remain.

o Regional bloc formation has produced fears of a new layer of protectionsim. While many protectionist pressures exist, global forces may make such action self-defeating.

3.8 'Outside' the core regions

The stretching of state interests across space is, then, very uneven. The most significant arrangements are north–north in orientation where global forces have greatest intensity and impact. In 1990, for example, 41 per cent of all forward direct investment was between the three so-called 'core regions' of the EU, North America and Japan (United Nations, 1993; see also **Allen, 1995a**). In 1993 merchandise trade across and between these regions accounted for 43 per cent of the world total (GATT, 1993). The need to manage this concentration of linkages has the present spotlight. But what of those areas outside the core regions, accounting for some 85 per cent of the world's population and where key future development issues lie? Population pressures in the developing world are difficult to exclude from debates on the sustainability of first world economic growth and lifestyles (**Sarre and Blunden, 1995**).

If we are witnessing the establishment of three core regions, we must also ask what this means for peoples and states that do not lie within this core. For better or worse it is debatable that areas in Central Asia, Africa and Central and South America will be able to develop an independence, any more than this was possible in the Cold War era. Indeed, there is every indication that they will continue to press for 'preferential trading' and other arrangements with the core regions. Such relations are likely to be marked by continuing unevenness, and accompanied by changing fields of influence and allegiance.

Allowing market access is one way in which the core regions and their lead states attempt to set the conditions, the uneven backcloth, within which global economic forces (in which they also play an active role) will operate to their advantage. Agreement under the Uruguay Round of the GATT to cut a wide range of tariff and non-tariff barriers from 1995 still left significant trading restrictions and distortions in place. Furthermore, increased trade liberalization will produce losers as well as winners and may cause key states and groups to rethink their positions. For instance, the relative openness of the US/NAFTA markets may be called into question as the USA is forced to deal more forcefully with its balance of payments problem.

What we will surely see is not a blanket opening or closure of markets in the core regions, but a continuous reshaping of uneven trading arrangements (in one guise or another) where preferred states and firms are given opportunities to export certain goods and services because this also serves the interests of the core regions. Who and what is preferred will depend on a wide range of factors: historical and cultural ties, military and security interests, energy needs and so on. All the time the development of *uneven* market access is tied to a drive for increasing strategic advantage. In the case of the EU, a complex 'pyramid' of trade preferences has been built up, focusing first on the rest of Europe, then Africa, the Caribbean and other selected areas. These arrangements reflect both regional strategic concerns and the legacy of Britain's and France's past colonial interests. The development of NAFTA has linked Mexico more closely and dependently to the USA, though the recent financial crisis in Mexico (linked to a collapse in the value of the peso from December 1994) threatens to undermine existing arrangements. Along with NAFTA, the USA has become active in developing a wider network of preferential trade deals to support cultural and geopolitical interests (see Reading B). The free-trade agreement with Israel in 1985 was a reflection of close links with the powerful US Jewish community and its business interests. The 1991 Enterprise for the Americas Initiative was intended to frame closer arrangements with emerging trade areas in Central and South America, to support geopolitical interest. In addition, the USA remains an important player in many Pacific co-operative initiatives (see Reading C), determined to help shape regional strategies and safeguard Pacific business and territorial interests.

Concerns over 'third world' migration and international debt have also been influential to wider trading arrangements. In general, migration pressure has been from less to more developed economies as migrants search for better job opportunities and living standards. In the EU and USA, migration was of great economic importance to growing post-Second World War labour markets. But from the 1970s slowing growth and new waves of (second generation) migration have combined to increase pressures on jobs and bring social tension. These tensions have not only produced further selective tightening of immigration policy (see **King, 1995**) but have influenced wider economic relations between states. Thus the EU gives preference to imports from low-wage economies in North Africa and Eastern Europe (rather than elsewhere), partly to stimulate job opportunities in these areas which in turn reduces pressures to migrate. Similarly, the NAFTA agreement with Mexico is designed to bolster economic development which may reduce migration pressures; the 1995 crisis in Mexico will test US support and what is achievable. International debt has also been influential to some regional trade arrangements. During the 1960s and 1970s countries in Central and South America ran up huge debts when interest rates were low, so that when rates rose a number of countries (Mexico, Brazil, Argentina and others) had to default on servicing agreements. Shared experience of indebtedness has been influential in new regional arrangements like Mercosur (see Figure 3.1 again) where emphasis is on increased competitiveness and export penetration, and not, as in earlier developments, to bolster protectionism through import substitution and trade diversion.

The uneven networks of preferred trading and other arrangements which link core regions with their 'client' states do not map out into sharply defined spheres of influence. Instead, the networks overlap and boundaries blur as core states attempt to set agendas and conditions which they hope will give them an edge.

Activity 8 Look back to Reading C and the related discussion in section 3.3. Note how diverse interests among Pacific Rim states have produced a series of overlapping regional arrangements, each with a slightly different character, agenda and membership.

The increasing complexity of these arrangements reflects the need to respond to globalized economic activity and its uneven impact. But in doing so they only serve to complicate further those activities. As indicated earlier, global forces have managed to develop a vitality and sinuosity in linking local developments and fortunes in different parts of the world. Many operate transnationally and appear largely outside the control of state and state-like formations. Increasingly, we see fortunes of local areas across the world tied through competition for investment, jobs and well-being. We see local areas linked through diverse cultural ties and environmental impact. The development of regional economic blocs is among varied attempts to stretch political relations to reflect and manage these forces. *What they succeed in doing is adding another layer of social structures to complicate patterns of uneven development further.*

References

ALLEN, J. (1995a) 'Crossing borders: footloose multinationals?', in Allen and Hamnett (1995).

ALLEN, J. (1995b) 'Global worlds', in Allen and Massey (1995).

ALLEN, J. and HAMNETT, C. (eds) (1995) *A Shrinking World? Global Unevenness and Inequality*, Oxford, Oxford University Press in association with The Open University (Volume 2 in this series).

ALLEN, J. and MASSEY, D. (eds) *Geographical Worlds*, Oxford, Oxford University Press in association with The Open University (Volume 1 in this series).

BHAGWATI, J. (1992) 'Regionalism versus multilateralism', *The World Economy*, Vol. 15, No. 5, pp. 535–55.

CRONE, D. (1992) 'The politics of emerging Pacific co-operation', *Pacific Affairs*, Vol. 65, No. 1, pp. 68–83.

DICKEN, P. (1992) *Global Shift: Industrial Change in a Turbulent World* (2nd edn), London, Harper and Row.

DUNFORD, M. and PERRONS, D. (1994) 'Regional inequality, regimes of accumulation and economic development in contemporary Europe', *Transactions of the Institute of British Geographers*, Vol. 19, No. 2, pp. 163–82.

EMMERIJ, L.J. (1990) 'Europe 1992 and the developing countries: conclusions', *Journal of Common Market Studies*, Vol. 29, No. 2, pp. 243–53.

EVANS, R. (1995) 'Brave new world order', *Geographical*, January.

FORD, R.E. and HUDSON, V.M. (1992) 'The USA and Latin America at the end of the Columbian age: how America "cut the Atlantic apron strings" in 1992', *Third World Quarterly*, Vol. 13, No. 3, pp. 441–62.

FRANKEL, J.A. (1991) 'Is a yen bloc forming in Pacific Asia?', in O'Brien, R. (ed.) *Finance and the International Economy 5*, Oxford, Oxford University Press.

GATT (1993) *International Trade 1993*, Geneva, GATT.

GIBB, R. and MICHALAK, W. (1993) 'The European Community and Central Europe: prospects for integration', *Geography*, Vol. 78 Part 1, No. 338, pp. 16–30.

GIBB, R. and MICHALAK, W. (1994) *Continental Trading Blocs*, Chichester, Wiley.

GREENWOOD, J., GROTE, J.R. and ROUIT, K. (EDS) (1992) *Organized Interests and the European Community*, London, Sage.

KING. R. (1995) 'Migrations, globalization and place', in Massey, D. and Jess, P. (eds) *A Place in the World? Places, Cultures and Globalization*, Oxford, Oxford University Press in association with The Open University (Volume 4 in this series).

LAFFAN, B. (1992) *Integration and Cooperation in Europe*, London, Routledge.

LANGHAMMER, R.J. (1992) 'The developing countries and regionalism', *Journal of Common Market Studies*, Vol. 30, No. 2, pp. 211–31.

LEYSHON, A. (1995) 'Annihilating space?: the speed-up of communications', in Allen and Hamnett (1995).

NUGENT, N. (1992) 'The deepening and widening of the European Community: recent evolution, Maastricht, and beyond', *Journal of Common Market Studies*, Vol. 30, No. 3, pp. 311–28.

PANIC, M. (1991) 'The impact of multinationals on national economic policies', in Burgenmeier, B. and Mucchielli, J.L. (eds) *Multinationals and Europe 1992*, London, Routledge.

SARRE, P. and BLUNDEN, J. (EDS) (1995) *An Overcrowded World? Population, Resources and the Environment*, Oxford, Oxford University Press in association with The Open University (Volume 3 in this series).

SCHOTT, J.J. (1991) 'Trading blocs and the world trading system', *World Economy*, Vol. 14, No. 1, pp. 1–17.

TAM, G. (1993) 'The next NICs of Asia', *Third World Quarterly*, Vol. 14, No. 1, pp. 57–71.

THE TIMES (1993) 'How world trade talks turned into a Hollywood cliffhanger', 14 December, p. 11.

UNITED NATIONS (1993) *World Investment Report 1993*, New York, United Nations.

VINER, J. (1950) *The Customs Union Issue*, London, Carnegie Endowment for International Peace.

WATTS, D. (1993) 'Lobbying Europe', *Talking Politics*, Vol. 5, No. 2, pp. 115–20.

WEBB, C. (1977) 'Introduction: variations on a theoretical theme', in Wallace, H., Wallace, W. and Webb, C. (eds) (1977) *Policy Making in the European Communities*, Chichester, Wiley.

WHALLEY, J. (1992) 'CUSTA and NAFTA: can WHFTA be far behind?', *Journal of Common Market Studies*, Vol. 30, No. 2, pp. 125–41.

YEARLEY, S. (1995) 'Dirty connections: transnational pollution', in Allen and Hamnett (1995).

Reading A: *Richard Gibb and Wieslaw Michalak, 'The European Community and Central Europe'*

[...]

Historically, the evolution of the EC [now EU] has been influenced by three, often competing, trends: widening, enlarging and deepening. Widening aims to expand Community competence in areas other than those explicitly mentioned in the Treaty of Rome. Over the past 20 years [1970s/1980s] the Community has been successful in introducing an EC dimension to regional policy, research and development, environmental and consumer questions and, with the Single European Act (SEA) of 1987, political co-operation in foreign policy.

The alternative priority of enlargement is concerned with the geographical expansion of Community space. Since 1957 the EC has gone through three enlargements [with a fourth in January 1995 when Austria, Finland and Sweden joined] [...]. Each enlargement involved complex, detailed and time-consuming negotiations. For example, the accession of Spain and Portugal on 1 January 1986, took place after eight years of intense and often acrimonious negotiations and included a 10-year transitional period, allowing time for their economies to adjust to new market conditions. The last priority area of deepening is concerned to see the Community consolidate its integration process. Traditionally, deepening has been associated with enhancing the common market, focusing on issues such as tariff barriers and impediments to competition. The principal aim of deepening is to create a genuine common market based upon the free movement of goods, people, capital and services.

The EC has in the past been unable simultaneously to pursue vigorously all three trends of widening, enlarging and deepening. It has therefore had to establish priorities which necessarily exclude major developments in other areas [Pelkmans *et al.*, 1988]. The EC's desire to establish an appropriate priority for the 1990s has focused attention on the conflict between deepening the Community, based on the SEA and progressive moves towards some form of economic and monetary union (EMU), and enlarging the Community to incorporate other European states. [...]

[...]

Deepening in the 1980s: the Single European Market

The second great phase of deepening the EC market started in 1985 with the publication of Lord Cockfield's White Paper [Commission of the EC, 1985] entitled 'Completing the Internal Market', which responded to the negative economic consequences arising from the enlargements of the 1970s and early 1980s. At the request of the Commission, the EC ruled out the prospect of any further enlargements until the Single European Market (SEM) had become fully operational in 1993. The fact that the second phase of deepening coincided with the democratization process in Central Europe has profound implications for EC–Central Europe relations. There are two main issues of concern. First, what access will Central European states have to the single market? And second, what effect will the deepening of the late 1980s and 1990s have on the chances of newly democratized Central European states joining the EC? In order to evaluate these concerns, it is first necessary to examine how the SEM will transform the character of the EC economy.

During the recession of the 1980s many Community states adopted economic policies based upon free-market principles as opposed to the interventionist, expansionist and reflationary policies adopted in the recession of the 1970s. With the exception of France, Community states adopted free-market policies based on privatization, deregulation and the cutting of public expenditure. European Community governments soon recognized that if the Community was to regain its competitive advantage in the global economy, there was a need for Community policies to complement market-oriented national policies. The 1992 programme therefore depended on increasing the supply-side efficiency of European economies, rather than the fiscal and monetary demand-side policies, and the recognition that such supply-side improvements are more powerful when enacted at the Community level.

The principle of mutual recognition is the cornerstone of the new Community rules designed to remove all impediments to the free movement of the factors of production in the EC. Put simply, mutual recognition insists that goods manufactured in one member state must be allowed free access into other member states. Where the selective harmonization of regulations and standards is considered unnecessary, immediate and full recognition of differing quality standards must be the rule. As such, there is no obligation on the vendor to prove the equivalence of a product produced according to the rules of the exporting state. Similarly, there is no obligation to submit such a product to additional technical tests nor to certification procedures in the importing state. It is the philosophy behind this policy initiative that gives the clearest indication as to the nature and purpose of the deepening process associated with the 1992 programme. [...]

The 1985 White Paper and much of the SEA is uncompromisingly technical and pragmatic. It is a liberal market solution to the EC economy's problems. The economic rationale behind the SEM is often perceived in quite narrow terms as the benefits emanating from the removal of non-tariff barriers to trade, the so-called physical, technical and fiscal barriers. However, the removal of these barriers is but the starting-point to a new and pervasive competitive environment. This increased emphasis upon deepening the Community with the use of competitive forces and free-market principles has important ramifications for Central Europe's hopes of joining the EC. The present deepening process will inevitably make the prospect of incorporating previously planned economies into the EC more difficult. Again, the conflict between deepening and enlarging is all too obvious.

Central Europe and the EC

The 1975 Helsinki Final Act of the Conference on Security and Co-operation in Europe (CSCE) proposed an improvement of European relations through increased East–West trade, freedom of movement, and guarantees for human rights [Maresca, 1985]. Unfortunately for Central Europe, the Final Act also *de facto* ratified the territorial and political *status quo*, in effect, recognizing formally for the first time the division of Europe into Eastern and Western spheres of influence. The Helsinki round of the CSCE was cynically exploited by the Brezhnev administration as an assurance of Soviet control rather than a starting-point of more open relations [Brzezinski, 1989]. It was only in 1989, after the collapse of the communist regimes, that a real breakthrough was achieved. During the G7 summit in 1989 and later the CSCE Conference held in Paris, November 1990, the possibility of reintegrating Central Europe into the rest of Europe was formally addressed. The Paris summit celebrated the dismantling of the Berlin Wall and the end of the Cold War. The 34 countries attending the summit agreed to institutionalize the CSCE, establishing a secretariat, a conflict prevention centre, and a parliamentary forum, the so-called 'Assembly of Europe'. However, the Paris summit did little to dampen the enthusiasm of Central Europe to join the EC.

[...]

[...] [T]he present difficulties surrounding the EC's decision-making towards Central Europe can be regarded as part of a more general dilemma threatening disunity in the Community [Wolnicki, 1989; Ungerer, 1990; Pinder, 1991]. The EC is now faced with an unprecedented number of states wanting EC admission or association. In 1989, it became apparent that several member states of the European Free Trade Area (EFTA) were seriously contemplating full Community membership. Anticipating the formal applications, the Commission launched a plan in January 1989 that proposed the creation of a European Economic Space (EES). [...] The primary objective of the EES was to allow EFTA states access to the EC market without the need for Community membership. The overriding paradox of the EES is that it was conceived as a way of sidestepping any immediate enlargement of the EC, but has in fact spurred countries to join the Community club. On 22 October 1991, an agreement was reached between the EC and EFTA to establish a 19-state 'European Economic Area' (EEA) stretching from the Arctic Circle to the Mediterranean [...]. The term 'space' has been replaced with 'area' at the insistence of the British, who considered the concept of an 'economic space' to be too abstract. If the sole reason for the EES/EEA was to forestall a string of applications for full Community membership, then it has been an unmitigated disaster. [...]

[...]

The major thrust of the Community's policy towards Central Europe appears to be designed to slow down the enthusiasm of new democratic leaders for full membership. The states of Central Europe perceive membership of the EC as essential not only to the successful transition from Soviet-style command economy to free-market, but also as a guarantee of long-term political stability [Michnik, 1990; Bleaney, 1990]. However, the Community envisages [...] a series of bilateral agreements which specifically exclude full membership as the ultimate objective [Pelkmans and Murphy, 1991; Kennedy and Webb, 1990]. The arguments of the European Commission against membership are based upon the political and economic immaturity of the newly emerged Central European democracies. In particular, the distorted nature of the Central European economies, which could not stand up to free trade within the EC, is seen as a serious barrier [Schröder, 1991]. In addition, Community member states are also fearful of a rush of immigrants from the former eastern bloc states into the EC. The southern Community states, particularly Greece, Spain and Portugal, are concerned that such an influx of unskilled, un-unionized and cheap labour would seriously threaten one of their main competitive advantages within the EC. Consequently, the idea of enlarging the Community to include the disadvantaged Central European states affronted many whose priority was the deepening of the existing Community.

The Commission insists that no membership provision is needed in the bilateral agreements since the Council of Ministers have made it clear that any democratic and free-market European country can apply for membership. In reality, the underlying aim of the Community is to rule out membership of any Central European country as an option in the foreseeable future. Paradoxically, exactly the opposite argument was used by the Community when it favoured enlarging the EC to admit Greece, Portugal and Spain. The membership of these countries was seen as vital in helping to consolidate democratic achievements after years of dictatorship. Clearly, the principle of the European Community has shifted since then. The present position of the Community seriously undermines the original founding principles of the EC. Although never spelled out formally, the very purpose of the organizations from which [the] EC evolved (that is, Organisation for European Economic Co-operation and European Coal and Steel Community) was to prevent another military conflict in the region as well as to act as a moderating force between conflicting parts of the continent [Jordan and Feld, 1986]. Instead, the exclusive policy of the Community towards EFTA and Central European countries in particular may achieve exactly the opposite.

If the present course of the EC were to continue, the likely scenario would be a break-up of Europe into [...] distinct and separate political and economic zones. [...] Although the outer zones of such an arrangement would undoubtedly benefit from economic co-operation with the Community core, they would remain politically inferior and isolated. It is highly doubtful that such a scenario could prove satisfactory for the newly liberated European countries. The existing attitude towards enlarging in the European Commission may become both politically and ethically untenable in the future. In fact, the present policy towards Central Europe has been already undermined by the speedy push towards German unification in 1990. The Chancellor of the former West Germany negotiated the conditions of the unification with the Soviet Union over the heads of both the European Commission and Central Europeans. Although the European Community has reluctantly accepted East Germany as a special case, the result was increased pressure from EFTA countries which found new support amongst EC member states for their membership.

The activities of the EC towards Central Europe, thus far, consist mainly of co-ordinating *ad hoc* economic aid and advice. The most tangible positive contribution is the establishment of the European Bank for Reconstruction and Development (EBRD) in 1990. The new bank will combine and co-ordinate the functions of the commercial-terms operations of the World Bank and its affiliate – the International Finance Corporation (IFC), which specializes in promoting private enterprise. The broad objective of this London-based institution is to help finance the rebuilding of ex-communist Europe. [...] Another example of the EC's involvement in Central Europe is the Phare [aid] programme, ironically instigated by the American administration rather than the European Commission. [...] Yet it is the establishment of trading agreements that will in large measure determine the nature of the EC's relations with Central Europe. Here, the Central Europeans argue that in order for the Community to secure the economic liberalization of the region it should put less attention on the supply of aid and credit and more emphasis on the opening up of the EC market to Central European goods. For the member states of the Community such association agreements produce considerable economic and social costs as the protected Community market is forced to compete with the steel, textile and farming products of Central Europe. As a consequence, although Central European membership is regarded as a necessary step towards the long-term political stability of this region, the economic and social consequences for the existing member states will be a major determining factor influencing future entry negotiations.

[...]

References

BLEANEY, M. (1990) 'Some trade policy issues in the transition to a market economy in Eastern Europe', *World Economy*, Vol. 13, pp. 250–62.

BRZEZINSKI, Z. (1989) *The Grand Failure: The Birth and Death of Communism in the Twentieth Century*, New York, Scribner.

COMMISSION OF THE EC (1985) *Completing the Internal Market*, Luxembourg, Office for Official Publications.

JORDAN, R.S. and FELD, W.J. (1986) *Europe in the Balance: The Changing Context of European International Politics*, London, Faber and Faber.

KENNEDY, D. and WEBB, D.E. (1990) 'Integration, Eastern Europe and the European Economic Communities', *Columbia Journal of Transitional Law*, Vol. 28, pp. 635–75.

MARESCA, J.J. (1985) *To Helsinki: the Conference on Security and Co-operation in Europe, 1973–1975*, Durham, NC, Duke University Press.

MICHNIK, A. (1990) 'The two faces of Eastern Europe', *New Republic*, Vol. 203, pp. 23–5.

PELKMANS, J. and MURPHY, A. (1991) 'Catapulted into leadership: the Community's trade and aid policies vis-a-vis Eastern Europe', *Journal of European Integration*, Vol. 14, pp. 125–51.

PELKMANS, J., WALLACE, H. and WINTERS, L.A. (1988) *Europe's Domestic Market*, London, Routledge.

PINDER, J. (1991) *European Community: The Building of a Union*, Oxford, Oxford University Press.

SCHRÖDER, K. (1991) 'Western financial assistance for reforms in Eastern Europe: conditions and risks', *Aussen Politik*, Vol. 42, pp. 326–35.

UNGERER, W. (1990) 'The development of the EC and its relationship to Central and Eastern Europe', *Aussen Politik*, Vol. 41, pp. 225–35.

WOLNICKI, M. (1989) 'Avoiding East European question', *Telos*, Vol. 81, pp. 41–51.

Source: Gibb and Michalak, 1993, pp. 16–30

Reading B: *Robert E. Ford and Valerie M. Hudson, 'The USA and Latin America at the end of the Columbian age: how America 'cut the Atlantic apron strings'* _____

Many rapidly changing political and economic forces have erupted throughout the world since the European revolutions of 1989. Particular note has been made of the economic and political significance of the EC 'single market' in 1992 as a harbinger of even more radical changes in global political and economic relationships [Quelch *et al.*, 1990; *The Economist*, 1991a,b]. Periods characterized by such radical restructuring are often referred to as 'sea changes' [Rizopoulos, 1990]. That this 'sea change' should also coincide with the 500th anniversary of Columbus' first voyage to America seems equally significant.

[…]

A fundamental realignment in the world's strategic relationships is now becoming apparent. The result will be that the long familiar North–North axis of world power, specifically the North Atlantic industrial and political centre of gravity focusing on the north-east United States and Western Europe, will give away and possibly even lose primacy to a new competing global core area whose axis is more North–South in orientation. In this new world order the old Atlantic links will continue but become increasingly weakened relative to strengthening cross-Pacific and trans-South Atlantic relationships […]. The primary and secondary core areas of this new global spatial structure will be located in the sunbelt/Pacific regions of North America and in Brazil and the southern cone of South America (Figure B.1).

[…]

Eurocentric 'Atlanticism' in American geopolitics and culture

A North–North 'Atlanticist' view of geostrategic relationships has dominated both American and European academic and political thinking for most of the twentieth century. If perceived 'alternative powers' threatened the Eurocentric hegemony, Europeans theorized as far back as the Dark Ages that this threat would emanate from East or Central Asia – the old 'Middle Kingdom' as expressed in either Chinese, Japanese or Russian hegemony (later as the USSR with its strategically centred Siberia). In much of this thinking emphasis was put on the centrality of Central Asia in world politics […]. Some have even posited an Islamic variant to that Eurasian hegemonic power that could link Middle Eastern oil power with the actual or potential nuclear power of now independent Central Asian states such as Kazakhstan.

Early in this century, this Eurasian threat perspective was most popularized by Mackinder's famous 'Heartland vs. Rimland' theory [Mackinder, 1904]. Subsequent to World War I, and particularly with the rise to superpower status of the USA after World War II, Mackinder's earlier limited version of Eurocentric/Anglo strategic thinking was expanded by himself and other writers to include the USA and Canada as part of the 'north Atlantic community' world core [Sloan, 1988; Hooson, 1964; Mackinder, 1904; Cohen, 1973; Spykman, 1944; De Severesky, 1941; Meinig, 1956; Bowman, 1946]. […]

Looking back, there is no doubt that the Cold War focused so much attention on the NATO/Warsaw Pact standoff that it became habitual for a whole generation of scholars and practitioners to perceive the primacy of the north Atlantic core as a geopolitical as well as geoeconomic bedrock principle. Several generations of 'Cold Warrior' US presidents including Truman, Kennedy, Nixon, Reagan and Bush based their whole world view and foreign policy on this 'Atlanticist' orientation.

This Atlanticist bias in geostrategic thinking can be traced back further than the Cold War – in the USA the influence and writings of Alfred Thayer Mahan, counsellor to Teddy Roosevelt and staunch Anglophile, were also significant [Mahan, 1898, 1900; Sloan, 1988]. […]

Mahan claimed, for instance, that the 'Yankee national character' – which was WASP (White-Anglo-Saxon-Protestant) and based in New England – was what made the USA a power to be reckoned with. It is now clear that he was

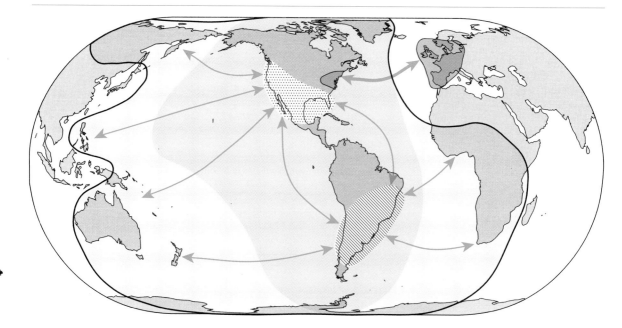

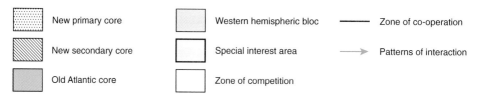

Figure B.1   *The new 'middle kingdom' zone of co-operation*

attempting to reify an Anglo-American version of nineteenth-century Victorian culture. [...]

But though this biased WASP perspective on American cultural and political hegemony may have reflected the political rationalizations of the nineteenth and early twentieth centuries, it no longer makes any sense whatsoever. Today, radical changes in sociocultural forces, primarily related to major shifts in American hemispheric population variables as well as global economic restructuring, are dramatically changing current and future political as well as social reality.

Yet it is not surprising, even in 1992, that the conventional though flawed perception of many US citizens is that 'America is Anglo'. It is true that many of the earliest immigrant groups who came to North America did have their cultural roots in north-west Europe, particularly in Britain (provided you ignore or undervalue the influence of the many non-northern European migrants who also came to the New World). But the reality was that the largely Atlantic-seaboard Anglo élite among these first migrants wrote the history and geography of the country as well taking control of the political arena. [...]

But migration is changing the regional geography and culture significantly – over the last three-quarters of a century, and particularly during the last 25 years, migration to the USA has seen a much greater influx from non-northern European regions including South and East Asia, Hispanic Middle and South America and transplanted African-Americans from places like Haiti and Jamaica. This most recent migration history, coupled with the influence of much earlier non-European migrations – that is, the African slaves – has begun to alter in both perception and reality, the primacy of the Anglo core cultural influence and has allowed underlying African, Asian, Hispanic and even native American (Amerindian) cultural elements to assert and make visible their equally significant contributions to the cultural and ethnic mix that exist in the western hemisphere as a whole and the USA in particular. As a consequence, a more appropriate contemporary analogy for this new demographic and polycultural reality is that of the USA as 'salad bowl' rather than the old WASP 'melting pot'.

[...]

It is also significant that many cultural elements now perceived around the world as uniquely 'American' are in fact products of cultural fusion and fission in this new core region. American cultural influences in general are rapidly supplanting European culture as the standard of reference worldwide. Anecdotal examples of the cultural hegemony of artefacts and practices originating in the new sunbelt/Pacific core region can be seen everywhere: Coca Cola from Atlanta and cartoon characters such as Mickey Mouse and Donald Duck from Walt Disney's Southern California and Hollywood. Think also of Louis Armstrong and New Orleans jazz, or Elvis Presley and Michael Jackson for rock and roll; even new cuisine such as Mexican, Cajun or San Francisco 'Chinese food' demonstrates the trend.

In the wider hemispheric cultural cauldron, examples abound which illustrate the resurgent influence of non-northern European influences on art, music, drama, literature: the revolutionary mural art of Siquieros in Mexico, reggae music from the Caribbean, the Lambada dance form (and la bamba) from Latin America, or African-American 'rap' music.

[...]

The current situation in American geopolitical thinking

Demographic, geographical and cultural evidence to the contrary, the Eurocentric/Anglo bias still dominates the thinking of the American and European political establishment. This is particularly obvious within the 'Beltway' of Washington DC. As recently as April 1991, Saul Cohen, one of America's leading political geographers, reiterated this in a post-Gulf War address to the Association of American Geographers in Miami, Florida [Cohen, 1991].

Essentially Cohen stated that the primacy of the North Atlantic – that is, NATO-centred – axis of world power would continue with the proviso that Japan now be included as part of the world core. The new world order, according to Cohen, will be a tripartite (North–North axis) global power structure consisting of the EC, NAFTA and Japan (along with its related 'Asian tigers'). But essentially, the centre of gravity in world power will still be the North Atlantic industrial heartland or 'trade-dependent maritime world'.

It is ironic that Cohen should have presented this essentially Atlanticist perspective on the New World Order in Miami, a city that exhibits so well the newly evolving cultural and political reality in the sunbelt/Pacific core region described earlier. One cannot help but ask: why does this Eurocentric bias still persist if the world is restructuring according to our scenario?

[...]

Unfortunately, a negative consequence of such geopolitical thinking, which attempts to retain the containment paradigm as its central tenet of faith along with its implicit Eurocentric orientation, could be that foreign policy analysis may give primacy to economic, military and geographical factors that no longer hold true or are at least less significant. Furthermore, though military, economic and industrial power do matter, we feel that those parameters of power basically reflect underlying demographic and cultural forces, not vice versa. Therefore, though the cultural and demographic forces of the nineteenth and early twentieth centuries did provide a certain rationale and impetus for an 'Atlanticist' geopolitical approach, current social and demographic facts are restructuring the world order in a way which mandates adoption of a new global strategy that is North–South and Pacific in orientation.

[...]

Benefits of creating a western hemispheric bloc

What benefits might come from pursuing a policy that encourages the formation of a western hemispheric bloc? First of all, it would create for the USA a trading counterweight to the European and Japanese trading blocs that may soon develop. The long-term benefits (for the USA) of forming such a bloc would far outweigh the short-term political and economic costs. The possible consequences of *not* carrying out this plan could be significant as well. But more significantly, we believe fostering hemispheric integration is also in the interests of Latin America and its third world partners.

Some regions like the Caribbean Community (CARICOM) are already moving in that direction, partly because they have no other choice – geography, migration trends and socioeconomic ties mandate this development [Braveboy-Wagner and Segal, 1991; Segal, 1990]. The USA currently has a free-trade agreement with Canada; in August 1992 it concluded negotiations with Mexico and will later move on to a possible agreement with Chile [Schuyler, 1991]. [...]

[...]

What other benefits to both the USA and its partners will flow from the creation of the western hemispheric bloc? First, because the region spans a whole range of climates and ecosystems on both sides of the Equator, great seasonal and ecological variability in the production of agricultural and other natural resource commodities is possible (tropical hardwoods, fibre crops, rubber, fisheries, cattle, natural oils, temperate fruits). In fact, most agricultural commodity market demands can be supplied by producers within the bloc. Already, the Inter-American Development Bank (IDB) reports that it has seen the export agricultural sector in Latin America diversify and grow significantly during the past 10 years, particularly in the export of non-traditional products, such as soya beans, fresh fruit and crustaceans.

[...]

As an overall policy goal, the USA should continue to espouse free trade, or at the very least fair trade. But it may be inevitable that trade relations with Japan and Europe will become more protectionist in the near future – there is no guarantee that former Cold War allies will remain such in the economic arena as well as the military one [Fallows, 1989]. Signs of economic nationalism are not hard to find today; the USA would be wise to plan for its worst manifestations. Therefore, in the event that the USA must pick and choose its friends in a world where 'beggar thy neighbour' economic policies become more attractive to narrow domestic political interest groups, having Latin America as a firm friend will be absolutely essential. And of course, many Latin American nations, to protect their own interests, may find it necessary to join or form a trade bloc of their own, particularly if the European single market should develop according to a more negative scenario [Brock and Hormatz, 1990; Lowenthal, 1990; Schott, 1989; Urquidi, 1988; Gilpin, 1987].

There is even the possibility that trading blocs will develop within Latin America that exclude the USA. In March 1991, the Inter-American Development Bank held its annual meeting in, of all places, Nagoya, Japan, ostensibly to seek more financial assistance from Japan and allow these nascent blocs to negotiate directly with it. Japan has become a major investor in Latin America, and it could soon surpass the investment of the USA. [...]

Significantly, the Inter-American Development Bank, though preferring development of a hemispheric free-trade zone with the USA as its leader, and strongly supporting Bush's 'Enterprise for the Americas', has noted with ambivalence the actions of the Andean Countries, the southern cone, Central America (CACM) and the Caribbean (CARICOM) to form their own regional trade blocs with independent links to Europe or Japan [*The IBD*, 1991; Will,

1991]. Whether these newly forming blocs will become integrated into the 'Enterprise for the Americas' process or go their own way, depends much at present on US attitudes and policy action. Unfortunately, the USA at present risks becoming a bystander in a potential negative trend toward regional protectionism, resurgent economic nationalism and old style 'America-bashing' that is in no one's interest.

[...]

Some may ask why the USA would want to target its world engagement toward the poverty-ridden countries of Latin America in the first place? Recent developments and trends seem to presage a brighter future. First, Latin America, particularly the large NIC economies of Brazil, Mexico, Colombia, Venezuela, Chile and Argentina, now represent a major sector of the world's production and consumption capacity [Frischtak, 1989]. Latin America could once again become the best outlet for US 'hi-tech' exports as well as for specialized agricultural products in which it has comparative advantage. After all, the region's population is still growing rapidly, including its middle class which is now heavily urban, industrial and better educated. This provides great opportunities for US participation and further development in their expanding labour and consumer markets.

[...]

And finally, there is another reason for the USA to co-operate closely with Latin America, particularly with the southern cone countries facing Antarctica and the South Atlantic/Pacific Southern Ocean region – the need to take a more expanded view of security that includes management of critical environmental zones, for example, Antarctica [Beck, 1990, 1988; Child, 1988; Gustafson, 1988]. The USA is also a major player in dealing with other critical ecosystem problems in the hemisphere; for example, forest resource management, ocean contamination and fisheries, global warming, and soil conservation. Though the Bush performance at the 1992 Rio summit was less than exemplary, these

regional and global problems will not go away – the only realistic way to deal with them is through collective action.

[...]

References

BECK, P.J. (1988) *The Falkland Islands as an International Problem*, London, Routledge.

BECK, P.J. (1990) 'Great power relations in Argentina, Chile and Antarctica', in Morris, M.A. (ed.) *International Relations in Antarctica*, New York, St Martin's Press.

BOWMAN, I. (1946) 'The stategy of territorial decisions', *Foreign Affairs*, Vol. 24, No. 2, pp. 177–94.

BRAVEBOY-WAGNER, J.A. and SEGAL, A. (1991) 'Preferential trade: leg-up or hand-me-down: the Caribbean, the European Community and the Caribbean Basin Initiative', paper presented to the Symposium on The Political Economy of Security and Democracy in the South in the 1990s, Dalhousie University, Halifax, Nova Scotia, Canada, September 1991.

BROCK, W.E. and HORMATZ, R.D. (1990) *The Global Economy*, New York, W.W. Norton and Co.

CHILD, J. (1988) *Antarctica and South American Geopolitics: Frozen Lebensraum*, New York, Praeger.

COHEN, S. (1973) *Geography and Politics in a World Divided*, Oxford, Oxford University Press.

COHEN, S. (1991) 'Geography and reordering the political order', Presidential Plenary Address at the Annual Meeting of the AAG, Miami, FL, 16 April 1991.

DE SEVERESKY, A.P. (1941) 'The twilight of seapower', *American Mercury*, Vol. 52, No. 2, pp. 647–58.

FALLOWS, J. (1989) 'Containing Japan', *Atlantic Monthly*, Vol. 17, May, pp. 40–54.

FRISCHTAK, C.R. (1989) 'Structural change and trade in Brazil and the newly industrializing Latin American economies', in Purcell, R.B. (ed.) *The Newly Industrializing Countries in the World Economy: Challenges for U.S. Policy*, Boulder, CO, Lynne Rienner Publishers.

GILPIN, R. (1987) *The Political Economy of International Trade*, Princeton, NJ, Princeton University Press.

GUSTAFSON, L. (1988) *The Sovereignty Dispute Over the Falkland Islands*, New York, Oxford University Press.

HOOSON, D.J.M. (1964) *A New Soviet Heartland?*, New York, Van Nostrand.

LOWENTHAL, A.F. (1990) 'Rediscovering Latin America', *Foreign Affairs*, Vol. 69, No. 4, pp. 27–41.

MACKINDER, H.J. (1904) 'The geographical pivot of history', *Geographical Journal*, Vol. 23, No. 4, pp. 421–44.

MAHAN, A.T. (1898) *The Interest of America in Sea Power, Present and Future*, Boston, MA, Little, Brown.

MAHAN, A.T. (1900) *The Problem of Asia and its Effect upon International Politics*, Boston, MA, Little, Brown.

MEINIG, D.W. (1956) 'Heartland and rimland in Euroasian history', *Western Political Quarterly*, Vol. 9, No. 2, pp. 553–69.

QUELCH, J.A., BUZELL, R.D. and SALAMA, E.R. (1990) *The Marketing Challenge of 1992*, Reading, MA, Addison-Wesley.

RIZOPOULOS, N.X. (ED.) (1990) *Sea-Changes: American Foreign Policy in a World Transformed*, New York, Council on Foreign Relations.

SCHOTT, J.J. (1989) *More Free Trade Areas?*, Washington, DC, Institute for International Economics.

SCHUYLER, G.W. (1991) 'Perspectives on Canada and Latin America: changing context … changing policy?', *Journal of Interamerican Studies and World Affairs*, Vol. 33, No. 1, pp. 19–58.

SEGAL, A. (1990) 'Small and poor countries in a world of big science and technology', *Science, Technology and Development*, Vol. 18, No. 3, pp. 224–33.

SLOAN, G.R. (1988) *Geopolitics in United States Strategic Policy, 1890–1987*, New York, St Martin's Press.

SPYKMAN, N.J. (1944) *The Geography of Peace*, New York, Harcourt Brace.

THE ECONOMIST (1991a) 'Too much good living', *The Economist*, 20–26 April, pp. 69–70.

THE ECONOMIST (1991b) 'Trade-block folly', *The Economist*, 20–26 April, pp. 11–12.

THE IBD (1991) 'New prospects for intraregional trade', *The IBD*, January–February, p. 10.

URQUIDI, V.L. (1988) *Free Trade and Economic Integration in Latin America: Toward a Common Market*, Berkeley, CA, University of California Press.

WILL, W.M. (1991) 'A nation divided: the quest for Caribbean integration', *Latin American Research Review*, Vol. 26, No. 2, pp. 3–38.

Source: Ford and Hudson, 1992, pp. 441–62

Reading C: Donald Crone, 'The politics of emerging Pacific co-operation'

The past decade has witnessed the delineation of a new political and economic grouping in the Pacific, which could be expected to consolidate into a significant bloc in the global system by the end of the century, setting a new framework for what has been widely touted as the 'Pacific Century'. This grouping ties together the Western industrial countries of the US, Canada, Australia and New Zealand, with Japan, the newly industrial countries of South Korea and Singapore, the next tier of Malaysia, Thailand, Indonesia, the Philippines and Brunei, with China, Taiwan and Hong Kong.

The forging of close relations between the industrialized countries and selected less industrial countries of the Pacific Basin has been expressed in a political process of constructing common organizations, most recently including the intergovernmental Asia-Pacific Economic Cooperation conference (APEC). This organizational network has not emerged smoothly, nor is it as yet fully defined. But it is a profound innovation in the Pacific, which has lagged behind every other world area in constructing explicit, co-operative arrangements, perhaps as a result of the high degree of diversity in cultures and economic levels found here. While these problems will continue to be relevant, the emergence of increasing levels and mechanisms of co-operation also signals greater cohesion, especially in economic affairs, a cohesion that may soon justify the term 'bloc', in parallel to the European bloc.

[...]

The setting: development of Pacific organizations

The roots of Pacific economic organization date back to the mid-1960s. Japan has been a consistent source of proposals and of support for resultant organizations, in part to balance fast institutional development in Europe. The first official proposal, from Japanese Prime Minister Miki in 1967 of a Pacific Free Trade Area, was based on a presumption that the shock of the impending completion of a European trade area would have a severe impact on the Pacific economies. However, the organizational responses were non-governmental in form, as the proposal was unable to garner wide support from either the other industrial country governments or from those of the developing countries of the region.

Two significant organizations were, however, formed. These were the Pacific Basin Economic Council (PBEC), established in April 1967 from national groups of business managers, and the Pacific Trade and Development Conference (PAFTAD), first convened in Tokyo in January 1968 as an economists' forum. PAFTAD, now headquartered at the Australian National University, has been a consistent producer of academic knowledge, especially on the economies of the developing countries of the region [Drysdale, 1984]. These two forums fostered greater contact among academic economists and business circles of the Pacific, and gradually widened the base of participants from a circle centred in Japan, Australia and the US, to include those from the developing economies of East and Southeast Asia. As strictly

non-governmental organizations, they could consider problems and policy issues, but could contribute little more to the process of community building; the many emerging problems were the exclusive domain of sovereign governments. [...]

A number of subregional intergovernmental organizations were also created during the 1960s, one of which was to become central, both to its members' foreign policies and, by default as there was no competition, to other Pacific powers. ASEAN, formed in 1967 among Indonesia, Malaysia, the Philippines and Singapore (Brunei joined in 1984) [...] came to provide a forum for a delimited sort of multilateral interaction by the 1980s; it also demonstrated some of the problems with attaining multilateral co-operation in, and outside of, the region. ASEAN had limitations as a vehicle for broader regional co-operation, especially in that its members set the agenda and form for the Post-Ministerial Conferences, structuring them essentially as bilateral forums between the ASEAN six and the outside five [Crone, 1988]. Still, as long as no alternative organization existed, ASEAN provided what focus there was to Pacific multilateral interaction.

By the late 1970s, the issue of regional co-operation was again raised. [...] Some form of association was vigorously pursued all around the Pacific littoral through numerous study groups, seminars, informal consultations, and published reports in 1978–1980. The result was the initiation of the Pacific Economic Cooperation Conference (PECC) in Canberra in September 1980, attended by the US, Japan, Canada, Australia, New Zealand, the Republic of Korea and the (then five) ASEAN members. PECC is a non-governmental organization, although representatives from government participate in an informal capacity, along with those from private business and academia; all are drawn from national committees for PECC in each member country which were gradually set up during the 1980s. A central secretariat was established in Singapore in 1990, and up to 1991 the original core members were supplemented by Brunei, China and

Taiwan; Hong Kong, Chile, Mexico and Peru were admitted in 1991. [...]

With an increasing number of problems to be solved [...], Australian Prime Minister Hawke, closely assisted by the Australian National Committee for PECC, launched close to a year of diplomacy to get a formative meeting for a governmental forum in early 1989. [...] The result was the founding meeting in November 1989 of the Asia–Pacific Economic Cooperation conference (APEC) in Canberra, with the US, Canada, Japan, South Korea, New Zealand and the six ASEAN members participating. The governments there agreed to continue their contacts, and work toward some form of regularization. A portion of the Pacific, after over twenty years of failed efforts, finally had an intergovernmental organization.

Driving forces: domestic and international change

[...]

Undeniably, a vast increase in economic transactions among the major countries of the Pacific increased the stakes. The scale of potential losses, and gains, and the importance and frequency of frictions all moved upward as the Pacific became an identifiable region in global economics. [...] However, a Pacific organization did not simply leap up to fill this need. Rather, several aspects of the domestic and international environments for Pacific states had changed during the 1980s, and these changes eroded the reluctance of some, and increased the enthusiasm of others, for a significant upward movement in the level of Pacific organization, from an informal and non-governmental one to a more formal organization, one backed by the authority of governments.

In the domestic arena, one factor that had contributed to governmental reluctance to engage in multilateral negotiations was the protected nature of many of the Pacific economies. This was true of the developing East Asian nations which had constructed dense walls from behind which they launched their export drives. As economic frictions emerged during the 1980s, partly because of the success of East Asian export drives, they

were often focused on these protectionist devices. [...]

[...] In the latter half of the 1980s, the intensity of these concerns about the possible agenda of a regional grouping was eroded by domestic liberalization programmes in some Pacific countries. Malaysia, Indonesia and Singapore all initiated privatization and deregulation programmes that had some effect in liberalizing their economies, and in deflecting pressures from the outside. South Korea and Taiwan became exemplars of successful outward-oriented development, and along with Indonesia each received praise and attention from international agencies, such as the World Bank and the IMF [International Monetary Fund], for their movement toward more open economies. Thailand's brief civilian regime, under Chatichai Choonhaven, pushed deregulation of business to the point of almost dismantling the Board of Investment and its incentives. Australia's Labour Party government started a programme of liberalization, partly out of concern at being marginalized in a changing world economic order, left by geopolitical reality with 'no choice but to adopt more outward looking strategies toward the region' [Yuen and Wagner, 1989; Higgott, 1987, p. 215; Drysdale, 1990]. The pressures of the recession of the early 1980s [...] was also instrumental in fostering the political will to dismantle some protectionist devices [for example, see Pangestu and Habir, 1989]. Ironically, having co-opted one area of concern, liberalization created another, being all dressed up for a party that no one else wanted to attend: liberalization in some states, as protectionism seemed to prosper in others, left liberalizing governments more vulnerable, with uncertain benefits, after a politically difficult exercise.

Domestic changes removed some of the blockages to consideration of a regional grouping, eroding the reluctance of some governments toward exposing themselves to more outside pressure. However, it was anticipated change in the global economy that created a sufficient threat to actually break the blockade that had existed for so long.

The issue was the apparent emergence of regional trading blocs all around Asia, particularly in Europe with its [...] connections to the new East Europe, and in North America. [...] The original Hawke proposal was seen as largely a counter to developments in Europe and North America, that were in contrast to what he characterized as the 'relatively benign' global economy of the 1960s and 1970s. In addition, at least some in Australia expressed concern that the US and Japan might arrive at an exclusive agreement to their mutual problems that excluded other Asia–Pacific interests, leaving Australia 'totally friendless' [Hàrris, 1989; Wanandi, 1989, p. 6; Hawke, 1989; *The Australian*, 9 November 1989; see also Evans, 1990]. That new regional trading blocs might harm those excluded from them became a common ASEAN perception during 1989. The emergence of a potential East European focus to the flow of West European capital, diverting finance from Southeast Asia, was one concrete manifestation raised by ASEAN, specific trade reciprocity, creating a 'fortress Europe', another. [...]

These sorts of domestic and international changes altered the governmental calculus on new organizations, from previous reluctance to a new, sometimes grudging acceptance. The ASEAN members had been the most negative. In the mid-1980s any new co-operative mechanism for the Pacific was sharply dismissed, with ASEAN having 'no intention' of considering such a forum, which was 'too difficult' and 'not practical'. The Malaysian charcterization was that such an organization could become a monster itself.[1] Australia, which had mooted forums in the past, undertook the APEC proposal only after long pressure from the national PECC committee.[2] By late 1989 ASEAN was providing lukewarm support for the idea, and Malaysian Prime Minister Mahathir was considering 'a try at it', as '[t]he nations of the ASEAN community ... must realize the limitations of their influence'. The 'new realities' of European integration and Eastern European change forced adjustment from earlier nationalistic reticence [Mahathir, 1989, p. 23].[3]

Some of these same issues affected the United States, but with its own particular slants. The traditional US position favoured universal economic forums over regional ones, and rejected the 1980 Japanese initiative on this basis plus concern over how to manage North–South conflicts in a merely Asia–Pacific forum. At the same time, some in the US government worried about the risk of exclusion from Pacific Basin organizations [...].

Japan, the premier promoter of Pacific organization, shared some necessity of reactive change. While earlier efforts to support organizations foundered primarily on the reluctance of others, Japan's own reticence to assume leadership contributed to their demise. But, at the turn of the 1980s decade, Japan's diplomacy entered what Saito characterizes as a far more politically oriented phase, that included a role as initiator of regional co-operation. This translated quickly into top level support for a wider Pacific community, focused on funding PECC and moving it toward a Pacific summit venue [Saito, 1990, pp. 54, 125; *Report of the Sixth Pacific Economic Co-operation Conference*, Osaka, 1988; Sudo, 1989]. Prime Minister Takeshita used the Group of 7 meeting in 1988 to raise regional trade integration as a major topic, essentially threatening an Asian bloc as a counter to European and North American ones. [...]

The principle of Pacific organization had been accepted, with some difficulty and only after some domestic adjustments and change in the international conditions that had allowed economic linkages to grow rapidly prior to the 1980s.

[...]

The Pacific rachet effect: form and competition[4]

One consequence of the increasing density of organizations in the Pacific is a more competitive environment. There are no more exclusive domains, but sets of overlapping memberships and forums that could provide alternative venues. Should one organization not provide outcomes suitable to some members, they can, within limits, take their business and loyalties elsewhere. This sense of potential competition has stimulated efforts on the part of several organizations to reinforce their position through upgrading their own institutional structures. A concomitant pressure has emerged to keep the organizational forms and processes as informal as possible, in order to reduce the potentials for governments losing control either to a central organization, or to each other.

The organization most threatened is ASEAN. Having long enjoyed an institutional monopoly, both PECC and especially APEC pose potential consequences of marginalization and pressurization to ASEAN. Members of ASEAN, especially Indonesia, have been influential in posing institutional constraints to other organizations as they have been proposed. PECC emerged as a non-governmental organization partially out of Indonesian reluctance to consider a more formal alternative. [...]

[...]

The climate of the 1980s changed [...] [as] real competition [...] emerged, and ASEAN seems more determined to preserve what it has built. Likewise, PECC has responded to the formation of APEC with new initiatives. APEC itself will have to move toward more substantive issues in order to preserve its own role. The level of Pacific organization is being ratcheted upward as each organization seeks to preserve, or define, a unique niche.

Whether the actual level of co-operation in the Pacific also rises remains to be seen. The organizational framework has been constructed. Few signs exist that the economic and political impulses to engage each other are transient. Thus far, the fears that inhibited co-operation have proved unfounded, although the economic and cultural diversity of the region remain significant sources of suspicion and potential misunderstanding. A foundation exists to support the launching of a Pacific century that will compete with the reinvigoration of the Atlantic. What remains is to furnish and inhabit the structure.

Notes

1 Indonesian Foreign Minister Mochtar speaking as chairman of the ASEAN Standing Committee, *FBIS Daily Reports*, Asia-Pacific, 6 July 1984, p. A1, and 12 July 1984, p. N1; *New Straits Times*, 16 August 1985 (Musa Hitam).
2 Author interview, Canberra, May 1990.
3 Lee Hsien Loon at the 21st ASEAN Economic Ministers Meeting, November 1989.
4 This section is based primarily on interviews with participants in the organizations in 1990 and 1991.

References

CRONE, D. (1988) 'The ASEAN Summit 1987: searching for new dynamism', in Ayoob, M. and Yuen, N.C. (eds) *Southeast Asian Affairs 1988*, Singapore, Institute of Southeast Asian Affairs.

DRYSDALE, P. (1984) *The Pacific Trade and Development Conference: A Brief History*, Pacific Economic Papers, No. 112, Canberra, Australia Japan Research Center.

DRYSDALE, P. (1990) 'Australia's Asia–Pacific diplomacy', *Current Affairs Bulletin*, Vol. 66, No. 10, pp. 14–21.

EVANS, G. (1990) 'Opening Statement', APEC, Singapore, 30 July 1990.

HARRIS, S. (1989) 'Regional economic cooperation, trading blocs, and Australian interests', *Australian Outlook*, Vol. 43, No. 2, pp. 19–20.

HAWKE, AUSTRALIAN PRIME MINISTER (1989) in 'Opening Statement', APEC Ministerial Meeting, Canberra 1989.

HIGGOTT, R. (1987) 'Australia: economic crisis and the politics of regional economic adjustment', in Robison, R., Hewison, K. and Higgott, R. (eds) *Southeast Asia in the 1980s: The Politics of Economic Crisis*, London, Allen and Unwin.

MAHATHIR, B.M. (1989) *Regionalism, Globalism and Spheres of Influence*, Singapore, Institute of Southeast Asian Studies.

PANGESTU, M. and HABIR, A. (1989) 'Trends and prospects in privatization and deregulation in Indonesia', *ASEAN Economic Bulletin*, Vol. 5, No. 3, pp. 224–41.

SAITO, S. (1990) *Japan at the Summit*, London, Routledge.

SUDO, S. (1989) 'Japan's role in the context of the emerging Asia–Pacific World', in Yuen, N.C. (ed.) *Southeast Asian Affairs 1989*, Singapore, Institute of Southeast Asian Affairs.

WANANDI, J. (1989) *The Role of PECC in the 1990s and Pacific Institutions*, Jakarta, CISS, p. 6.

YUEN, N.C. and WAGNER, N. (eds) (1989) 'Privatization and deregulation in ASEAN', *ASEAN Economic Bulletin*, Vol. 5, No. 3.

Source: Crone, 1992, pp. 68–83

Global options: Islamic alternatives

by Brian Beeley

Chapter 4

4.1   Introduction

In 1099 Crusaders from Europe seized Jerusalem butchering many of its inhabitants, and Palestine became one of five Christian-ruled states in the eastern Mediterranean. In 1187, an outstanding Muslim ruler, Saladin, retook the Holy City without the brutality shown by Western armies nearly a century before. Elsewhere, as well, Christian forces were pushed back. For both sides the conflict was 'holy': Crusaders invoked the Cross of Christ; Muslims proclaimed *jihad* (holy war). Ostensibly, the wars were about control of places and spaces in Palestine holy to both Christians and Muslims – particularly in Jerusalem. By the skilful use of what we would today call propaganda, the leaders of the two sides built up *images* in the minds of their followers of the threat posed by the other side. More durable than military and political outcomes, these perceptions of the 'other side' are perhaps partly responsible for present-day Western perceptions of Muslims and Muslim perceptions of the West – often as strongly felt as they are denied by the facts.

The above glimpse of long-ago events illustrates the reality of image and the importance of choice of words: presumably the European knights fighting in the name of the Christian Cross did not see themselves as 'butchers' but as defenders of Christianity. Was the conflict really a religious one or were sacred labels attached to what was in fact a wider struggle for wealth and territory between Christendom and Islam? The example above also illustrates how history often oversimplifies events. And perhaps Saladin's view of what he was doing was quite different from that of the foot-soldiers in his armies or of Muslim holy men. Perhaps Richard I of England had an image of Islam at odds with that of the rank and file of troops with him on the Third Crusade in the Middle East.

Whatever the motives given for the Crusades, in the end they involved places and land. The principal prize, Jerusalem, was 'ours' to both sides. The late twentieth-century equivalent of this is that today the Holy City is held by (Jewish) Israelis and claimed by (Muslim and Christian) Palestinians – which reminds us that there is a time dimension as well as a spatial one.

This chapter however is not about the past: it is about the present and future role of a religion – *Islam* – in shaping the political map of states. Islam has been chosen because it provides an example of a cultural force which is in conflict with the dominant Western culture. Sometimes it questions 'Western' ways of organizing political space. One-quarter of the member states of the United Nations are Islamic and one person in five of the world's population is a Muslim. With such a case-study, the purpose of this chapter is to see how far a faith can be an alternative basis for the mobilization of global order. In other words, are there non-Western ways in which political space can be organized (**Allen, 1995**)? Will future first-rank contenders in the evolving global system depend on economic power *or* on some other force – such as ties of culture and religion? In this approach, we confront directly the power of ideas. Of course, the characteristic features of the 'European' state system (see Chapter 1) emerged during centuries of debate and change grounded largely in what is conventionally called the Judeo-Christian tradition. Can another tradition, perhaps that of Islam, be similarly influential as a motor of

image

Islam

change in the world political system? As Worsley puts it after a wide-ranging survey of *Models of the Modern World-System* (1990):

None of the models so far discussed takes culture into account. All of them are variants of one kind or another of political economy, though without the cultural dimension it is impossible to make sense of a modern world in which nationalism, religion and inter-ethnic hostility have been far more important than internationalism and secularism. Models based on political economy alone, therefore, are quite incapable of explaining such phenomena as the rise of a modern version of Islam which is wrongly labelled 'fundamentalism', or the contradiction between the claim of that religion to universal community and the reality of the harnessing of Islam to the interests of the nation-state, notably during the Iran–Iraq war.

fundamentalism

[...]

All the models we have discussed ... take the nation-state as their unit of analysis. Yet all of us belong to communities which are both smaller and wider than the nation-state. Hence, as one anthropologist has put it, as long as there are 'ten thousand societies inhabiting 160 nation-states' which refuse to recognize their cultural and political rights, minority peoples will continue to struggle to run their own affairs, by force of arms if need be.

Conversely, the modern world has been shaped by cultural communities, from the Catholic Church and Islam to secular ideologies and movements like communism which transcend the boundaries of even the largest and most centralized state.

(Worsley, 1990, pp. 92, 94)

This chapter examines both the 'overlap' of the West in the Islamic world *and* the growing presence of Islam within the West. It is built round the key questions: to what extent does Islam constitute an alternative means of political mobilization and what is its impact as a transnational cultural force? Put geographically, the question is: can space be organized politically in terms of Islam rather than on the basis of the Western concept of the state? Muslim views of the West are as real as Western images of Islam. Neither image is standard for all for whom it depicts the 'other side'. Each varies according to the location, experience and social status of the viewer. Indeed, to talk of a 'Western' view, as if there were only one, is itself part of the problem of representation. Similar variety characterizes Muslims' views of their own faith.

This chapter takes forward the focus in this book from sub-state regionalism and nationalism (Chapter 2) and from economic forces and global-scale regionalization (Chapter 3) to look at transnational cultural identity. Then, in the following chapter (Chapter 5) the focus moves to another transnational area – that of environmentalism.

The chapter is organized in five main sections. Two look at cultural and spatial contrasts, one examines Western and Islamic perceptions of each other, and two more try to assess the outcomes for Islam – divisive or unifying. In section 4.2 we look at different types of geographical space, notably conventional space, and the religious and cultural space which is harder to map because it exists in a representational rather than a physical form (see **Massey, 1995b**). Section 4.3 briefly gives a picture of the scale and extent of Islam while section 4.4 argues that perceptions – or representations – are at least as significant as 'reality' in influencing the aspirations and actions of groups. Sections 4.5 and 4.6 assess the role of Islam in processes of political realignment within continuing globalization.

4.2 Cultural contrasts

4.2.1 The geography of culture

At first glance, geography and religion seem to be curious bedfellows. However, even a brief reflection reveals a myriad of ways in which the two interact – religion affects people and their behaviour in many different ways, and geographers have traditionally been concerned with the spatial patterns, distributions and manifestations of people and environment.

(Park, 1994, p. 1)

religious culture

This chapter is, in these terms, about the interface of religious and political space (Levine, 1986; Rowley, 1989; Scott, 1991). It accepts that people identify 'their own' places and spaces and attach importance to locations with special cultural value for them (**Massey, 1995b**; **Rose, 1995**). Cultural spaces demarcated in this way are built on formal and informal links and networks stretched over them (**Massey, 1995b**), and they have limits or edges which are often imprecisely defined and may change over time. Communities may concern themselves with quite limited spaces, differentiating a 'home' area such as a village or local community or region from the 'world beyond' constructed in the minds of members of a group. Images of both *our* space and the *other* space are developed over time and received by individuals from family, school or community (**Massey, 1995a**). Such cultural baggage has the permanence of the group to which it attaches: individuals making up a group are the temporary custodians of such baggage during their lifetimes. An unchanging society is one in which individuals bequeath to their own children more or less the same sets of views, the same constructions of cultural space, which they inherit. Late twentieth-century cultures are often far from unchanging within the lifespans of individual members. Sometimes change is fundamental, even violent, as individuals, and thereby the groups of which they are part, alter their images of themselves, their own communities and networks and of such 'other' communities as are relevant to them.

Of course, there have always been changes in the lives of people which brought about substantial modifications in the 'world-view' of individuals and groups. The emergence of new religious movements or some technological innovation may have produced change so basic that, with hindsight, we differentiate distinct phases or eras. Examples might be the differentiation in time of pre-Christian and Christian or of pre-industrial and industrial. What is characteristic of the run-up to the end of the second (Christian) millenium is frequency of change, its scale and its range of implications for increasing numbers of people. In other words, change is now widespread and, because of the expansion of networks of interconnection worldwide, there may be significant and speedy repercussions far away from the source of the change (for example, see **Allen and Hamnett, eds, 1995**). In past ages, substantial empires rose and fell and distinctive cultures waxed and faded without other empires and cultures being very much affected – or even being aware of such changes. Such is the interdependence of changes today, within a shrinking world, that it is inconceivable that a cultural tradition or the modern-day equivalent of an empire could be lost without the rest of the world knowing about it. The kind of loss which threatens peoples today – or is believed by them to be threatening – is the loss where one culture is absorbed into another culture or is even obliterated by it. Far from happening in some 'unknown' corner of the globe, such change may be well publicized over a very wide area. Increasingly, people nowadays can have information on the basis of which they may identify with faraway groups in terms of perceived bonds and shared cultural priorities. Such common-feeling may be based on perceptions of shared ethnic origins, or of exploitation, or of cultural features such as language, religion or nation.

Activity 1 Think about how religion influences your own views about places and social spaces. If you identify with a religious denomination, is your religious link more nominal than pro-active? Do you have a particular political affiliation? (If so, why *do* you vote the way you do?) Where do you come from (– identify the place)? Have you changed your allegiance to place or community? If you live in the United Kingdom, do you think of yourself as British, Scottish, Geordie etc., or as 'foreign'? Are any international affiliations important to you? Do not spend too long on these questions; they are designed simply to open up some of the areas of enquiry in this chapter. Answer them quickly and then move on.

The discussion so far has been about overlapping dimensions. One is the territory – the geographical, physical space – which a group occupies. The other is made up of the specially valued places and areas which a community occupies *or hopes to occupy* because of their religious or cultural importance. Thus, for example, a religion has a spatial dimension to the extent that the adherents of that faith value certain areas – perhaps including points of special religious importance such as sacred cities or shrines or places associated with major past events. This sort of religious space is comparable to the sense of national space shared by a group, whether or not the national area perceived by members of the group is coterminous with the nation-state in question. For example, the seventeen million Hungarians may identify with their national space, being the areas in which Hungarians live in several states in central Europe, while being aware that only some eleven million of their number live within the state of Hungary. For their part, Muslims distinguish states where they are dominant from areas within 'non-Muslim' countries where their co-religionists constitute minority communities. In both the Hungarian and the Islamic examples, the cultural area identified is more extensive than the related pattern of states.

If both physical and cultural spaces are seen as parts of a 'horizontal' dimension, we can recognize a third or 'vertical' dimension – that of social character – within the communities of people making up groups, religious sects, nations and so on, in that the involvement of individuals in their communities and cultures differs according to class, gender, age and education. On this basis, perceptions about such things as 'our' nation, or territory, or group, or faith may vary in ways which have potentially important outcomes. Just one example of this is that the view of religion among one section of a community may differ markedly from that of the leaders of that community who may consider themselves as having a priority position.

Traditional Islam – Ka'aba, Mecca – the central place of Islam

Alongside the horizontal and vertical dimensions of culture is another – that of time. If rapid and substantial change is now the norm, this is likely to reflect increasingly frequent adjustments and realignments in the interrelationships of groups within wider groups – and to result in changes to patterns of national and cultural identity. But while change is now the norm, the prospect that there is an underlying move away from reliance on nation-states prompts us to select one culture – that of Islam – as a focus for this enquiry.

4.2.2 The Islamic alternative

The contemporary world political system is viewed by realists as including a spatial mosaic of separate, 'sovereign' states (Piscatori, 1986; Vatikiotis, 1991). Some are large, some small, some able substantially to influence other states and some weak and vulnerable. This system has spread from Europe, where it emerged in its present-day form in the seventeenth century, to become the dominant basis for the spatial arrangement of government across the world. In most cases, boundaries imposed by Europeans have stayed in place even after the retreat of formal colonial rule. Fundamental to the character of the state system built up in this way is the European culture which generated it in the first place.

A look at a non-European culture may provide a useful basis for comparison, to understand more clearly why the 'European' state system seems not always to sit comfortably in other world regions (indeed it does not always sit comfortably within Europe itself). Perhaps non-European alternatives to the state system might be developed in other cultural areas in which people construct differently the spaces which are important to them. This raises the prospect of a cultural duality in which individuals are required to construct their image of political space both in West-led terms (because it is a West-led system) *and* in terms of their own cultural inheritance. The result may be a double image of two overlying patterns where the 'fit' may be far from exact. In this context we can look to specifically 'Islamic' images and representations of what is or what should be to understand what people who accept Islam may expect to see in systems which affect them. We would expect to find still further differences of priority and perception if we were to look at Buddhist, Hindu or other non-European traditions.

The significance of Islam is brought into sharper relief because its core region is adjacent to Europe. To Europeans over many centuries it has evoked thoughts of 'threat', of valiant Crusaders or Knights of St John 'holding back the tide' of encroachment by Muslims into Europe's space. Much of such feelings about 'them' (versus 'us') features in notions of the Orient as the uncivilized 'other' of the civilized West. Said (1978) presents this notion, arguing that a European definition of another – neighbouring – culture area helps Europeans to define their own space – be it Europe or, more broadly, the West (see also **Rose, 1995**). Today, of course, this us-and-them view of Islam from Europe is blurred by the emergence within Europe itself of substantial communities of Muslims with varied sets of wider connections: four million live in France, two million in Germany and nearly that number in the United Kingdom. To some extent then, Europe has to internalize its image of Islam and of the Muslims who represent it as 'the Other' *within* the West (Nielsen, 1992).

One feature of Islam which provides a striking contrast with modern Western culture is the stress placed on the completeness of the Islamic message as a basis for living lives. Islam teaches that there is no distinction between an area of human existence which is that of the faith and another which is secular or beyond the faith. Ultimately there cannot be a distinction between civil and religious law since all law is Islamic (that is taken, directly or by inference, from the statements of faith in the Qur'an [Koran] or the Hadith [pronouncements made by the Prophet Mohammad in the seventh century AD]). Medieval Christianity also saw all authority derived from God (see Chapter 2) but the distinction between church and state which has taken hold within the European state system (and in its exported versions) during the past few centuries is still lacking in the *Islamic* presentation of the world and social order. Of course, different compromises between the prescriptions of Islamic and of the West have emerged – and are continuing to emerge – in different places across a world which is not only shrinking but is shrinking unevenly (**Allen and Hamnett, eds, 1995**). Hence relations between parts of the world are also uneven.

Clearly, while there is one Islam, conveyed from God in the Qur'an, there is now a wide variety of interpretations of that message and therefore different cultural outcomes across Muslim societies in an uneven mosaic. In areas where Muslims are in control they show different approaches to political action and state behaviour: elsewhere minority communities make up the Muslim diaspora (**Hall, 1995**). At this point it is enough to stress the obvious which is that there is no one way in which Islamic culture is expressed in political action today any more than parallel generalizations could realistically be made about the outcomes of Christian cultural traditions. Yet generalizations by Europeans about 'others' or by Muslims about Europeans are important even though they may be patently misleading in terms of hard evidence because they guide the way in which members of one group view members of another group (the differentiation between *us* and *them*). It is not essential that perception of difference between *us* and *them* involves any detailed real knowledge of what is represented by the differentiating characteristic – in this case Islam. It is enough that there is perceived to be a difference. Antagonisms within communities in Europe operate at the local scale but here we are also concerned with the implications of antagonisms at the greater level of the world system of states.

Linking the two levels is the notion of scale. This leads us into the next section which looks at the world scale of Islam today but does this recognizing that, above all, images based on simplistic generalization must give way to the recognition of spatial and social unevenness within patterns of global inequality.

Summary of section 4.2

o The state system which is today the basis of the organization of political space is a product of 'Western' culture which has been exported across the world. A look at a non-Western culture – Islam – enables us to sharpen the focus of our assessment of the state system by suggesting how political space might be organized differently.

o 30 per cent of Muslims now live in the diaspora in Western and other 'non-Islamic' countries. Thus Islam, an 'other' in Western images since the Crusades, is now also *within* the West.

o Evidently a culturally defined community of more than one billion people dominant in over fifty states and substantially represented in many others will be reflected by complex overlapping transnational and inter-state networks in the name of Islam. Islam in coming transnationalism years might be more influential – or undermining – *transnationally* on the world political scene than as 'Islamic states' within a still West-led system of states.

4.3 Spatial contrasts

4.3.1 The map of Islam

As we have seen, a religious tradition has a geographical expression because its believers occupy areas and places. Firstly, we can identify some fifty states as 'Islamic' because they claim to be such or because a majority of their inhabitants are Muslim (Table 4.1). On this basis the Islamic realm comprises northern and eastern Africa, south-west, central and much of south and south-east Asia, plus small parts of Europe (Figure 4.1).

Predominantly Muslim

Significant outlying Muslim communities

International boundaries

Figure 4.1 The realm of Islam

Table 4.1 Islamic countries

Region	Sub-region	Country (a)	Population Millions (b)	Population % Muslim (b)	Political independence	Previous colonial influence	Principal language	(c)							GNP per capita US$ (b)
AFRICA	WEST	Gambia	0.9	85	1965	UK	English	I	B		A		C	N	360
		Senegal	8.0	91	1960	France	French	I	B		A			N	720
		Guinea	7.3	79	1958	France	French	I	B		A			N	450
		Nigeria	115.8	55	1960	UK	English				A	O	C	N	290
	SAHEL	Mauritania	2.1	98	1960	France	French/ Arabic	I	B	L	A			N	510
		Mali	9.4	90	1960	France	French	I	B		A			N	280
		Niger	8.0	90	1960	France	French	I	B		A			N	300
		Chad	6.3	<50?	1960	France	French/ Arabic	I	B		A			N	267
	EAST	Eritrea	3.5	50	1993	Italy, Ethiopia	Tigrinya				A				77
		Ethiopia	52.0	<50?	1941	Italy	Amharic				A			N	120
		Djibouti	0.5	94	1977	France	Somali/ French	I	B	L	A			N	475
		Somalia	8.1	99	1960	Italy, UK	Somali	I	B	L	A			N	200
		Comoros	0.5	98	1975	France	French/ Comoran	I	B		A			N	500
	NORTH (Arab countries)	Morocco	25.7	98	1956	France, Spain	Arabic	I	B	L	A			N	1030
		Algeria	26.6	98	1962	France	Arabic	I	B	L	A	O		N	2020
		Tunisia	8.4	96	1956	France	Arabic	I	B	L	A			N	1450
		Libya	4.0	97	1951	Italy	Arabic	I	B	L	A	O		N	5410
		Egypt	57.0	92	1922/54	UK	Arabic	I	B	L	A			N	620
		Sudan	31.0	72	1956	UK	Arabic	I	B	L	A			N	400
ASIA	ARABIA (Arab countries)	Saudi Arabia	16.9	99	Old	–	Arabic	I	B	L		O		N	7070
		Kuwait	2.1	90	1961	Ottoman, UK	Arabic	I	B	L		O	O	M	16380
		Qatar	0.5	95	1971	UK	Arabic	I	B	L		O	O	N	15857
		Bahrain	0.5	88	1971	UK	Arabic	I	B	L				N	6910
		UAE	2.1	92	1971	UK	Arabic	I	B	L			O	N	19900
		Oman	2.1	97	1971	UK	Arabic	I	B	L				N	4666
		Yemen	13.0	99	1919/67	Ottoman, UK	Arabic	I	B	L				N	540
	FERTILE CRESCENT (Arab countries)	Syria	13.4	90	1941	Ottoman, France	Arabic	I	B	L				N	1110
		Lebanon	2.8	60	1941	Ottoman, France	Arabic	I	B	L				N	1120
		Jordan	4.0	93	1946	Ottoman, UK	Arabic	I	B	L				N	2140
		Iraq	19.4	96	1932	Ottoman, UK	Arabic	I	B	L		O		N	2140
	SOUTH WEST	Turkey	59.9	99	Old	–	Turkish	I	B	E		O	T		1820
		Iran	55.8	96	Old	–	Persian	1	B	E		O		N	2320
		Azerbaijan	7.2	88	1991	Russia	Azeri	I		E			R		1670
		Afghanistan	16.6	99	Old	–	Persian/ Pashtu	I	B	E				N	250
		Pakistan	119.1	97	1947	UK	Urdu/English	I	B	E			C	N	400
	CENTRAL	Kazakhstan	17.0	<50?	1991	Russia	Kazakh			E	E		R		2470
		Uzbekistan	21.2	88	1991	Russia	Uzbek			E	E		R	N	1350
		Turkmenistan	3.8	85	1991	Russia	Turkmen			E	E		R		1700
		Kirgizia	4.5	68	1991	Russia	Kyrgyz	I		E	E		R		1551
		Tajikistan	5.5	93	1991	Russia	Tajik				E		R		1050
	SOUTH/ SOUTH EAST	Malaysia	19.0	55	1957	UK	Malay/ English	I	B				C	N	3625
		Bangladesh	118.7	85	1947/71	UK	Bengali/ English	I	B				C	N	220
		Maldives	0.2	100	1965	UK	Divehi/ English	I	B				C	N	460
		Indonesia	187.8	88	1949	Netherlands	Indonesian	I	B			O		N	3265
		Brunei	0.4	64	1983	UK	Malay/ English	I	B				C	N	9600
		India (a)	846.3	11	1947	UK	Hindi/ English						C	N	330
EUROPE		Albania	3.3	70	1912	Ottoman	Albanian	I							930

Notes to Table 4.1:

(a) Countries listed have 50 per cent or more Muslim populations, except for India (listed because of its very large Muslim minority). Seven countries with Muslim populations less than 50 per cent are excluded although they are members of the Organization of the Islamic Conference, the Islamic Development Bank and of the organization of African Unity (the seven are Benin, Cameroon, Gabon, Guinea Bissau, Sierra Leone, Burkina Faso and Uganda). Zanzibar is also a member of the OIC and Mozambique has observer status.

Also not listed are:

• *Bosnia-Hercegovina:* The Muslim element (44 per cent of the total population of 4.36 m) is now substantially greater than 50 per cent in the reduced area still under Bosnian government control (June 1995).

• *Mayotte* (Comoros) (pop: 0.1m; 97 per cent Muslim): a French 'Territorial Collectivity' from 1976.

• *Turkish Republic of Northern Cyprus* (pop: 0.2m; 98 per cent Muslim): part of Republic of Cyprus from withdrawal of UK in 1960 to secession in 1974, recognized only by Turkey. Has observer status of OIC and is a member of the Islamic Development Bank.

• *West Bank and Gaza* (Palestine) (pop: 2.1m; 92 per cent Muslim): occupied by Jordan (West Bank) and Egypt (Gaza) after UK withdrawal from Palestine in 1948; occupied by Israel in 1967, Jordanian link severed in 1988. Member of the League of Arab States, the Islamic Development Bank, the OIC and the Non-Aligned Movement. Gaza and Jericho gained limited autonomy in 1994.

• *Western Sahara* (pop: 0.2m; 100 per cent Muslim): occupied by Morocco after withdrawal of Spain in 1975. Referendum envisaged (1995).

(b) Latest estimates available (1994).

(c) Membership of selected organizations:

I   Organization of the Islamic Conference (OIC)

B   Islamic Development Bank

L   League of Arab States

A   Organization of African Unity

E   Economic Co-operation Organization

O   Organization of Petroleum Exporting Countries (OPEC)

C   The Commonwealth

R   Commonwealth of Independent States (ex-USSR)

T   Turkey is a member of the North Atlantic Treaty Organization (NATO), the Organization for Economic Co-operation and Development (OECD), and is an Associate Member of the European Union (EU).

N   Non-Aligned Movement.

At this level the main division is between a large area where Islam appears to be dominant and the rest of the world where Muslims form outlying communities. Some of these outliers are large: India has a 'minority' far in excess of 100 million Muslims. Across the world the mosaic of post-colonial boundaries leaves groups as minorities. Many Muslims in Indian-controlled Kashmir are demanding to be included in an Islamic state, just as many non-Muslims in Islamic Sudan would prefer not to be ruled from Khartoum. There is a spatial mis-match between the pattern of distribution of Muslims and the mosaic of political states within which they live.

No such political/spatial fragmentation was part of the initial message of Islam in the seventh century AD. Islam *was* (and *is*) one space in terms of all aspects of Muslim life, including that of being governed. Government, law and sovereignty derived from God, as did other aspects of people's lives. Since it was necessary to have structures of government, there were rulers but they were required to rule for God rather than for the secular interests of

Dar ul-Islam
Dar ul-Harb

states. This traditional Islamic view of government is relevant, even though all Muslims nowadays live within the boundaries of political states, because it influences views which Muslims hold about states and about how they should be governed. Also relevant is the Islamic distinction between the 'Realm of Islam' *(Dar ul-Islam)*, and the 'Realm of Conflict' *(Dar ul-Harb)* which is the 'zone beyond' where Muslims constitute outlying groups under non-Islamic rule (Parvin and Somner, 1980). Britain's Muslim community is one example of this.

However, present-day Muslims live within a mosiac of fifty states, showing unevenness of territorial size, population and resources (see Figure 4.1 and Table 4.1) The largest Islamic country is Indonesia with 175 million Muslims and the smallest is the island republic of Maldives with 200,000. Most Muslims live in south and south-east Asia compared with the relatively smaller numbers who live in the Middle East, the place of origin of the faith. Second in size, with Muslim populations near the 120 million mark are Pakistan and Bangladesh although, as we have seen, a similar number form a minority in India. Egypt, Iran and Turkey have between 60 and 65 million Muslims each and a similar number live in Nigeria where they are thought narrowly to outnumber non-Muslims. A number of Islamic countries have nearly 100 per cent Muslim populations. Most of the states of Arabia and north Africa fall into this category. But still more have substantial non-Muslim minorities – for example, Malaysia, Sudan, Ethiopia, Lebanon, and some of the republics of central Asia (Table 4.1).

The Islamic realm varies from the Balkans (for example, Albania) and the Mediterranean (Morocco, Libya, etc.) to tropical mainland Africa (Guinea and Djibouti) and island states in the Indian Ocean (for example, Comoros). In Asia the range is from interior upland Tajikistan and Afghanistan to crowded states of the tropical coasts (Bangladesh, Brunei). Islamic states vary in resources as much as in size. Some are rich in minerals (for example, Malaysia, Turkey), others not (Chad, Somalia). Richest of all are some of the smallest Muslim states where there are major deposits of oil (Qatar, Kuwait). Within states this pattern of unevenness extends to disparities between class and ethnic groups and between town and country.

Activity 2 The following questions draw your attention to some of the variety and experience of Islamic states.

Using the data in Table 4.1 and Figure 4.1, try to answer the following questions:

1 Which four countries have the largest Muslim populations?

2 Give (approximately) the total population of all Arab countries: state the number of Arab countries and their location on the world map.

3 Using GNP (gross national product) per capita as an indicator, identify on the map where the six 'richest' Islamic countries are and where the six poorest are.

4 In which decade did the largest number of Islamic states achieve political independence?

5 From the data in Table 4.1, can you suggest a ranking of the one-time imperial powers in terms of their involvement in the Islamic world?

(Table 4.1 and Figure 4.1 aim to show you the scale and variety of the Islamic world. You are not expected to memorize detail.)

4.3.2   Cultural patterns

Islam emerged in what is now Saudi Arabia in the early part of the seventh century AD and spread rapidly into areas to the east and south of the Mediterranean. Expansion into the rest of Asia was slower, while in a few areas, such as the Iberian Peninsula, the spread of Islam was subsequently reversed. In each case there was a fusion of pre-existing cultures with that brought by incoming Muslims, producing a pattern of fragmentation centuries ahead of the new wave of division in response to Western interference. In some cases early converts to Islam adopted the language of the Arabs who brought the faith from Arabia, but in most of the world Muslims retain local tongues and regard Arabic as having a special status as the language of the Qur'an.

To such contrasts from place to place across the Islamic realm was added the divisiveness of European colonialism. Strangely perhaps, the first major colonial penetration into Muslim lands was in places most distant from Europe – the East Indies – and the most recent was into North Africa, central Asia and the Fertile Crescent. The principal European intruders were Britain, France, the Netherlands and Russia, lesser ones were Italy and Spain. Since 1971 formal European control has gone from almost all Muslim territories although large – and, in some cases, increasing – populations of Muslims remain outside the now independent Islamic states (Table 4.2).

As well as their language, system of administration, and demands on local populations and resources, the Europeans took ideas to their Islamic territories. The resulting impact tended to divide even neighbouring Muslim countries from one another so that, for example, ties might develop between France and the Ivory Coast and between Britain and the Gold Coast (Ghana) more effectively than between these two neighbouring territories in West Africa. The extent and character of the European impact depended on the duration of the colonial stay: the British, for example, occupied parts of south Asia for two centuries but Iraq and Jordan for little more than two decades. The Dutch ruled much of what became Indonesia for centuries but the Italians held Eritrea and Somalia only briefly this century. The impact also varied in purpose. If Britain's penetration into what had been the Muslim Mogul Empire in India was imperialism in some grand sense, Dutch moves into the East Indies were more straightforwardly commercial. By contrast, the United Kingdom's hold on Aden (Yemen) and on Egypt's Suez Canal were matters of strategic benefit to the British Empire, while Italy's brief colonial forays into Africa had a lot to do with that European country's wish simply to join the 'top table' of European imperialism.

Another cultural feature has to do with Islam itself and not with intruders from outside. As in Christianity, there are sects, orders and other distinctive traditions within Islam, the origins of which can be found in past splits and local factors. Over 80 per cent of Muslims identify with the *Sunni* tradition of Islam, while the second most numerous sect is that of the *Shi'a*, who constitute the ruling group in Iran today, but are also found elsewhere, notably in parts of Iraq, Lebanon and Yemen. To these major sects can be added numerically very small groups which can be distinguished by either their strictness, fundamentalism or mysticism. Such divisions within Islam add another basis for differentiation between Muslims in different places. One result of this is that different groups of Muslims see things in different ways.

Generally speaking, the European presence was felt most by those who worked with or for the outsiders in commerce, government, education or the military. Such people tended to be urban rather than rural and men rather than women. Where the colonial presence was short-lived, the social divisiveness might be limited to the European language being learned by a small section of society. Where the stay was longer, as in 'French' Algeria or 'British' India, local people had a chance to gain substantial insights into the alien culture – even to the extent where some local Muslims came to develop a sense of identity with both their indigenous *and* imposed cultures. This made it possible for some Algerians and some Muslim Indians to immerse

Table 4.2 Islam and types of European colonialism

	Pre-colonial	Date of colonization	Colonial	Date of independence	Post-colonial	Muslim population* (millions)	Examples
Long-term colonial	Competitive European involvement • plunder • trade	17th century	• conquest • control • investment	1957	• investment • multinationals	402	Indonesia (resource-rich; large population)
Arab world	Limited European involvement Ottoman Empire	1830	• settlement (e.g. Algeria) • oil (e.g. Iraq) • strategic (e.g. Yemen)	1971	• oil money • rapid industrial modernization	210	Qatar (oil-rich; small population) Egypt (oil-poor; large population)
Black Africa	Competitive European involvement • slavery • trade, forts, missions	c.1870	Competitive European involvement • raw materials • imperial prestige	1965	Continuing dependence • primary products • multinationals	137	Nigeria (resource-rich; large population) Chad (resource-poor; small population)
Central Asia	Limited European involvement	c.1840	Conquest • Russification	1991	• re-alignments • continuing links with Russia	44	Uzbekistan (mixed resources; Turkic) Tajikistan (agricultural; Iranic)
Non-colonial	Limited European involvement		Informal colonialism		Varying reactions • investment • multinationals	132	Turkey (secular; pro-West) Iran (Shi'ite; anti-West)

Note: *1994 estimates.

themselves in the understanding of the language and ideas of their rulers, possibly even more effectively than in their own culture.

Since political independence from direct European rule, Muslims (like other ex-colonial subjects) have had more freedom to choose their models for thought and action. But the types of legacy noted here combine to generate an inertia to maintain earlier contacts. This is specially true where languages have been learned and administrative and other procedures absorbed. Hence the paradox that while West-led modernization, during and since the colonial period, has created unevenness and divisions between places and among affected people, it has also spread a worldwide political structure based upon the state and upon 'universal' human rights (Modelski, 1972). In other words, there has been both differentiation *and* standardization. This *uneven globalization* is examined in the next section from Islamic and Western perspectives.

Summary of section 4.3

o   Muslim people occupy a vast part of the earth's surface, larger indeed than the combined areas of the states which identify themselves as Islamic. Several factors combine to make the 'Islamic world' uneven – fragmented spatially and culturally.

o   At the same time, however, Islam as a tradition offers a unity of teaching and religious practice. Islam existed before there were modern states and continues as a potential alternative focus for allegiance. Islam, to this extent, works against fragmentation: it draws Muslims together – but as Muslims or as nationals of states?

4.4   Perspectives on globalization

4.4.1   Images and realities

The European-type state (see Chapter 1) which is now dominant throughout the world possesses precisely defined territory and authority, both of which assume that possession of such a state resides with its people. The central element in this model is the notion that places and areas – that is, land and, by extension, property of various kinds – are owned by individuals, either in the sense of personal property or the wider notion of shared possession of the national property. Thus, today we have a world political mosaic defined in terms of European views of the state as these have emerged during the centuries when Europeans have been in a position to export their model. The links, in this model between the individual and the state and between the individual and property, have come to be seen as good, as modern, and as progressive. Non-European images and ideals about how things should be can be dismissed as 'pre-modern' or even primitive. When Europeans have had the power to disregard the procedures of others, they have been able to establish a 'European' system as if in a vacuum. When Europeans have found political structures with which they could at least identify, there has often been compromise with local interests adapted to suit those of the imperial power. On this basis, elements of pre-colonial political systems have survived in parts of Asia and Africa into the present period of political detachment from Europe. Pre-colonial monarchies, for example, have survived in Morocco, Nigeria and Malaysia.

The twentieth century has seen the steady disengagement of Europeans from the formal political control of other parts of the world and the re-assertion of links within the continent itself. A Europe has emerged which is not dominated by mutually competitive colonial powers (though the legacy of those eras remain) but is spending the last years of the twentieth century attempting to harmonize intra-Europe ties, making it possible to see Europe as an ascending multi-state force (see Chapter 3). The European Union shares its 'first world' status with the United States and Japan, while there are prospects of other superstates, such as China and India, emerging. Smaller countries, without the size or resource base for individual front-rank status, may attempt 'safe-haven arrangements' within expanding multi-state blocs (see Chapter 3). Can Islam be the basis of such a bloc or can it operate politically as a transnational force to undermine existing arrangements? Some discussion of mutual images can be a start towards answering this question.

4.4.2   The Euro-view of Islam

The view of Islam from the West is dominated, firstly, by the experience of European colonial rule over Muslim (among other) areas and, secondly, going back before the Crusades, by Europe's largely Christianity-based feelings of competition with Islam (Daniel, 1993). Thirdly, in the contemporary, post-colonial phase there is an uncertainty about Islam which is seen variously as an anachronism or a threat. Perhaps the very geographical proximity of Islam to Christendom in earlier times contributed to European feelings of distrust in ways not seen in respect of Hinduism, Buddhism and other faiths and cultures far enough away to be ignored. After its rise in the seventh century AD, Islam split the Mediterranean into Muslim south and Christian north shores, though Islam did not finally replace the Byzantine inheritors of Greece and Rome in what is now Turkey until the fifteenth century. It has long been supposed that Islam 'blocked' the landward route east across Asia to the Orient and thus contributed to the early efforts by Portuguese and other European sailors to find another route to the East. Significantly it was the East that was the target, rather than the Muslim lands in-between. The notion that Muslims really wanted to bar Europeans from trade-routes across Asia may have limited foundation in fact, but it was certainly characteristic of the 'them-and-us' view of Europeans who saw Islam as delimiting Christendom. Here is the origin of European views of the 'Orient', as mysterious if not menacing.

Rose (1995) in discussing Western views of the 'Orient' – that is the Middle East and North Africa – draws on the work of Edward Said, a Palestinian, who catches the essence of Orientalism when he notes that, 'On June 13, 1910, Arthur James Balfour lectured the House of Commons on "the problems with which we have to deal in Egypt". These, said Balfour, "belong to a wholly different category" than those "affecting the Isle of Wight or the West Riding of Yorkshire"' (Said, 1978, p. 31). What is 'Orientalist' here is the notion that problems in Egypt have to be dealt with in London. No true Orientalist would dream that Cairo should concern itself with circumstances within Britain – and should 'problems' in Egypt be problems for British outsiders rather than for Egyptians?

Sometimes Orientalist approaches were benign – to preserve that which was supposed to be exotic – rather than the pragmatic needs of Balfour and Cromer who wanted to rule a worldwide empire from London. **Rose (1995)** refers to the romanticized view of the Orient, much of it judged in terms of perceived European Christian analogues.

In the European mind that which is more different is more significant. Many Europeans see the 'outmoded' reliance on the Qur'an as the basis of law in Saudi Arabia but fail to notice secular Turkey. Many are quick to make judgements about restrictions on Muslim women, overlooking the fact that women have been prime ministers in Turkey and Pakistan. The variety and unevenness of the Islamic realm is collapsed into placing stress onto those visible features which are most 'un-European'. 'Modern' Islam is that which looks most Western and traditional Islam is that which seems to be most alien. Taken to an extreme, alien Islam can become the new great threat to the West, replacing that of Soviet communism. Between the extremes are fundamentalists, vehemently Islamic people who become fanatics if they challenge Western interests and terrorists if they oppose them violently.

The Muslim communities now established in Western Europe arouse concern if they do not learn the local language and dress and behave as Europeans. It rarely occurred to Europeans living in Islamic lands in colonial times to act like Muslims because they were there as rulers or, at least, as people in command. In such ways can power relationships contribute to uneven development. For their part, British Muslims see inconsistencies around them: for example, they do not receive support for Islamic schools from the British state – which provides help for sectarian schools run by Roman Catholics, Jews and others. When Muslims burned copies of *The Satanic Verses* by Salman Rushdie in 1988 because, they said, it contained blasphemy, they found that Britain's laws covering blasphemy related only to Christianity. Rushdie, they pointed out, had the 'freedom of speech' in English law to blaspheme against the Prophet Mohammad.

The *fatwa* from Iran's Islamic leadership condemning Salman Rushdie, a British citizen, did much to sharpen the focus on the Islamic 'other' *within* the United Kingdom. A Muslim in some distant land was calling for the death of someone 'here' in a threatening international, intra-Islamic link between 'the Other' non-Western world and Britain itself. Muslims in Britain were not a new development. What seemed to matter in the Rushdie case was the element of interference in the UK where, at worst, Britain's Muslim population became a potential fifth column with an agenda in which freedom of speech (for example, writing *The Satanic Verses*) was to be called into question.

Yet Muslims had been established in Britain for some time. Communities of Yemeni Arabs have, for example, been established in north-east England and elsewhere for several generations. The Yemenis, though Muslims to the wider British public, have been differentiated from others of their faith by their history, and by local loyalties and experiences.

Activity 4 At this point you should look at Reading B, an extract from Fred Halliday's (1992) book, *Arabs in Exile*. As you read:

(a) Look for implications of linkages and of unevenness within the group and for transnational connections.

(b) Consider the picture given by Halliday in terms of the notion of hybrid cultural development (compare **Hall, 1995**).

The Yemeni Arab Muslims studied by Halliday constitute a small part of an Islamic community in Western Europe numbering nearly eight million. In France, as in Britain, Germany and elsewhere, the politicization of concerns about Muslim immigrants appeared as early as 1970.

Activity 5 Now read Reading C, 'The age of migration' by Stephen Castles and Mark Miller in which they assess the problems of integration into France of Muslims, mostly from ex-French North Africa.

4.4.3 The view from Islam

Images of Europe or, more widely, of the West held by Muslims seeking to fund Muslim schools in Bradford vary greatly from the images held by Muslims who have had little or no direct contact with Europeans. Such images further vary by sect, educational attainment, age, gender, and so on. But there are some general themes common to all the images. One is due to all Islamic lands having, directly or indirectly, come under European control in recent times. All Muslims share a sense of this legacy of occupation which is found throughout the post-colonial world. Muslims are conscious of the extent to which West-led modernization has made inroads – unevenly – into their cultural priorities and into the ways in which they organize their lives (Ahmed and Donnan, 1994; Al-Azmeh, 1993). Some Muslims – notably the so-called fundamentalists – now seek to reject what they see as alien, as Western, as 'modern', even as Christian, and to redefine intercultural boundaries. Others have accommodated to Western and European institutions and ideas.

The Islamic view of the West is evidently an uneven one, moulded in different settings by local legacies, colonial contacts and present-day issues and continuing economic dependence. A common theme is one of Islamic resurgence or the reaffirmation of the non-Western identities of most Muslims. Since the state pattern within which such an Islamic dimension operates is part of the West-led world system, some of the resurgence is directed at questioning why Muslim states are as they are now.

Activity 6 Turn now to Reading D, 'The word of Islam' by John Alden Williams, noting in particular how he develops the notion that the Islamic resurgence includes the rejection of Western models – such as state models – and that Islamic resurgence is thus both reactive and proactive.

It is worth noting in passing in this discussion that the status of Europe and of the United States is a matter for distinction from the viewpoint of Islam. Europe is the closer part of the 'West' to Muslims and has longer links with

Modern Islam – two Muslim women at a bus-stop in Bradford

Islam. Though it was not among the imperial powers of Europe, the United States has acquired a neo-colonial image, most notably as a result of its support for Israeli occupation of the Holy Land but also, more generally, for its apparent support for some illiberal regimes in the interests of 'stability'. At the level of Islam and the West, it is recognized that the USA has become the leading power, especially since the collapse of the Soviet Union in 1991. In one sense, however, it makes little difference to Muslims that the leadership of the West has moved across the Atlantic to Washington. In either location the centre of world power was, and is, outside the Islamic realm. The view of the wider 'West' varies importantly from Muslim country to Muslim country and within national societies. At worst, Muslim accommodators, who work with or are supported by the West, are seen as traitors by those within their own state systems who argue for the rejection of non-Islamic forms and procedures. We shall look at some examples of the translation of competing Islamic images into conflict in the next section.

Muslim 'rejectionists' are quick to put 'Christian' labels on Western influences which they oppose, though labelling works equally in the other direction. For example, opponents of Israel's expansion in Palestine become (Muslim) fundamentalist fanatics according to Western labels. They may even be said to be anti-Jewish, although they would have opposed the loss of control of the Islamic (as well as Christian and Jewish) Holy Land to any invading group irrespective of its religious complexion.

Reference to the Holy Land underscores another spatial aspect of the social construction of images of place. Notions of 'this land is our land' become powerfully strengthened when place has some central religious significance. The pre-eminent example is, of course, the city of Jerusalem, holy to more than one culture. Muslims who aim to re-assert Islam as the basis of human – including political – organization view the loss of Jerusalem (to Israeli occupation and annexation) in a way quite different from their feelings about other territory – even territory in Palestine. If anything about representations of places and spaces is certain it must be that few Muslims would be able to come to terms with the indefinite loss of Islamic control of sacred sites such as the Dome of the Rock in (East) Jerusalem. That Israel's policy is to retain its own control of Jewish holy places – such as the Western Wailing Wall which lies *beneath* the Dome of the Rock – underlines the basis for conflict at such points.

Summary of section 4.4

o Islam is unlikely to become the basis of a multi-state bloc because international links which are most important to Islamic states continue to be with non-Islamic, Western states.

o Islam is, however, likely to be influential politically as a transnational force precisely because it links Muslims in a way which is non-state, supra-state and pre-state.

o Muslims now constitute substantial minorities in many countries – including some in the West – which raises questions about the extent to which they will be assimilated or will continue to be identified with 'the Other' (world of Islam).

4.5 Anti-global Islam?

Islam is evidently universal as a cultural prescription though Muslims recognize the divide between the 'realms' of Islam and that which lies 'beyond' (that is the *Other* from the standpoint of Islam). We have seen that the Islamic reality is one of unevenness from place to place brought about by local contrasts and by varied influences from outside. And it seems that Islam does not undermine the present state system, however much some Muslims proclaim that it should. Nevertheless this does not rule out the prospect that Islam might tend to undermine the state system in future through transnational links and realignments.

4.5.1 Islam and states

Chapter 2 looked at threats to the state system to fragment and divide rather than to unify and to combine. Our discussion of images of, and from, Islam suggests that unevenness across the Islamic world is of such a level that there is no realistic prospect of any change other than further sub-division.

We can usefully return to the paradox that globalization has *both* created divisions from place to place and within societies *and* has spread the uniformity of notions such as that of the central role of the 'sovereign' state and the common rights of individuals (Modelski, 1972, chapter 3). One outcome of this paradox is that where Muslims make demands for modern (or Western) treatment, they have to direct their demands to state authorities within a state system which is West-derived anyway. So there are possibilities for fragmentation to occur at both state and sub-state levels.

In 1923 the then new Republic of Turkey, led by Mustafa Kemal Ataturk, made a state-level decision to break with the Islamic orientation of the country up to that time. The Sultan of the previous Ottoman Empire had been also Caliph (central religious figure) of Islam until the role was abolished by republican Turks (in 1924). Behind this re-orientation by the newly defined Turkish state was the decision by its then leadership that the best interests for the future of the country lay in *joining* the non-Islamic West (Toprak, 1981). For Ataturk, Western progress was the model which could work for Turkey – because his image of Turkey's future was of a 'European' country. His government set in train reforms to displace Islam as the framework for state operation. In fact, Islam in Turkey became a department of government for operational purposes and *secularism* was established as a central ingredient of the state. Arguably, this reform has been accepted by most Turks, though Islamic opposition – even to some of Ataturk's reforms – has increased during the 1990s (Öğütçü, 1994).

secularism

In neighbouring Iran, in 1979, a quite different change of direction took place when the Islamic religious leader Ayatollah Khomeini led a revolt which replaced the monarchy with an 'Islamic Republic'. The revolution, which was inspired by the back-to-Islam message from the Ayatollah, set out to undo what it saw as changes away from strictly Islamic forms which had been introduced, in the name of modernization (that is Westernization), by the Shah. The extent of the change was as clear cut as that in Turkey in the sense that the retreat of the Shah brought to an end two and a half millennia of Persian monarchy. The reaction of Western states was one of dismay that the clock of progress (that is Westernization) seemed to have been turned back. Brutal behaviour by Iranian authorities towards certain groups and individuals confirmed suspicions in Europe and the United States that 'fundamental', 'fanatical' Islam had taken over control of the state in Tehran.

Activity 7 Reading E by Peter Beyer is on the 1979 Islamic Revolution in Iran and looks at it in the context of globalization today. What seem to be the distinctive Iranian (or Persian) features of the case and which aspects appear to have a more widespread resonance across the Islamic world today? How far was Khomeini's Revolution about struggle for influence over Iran's pattern of modernization between Shi'a Islam and the Shah's West-supported monarchy? And how far was it about a wider struggle between Islam and the West?

Egypt is one of those predominantly Islamic countries internally divided to the extent that a 'rejectionist' Islamic element opposes the state leadership because it is seen as accommodating – at the expense of Islam – to a West-led state system. The origins of such a movement in the name of Islam go back to the opposition from the Muslim Brotherhood which emerged when Britain ruled in Cairo. Egypt's establishment might see itself as pro-Egypt rather than pro-West, but in fact their patriotism is couched in national, rather than in Islam-first, terms. The bitterness of rejectionists has been directed in a general way against the spread of un-Islamic culture within Egypt and, more specifically, towards major social problems such as poverty and unemployment and towards the problem of the Holy Land. 'Rejectionists', for example, regard their country's treaty with Israel in 1979 as a sell-out by the ruling establishment in Cairo in return for immense financial subventions from the United States (seen as having bought off Egypt as part of US support for Israel).

In Algeria an election scheduled for 1992 was abandoned in face of the prospect of a victory by the Islamic Salvation Front (FIS). Initial relief in Western capitals at the removal of the 'threat' of a stridently Islamic government in Algiers gave way to dismay at the growing violence in the country. The campaign by FIS against their secular rulers seemed, by 1994, likely to develop into another bloody 'liberation' struggle reminiscent of that which led to the end of French rule in Algeria in 1962. Inevitably, growing numbers within the Algerian establishment saw scant hope for a political solution without great suffering and destruction. Inevitably, too, a developing struggle in Algeria could spill over into France which has Western Europe's largest Muslim community – mostly from Algeria. Within Algeria the non-Arab Berber people feel they might be caught between Islamists and the government. Berbers hope for at least a sort of neutrality which might keep violence out of the areas where they are concentrated.

Sudan, within the 'colonial' boundaries it has had since independence in 1956, has a Muslim north and a non-Muslim south. The political capital of the state, Khartoum, lies in the Muslim Arab north which accounts for a majority of the country's population. Many southern Sudanese are Christians, as a result of missionary activity during the colonial period. There has been continuing struggle, between southerners who reject the political expression of Islam in 'their' area of the country and those northerners for whom the state – all of it – should be Islamic.

The basis for conflict and fragmentation of this sort lies in the location of Sudan across the divide between Muslim-majority and Muslim-minority space but with control of the whole state area effectively handed over to a post-colonial government in the north. Potential for conflict involving Muslims and non-Muslims exists in several other states on the Islamic borders. Examples are Kazakhstan (Russian minority) and Nigeria (Muslim north and Christian south). Lebanon is one Arab country where Muslim–Christian tension has exploded into a destructive civil war in recent times; Bosnia is a European example.

4.5.2 Nationalism versus religion

There can be conflict between Muslim groups as readily as between Muslim and non-Muslim ones. In both cases it appears that it is nationalism – as the expression of group identity with territory within the state system – which is stronger than religion as a demarcator of allegiance. Thus conflicts within Sudan or Lebanon – or in Bosnia or Ethiopia – arose *not* because one of the 'sides' in each of those cases was Muslim but because there were two (or more) groups in search of some form of territorially based independence. In this sense the 'Orientalist' view from the West of the Islamic world is unhelpful in understanding conflict. It asserts that Islam is central in the – political – lives of (correct) Muslims and that Islam and political power occupy the same socially constructed space. The contrary view is that Muslims, however devout, demand improved material well-being and political rights from the governments of the states in which they live. If such articulation of demands by Muslims is expressed in terms familiar in the 'West', so can be the secular reaction to them. State authorities may seek to suppress 'fanatic' and 'fundamentalist' Islamic movements for the same

Modern Islam – a man prays in the hall of Algiers airport. On the wall is a picture of a petro-chemical plant

189

reasons that they would suppress secular or separatist elements – that they threaten the integrity, including the spatial/geographical integrity, of the state.

In the context of the suppression of dissent one group may benefit from efforts by the state to weaken rivals. In Iran during the last years of the monarchy prior to the 1979 Islamic Revolution in that country, it seems that the very success of the Shah's government in suppressing 'left-wing' elements (among urban intellectuals, including university students) and in weakening traditional tribal power centres (for example that of the Qashqai in Fars Province) made it easier for Islamic forces to seize power in Tehran. To many onlookers, the revolution in Iran came as no surprise. What was surprising was that the take-over was in terms of Islam rather than of the secular opposition which had been far more visible in the run-up to the overthrow of the monarch and his pro-West system.

The evidence is that Islam, as a faith and culture, *can* be a basis for questioning the state pattern. In other words, Muslims can be as effective as other groups in fragmenting the states in which they find themselves. But Muslims seem, in these terms, to operate much as other groups, even to the extent that Muslim groups may compete with each other in efforts to de-stabilize and break up state patterns. However, while Muslim groups compete for change alongside other Muslim and non-Muslim groups, there *is* a transnational dimension to Islam which, arguably, could make it a force for both fragmentation and consolidation in the globalizing state system. In other words, the pattern of Islamic unevenness is likely to be changed, at different levels, by new groupings of states sharing a perceived Islamic national character *and* by the increasing importance of transnational Islamic movements possibly threatening *both* Islamic state structures *and* the perceived interests of the West. The question of whether there can be any Islamic alternative in a global sense if reaction is on a state-by-state or class-by-class basis leads into the final section of this chapter.

Summary of section 4.5

o   States within the Muslim world have made, and continue to make, different accommodations with the West-led state system. The range is from Saudi Arabia, which remains formally Islamic in law and in economic and social practice, to Turkey which has accepted a Western state structure in which Islam has no formal role.

o   Both nationalism, in Western state-centred terms, *and* Islam figure – and may compete – within states with Muslim majorities. In other words, the balance between Western and Islamic options *within* states divides them internally.

4.6   Global Islam?

4.6.1   Muslim unity

The answer to the question as to whether a faith such as Islam can constitute an alternative means of mobilization of global order seems to be 'not much', given the extent of continuing Western influence in the Islamic world. Muslim states go to war with each other or join alliances with non-Muslim powers against other Islamic states. Some states base their law on the Qur'an; others effectively disestablish Islam. Islamic states find it hard to make common political cause. Yet enough people proclaim Islam as a link for us to look more closely at the extent to which the faith can be a transnational force, either as a sort of cultural multinational corporation or as a more loosely structured 'grass roots' movement.

Islam has a comprehensive self-image as a basis for political – and all other – organization. Unlike Western paradigms of political order, such as Marxism or Liberalism, however, Islam is founded not in notions of human rights but in the word of God. Its teachings derive not from principles of equality between people – expressed in demand for 'justice' and 'basic standards' due, ideally, to all people – but to a statement of world order prescribed by God through the Qur'an and through the teachings of God's Messenger, Mohammad. Yet Muslims learn non-Islamic views of themselves and of their cultural and material environment within the state system which now organizes the world politically in ways which emerged in Europe.

One feature of the universalist character of Islam deserves special mention. This is the concept of *ummah* which is the recognition of a bond linking   *ummah*
Muslims everywhere and even over all time. There is no equivalent in Christianity to the sense of 'togetherness' implied in *ummah*. It is possible to see this sense of relationship when Muslims identify with fellow Muslims (as, for example, in Bosnia from 1993) and empathize with their sufferings in terms of the perceived Islamic link. The sympathy of Western Christians for their co-religionists suffering in Israeli-occupied areas or in southern Sudan lack the kind of specifically religious bond exemplified by the *ummah* for Muslims.

But the perception of *ummah* among the world's billion Muslims varies (partly as a consequence of Western influence), as does their view of the practical reality of their faith more generally. This produces the evolving pattern of spatial and social unevenness. Such unevenness may be economic (for example, oil-rich or oil-poor) or political (compare 'traditional' Saudi Arabia and 'Westernized' Turkey) and it may differentiate individuals by gender, age, etc. within local communities, states and wider groupings. But such changing patterns of differentiation exist within a shrinking world of intensifying consciousness (Robertson, 1992, p. 8, quoted by **Yearley, 1995**, p. 147) which produces greater complexity to the extent that 'the operation of states in an ever more complex international system both limits their autonomy and infringes ever more upon their sovereignty' (Held, 1991, p. 157). How does a culture such as that of Islam react to shrinking and complexity? And how is its reaction perceived outside the faith?

4.6.2   Islamic resurgence

How far is greater international and transnational interdependence, in the context of a more complex shrinking world, *causing* the movements which are nowadays seen by Muslims and others as demanding some expression of back-to-Islam change? Are those who angrily call for reform demanding that West-led globalization must accommodate 'other' cultures such as Islam or are they calling for the replacement of that Western system by another which existed previously or is at least 'Islamic' in terms which make sense to Muslims? So insistent is much of the resurgent opposition in the name of Islam that inevitably it seems to threaten the West and its clients.

The perceived Islamic threat may have at its foundation the historic clash that took place between Europe as Christendom and Arab, later Ottoman Turkish, power which was Islamic. In the millennium of Arab and Ottoman power, their threat to Europe was both physical – in South and Central Europe – as well as intellectual–ideological, or rather Islamic. With Ottoman power on the wane, the potential threatening influence of Islam receded. At the close of the twentieth century, however, there has been a revival of the idea of an Islamic threat. Exactly what constitutes this threat is not obvious. The form it has taken is multifarious.

(Roberson, 1994, p. 290)

Present-day concern about an Islamic threat dates from the 1979 Revolution in Iran when a pro-West monarch, Shah Mohammad Reza, was replaced by an Islamic Republic under Ayatollah Khomeini. But:

Although revolutionary Iran was said to threaten regional security, the aspirations of Ayatollah Khomeini, when one abstracts the excesses of revolutionary rhetoric and places ambitions in the context of capabilities, do not differ greatly from the aspirations and ambitions of the shah; it has been argued that the shah wanted to make Iran a regional superpower. The United States, however, viewed the shah's aspirations and capabilities as compatible with US global strategy, but the Islamic Republic of Iran has been regarded as a threat to regional order and Western interests. While Islam formerly was viewed in the West as one of the ideological bulwarks against atheistic communism, in communism's absence Islam is seen as expansionist.

(Roberson, 1994, pp. 290–1)

Activity 8   John Esposito in Reading F takes the discussion further to focus on the position of the United States, within 'the West', in face of the threat posed by 'Islamic fundamentalism'. As you read, note that Esposito recognizes the reality of Islamic threats to state authorities and he points to the United States' attitude which equates extremist Muslims with Islam as a whole. Americans, he points out, do not blame all Christians for the violence of some and they do not condemn the mixing of religion and politics in Israel and elsewhere.

Thus one of the most significant features of the anger of 'fundamentalists' or other groups who claim to represent Islam is the degree to which their animosity and, increasingly, violence is directed towards governments which see themselves as Islamic (Choueiri, 1990). Tourists in a Muslim country may be attacked to weaken a government which wants the revenues from tourism, and to draw attention to the extent to which that state authority is dependent on non-Islamic, largely Western, sources of income. Muslim fundamentalism is reported in the Western media when it explodes into violence in such ways. Best reported of all may be direct violence against Western people or businesses. Attacks on state and other authorities in Islamic countries alarm Westerners because they threaten to undermine stability – defined as the status which best supports Western interests. At worst, all Muslims are seen in the West as potential fanatics provoking new Crusades by Christians to protect their interests. Fundamentalism which is not violent but stresses piety and devoutness arouses little interest.

The outcome of this enquiry into the prospect of Islam moulding new dimensions of globalization in the short- and medium-term is probably that Islamic states are moving towards increased co-operation rather than to merger and political union. But this may well be accompanied by conflict and competition between states and increasingly co-ordinated transnational – or 'grassroots' – movements in the name of Islam. Western pressures push Muslims together but cross-currents and differing wider international interests make it difficult for them to co-operate in meaningful ways.

An example of state-level co-operation is provided by the Organization of the Islamic Conference (OIC) which has held periodic meetings since 1969. This association of states which identify themselves as Islamic accepts that it is just that – a group operating within the West-led state system. It proves incapable of resolving conflict *between* Muslim states – such as that between Iraq and Kuwait before and during the Gulf War when Islamic states ranged against Baghdad found themselves subordinate to non-Muslim, Western allies (see Chapter 1). But criticism of the OIC that it is ineffectual may be unfair insofar as no grouping of any kind becomes influential simply by existing. The once-British Commonwealth is no more effective than the OIC in resolving conflict between states, members or not, but no one would expect it to be. Even the United Nations achieves change only when it is backed by powers with an interest in specific change and the means and commitment to bring it about.

There is the possibility that sub-set groupings of Muslim states may play a more important role in future in the move towards the globalization of political systems. The most obvious such grouping is that of the twenty-five Arab countries among which the Islamic connection is strengthened by a common language – and the language of the Qur'an at that (Table 4.1). Other factors, too, characterize this group, from its proximity to Europe to its most direct concern with the take-over of the Holy Land by a non-Islamic, Western-style state – Israel. For their part, the Muslim countries of the north of Africa have some basis for common interest with other states in that continent. But there are also bases for conflict in the Islamic peripheral zone across the Sahara and the Sahel where state boundaries straddle the line between the Realm of Islam and the Realm of Conflict to produce the basis for the split-state struggles seen in Sudan, Nigeria and elsewhere.

Turkey, as seen above, chose to identify with Europe and the West. Rejection of some of its advances – notably the application for membership of the European Union – has, however, contributed to Turkey's looking at other options for wider grouping and connection. One new opportunity is in central Asia and part of the Caucasus where the collapse of the Soviet Union has left a number of new and assertively Islamic states, most of them speaking Turkic languages. They may, however, prefer to link among themselves rather than with Turkey or with Iran, their revolutionary Islamic neighbour to the south which offers an Islamic dimension very different from that of Turkey.

In south-east Asia there is a variety of Islamic states, relatively remote from those of south and south-west Asia but including the biggest of all – Indonesia – along with rich but tiny Brunei and mixed Malaysia which has clear economic potential if it can resolve the challenges arising from its ethnic and cultural diversity. The prospects for an Islamic sub-set grouping in that part of the world seem less than in the other areas identified because of the 'mix' of states there.

Summary of section 4.6

o   Islam is not likely to become the basis for global political mobilization by uniting states into super-state blocs. This is because even Islam, as compelling in demands and extensive as it is, operates within – and is itself undermined by – the present state system.

o   Islam is, however, likely to gain influence as a transnational force linking elements within and between states.

o   Within Muslim states, Islam may increasingly be the 'opposition' to national, secular and pro-West establishments.

o   In states where Muslims constitute minorities, Islamic priorities are likely increasingly to figure in national politics and in links to other countries.

4.7   Conclusion

If we consider the possible future of the state system as a spectrum ranging from greater fragmentation at one end, to unity at the other, where do we locate Islamic countries as constituted today? To the extent that 'unity' implies a continuation of the logic of the West-led state system, there is likely to be greater conflict between pro-West Muslim governments and staunchly Islamic groups within them. These latter are likely to stress *international* links, certainly in terms of rhetoric but also sometimes in mutual support. But conflict over resources is likely to be as prominent as dispute over ideology. Shortage of water will lead to conflict between Muslim countries as much as between Muslim and non-Muslim. In many cases there is potential for migration stimulated by relative levels of poverty and promise. Where countries feel threatened in ways such as these they are likely to respond nationally rather than in terms of Islam.

We seem, therefore, to be concluding that Islam – with its evident diversity and unevenness – cannot mobilize a political alternative to the state system and that Islamic states are caught up within it, however much some Muslims may argue for non-Western alternatives. But the scene is more complicated than this. Islam extends over much more of the world than the territory of some fifty Islamic states and draws together substantial Muslim communities in Western as well as Islamic lands, offering the possibility of an Islamic

Traditional Islam – Muslim girls praying

'global world' alongside others (see **Allen, 1995**). Such transnational links are likely to figure prominently in the rearticulation of politics and political space discussed in Chapter 1. This rearticulation sees a state system juxtaposed with an evolving global society where political space is not only and necessarily delimited by state boundaries. The implication of this is for overlapping authority and multiple loyalties, where a transnational framework of linkages can exert influence across continuing international boundaries even though it is not constituted in a formal international sense like the European Union (see Chapter 2).

Within individual states Islam can be both unifying and divisive. Unifying in that it can be a focus for 'national unity' – where Islam is invoked to justify action (for example, Holy War) or simply to legitimize practice (for example, laws based on Islamic prescriptions). Signs are that the divisive effect of Islam within states is likely to grow as national populations split between modernizers and Islamists. One type of modernization is that which welcomes Western ways of organizing society as well as the state itself. Another is the Muslim modernizer who sees a need to reassert Islam itself in a more ideal form as the basis for social and political order. Ayatollah Khomeini led a major example of this type of modernization which, of course, looks like retrogression – the antithesis of modernization – to Westerners or to Muslims who aim at secular priorities. In Iran Khomeini's 1979 Revolution took over control of decision making. Elsewhere (for example, Egypt) conflict between secular modernizers and Islamic purists becomes a persistent part of the political culture. Even in committedly secular Turkey, there is now a growing element of reaction in the name of Islam. Evidently, despite the linkage of *ummah* uniting Muslims, different forms of nationalism, within the world pattern of unevenness, mobilize Islam differently in different state contexts. Such sub-state unevenness militates against state cohesion (see Chapters 2 and 3) as much as contrasts between states reduce prospects for multi-state co-ordination.

The variety of trends and realities in Islamic countries and in the status of Muslim communities elsewhere adds up to one aspect of the unevenness identified throughout this book. In other words, there are different responses to modernization in different places and they change over time. There may indeed be important contrasts between class or ethnic groups, or between genders and generations, as well as between those elements which are spatial as well as social. All of this seems to support the argument that Islam is unlikely to *replace* the state system as such but it leaves open the possibility of growing international and intra-national influence in the name of Islam. In other words, *culture* can provide a transnational dimension to patterns of governance – just as does the environment which is the theme of the next chapter.

References

AHMED, A. and DONNAN, H. (1994) *Islam, Globalization and Postmodernity*, London, Routledge.

ALLEN, J. (1995) 'Global worlds', in Allen and Massey (eds) (1995).

ALLEN, J. and HAMNETT, C. (EDS) (1995) *A Shrinking World? Global Unevenness and Inequality*, Oxford, Oxford University Press in association with The Open University (Volume 2 in this series).

ALLEN, J. and MASSEY, D. (EDS) (1995) *Geographical Worlds*, Oxford, Oxford University Press in association with The Open University (Volume 1 in this series).

AL-AZMEH, A. (1993) *Islam and Modernities*, London, Verso.

BEYER, P. (1994) *Religion and Globalization*, London, Sage.

CASTLES, S. and MILLER, M.J. (1993) *The Age of Migration: International Population Movements in the Modern World*, Basingstoke and London, Macmillan.

CHOUEIRI, Y.M. (1990) *Islamic Fundamentalism*, Boston, MA, Twayne Publishers.

DANIEL, N. (1993) *Islam and the West: The Making of an Image*, Oxford, Oneworld Publications.

ESPOSITO, J.L. (1992) *The Islamic Threat: Myth or Reality?*, Oxford and New York, Oxford University Press.

HALL, S. (1995) 'New cultures for old', in Massey and Jess (eds) (1995).

HALLIDAY, F. (1992) *Arabs in Exile: Yemenis in Urban Britain*, London and New York, I.B. Tauris.

HALLIDAY, F. (1993) 'Orientalism and its critics', *British Journal of Middle Eastern Studies*, Vol. 20, No. 2, pp. 145–63.

HELD, D. (1991) 'Democracy and the global system', in Held, D. (ed.) *Political Theory Today*, Cambridge, Polity Press.

LEVINE, G.J. (1986) 'On the geography of religion', *Transactions of the Institute of British Geography (New Series)*, Vol. 11, No. 4, pp. 428–40.

LEYSHON, A. (1995) 'Annihilating space?: the speed-up of communications', in Allen and Hamnett (eds) (1995).

MASSEY, D. (1995a) 'Imagining the world', in Allen and Massey (eds)(1995).

MASSEY, D. (1995b) 'The conceptualization of place', in Massey and Jess (eds)(1995).

MASSEY, D. and JESS, P. (EDS) (1995) *A Place in the World? Places, Cultures and Globalization*, Oxford, Oxford University Press in association with The Open University (Volume 4 in this series).

MODELSKI, G. (1972) *Principles of World Politics*, New York, Free Press.

NIELSEN, J. (1992) *Muslims in Western Europe*, Edinburgh, Edinburgh University Press.

ÖĞÜTÇÜ, M. (1994) 'Islam and the West: can Turkey bridge the gap?', *Futures*, Vol. 26, No. 8, October, pp. 811–29.

PARK, C.C. (1994) *Sacred Worlds: An Introduction to Geography and Religion*, London, Routledge.

PARVIN, M. and SOMNER, M. (1980) 'Dar al-Islam: the evolution of Muslim territoriality, and its implications for conflict resolution in the Middle East', *International Journal of Middle East Studies*, Vol. 11, No. 1, pp. 1–21.

PISCATORI, J.P. (1986) *Islam in a World of Nation States*, Cambridge, Cambridge University Press.

ROBERSON, B.A. (1994) 'Islam and Europe: an enigma or a myth?', *Middle East Journal*, Vol. 48, No. 2, pp. 288–308.

ROBERTSON, R. (1994) *Globalization: Social Theory and Global Culture*, London, Sage.

ROSE, G. (1995) 'Place and identity: a sense of place', in Massey and Jess (eds) (1995).

ROWLEY, G. (1989) 'The centrality of Islam: space, form and process', *Geo-Journal*, Vol. 18, No. 4, pp. 351–9.

SAID, E.W. (1978) *Orientalism*, London, Routledge & Kegan Paul.

SCOTT, J. (1991) *Sacred Places and Profane Spaces*, Westport, CT, Greenwood Press.

TOPRAK, B. (1981) *Islam and Political Development in Turkey*, Leiden, E.J. Brill.

VATIKIOTIS, P.J. (1991) *Islam and the State*, London, Routledge.

WILLIAMS, J. (1994) *The Word of Islam*, London, Thames and Hudson.

WORSLEY, P. (1990) 'Models of the modern world-system', *Theory, Culture and Society*, Vol. 7, pp. 83–95.

YEARLEY, S. (1995) 'Dirty connections: transnational pollution', in Allen and Hamnett (eds)(1995).

Unlike Balfour, whose theses on Orientals pretended to objective universality, Cromer spoke about Orientals specifically as what he had ruled or had to deal with, first in India, then for the twenty-five years in Egypt during which he emerged as the paramount consul-general in England's empire. Balfour's 'Orientals' are Cromer's 'subject races', which he made the topic of a long essay published in the *Edinburgh Review* in January 1908. Once again, knowledge of subject races or Orientals is what makes their management easy and profitable; knowledge gives power, more power requires more knowledge, and so on in an increasingly profitable dialectic of information and control. Cromer's notion is that England's empire will not dissolve if such things as militarism and commercial egotism at home and 'free institutions' in the colony (as opposed to British government 'according to the Code of Christian morality') are kept in check. For if, according to Cromer, logic is something 'the existence of which the Oriental is disposed altogether to ignore', the proper method of ruling is not to impose ultrascientific measures upon him or to force him bodily to accept logic. It is rather to understand his limitations and 'endeavour to find, in the contentment of the subject race, a more worthy and, it may be hoped, a stronger bond of union between the rulers and the ruled.' Lurking everywhere behind the pacification of the subject race is imperial might, more effective for its refined understanding and infrequent use than for its soldiers, brutal tax gatherers, and incontinent force. In a word, the Empire must be wise; it must temper its cupidity with selflessness, and its impatience with flexible discipline.

[...]

Cromer makes no effort to conceal that Orientals for him were always and only the human material he governed in British colonies. 'As I am only a diplomatist and an administrator, whose proper study is also man, but from the point of view of governing him', Cromer says, '... I content myself with noting the fact that somehow or other the Oriental generally acts, speaks, and thinks in a manner exactly opposite to the European.' Cromer's descriptions are of course based partly on direct observation, yet here and there he refers to orthodox Orientalist authorities [...] to support his views. To these authorities he also defers when it comes to explaining why Orientals are the way they are. He has no doubt that *any* knowledge of the Oriental will confirm his views, which, to judge from his description of the Egyptian breaking under cross-examination, find the Oriental to be guilty. The crime was that the Oriental was an Oriental, and it is an accurate sign of how commonly acceptable such a tautology was that it could be written without even an appeal to European logic or symmetry of mind. Thus any deviation from what were considered the norms of Oriental behaviour was believed to be unnatural; Cromer's last annual report from Egypt consequently proclaimed Egyptian nationalism to be an 'entirely novel idea' and 'a plant of exotic rather than of indigenous growth'.

We would be wrong, I think, to underestimate the reservoir of accredited knowledge, the codes of Orientalist orthodoxy, to which Cromer and Balfour refer everywhere in their writing and in their public policy. To say simply that Orientalism was a rationalization of colonial rule is to ignore the extent to which colonial rule was justified in advance by Orientalism, rather than after the fact. Men have always divided the world up into regions having either real or imagined distinction from each other. The absolute demarcation between East and West, which Balfour and Cromer accept with such complacency, had been years, even centuries, in the making. There were of course innumerable voyages of discovery; there were contacts through trade and war. But more than this, since the middle of the eighteenth century there had been two principal elements in the relation between East and West. One was a growing systematic knowledge in Europe about the Orient, knowledge reinforced by the colonial encounter as well as by the widespread interest in the alien and unusual, exploited by the developing sciences of ethnology, comparative anatomy, philology, and history; furthermore, to this systematic knowledge was added a sizable body of literature produced by novelists, poets, translators, and gifted travellers. The other feature of Oriental–European relations was that Europe was always in a position of strength, not to say domination. There is no way of putting this euphemistically. True, the relationship of strong to weak could be disguised or mitigated, as when Balfour acknowledged the 'greatness' of Oriental civilizations. But the essential relationship, on political, cultural, and even religious grounds, was seen – in the West, which is what concerns us here – to be one between a strong and a weak partner.

Source: Said, 1978, pp. 36–7, 39–40

Reading B: *Fred Halliday, 'Arabs in exile'*

The Yemeni migrants shared with those from Pakistan and Bengal not only their motivation in coming to Britain, the pattern of migration and settlement itself, and the working and social conditions they endured, but one further defining characteristic, namely their adherence to the Islamic religion. There is, however, a need to be cautious about invoking this as an explanatory or definitional concept, since it conceals a great deal of diversity and interlocks with other, secular, forms of identity. In much of the literature on the Islamic religion, equally in that produced by Muslims and by non-Muslims, there is a belief that 'Islam' can be treated as a single body of faith and that, more so than with Christianity, its tenets and attitudes determine the lives of those who adhere to it. 'Islam' is said to be all-encompassing and sets the outlook of those who uphold it apart from the non-Muslim world. Moreover, on the basis of this faith, Islamic migrants in Britain share a common identity, such that they can be said to be part of a 'Muslim community' in Britain[...].

There is, however, another way of looking at the relationship of migrants to Islam and it is one which, applied equally to Yemenis as to other Islamic migrants in Britain, may provide as many insights as the more conventional total view[...]. All Muslims do share certain tenets in common and in this minimal sense there can be said to be a 'Muslim community' in Britain. But, as with Christians, the unity ends there. First, there are different shades of belief and patterns of organization: between the Shi'ite merchants of Gujarati origin who came from East Africa in the 1960s and the Bengali and Pakistani migrant workers there is as much of a divide as between the Church of England and West Indian Pentacostal churches. Moreover, while all profess adherence to a single religion, their religious practice in the migrant situation is to a great extent shaped by non-religious factors, by ethnic and sub-ethnic associations. Muslim migrants all go to mosques but the places where they choose to worship are chosen on a particularist basis: as was shown in a study of Muslims in Birmingham, the thirty-odd mosques there are attended by communities defined almost entirely, and divided almost entirely, along ethnic and regional lines.

In the case of the Yemenis the same differentiations apply. The Yemenis who came to Britain were almost wholly Shafe'i Muslims from North and South Yemen and had therefore a common and distinct religious culture, not just vis-à-vis non-Muslims but within Islam itself [...]. If 'Islam' served, therefore, as in some measure a common characteristic that linked Yemenis to some other Asians, it did little to promote an integration or co-operation of the Yemenis with these others. Beyond the modicum of theological identity, ethnic and linguistic diversity prevailed.

[...]

The first distinct aspect of the Yemenis was their history. The great majority of the third world immigrants into Britain came after the Second World War: this was true of the West Indians and the South Asians of all kinds. None of these communities had existed before in any significant numbers. They came as passengers on ocean liners, and later by plane, and were employed in the new industrial openings of the post-war boom. The Yemenis, while caught up in this process, and employed in some of the industrial cities, had been in Britain since the First World War and had developed a network of residence, employment and collective organization well before these later immigrants arrived and settled [...].

The second distinctive characteristic is their shifting identity in terms of how non-Yemenis perceived them. All people, and not least migrants, have multiple identities, born of the combined characteristics of where they come from and where they settle, and of the fact that everyone has multiple determinants – of place, region, gender, race, religion, nationality, political condition, and so forth. However, the degree of identity shift on the part of the Yemenis was especially marked and significant. This can be seen from the very wide range of terms used to identify Yemenis over the eight or so decades that they were present in Britain: as lascars, coloureds, blacks, negroes, Arabs, Adenis, Mediterraneans, Muslims, Asians, South Asians, Pakistanis, Yemenis. Among themselves a different process of identification took place [...].

The fluidity of identities accounts in part for one further striking characteristic of the Yemenis, namely their invisibility. An obvious reason for this was simply that there were not that many of them: 15,000 at most compared to hundreds of thousands of West Indians and South Asians. But the invisibility of the Yemenis had other causes as well.

One was the result of the shifting identities already mentioned: most of the time there was some larger identity into which they could easily be assimilated. In most cases there was an element of

validity in this inclusion – lascars, Muslims, Arabs being cases in point. The characterization of them as 'Asians' or 'South Asians' was to some extent justifiable, but was not strictly accurate, since these geographical terms normally excluded the Middle East. The terms 'coloured', 'negro' and later 'black' were even more dubious, in that, in most political discourse, they applied to people of African or West Indian descent, although in the late 1980s the term 'black' did come to be applied to all non-whites, in particular to characterize those liable to white racist harassment. In some cases the Yemenis were simply classified in misleading residual categories – 'Mediterranean', in other words like Maltese and Cypriot, being one example. Similarly, in areas where they lived near Pakistani migrant communities, it was quite common to see Yemenis classed as Pakistanis: this was as much the case for those who, in the racist idiom of the 1980s, abused Yemenis as 'Pakis', as it was for Pakistanis themselves who had to have it explained to them by the Yemenis that they could not speak Urdu or Punjabi as their interlocutors initially supposed.

There was, however, one further reason for the invisible character of the Yemenis or, to put it more accurately, for their remaining invisible until the emergence of explicitly Yemeni community organizations in the 1980s. This was, quite simply, the feeling on the part of the Yemenis that they would benefit from being as little noticed as possible. This was one part of the process of 'incapsulation' already noted, whereby immigrant community and host society together combine to insulate the migrants from the world around them. [...]

Source: Halliday, 1992, pp. 137–42

Reading C: Stephen Castles and Mark J. Miller, 'The age of migration' _____

By 1970, Islam was the second religion of France. By 1990, it was the second religion of the French. There were perhaps six million Muslims in Western Europe by 1990, including over three million in France alone, and virtually this entire presence could be attributed to post-1945 immigration. [...]

[...]

The French reaction to Islam was both irrational and grounded in concrete immigration-related problems. The irrational dimension stemmed from the trauma of the Algerian war and the association of Islam and terrorism. In 1982, following a series of crippling strikes in major car plants in the Paris region which principally involved North African workers, French Prime Minister Mauroy insinuated that Iran was trying to destabilize French politics by backing Islamic fundamentalist groups involved in the strike (*Le Monde,* 1 February 1983). While no evidence of an Iranian involvement was produced, it was clear to all that Islamic groups were heavily involved in the strikes, with the French Communist Party and its trade union affiliate, the CGT, desperately trying to regain control of the strike move- ment [...]. Islam was seen by many French as incompatible with democracy because no distinction was made between church and state in Islam. Moreover France's Muslims were portrayed as heavily influenced by Islamic fundamentalism when, in fact, only a small minority of France's Muslims consider themselves fundamentalists and they are divided into multiple and often competitive organizations [...].

The integration problems affecting France's Islamic minority were perhaps more central to the politicization of immigration issues [...]. Immigrants, and particularly North African-origin immigrants, [disproportionately] live in inadequate housing. As settlement and family reunification proceeded, more and more immigrants applied for subsidized governmental housing, causing severe friction when numbers of immigrants grew while non-immigrant residents diminished. Before long, entire buildings came to be viewed as immigrants'

quarters. [...] By the 1980s, primarily North African Muslim-origin youths, most of whom probably were French citizens, became conspicuously involved in urban unrest that was deeply unsettling to the French.

[...]

Illustrative of the broader issue was the question of the *foulards* or Islamic headscarves worn by some young girls to school in the late 1980s. In a country where the tradition of the separation of church and state is deeply rooted and politically salient, wearing of the headscarves appeared to many French as incompatible with the very principles of the French Republic: French republican tradition prohibited the wearing of religious articles, and no exception should be made for Muslims. On the other side of the debate was the claim that the choice of wearing a headscarf was an individual's prerogative, a private matter of no consequence to public authorities. In the end, French authorities ruled in favour of the girls, but not before the question had become a *cause célèbre.* Should school cafeterias serve *halal* food, that is food prepared in accordance with Islamic ritual prescriptions? Should Muslims be granted representation in French politics – as Roman Catholics are through governmental consultations with the bishops and French Jews are through the consistory? Should factories honour Islamic holidays in addition to Catholic feast days? As Islam was affirmed, a host of long latent issues came to the fore, with major consequences for the French political system.

[...]

Despite the separation of church and state in France, many French local governments supported the construction of mosques as part of integration policy. The building of mosques was often violently opposed, and several were bombed. Other Western European governments also fostered Islam through policies which brought Islamic teachers to Western Europe. These policies usually stemmed from provisions of bilateral labour agreements which granted homeland governments a role in educating migrant children in Western Europe. Many so-called Koran schools in Germany, for example, were controlled by Islamic fundamentalists. Such institutionalization of Islam in Western Europe has probably progressed the furthest in Belgium.

Most of Western Europe's Muslims saw their religion as a private matter. The Rushdie Affair made Islamic identity more of a political problem than, say, Roman Catholicism or Protestantism. [...] Much-publicized anti-Rushdie demonstrations by Muslims in England, France and Belgium confirmed the incompatibility of Islam with Western institutions in the eyes of some critics of the Islamic presence in Western Europe. [...]

While the vast majority of Western Europe's Muslims eschewed fundamentalism, Western Europe certainly was affected by the upsurge in fundamentalism and religious piety that swept the Muslim world in the 1980s. Islamic fundamentalism often had the greatest appeal in areas beset by high unemployment, poverty, educational failure and social marginalization. The integration problems facing Western Europe's immigrants in general were most deeply felt in Islamic communities. The depth of these long-term problems virtually ensured that Islam would remain a key Western European political concern for a long time to come.

Source: Castles and Miller, 1993, pp. 239, 240–3

Reading D: John Alden Williams, 'The word of Islam'

Islam has been at least three things: it is a religion, pointing the way to human salvation; it was one of the world's great civilizations, producing art, architecture, literature, and material culture which have been the envy and admiration of the world; and it is a community which seeks for governance: a polity. Thus a resurgence in Islamic religion will necessarily be a political fact as well.

Today Islam is reasserted in the public and personal lives of Muslims in a way it has not been for many years. Their dress – especially that of women – reflects this, whether in the streets of Cairo, Istanbul, or Jakarta. Islamic banking, taxes, laws, and punishments are being introduced in many Muslim lands. Islam is reflected in politics from Morocco to Mindanao. The revival of Islamic practice involves an increased emphasis on religious identity; more faithful attendance at mosques; increased avoidance of alcohol, dancing, and gambling; the growth of new Islamic associations; and the proliferation of Islamic literature and media programmes. There is also renewed vitality in Sūfism.

Cultural authenticity in Islam today is seen as involving religious orthopraxy, and it is seen as normal to mix religion and politics, even though this may at times seem to observers to involve manipulating and controlling people.

Rulers in Muslim lands increasingly use Islam to bolster their legitimacy and justify their policies, and their opponents use it to impugn them for not being Islamic enough.

The Western world, particularly the United States, has been slow to grasp how much the world has changed. When North America was colonized in the seventeenth century, Europeans had been in direct and continuous contact with the civilization of Islam for nearly a thousand years since Muslims invaded and conquered Spain in 711. During all that time, the Muslims had usually demonstrated an easy sort of superiority over the West, in terms of seapower, productivity, trade, gracious living, science, and intellectual achievements. Western Europe could usually hold its own militarily, but it frequently lagged behind culturally. Islam was always the great challenger.

[...]

With the eighteenth century, however, Europeans began to demonstrate a growing technological and organizational edge over the Muslims. That gave Europe a great sense of confidence and optimism. The United States was born in a world in which the power of Islamic civilization appeared to be breaking down. For two hundred years, the United States was isolated from the Islamic sphere and buffered by great oceans from the world that its ancestors in Europe, Asia, and Africa knew. Islam appeared to be a spent force, politically speaking. Today no rational person could hold that view. However, US leaders have been poorly prepared to deal with the Islamic resurgence of the late twentieth century.

[...]

During the period of Western colonialism, [...] Muslim decision makers for the most part became convinced that their best hope was to modernize by imitating the West; to introduce secular law (independent of religion), parliamentary systems, Western dress, Western architecture, and Western institutions; and to emphasize nationalism rather than Islam. After World War II, this was varied occasionally with imitation of East European socialist states, because these states seemed to be successful in achieving progress and independence from Western control. In all cases, it was essentially a period of imitation, in which inspiration came from outside Muslim society.

This period came to an end in the 1967 Middle East War, in which the state of Israel, created in 1948, backed morally by the West and materially by the United States, quickly and decisively defeated its Arab neighbours (who had taken up threatening positions) in a carefully planned pre-emptive attack. Old Jerusalem with its shrines, third holiest city of Islam, was lost to Israel. The West Bank, the Gaza Strip, the Jawlān (or Golan) of Syria, and Egypt's Sinai Peninsula also fell under Israel's control.

[...]

That year, 1967, was when disillusionment with imitating the West or socialism began. It picked up speed, particularly in the 1970s. One of the events that gave the Muslim world the sense that new hope was on the horizon was the 1973 war, in which Egypt demonstrated the ability of a Muslim government to wage a modern war. It did not win, because the United States was aiding Israel politically and materially, and Israel had one of the best armies in the world in any case. But the war at least demonstrated that Muslims could fight a war with modern weapons. It was something that the world, and not least the Muslim world, needed

to learn. Moreover, the war was fought in the holy month of Ramadān, when the Muslims of the world were fasting, and it was accompanied by a great outpouring of prayer and religious devotion. Egypt's president, Anwar Sadat, portrayed the war as a Muslim struggle against oppression. Its gains seemed the answer to prayer.

Along with this went the success of the Arab oil embargo. To prevent the West from backing Israel completely in the war, the other Arab states managed successfully to deny a critical part of their oil resources to the industrialized world, dependent on these oil imports. After the war, they managed with the help of the shah of Iran to hold out for better prices for their undervalued product. This too suggested new power, new hope.

The second major event was the 1978 overthrow of the shah of Iran, a man widely regarded by the Iranian people as a cruel tyrant. The shah was backed by the American presidency, by the CIA, the US military establishment – backed, in fact, by the United States, wholly and uncritically.

[...]

The Gulf War of 1991, with its terrifying revelation of what Arabs were willing to do to 'brother Arabs', was very damaging to the idea of Arab nationalism and, to some degree, nationalism in all Muslim lands, Islamic solidarity then appears as the correct alternative.

A part of the Islamic resurgence today is the rejection of the idea that Muslims can find any satisfactory model in the Western world. Muslim attitudes toward the United States are ambivalent: they admire its material well-being and ease of existence as well as its professional ideals, but they regard it and most of the West today as a violent and bedeviled society which deserves to be pitied, not emulated; one whose people are prey to crime, promiscuity, addiction, and deep sexual confusion. They watch American television serials and know that they do not wish to be the sort of society depicted in them. Certainly economic frustration and urban alienation play their roles, attractive for neo-Marxist observers' analysis. Muslims also resent the hypocrisy and manipulation that the West has used on them, symbolized in such matters as the forcible colonization of Palestine by Europeans with the aid of the United States.

Muslims are also deeply apprehensive at the threatening and fearful image that they and their religion are often given in Western media. They fear that now that the Soviet empire no longer exists, Islam will be cast in the role of a demon by aggressive Western leaders who want an enemy in order to socially manipulate their own people.

Source: Williams, 1994, pp. 211–15

Reading E: Peter Beyer, 'The Islamic Revolution in Iran'

As an event in contemporary global society, the Iranian revolution represents an effort to give a marginal, 'third world' region greater access to the perceived material and cultural (such as prestige, recognition) benefits of globalized systems, but in such a way as to enhance the cultural particularity that hitherto has been associated with its marginalization. In other words, Iranians want to be richer, more powerful, and generally more influential through a *revitalization* of their cultural difference, not at the cost of it. It is an example of a general moment of the globalization process. In this case, movement participants have looked to religion (Twelver Shi'a Islam) both as an instrument for reaching this goal and as the name of the goal itself. Moreover, that goal has had a large this-wordly component and has been consistent with certain of the key values historically resonant with the global spread of the more prominent instrumental systems, above all, progress and equality.

Among the important things we can learn from the Iranian revolution, however, is that its religious nature, while a decisive mobilization strategy, also introduces certain characteristic difficulties. As has been the case for Latin American liberation theology, the religion involved has strong other-wordly tendencies, reflecting a high degree of functional differentiation and specialization of the religious system. This has led to a certain inner-religious tension which manifests itself in pressure to differentiate the revolutionary movement from that religious system. Correspondingly, while religious holism is precisely what makes religion suitable for framing the sort of identity question that informs the Iranian situation, it also runs counter to the fractionalization of goals attendant upon the structural dominance in global society of several functionally specialized societal systems, *including* the religious. The result of this latter consideration is that the revolution has come under pressure to differentiate its activity and translate it into the respective idioms of different systems, above all the political and legal, the economic, and the educational. That fractionalization, in turn, pushes the properly religious again in a differentiated and more privatized direction.

In the Iranian case, these theoretical predictions are particularly salient because, at least according to the victorious Khomeinists and their substantial following among the Iranian people, the revolution was to negate and reverse precisely these tendencies. Such differentation or secularization was for them at the heart of the Western imperial threat. This was the evil that wished to obliterate Islam. Accordingly, the Khomeinists took a fairly consistently conservative religious direction. They emphasized the preservation of what they saw as the received 'fundamentals' of their Shi'a tradition, insisting that these must guide the formulation of solutions to contemporary problems. Everything that happens in society was to be judged according to traditional religious principles and, to the extent that it was not in accord with them, proscribed. There ought to be a specifically and traditionally warranted Islamic way of doing everything. Globalized values, so central to Shariati and his followers, were to be pursued only to the extent that they were also manifestly Islamic values. Not surprisingly, this Shi'a conservatism is also religiously particularistic. Khomeini and his followers have not only rejected all other religions as at best inferior; even their pan-Islamism is so strongly coloured in traditional Twelver Shi'a idiom as to make it difficult to export to otherwise sympathetic non-Shi'is [...].

Correspondingly, for these revolutionaries, the explicit rejection of the relativizing implications of globalization meant that Iran would only be the beginning. From there, the Islamic revolution would spread to all Muslim lands and ultimately around the whole world, thereby inflicting a final defeat upon the evil that threatened them.

To a significant extent, the Khomeinists succeeded in implementing this vision, at least within Iran. As they defeated their erstwhile allies, they gradually dissolved the structures of revolutionary mobilization or absorbed them into the state power structures now firmly in their hands. One after another, the Revolutionary Council, the Islamic Republic Party, the revolutionary committees, and the Revolutionary Guard disappeared or were normalized. By the early to mid-1980s, the Islamic revolution had become the Islamic government. This was a rather different situation from the mobilizing for the overthrow of the old order. Yet with this institutionalized power now under their control, they also faced the logic of its structures and the global context in which these had developed. Implementing Islam would have to occur under these conditions.

[…]

Above, I mentioned the extent to which the victorious Khomeinists in Iran insisted on the priority of traditional Islamic values and forms over global ones. Three central manifestations of this direction of the revolution can serve here as introduction to the kinds of changes that have happened as the policies confronted the globalized context.

The first concerns governmental (political and legal) structures. The 1979 Constitution set up what one can best describe as a mixed system of government. On the one hand, one sees globally common republican items like an appointed supreme court and a popularly elected president and legislature (Majles). While these do not contradict traditional Islamic laws and precepts, they are definitely Western in origin and form. Along with the elaborate bureaucracy built up under the Pahlavi shahs, the revolutionaries evidently kept these structures because of the political/

administrative control they afforded over the country. Not to follow the dominant globalized pattern here would have been to doom the revolution and its theocratic turn to failure. [...]

A second manifestation of the Islamic priorities of the revolution was the policy of exporting the revolution, of mobilizing the Iranian people for the purpose of spreading the Islamic impulse to other Muslim countries and eventually the whole world. What we have here is a direct and conscious attack on both the propensity in global society towards [...] the relativization of particularisms, and correspondingly a clear favouring of Islamic values like martyrdom and *jihad* for the faith over secular and global values like progress, equality, and inclusion. The major although not sole occasion for putting this policy into action was, during most of the first decade of the republic, the Iran–Iraq war. [...]

The third manifestation is more of a negative one: the lack of any clear economic direction. Although there now exist in the Muslim world numerous writings proclaiming an Islamic economics, it is unclear whether this amount to more that the application of Islamic constraints on what is otherwise a modern market economy. A properly Islamic theory or mode of production and consumption seems to be missing. [...]

Turning now to the fate of these attempts at Islamization over the first decade of the republic, it is important to recall that by no means everyone in Iran has had the same conception of the goals of the revolution, or of what Islam implies. Even among the clerics in power, there was a sharp difference of opinion on such central matters as the degree of state intervention in the economy, and how aggressively the revolution should be exported. In these and similar matters, a point at issue was whether, at root, 'Islam' meant 'progress and equality' or 'received tradition'; whether the revolution was essentially a modern nationalist one with Islamic details or one that implemented received Shi'a Islam, period. For a great many Iranians, of course, it was both; that, however, only begs the question of their degree of compatibility.

Source: Beyer, 1994, pp. 174–9

Is there an Islamic threat? In one sense, yes. Just as there is a Western threat or a Judaeo-Christian threat. Islam, like Christianity and Judaism, has provided a way of life which has transformed the lives of many. At the same time some Muslims, like some Christians and Jews, have also used their religion to justify aggression and warfare, conquest and persecution in the past and today. Political Islam, like the appeal to any religion or ideology, can be effective but also dangerous. Secular ideologies have proven vulnerable to manipulation. Spreading God's will, like spreading democracy, can become a convenient excuse for imperialism, oppression, and injustice in the name of God or the state.

[...]

The reality of Muslim societies today contributes to a climate in which the influence of Islam and activist organizations on sociopolitical development will increase rather than diminish. Muslim states continue to exist in a climate of crisis in which many of their citizens experience and speak of the failure of the state and of secular forms of nationalism and socialism. Heads of state and ruling elites or classes possess tenuous legitimacy in the face of mounting disillusionment and opposition, in the expression of which Islamic activists are often the most vocal and effective. The extent to which governments in predominantly Muslim countries fail to meet the socioeconomic needs of their societies, restrict political participation, prove insensitive to the need to effectively incorporate Islam as a component in their national identity and ideology, or appear exceedingly dependent on the West, will contribute to the appeal of an Islamic political alternative.

The political strength and durability of Islamic movements and their ideological impact are reflected in a variety of ways. They have forced government changes and, where permitted, have successfully contested elections. Rulers from Morocco to Malaysia have become more Islamically sensitive and sought to co-opt religion or suppress Islamic organizations. Many have employed Islamic rhetoric and symbols more often, expanded support for Islamic mosques and schools, increased religious programming in the media, and become more attentive to public religious observance such as the fast of Ramadān or restrictions on alcohol and gambling.

When free from government repression, Islamic candidates and organizations have worked within the political system and participated in elections in Algeria, Tunisia, Turkey, Jordan, the Sudan, Egypt, Kuwait, Pakistan, and Malaysia; activists have even held cabinet-level positions in the Sudan, Pakistan, Jordan, and Malaysia. In countries such as Algeria, Tunisia, Egypt, Jordan, and Pakistan, Islamic organizations have been among the best-organized opposition forces, and are often willing to form alliances or cooperate with political parties, professional syndicates, and voluntary associations to achieve shared political and socioeconomic reforms. Islamic student organizations successfully compete in student elections in the universities and lead student strikes and demonstrations.

While the vast majority of Islamic organizations are moderate and work within the system, clandestine radical organizations that advocate the violent seizure of power to establish an Islamic state continue to exist. A minority of militant Islamic organizations with names like al-Jihad, the Party of God, Salvation from Hell, the Army of God, and the Islamic Liberation Organization will continue to resort to violence and terrorism.

[...]

American support for repressive regimes will intensify anti-Americanism, as events in the Shah's Iran, Lebanon, Nimeiri's Sudan, and the West Bank and Gaza have demonstrated. One can neither deny nor overlook the fact that there is often a strong anti-Western, and especially anti-American, sentiment among many moderates as well as radicals, secular as well as Islamic. It is manifested in a tendency to regard the United States as anti-Islamic and uncritically pro-Israeli, and to blame the ills of Muslim societies upon Western political, economic, and sociocultural influences. At the same time the double equation of 'Khomeinism' with 'Islam' and of 'violent radicalism' with 'fundamentalism' results in the assumption that Islamic movements are naturally or inherently anti-Western, thus obscuring the causes of anti-Americanism and radicalism. Movements are more often motivated by objection to specific Western policies than by cultural hostility. Differences between Western and Muslim societies can best be explained by competing political, socioeconomic, and cultural interests. US presence and policy, not a genetic hatred for Americans, is often the primary motivating force behind acts against American government, business, and military interests. American interests will best be served by policies that walk the fine line between selective, discreet, low-visibility cooperation with friendly Muslim governments, and a clear, consistent public policy concerning the rights of citizens to determine their future democratically.

The assumption that the mixing of religion and politics necessarily and inevitably leads to fantacism and extremism has been a major factor in our concluding that Islam and democracy are incompatible. Failure to differentiate between Islamic movements – between those that are moderate and those that are violent and extremist – is simplistic and counter-productive. The American government does not equate the actions of Jewish or Christian extremists leaders or groups with Judaism and Christianity as a whole. Similarly, the American government does not condemn the mixing of religion and politics in Israel, Poland, Eastern Europe, or Latin America. A comparable level of discrimination is absent when dealing with Islam. [...]

[...]

Islamic movements are indeed a challenge to the established order of things, to the presuppositons that have guided many governments and policymakers. The tendency to focus on the more Western-oriented and secular élite minority, and to transform secular predispositions into guidelines for sociopolitical development, blinded many to deeper social realities. In many Muslim societies religion remains a pervasive, though at times diffuse, social force, and popular political culture is far less secular than is often presumed. The power of an idea or belief, when coupled with the economic and political failures of established governments, was neither anticipated nor comprehensible for those more accustomed to secular isms – nationalism, socialism, communism. As a result, the shock of the Iranian Revolution and more recently the electoral strength of Islamic movements in Algeria, Tunisia, Egypt, Jordan, and the Sudan forced many to confront the unthinkable. This challenge in the name of Islam to the conventional secular worldview which has constituted our norms, is often dismissed as deviant, irrational, extremist. For liberal, secularly informed Western intellectuals, policymakers, and experts as well as many elites in the Muslim world, religion in public life necessarily constitutes a retrogressive fundamentalist threat, whether it be Muslim or Christian. For many governments in the Muslim world, whose legitimacy is tenuous and whose power is based upon coercion, the combination of 'uncontrolled democracy' and Islam is indeed a formidable threat. For Western governments, long accustomed to pragmatic alliances with regimes which. however undemocratic or repressive, were dominated by Western-oriented élites, the leap into the unknown of a potential fundamentalist government is far from attractive. As a result, the challenge of contemporary Islamic revivalism to the political and intellectual establishment is easily transformed into a threat.

Source: Esposito, 1992, pp. 205–8, 210–11

The transnational politics of the environment Chapter 5

by Steven Yearley

5.1 Introduction

5.1.1 Global warming and the range of political responses

Carbon dioxide and other 'greenhouse' gases are accumulating in the atmosphere, leading to a growing danger of unprecedented atmospheric warming – warming which could disrupt climate systems, upset agricultural production, cause catastrophic flooding and result in significant loss of natural species. Following the United Nations' Earth Summit in Rio de Janeiro in 1992, the vast majority of countries publicly accept, at least in principle, that policies need to be put in place to prevent this problem from becoming disastrous. Furthermore, these countries agree that they have to co-ordinate their responses since greenhouse gases are highly mobile so that, for example, Russian emissions can affect any other country and any other country's emissions can affect Russia. It makes no sense for countries to look only to their own interests.

But this is no easy matter. The regulation of greenhouse gas emissions goes right to the heart of domestic policies in these countries since it requires alterations to energy, transport and industrial policies. In the absence of a global authority, countries have to consent to work together. In essence, they are sovereign actors who have to bargain until an approach is agreed; then they have to rely on diplomatic pressure to ensure that others adhere to the agreement. Most countries can be relied on to approach these negotiations selfishly, wanting to secure as advantageous a deal for themselves as possible. Monitoring agreements can also be costly and countries are unlikely to want to spend more than the minimum on civil servants and scientists to check that they are sticking to the agreement. Obviously, international agreements are not new: as you know from Chapter 1 governments have long co-operated over very many issues, but this is a new issue which requires a considerable surrender of sovereignty over matters central to the business of the modern state. Accordingly, some commentators have claimed that global warming and other global environmental problems give rise to a new transnational politics of the environment.

Governments are not the only parties to these worldwide negotiations. Most obviously various supranational political entities are involved, including the United Nations (UN) and the European Union (EU). Whereas the constitutional and legal status of nation-states is long established, the standing of supranational bodies is generally much more debatable and contested, as you saw in Chapters 2 and 3 of this volume in the case of the EU. Although there are some cross-national bodies which were established expressly to deal with environmental management issues, the most significant supranational agencies have primarily economic and political objectives. All the same, as we shall see, such bodies have played an important role in proposing and brokering agreements on transnational environmental issues.

Nor are supranational bodies the only other political entities which exert an influence over the negotiations between state governments: sub-state bodies have also played a key role in responses to global warming and other transnational problems. As we shall see later on, some regional authorities and city councils have embraced the opportunity to act on international environmental problems, whether by putting pressure on their national governments or by introducing policy measures of their own.

In addition to these official political bodies, there are at least four other types of participants. First, there are pressure groups and campaign organizations such as Greenpeace which draw support from citizens of many different countries and which aim to represent common interests in the environment. Such groups can achieve levels of cross-national agreement and co-ordination which are often beyond national governments. Generally, such groups campaign for tighter controls and better enforcement, and for the wealthier countries to bear a greater share of the burden. Second, there are transnational networks of scientists (atmospheric chemists, biologists, economists and so on) working for universities, research institutes, governments and pressure groups, who offer expertise on environmental quality targets and on the mechanisms for meeting them. As global warming is a hugely complex technical matter, there is a good deal of scientific co-operation. If scientists arrive at an international consensus it is difficult for national governments to adopt a conflicting view without seeming to be guided by suspect motives. Third, there are private companies and corporations which have a transnational reach. They form hugely powerful lobbies which can directly influence the policy options of governments. Their international spread also means that, in practice, they restrict the sovereignty of governments since governments will not wish to introduce policies which may encourage companies to relocate their businesses elsewhere. The fourth category of participants comprises local groups, community associations and small-scale initiatives concerned with some aspect of policy tied to global warming, for example local afforestation projects or proposals for small-scale wind power. They can draw on global-level justifications for their local action, thus winning themselves some independence from national authorities.

5.1.2 Transnational environmental politics as an insight into globalization

Global warming has elicited political responses at a variety of levels, from the local through the national to the transnational. The example of global warming crystallizes the theme of this chapter, whose purpose is to use the example of various political institutions and groups concerned with environmental issues to further our understanding of the dynamics of globalization and political re-ordering. It illustrates some of the points made in Chapter 1 about transnational organizations, regulatory regimes and communities of interest which span territorial boundaries. As was noted in Chapter 2, 'global ecology' has very significant 'transformative potential' for the 'unbundling' of territoriality.

Environmental issues are a particularly good vehicle for studying global political re-ordering, for several reasons. First, people concerned with the environment have made strenuous efforts to argue that environmental concerns are global in scale. For example, well-known and successful organizations have given themselves such names as Friends of *the Earth, World Wide* Fund for Nature and *Earth First!* Each of these names invokes the worldwide nature of environmental concerns and implicitly claims that ecological problems have to be treated at the level of the planet as a whole. This case offers the opportunity to assess exactly how global the allegedly 'global' issues really are.

Second, in recent years a number of environmental issues have been addressed through international agreements, often brokered by agencies such as the UN or the EU. Such developments reached a temporary peak in the Earth Summit of 1992. Furthermore, the world's leading environmental movement organizations have also begun to develop cross-national co-operation. The growing importance of such supranational action, whether by groups of governments, by consortia of influential campaign bodies or by industrial groups and their lobbyists, indicates that in a globalizing world, political initiative and political control can begin to pass away from the nation-state and into the hands of supranational actors. It is important to ask whether these activities are signs of the emergence of a new transnational politics.

Third, at the same time the stimulus to a great deal of environmental campaigning remains local, whether opposition to landscape destruction resulting from road building or to the dangers from chemical or nuclear plants. As we shall see, there are local environmental protests the world over, the participants in many of which resist incorporation into the programmes of larger, national or even international bodies. Acutely local concerns persist as a stimulus to environmental activism; they also remind us of two important things. Despite trends towards globalization, the world is not necessarily becoming the same everywhere. As is argued throughout this volume, global processes can have uneven consequences and result in fragmentation rather than global uniformity. The persistence and sheer variation which characterize local environmental protests remind us of this point. Furthermore, local environmental campaigns and protests pose their own distinctive threat to the sovereignty and coherence of the nation-state. Such protests thus affect the dynamics of global politics, both because they may fit into supranational patterns of environmental activism, and also because they tend to 'chip away' at the state from 'below'.

As has already been implied by the idea that differences and uneven experiences can accompany globalization, one cannot claim that environmental problems are 'obviously' or 'inevitably' global. Accordingly, the next part of this section looks at the way in which environmental problems have come to be presented as 'global'; the subsequent section reviews the underlying geographical and socio-economic bases of global environmental problems and assesses the extent to which they merit the term 'global'.

global environmental problems

Whether or not all *'global' environmental problems* have genuine worldwide standing, there are patently many transnational environmental problems and it is the responses to these which occupy the final two sections of the chapter. Section 5.3 looks at the responses of governmental actors. In some cases, national governments have negotiated *ad hoc* arrangements with neighbouring states in response to environmental hazards. However, the increasing trend is for international agreements to be brokered and, in some cases, enforced by supranational agencies such as the EU.

Crucial to the solution of environmental problems though they are, governments are not the only influential actors responding to global environmental issues. Section 5.4 deals with other sorts of transnational actors – organized campaign groups, transnational business interests and alliances of local agencies. All three show, in different ways, how environmental problems are stimulating new forms of transnational political action. They show how this action is re-ordering the global world of political power, re-shaping and often diminishing the political autonomy of national governments.

5.1.3 Making out a global interest in the environment

Advocates of all political movements tend to claim that their philosophy is in the common interest. Thus, nationalists argue that people are happier and more satisfied if they live with their co-nationals; socialists have typically argued that public ownership of the chief engines of the economy advances the common good. Many environmentalists have chosen to make a similar claim for their beliefs too: they assert that environmental degradation is a problem that humankind faces in common and therefore environmentally beneficial objectives can be expected to be favoured by everybody. This section reviews the evidence and the kinds of arguments that environmentalists have used to make this case and evaluates how robust the case actually is.

On the face of it, environmentalists seem to have it easier than others when it comes to advancing a common interest argument. Socialists, for example, have to persuade people to view their class identity as an important, common characteristic, but, all too frequently, people have reverted to racial, ethnic or gender divisions, and class solidarity has been forsaken. Environmentalists tend to think that they enjoy an advantageous position because the common interest they speak of is – in their view – a material and palpable thing. It is not common consciousness they are promoting but a common response to the physical and health-threatening effects of air pollution or to the threat of shortages if the world's resources are used up. People have good physical grounds (or so it is argued) for viewing things the environmentalists' way.

Furthermore, thanks to industrialization and the spread of Western techniques throughout the globe, the physical threats to the environment are becoming more similar the world over. Air pollution problems are common to virtually all large-scale cities whether in rich or poor countries, irrespective of political systems or geography. Similarly, urban sewage disposal is a worldwide management problem. Accordingly, the idea that the world's population has common environmental interests seems to be becoming more credible.

The case can be made out even more readily in those instances where the environmental threats are themselves transnational. Air pollution caused by vehicles is a large problem in most of the world's major cities, but it is locally produced pollution that causes the local hazard. So if, for example, Sydney or Bangkok changed their ways, they would remedy their own problems. Although cities are all in the same boat at the moment, each one could jump ship individually. Other problems do not have this character: some air pollution problems are global in scale (see, for example, **Yearley, 1995**).

Carbon dioxide (CO_2) emitted in one country is as likely to upset the atmospheric balance in another country as in the area in which it was emitted. The dangers resulting from the destruction of the ozone layer follow the same logic. The world shares one ozone layer and the pollutants released by each of us act cumulatively to deplete it. With global forms of pollution the arguments for there being a collective interest in pollution control appear even stronger. No-one can meaningfully go it alone, so the only reasonable political responses depend on co-operation. We have a common interest in protecting the global environment and can recognize good grounds for acting concertedly to protect it.

Svanemøllevaerket power plant in Denmark: a small country contributes to global air pollution

'Green' political thinkers have tried to take this process one step further. They have sought to suggest that people should see themselves not as citizens of a particular country, nor as members of an ethnic group, nor as comrades within a class, but as 'citizens of planet earth'. Environmentalists have used visual and poetic representations of the earth to promote and engender this process of planetary identification. The well-known photographic image of the globe viewed from space has been used repeatedly to evoke the earth's isolation in space, its fragility and wonder, and the sense that the beings on it share a restricted living space surrounded by an unwelcoming void.

Photographs of the earth taken from space have had an unexpectedly significant and yet contradictory influence upon the development of 'global consciousness'. The image of the world as a small, discrete, living organism has led to 'new age' and 'Gaia'-based philosophies which view humanity as one strand in the web of nature. Yet the global image also distances humans from the earth, enabling a new role for the human race – that of observer, manager and planner of the 'Blue Planet'.

Some 'green' political writers have attempted to underwrite these convictions with the support of scientific evidence. According to the analysis of Jim Lovelock, a reputable but maverick scientist, the earth itself and the life on it should really be seen as a 'superorganism', a superorganism he has represented as 'Gaia' (see **Sarre, 1995**). He argues that life on earth has somehow collectively organized itself to withstand external shocks and internal malaise. For example, during the history of the planet, the sun has aged and the heat energy coming from it has fluctuated. Yet the temperature of earth has not changed correspondingly; it has been maintained at more or less its previous level by the operations of the various forms taken by life on the planet. Lovelock draws the comforting conclusion that just as ordinary organisms have defence mechanisms to cope with ill health and changing environments so Gaia has the capacity to withstand changes at the planetary level. Of course, certain species may become extinct (potentially including human beings) but the living planet as a whole is likely to find ways to adapt.

Scientists are conspicuously divided over Lovelock's 'Gaia hypothesis'. For many, it seems to amount to a claim that the earth is – in the words of the favourite *Star Trek* phrase – '… life, but not as we know it!' But whatever the eventual verdict of the scientific community on Lovelock's innovative hypothesis, some Greens have seized on this representation of global interconnectedness as a legitimation for the idea that the planet has real 'oneness'. In this view, the planet as a whole is a real, coherent entity – a superorganism. This is perhaps the strongest possible basis for the claim that the earth should properly be considered as a global whole. It is a scientific and realistic basis on which intellectuals and populists of the environmental movement have sought to promote the idea that our ecological problems demand global solutions and global awareness.

In their book, *The Coming of the Greens*, Porritt and Winner give expression to the radical green view which, they claim:

… seeks nothing less than a non-violent revolution to overthrow our whole polluting, plundering and materialistic industrial society and, in its place, to create a new economic and social order which will allow human beings to live in harmony with the planet. In those terms, the Green Movement lays claim to being the most radical and important political and cultural force since the birth of socialism.

(Porritt and Winner, 1988, p. 9, emphasis added)

Activity 1   In the light of Porritt and Winner's claims about living in harmony with the planet, assess the claims for the 'universality' of environmental concerns. Can we reasonably expect environmental problems to appear pressing to all people, women and men, old and young, privileged and poor, from the 'third world' and the first world? What factors are likely to affect the seriousness with which people view the environment? If there are differences in people's views, is the environmentalists' case for common global interests convincing?

It has clearly been in the interest of environmental philosophers and activists to claim that they are working for a global mission and that they represent the interests of the whole of humanity, perhaps the whole of the biosphere. But some of these claims are open to question. Even apparently global physical problems, such as the depletion of the ozone layer, are more severe in some areas (at the poles) than in others. Claims about humankind's universal interest in solving environmental problems cannot necessarily be taken at face value.

Having set the rhetorical and political scene for claims about the global nature of environmental problems, the next sections will look at processes and practices which have shaped how environmental problems have been interpreted and analysed. Some of these relate to the nature of the issues themselves, others to the geography of environmental problems, or the practicalities of policy-making, while yet others are more sociological.

5.2   Environmental concerns and the 'globality' of environmental issues

5.2.1   The geographical bases of 'globality'

Let's start by looking at some of the practical and physical reasons why environmental problems have come to be seen as problems for the entire human race or for the globe as a whole. To re-emphasize some points made in the last section, one can find grounds for globalization in the character of environmental phenomena themselves. Environmental threats are themselves often international in character. No matter who pumps them out, chlorofluorocarbons (CFCs) will affect the ozone layer. The USA or Europe cannot attend to its own interests in this matter (although this is not to say there are no disputes over the first world's and the 'third world's' differing views of humankind's ecological interests). The same is true for global warming, to some extent for acid rain and even for marine pollution. Rivers and water resources are typically shared between countries, as the current concerns over access to and pollution of the Danube, the Rhine, the Jordan and the Euphrates demonstrate.

Other environmental hazards are *potentially* international. For example, many environmentalists worry about the likelihood of accidents at nuclear power stations after the experience of Chernobyl and the scare over Three Mile Island. While the power stations are working normally, the global radiation pollution is low (whatever the adverse consequences close to the plant may be), but failures at any nuclear installation could have catastrophic consequences over large tracts of the globe.

So far, the environmental threats we have considered have been *pollution* problems (these are reviewed at greater length in **Yearley, 1995**) but it is important to appreciate that environmental problems are wider than just pollution problems.

Activity 2 Global warming, ozone depletion and contaminated seas are all environmental hazards caused by pollution. Briefly list any examples of transnational environmental problems you can think of that are caused by factors other than pollution.

Additional transnational environmental problems can usefully be grouped under two headings. First, nature conservationists are increasingly worried about a loss of 'biodiversity' – in other words the shrinking numbers of species left as humans eliminate natural habitat. In this case it is clear that many individual species are not international. Europe, for instance, is not directly affected by threats to the rhino or to sloths. But the term 'biodiversity' allows us to generalize this concern to a global level. Biodiversity refers to the amount of genetic diversity existing on the planet; how many insects there are, how many types of parrot, how many varieties of maize and so on. Through modern agricultural practices and through the destruction of habitats, humans are rapidly decreasing this biodiversity. This may well rob humans themselves of the biological riches manifested in these disappearing species – for example, it is often suggested that the loss of rainforest plants may deprive us of as-yet-undiscovered medicines or that vanishing varieties of wheat may contain genes which would benefit

Burning forests to enlarge cattle ranches in the vicinity of the Rio Branco in Amazonia, Brazil, causes a loss in biodiversity

agriculture in years to come. Furthermore, we may not only be, so to speak, killing off the genetic geese before they lay their golden eggs, but also endangering the adaptive capacity of large sections of the natural world itself.

Second, environmentalists are also commonly concerned about dwindling natural resources. In particular, energy resources can only be used once (apart, that is, from 'renewables' such as wind energy). The world contains only a finite amount of petroleum, natural gas and coal so resources on a global scale are necessarily limited. The same, of course, applies to minerals – metals, precious stones, building stone, sands and gravel and so on. In some cases, though, the amounts of these materials are so large as to make the problem an academic one. Sand, for example, is not scarce. In any case, minerals can be recycled. Old ships can be disassembled and reworked into ploughshares or guns. The metals from batteries can be recovered and re-used. Even old road surfacing can be recycled into new paths and roads. Recycling demands energy but, in principle at least, nearly 100 per cent recovery rates can be achieved. Another kind of resource is water, often ignored but of great importance (see **Sarre and Blunden, eds, 1995**). Evidently, the world contains an awful lot of water. And there is a natural cycle: rain falls, runs off and through the land ultimately into the seas, and evaporates to fall as fresh rain. Natural processes constantly deliver fresh water to land-bound humans. But in many places we have been consuming it faster than it is renewed. Frequently, human settlements draw on water from artesian sources, sources which have accumulated over thousands of years but which are fed only slowly by rain. On average, we are using these up faster than they are being renewed (see Box 5.1).

As is indicated in Table 5.1, the 'water cycle' is believed to involve nearly 1380 million cubic kilometres of water. But nearly 98 per cent of this water is held at any one time in the oceans. The bulk of the rest is retained in ice.

Much less than 1 per cent of the water in the ocean evaporates per year and, in any case, the great majority of that falls back into the oceans as rain. Thus, while water is plainly not scarce, the amount 'delivered' onto the land regions of the globe each year is very limited. It also varies greatly from region to region. As consumption by industry and private citizens continues to grow, water shortages can be expected to intensify even though, at a global level, the earth is a very wet place (these figures are also discussed in sections 4.6 and 4.7 of **Blunden, 1995**).

Table 5.1 Estimates of the quantities of water in various compartments of the water cycle

Compartment	Volume of water (10^6 km^3)
Oceans	1350
Lakes and rivers	0.2
Ice	29
Organic matter	0.0006
Atmosphere	0.013
Total (approx.)	1379

Source: Silvertown, 1990, p. 74

Box 5.1 Global warning: is the water running out?

'All land-bound life has to share one ten-thousandth of the planet's water. Less than three per cent of the world's water is fresh, and more than three-quarters of that is frozen, mainly at the poles. Ninety-eight per cent of the rest lies deep underground.

The tiny fraction that remains should still, in theory, be more than enough. Every year about 27,000 cubic miles of rain fall on the continents, enough to submerge them under two and a half feet of water. But nearly two-thirds of it evaporates again, and two-thirds of what is left runs off in floods. Even the remaining 3,400 cubic miles of rainfall could still sustain more than double the world's present population – if only it would fall evenly where people live. But while Iceland gets enough rain every year to fill a small reservoir for each of its quarter of a million inhabitants, Kuwait, with seven times as many people, scarcely gets a single drop to share between all of them.

In all, 26 of the world's countries – including many of those in Africa and the Middle East – get less water than they need. Over the next 30 years another 40 nations are expected to join them, as their populations outstrip their rainfall. The number of people affected is expected to grow tenfold from the present 300 million to three billion – one third of the projected population of the planet.

[...]

Money, of course, counts for even more than nature. Phoenix, Arizona, gets the same amount of rain as the dusty town of Lodwar in the far north of Kenya, yet its people use 20 times as much water. Immense sums have been spent on water in the western United States. Not a single drop of the great Colorado River – which carved the world's largest gorge at Arizona's Grand Canyon, and drains a fifth of the once-wild West – now reaches the sea. It has all been dammed and used for cities and agriculture. US water engineers have finally succeeded in fulfilling the command of a 12th century King of Sri Lanka, Parakrama Baku the Great: "Let not even a small quantity of water obtained by rain go to the sea without benefiting man."

The Colorado also supplies Los Angeles, more than 200 miles away across the Mojave desert. The city draws further water from northern California, 300 miles in another direction. Yet rationing is so tight that the city's restaurants break the law if they offer a customer a glass of water before he or she specifically asks for it. Virtually every river in the western United States is heavily exploited. But even so it has had to go in for water mining on an alarming scale. The West has been saved by a vast and ancient underground sea – the Ogallala aquifer, which contains as much water as one of the Great Lakes and stretches for 1,000 miles under eight Great Plains states from South Dakota to Texas [see Figure 5.1]. One out of every six ears of grain grown in the United States now depends on it, and so does most of the world, for the Midwest helps to feed 100 nations. But this is fossil water, laid down ages ago, which cannot be quickly replenished. Every year pumping draws down the level of the hidden sea by more than four feet, while only half an inch percolates through the rock to replenish it. At the present rate of depletion, the agricultural abundance of the Great Plains is expected to last for only another 20 years.'

Source: Lean, 1993, p. 18

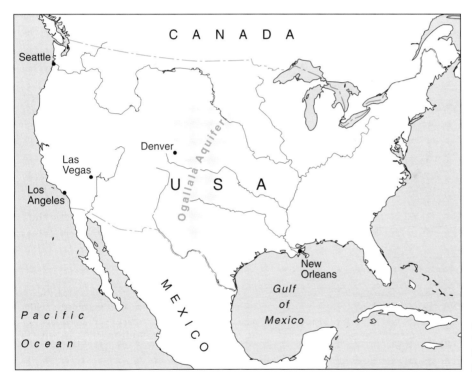

Figure 5.1 The Ogallala Aquifer (Source: Lean, 1993, p. 22)

Of particular interest in these cases of resource depletion is the point that, though we can meaningfully talk of a global amount of these things, in fact they are very unevenly dispersed around the globe. Thus, while the world is currently estimated to have around 300 years' worth of coal at present consumption rates, the Latin American countries between them have rather little of that while the former Soviet Union sits on around ten times as much (see Figure 5.2).

Thousand million tonnes

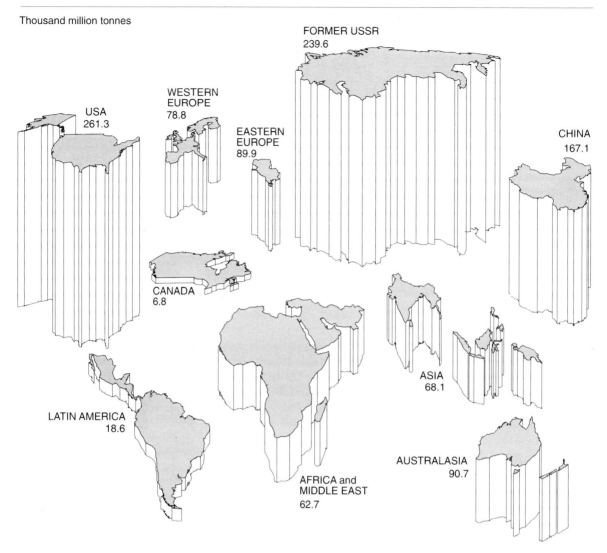

Figure 5.2 Coal: proved reserves. Map representing global distribution, 1989. The height of the columns indicates the relative extent of reserves (Source: Reddish, 1991, p. 10, Figure 1.3)

Of course, these estimates depend on calculations from 'proven reserves' and will not take into account new discoveries nor the matter of how likely mining operations are: there may be coal under Oxford but it is hard to imagine a policy of mining there. Other resources are also less easy to pin down than coal. Natural gas, for example, is mobile: if it is extracted from one end of a gas field, more tends to flow to that end. Thus the Anglo-Dutch gas fields, for example, are not easily divisible into British and Dutch components since the gas itself can switch allegiances. Still, it is clear that 'global' stocks are not likely to be available on a globally equal basis (see Figure 5.3). The countries or companies which control them are likely to appropriate the lion's share of the benefits.

Lastly on this point, by no means are all environmental problems global in themselves. As we have mentioned, air pollution from vehicles is

Trillion cubic metres

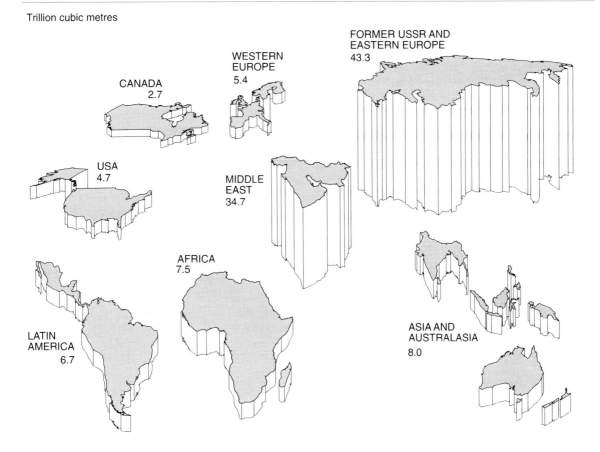

Figure 5.3 *Natural gas: proved reserves. Map representing global distribution, 1989. The height of the columns indicates the relative extent of reserves (Source: Reddish, 1991, p. 9, Figure 1.2 (a))*

predominantly local. The dust, noise and loss of visual amenity associated with quarries is local. The greatest effects of discharges from chemical works are usually felt only locally. And even apparently major environmental catastrophes such as large tanker wrecks have their predominant impact in a restricted area.

Of course, if such 'local' processes are repeated all over the world they do, in a sense, become global phenomena. There can meaningfully be international federations of anti-mining campaigners, for example. Coastal communities the world over can join in their concerns about marine pollution from oil tankers. Such alliances make particular sense when the campaign target is an international firm or industry. Thus Rio Tinto Zinc, a huge transnational mining concern which has been the target of many anti-mining actions, forms a focus for international action at the local level. Local community groups facing the prospect of having waste incinerators built in their region can collaborate internationally, exchanging data and tactical information.

But this should not lead us to assume that the local is always global. In some sense and with enough ingenuity, all environmental problems can be made out to be global but, one might be tempted to say, some are more global than others. Furthermore, as we will see below, one has to take into account

221

the fact that it benefits some people to advance claims about 'globality'. Clearly, environmentalists look more important if, instead of complaining about a local grievance, they can lay claims to global concerns. They benefit from upping the stakes. But, more insidiously, a nation or a company which benefits from a particular environmental policy or reform may want to see that policy adopted as broadly as possible, in which case a 'global' label is very handy. In other words, certain groups may have an ideological interest in having specific environmental problems treated as though they were global and therefore special. To put it crudely, there may be other reasons than pure environmental concern for wishing to see certain environmental problems handled as matters of international priority.

5.2.2 How global is 'global'?

globality In this section we take a critical look at claims about *globality*. As we have seen, there are good physical grounds for regarding some environmental problems as global. Some processes genuinely do have global reach and global impact. If the sea-level rises, it rises everywhere; a radiation cloud from a nuclear accident could travel for thousands of kilometres in any direction. There are also grounds for accepting that the globalization of production and commerce tends to spread even local environmental problems until they are global in scale. In addition, there are philosophical and principled reasons for accepting that the green message has a global flavour. All over the globe, humans are threatening the well-being of other species by disturbing or removing their habitats. Some form of co-ordinated response will be required if the earth's other inhabitants are to get a chance to prosper. Equally, it is clear that – one way or another – energy and mineral resources are limited. For the sake of long-term survival, lifestyles which do not recognize these limits need to be altered worldwide. But, as mentioned at the end of the last section, there are pressure groups and companies whose interests would be served by the widespread acceptance of the idea that all environmental problems are truly global. We must accordingly be careful about accepting claims about 'globality' at face value, and when people make such claims we should examine their arguments carefully.

Two partially related factors tend to mitigate against the overall tendency towards globalization. First, as argued in Chapter 2 of this volume, globalization is often accompanied by fragmentation. The very forces producing some measure of global uniformity tend to undermine the coherence of cultures and policies at the national level. The worldwide sales of Toyota cars do not make for uniformity, but for greater inequalities in transport opportunities in poor African countries as the elite will be able to travel further and faster than everyone else. At the national or regional level, global trends may create disorder where relative order existed before. Accordingly, just because an environmental threat may be viewed as global by an expert commission or by international campaigners, this does not mean that the perception of the issue will be globally uniform. Second, supposedly 'global' processes may not in fact be as global as they are made out to be.

The significance of these points can be demonstrated and developed as two strands: the unevenness of global impacts, and the implications of this unevenness for developing common global interests and policies.

Uneven global impact

Even global phenomena have different impacts at different places on the globe depending on geographical and economic differences. Thus, ozone depletion is one of the best candidates for the status of a 'global' problem, but physical processes ensure that, in fact, the ozone layer is depleted most at the poles. In many respects, equatorial countries have less to worry about than near-polar ones. Global warming demonstrates the same variability. In this case the uncertainty of the consequences of atmospheric warming means that it is harder to pick winners and losers, but, if a rising sea-level is a leading anxiety, the Swiss clearly have less to worry about than the Dutch.

Other geographical variables can exert an influence on transnational pollution problems too. Thus, acid precipitation causes less of a problem where soils and bedrock are slightly alkaline and can therefore neutralize the impact of the acid than in areas where the earth's surface is already neutral or mildly acidic, such as large tracts of Scandinavia. But in addition to variations in geography and the earth's physical processes, there are variations due to wealth. Large areas of The Netherlands are already below sea-level; clearly the Dutch have learnt to cope with this problem. Further sea-level rises will cause great expense but engineers can envisage ways of managing them. Countries of the 'third world' faced with the same threat cannot feel so sanguine. Bangladesh is already subject to frequent flooding; the Maldive Islands stand only a few metres above sea level at their highest point. Both lack the financial resources and the decades of engineering experience needed to counter the effects of global warming. A supposedly global process will impact very differently even among the low-lying countries of the world.

Given the significance of these differences in geography and, particularly, in wealth, talk of global 'challenges' and calls for united, global responses can be seen as misleading and tendentious. The emphasis on the global nature of current environmental problems tends to imply that there is much more of a common interest in combating them than is, in fact, the case. This false implication mirrors an ideological problem which Dobson (1990) identifies at the heart of green politics.

Activity 3 Read the passage from Andrew Dobson's *Green Political Thought: An Introduction* which can be found as Reading A at the end of this chapter.

Is anything wrong with the Greens' answer that 'everyone' will be motivated to bring about the necessary social reform? Are divisions of wealth, culture and ethnicity going to be overcome by the common need for environmental reform?

So far, Green parties have mostly operated in national and regional elections where 'everyone' effectively means all citizens of a nation (or group of similar nations such as the EU). Are the Greens' problems multiplied if 'everyone' is taken to mean literally every living person on the planet?

As Dobson correctly points out, it is Utopian to suppose that there will be consensus on environmentally far-reaching reforms *even within the context of an industrialized nation*. How much more unrealistic, then, is the assumption that global problems will call forth a unified international response, across all the disparities of wealth, geography, religion and ethnicity of the globe.

Implications of uneven global impact

But if differences of geography and wealth threaten to break down the apparent uniformity and universality of 'global' processes, is there a danger that the very idea of common global interests will break down and common global responses will become impossible?

The answer appears to be that in many instances 'global' policies have been perceived as attempts by first world governments to solve their own problems at the expense of the development potential of the 'third world'. This accusation is made by, for example, Middleton *et al.* (1993), who argue that at the 1992 Rio Earth Summit, by giving priority to '... an environmental agenda, the North has once more concentrated on its own interests and has called them "globalism"'. This issue has come to the fore particularly over the management of global warming. The gas principally responsible for global warming is carbon dioxide (CO_2) which is produced by fossil-fuel burning power stations, furnaces, boilers, vehicles and fires. The most appropriate policy for combating global warming appears to be limiting and then reducing overall CO_2 emissions. But limiting emissions is far from easy since the gas is a direct product of key economic activities such as generating power and running factories. If the countries of the 'third world' are to increase their economic production using similar technologies to those employed in the first world, overall world CO_2 emissions will rise rapidly. From the perspective of the 'third world', proposals to limit these emissions threaten to impose a brake on their economic development prospects, as is made clear by the data in Figure 5.4.

Thus when official agencies and campaign groups in the first world propose that overall CO_2 production must be stabilized and then cut, the key question in the 'third world' is, how is that 'cut' to be divided? Proposals to limit carbon dioxide emissions from the 'third world' which are not matched by drastic reductions in the first world's output are seen as merely hypocritical. Voices from the 'third world' argue that the industrialized world has enjoyed two hundred years of wealth based on carbon emissions. Now, they say, it is their turn. Officials in the first world are more inclined to

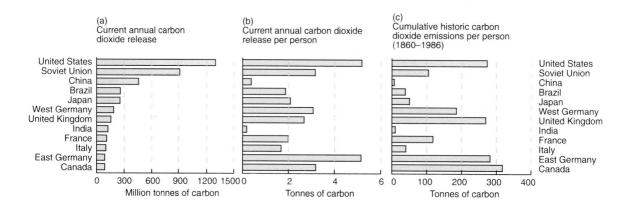

Figure 5.4   *Indicative carbon dioxide emissions for selected countries calculated in varying ways (Source: Friends of the Earth, 1994)*

Note: These figures are based on data gathered in the late 1980s – prior to the collapse of the Soviet Union and the unification of Germany.

favour pollution limits based on current emission levels which – as is shown in Figure 5.4(a), (b) and (c) – lead to a very different view. But any such proposal tends to reinforce today's economic inequalities by restricting the scope for industrialization in the 'third world'. This is because it is hard to see how underdeveloped countries can advance their industries and raise living standards without at least approaching the per capita emission levels of the industrialized world. As is clear from Figure 5.4(a) and (b), if per capita emissions in India (currently around one fifth of a tonne per year) were to rise to even half those in France, overall Indian output would rise five-fold, and India would become the third largest polluter. It is significant in this context that the figures for per capita emissions in the countries of the former Soviet bloc are about the same as those in Western countries, even though their economic productivity is lower. Since, typically, industrializing countries have sought to develop their economies in part through encouraging heavy industry – shipbuilding, heavy engineering, vehicle manufacture – it is likely that they will be relatively heavy emitters of carbon dioxide. Eastern European countries were exceptional in their commitment to heavy – and thus highly polluting – industry, but there is no reason to believe that today's developing economies will be able to move directly to the highly efficient, low-energy practices now being advocated in the leading Western nations. Furthermore, the way that these negotiations are conducted *within* countries can actually lead to a situation of stasis:

Demands for huge amounts of climate aid [that is, aid directed at carbon dioxide abatement measures and for alternative technologies] for the Third World give First World governments an excuse to do nothing except point out to their electorates the huge costs of dealing with the problem and enable them to shift the blame for global warming from the historic and present high emissions from industrial countries onto the projected future emissions from the Third World. It also gives Third World governments the excuse of not doing anything because they can claim it is too expensive and the First World will not stump up the money.

(McCully, 1991, p. 251)

Through suggested official initiatives such as climate aid, the world is being offered measures of an apparently universalistic nature which may not actually operate in anything like the common interest.

The World Bank's Global Environment Facility (GEF), a fund reserved for development-related environmental projects, has been subject to similar criticism (Tickell and Hildyard, 1992). Two sorts of argument have been made. First, the GEF can go to redressing the environmental damage caused by the sort of development projects the Bank might well have funded before ecological issues came to the fore; for instance, the GEF could be used to lessen the environmental damage associated with dam construction. So, rather than preventing ecological damage, it could seek to compensate for it. Implicitly, the critics argue, this means that the GEF will allow environmentally damaging projects to go ahead which, in the absence of the GEF, might have been opposed. Second, and more subtly, it is argued that the GEF only directs funds to ecological problems which are construed as 'global'. But, as we have already seen, the globality of environmental problems is not an inherent or obvious quality; in effect, the Bank gets to define what is 'global' and what is not. And the Bank's 'third world' critics argue that it has been constructed to coincide with those environmental problems seen as most pressing in the first world, and not those – such as poverty – which groups in the 'third world' might try to present as global.

5.2.3   Globality and the discourse of science

A further factor contributing to the globalizing of environmental problems stems from the central role that scientific reasoning and expertise play in the diagnosis and management of environmental problems. It is only through science that we can know of the potentially harmful effects of ozone depletion or work out whether global warming is likely. Given the centrality of science, it is understandable that the discourse of science will affect the way in which environmental problems are approached. Typically, science aspires to universal generalizations. Unless there are powerful reasons to the contrary, scientists assume that natural processes are consistent throughout the natural world. The very term 'biodiversity' that was introduced earlier displays this universalism. The notion of biodiversity takes for granted the idea that all living beings are composed of related genes and that there can be a measure of genetic variability which is applicable across the globe.

scientific universalistic discourse

It is not that scientists are always very internationally minded or that there is good scientific collaboration around the globe (though these things are often true) – rather the point is that science aspires to universally valid truths, truths which apply the world over. Science is a universalizing discourse. Scientists claim to speak a universally valid truth. This orientation has left its stamp on the overall international discourse of environmental management.

Suspicion of the first world's interpretation of global interests has been tied up with the use of the universalistic discourse of science to diagnose the globe's problems. This is an intricate point best introduced through an example. In 1991 the World Resources Institute (WRI), a not-very-radical US-based environmental lobby group, sought to produce figures – similar to those used in Figure 5.4(a), (b) and (c) but much more detailed – indicating each country's CO_2 emissions and thus their contribution to global warming. The WRI had shown an early interest in global warming and had been especially influential in publicizing an emissions-reduction target against which governments' policies could be assessed (Pearce, 1991, p. 283). Their next task was to provide data on each country's performance, allowing the appropriate amounts of 'blame' to be attached.

This task faced many practical difficulties: the data were hard to come by and countries had good reasons for concealing the extent of their pollution. But, in principle, the task seemed straightforward. From the point of view of global warming, one molecule of CO_2 is, scientifically speaking, the same as another. But the WRI study stimulated a fierce attack from Indian researchers (Agarwal and Narain, 1992). Their argument was not only that the figures were defective (owing to problems of data gathering and the like), but that the scientific discourse and apparent objectivity of the report listing nations' respective contributions concealed two issues. First, like any model, the WRI report had to make assumptions. For example, countries with coasts conventionally lay territorial claim to some of the sea. Just how much of this is counted will have a considerable impact on a country's CO_2 output since the oceans act as a carbon sink. India's 'performance' as a CO_2 emitter depends on the amount of ocean attributed to India. Thus, the apparently accurate 'facts' depended to a considerable degree on geographical and political conventions.

The second and more important point is that the WRI figures made no distinction between sources of CO_2. Gases emitted from the exhausts of people driving a short distance to the grocery store (when they could have cycled or taken public transport) were – scientifically – equated with people breathing out or with people burning fuel for cooking. The apparent universality of the scientific rendering of this issue was presented as inaccurate and immoral.

In other words, the Indian researchers challenged the suitability of scientific comparisons as the base-line method for comparing countries' contributions to pollution. Scientific methods gain much of their power through their appeal to universal standards. But, in this case, it was argued that moral and ethical considerations should have also played a part. Science, perhaps the leading intellectual tool for analysing the globality of environmental problems, was presented as unsuitable. Though science was held to be unsuitable for the case in hand, it should be noted that this critique of the 'universalistic' pretensions of science has the potential to be developed into a broader opposition to 'universalism' as described in Chapter 2, section 2.6.2.

Summary of section 5.2

o   In the contemporary world there are many forms of transnational environmental problems. These include pollution problems but also encompass loss of species and diminishing resources of energy, minerals and water.

o   Increasingly, these transnational issues are interpreted as 'global' problems. In some cases, their globality arises from the nature of the problem itself (for example, the globe has a protective ozone layer which is suffering depletion); in other cases, environmental problems rise to global significance because – like habitat loss – they are repeated the world over.

o   However, the status of 'global' problems is far from straightforward. Being global, one might suspect that everyone should worry about them equally. But, in fact, global problems turn out to have different impacts and implications, depending on geographical and socio-economic factors. Even the most inherently global hazards, such as 'global warming', turn out to have differential impacts. Because of climate, altitude and other geographical factors, their impacts will be greater in some areas than in others. Furthermore, on average, wealthier societies and the wealthier people in societies will be better placed to withstand their impacts than will other groups.

o   Accordingly, the label 'global' can itself come to be disputed. Organizations come to refer to a problem as global when they want it to be taken especially seriously and when they want to present its solution as in the 'common interest'. In some cases, spokespersons from underdeveloped countries have argued that the West's identification of 'global' environmental problems is very selective (for example, the West has tried to give priority to its concerns over air pollution) by implying that these problems are the most urgent for the *globe as a whole*.

o   Scientific analysis has been central to the identification of global environmental problems, such as ozone depletion and loss of biodiversity. However, some commentators have argued that the assumptions associated with scientific analysis (for example, that one molecule of carbon dioxide is the same as another) are not always appropriate for the just interpretation of international environmental problems.

5.3   Governments and the supranational response

5.3.1   Supranational co-operation

One leading stimulus to global or, at least, supranational responses to environmental problems arises almost immediately from the geographical bases of globality described above. Just as many environmental phenomena have been international, policy responses have also had to be cross-national. Governments have realized that policies towards the environment need to be co-ordinated above the national level or, to express it in a less favourable light, governments have learned that they need to worry about their neighbours' policies. In what is probably the most cited European example, Scandinavian governments were concerned about damage to their forests attributed to acid rain stemming, to a large extent, from British power stations. The Swedish government could not act to protect its own timber resources because the problem was being brought in from Britain by the prevailing winds. They had to combat the pollution problem through international negotiations since they had no direct legal control over British industry or the principal electricity generating company. Though this example concerns pollution, similar problems arise over resources. As Box 5.1 above on water resources indicated, access to water supplies is a growing problem and many of the world's most significant rivers cross or run along national boundaries. Countries therefore, cannot act alone to safeguard such resources (see **Blunden, 1995**).

Governments seldom have 'pure' interests in environmental quality. The protection of the countryside is commonly related to the tourist business and states may have concerns about the health consequences for their citizens of neighbouring countries' pollution. In the Swedish case just mentioned, the state had a direct economic interest in the condition of its forests. However, governments' interests in environmental policy issues stretch even wider than this. For example, governments are aware that industries in countries with lower pollution control standards than their own will typically have lower expenses. Therefore, it is in the industrial interests of the leaders in environmental policy to demand that others raise their standards; otherwise they will risk being undercut. These considerations have played a large part in the drive for rising and uniform standards in the EU; in a single market, countries with low environmental standards ought to perform better economically. Exactly the same considerations have played a part in the negotiations over the North American Free Trade Agreement (NAFTA) where low Mexican environmental quality was cited as a threat to US industrial performance. In other words, some governments favour the widespread imposition of high environmental standards not so much for the environment's sake but to ensure that costs of industry are similar in competing countries.

5.3.2   Supranational agencies

In some cases, governments' perceptions that they would benefit from working together have led them to establish bodies with powers to propose and agree common policies. Such acts of *intergovernmentalism* (Chapter 2) can be illustrated through one of the best-known examples, the Mediterranean Action Plan. Around twenty states border on the Mediterranean; some (such as France and Italy) are wealthy and industrialized, others (such as Egypt and the Lebanon) are much poorer. Some fish it, nearly all use it for leisure and tourism, most dump human sewage into it and all pollute it to some extent by industrial and agricultural practices. Several of the bordering countries are members of the EU and can, therefore, be expected to have more or less harmonized policies with one another. Others, however, are separated from the wealthier countries, such as France and Italy, by great cultural and economic differences. Yet all, to some extent, have an interest in managing the environmental quality of the Mediterranean. Thus, from its inception in 1975, the Mediterranean Action Plan has grown both in terms of the number of subscribing countries and in the extent of the agreements made.

intergovernmentalism

Although the Mediterranean Action Plan could have grown up simply as a pact between governments, it was brokered through the United Nations Environment Programme. This fact points to a further, very significant stimulus to supranational environmental action: the involvement of international bodies such as the EU (in particular the Commission and the European Parliament) and, most notably, the UN. Though they were not originally established with environmental objectives in mind (indeed the EU had to take a very loose reading of its original constitution to justify its earliest environmental measures), such bodies have fastened onto environmental issues as a way in which they can act in the 'common good' and thereby augment their influence. The environment appeals to these bodies because they can argue that it is inherently international and therefore precisely within their purview, and because it can be presented as a public interest issue. If, for example, the UN is putting forward proposals which supposedly advance the global environmental good it is hard for national politicians to oppose these without seeming to argue out of national self-interest and thus surrender the moral high ground. In the case of the EU it is not only the 'moral' high ground since European legislation impacts on domestic law, and campaign groups have used legal remedies to enforce governmental compliance with EU legislation. Looking ahead to section 5.3.3, this means that environmentalists may find that these international bodies afford a 'softer' lobbying target than national governments. However, it should be noted that the costs and administrative demands of lobbying at this level tend to screen out smaller environmental organizations and thus to favour the larger campaign groups.

Sugar Loaf Mountain, Rio de Janeiro. The Greenpeace poster, erected during the Earth Summit in 1992, warns that the earth is being 'sold'

Activity 4 The United Nations has played a key role as a forum in which international environmental issues can be aired, as indicated in Reading B, 'The road to Rio' by Neil Middleton, Phil O'Keefe and Sam Moyo. Read this extract now.

Because they are supposed to have a vantage point above the level of single countries, supranational agencies are often regarded as being in a position to analyse transnational problems. Apart from seeing the patterns of cross-national environmental damage, are there any other advantages supranational agencies have when it comes to analysing transnational environmental problems?

As explained in the reading, as well as providing a focus for providing authoritative documentation of cross-national environmental problems, UN committees have had a key role in introducing the vocabulary and conceptual tools for the development of environmental policy. Thus, the concept of '*sustainable development*' was publicized through the Brundtland Report of the World Commission on Environment and Development (see **Sarre, 1995**). And though many authors (including Middleton *et al.*) have reservations about the precision and utility of this concept, it is notable that it has attained considerable practical importance. Sanctioned by the UN, the term has gained international legitimacy. It provides campaign groups with an officially sanctioned yardstick by which they can gauge governments' performance and it is a concept that has been publicly adopted by individual states and by the EU as the stated objective of their environmental policies.

sustainable
development

Activity 5 Turn now to Reading C and Reading D on the role of the United Nations. Both readings are taken from *The International Politics of the Environment* edited by Andrew Hurrell and Benedict Kingsbury.

These two excerpts show the role of the United Nations' Environment Programme (UNEP) in gaining acceptance by various countries of the 'Montreal Protocol' in order to combat transnational pollution. Some people have argued that this success can stand as an exemplar for the treatment of other environmental hazards.

Is this view correct or are there special features to the problem of ozone-depleting pollution which make this instance atypical?

5.3.3 Policy problems of agreeing what constitutes the 'environment'

Even where policy-makers appear to be in agreement about a desire to take action on 'global' environmental problems, difficulties have arisen over the interpretation or definition of the term 'environmental' itself. The first question has been what is to count as an 'environmental' issue in which we all, supposedly, have a common interest? Certain issues, such as air pollution, biodiversity and water pollution, have come to occupy the centre ground of the environmental agenda. But other items are more often on the fringes. For some officials and campaigners in the first world, population is taken as an environmental issue. Others see population as a comparatively marginal issue, for them it is the use of resources not the size of the population that matters. Similarly, campaigners in the 'third world' have often tried to argue that poverty itself is an environmental problem. Officials in the first world have tended to deny this. Since people appear unable to agree about what *is* an environmental problem, it seems unrealistic to believe that we could find agreement over humanity's supposed common environmental interests.

A demonstration at the 1992 Earth Summit in Rio de Janeiro, Brazil

231

A second, closely related issue concerns the relationship between environmental topics and other social and economic priorities. For example, while people still demand cars, while companies still benefit from selling them, while the motor lobby still campaigns on their behalf and while national fortunes still depend, as Margaret Thatcher said, on the 'great car economy', environmental policies will not be assessed in their own right but in relation to the value people place on cars. There are few areas of environmental concern which can be considered in relative isolation. Energy policy might be one. If people can light and heat their houses equally well with energy-saving methods, then they are able to adopt them without altering their lives and their values all that much. But most other aspects of environmental policy impact in a broader sense on the way in which people live their lives, organize their work and conduct their personal relationships. Even if all environmental problems were straightforwardly global (in the way that ozone depletion almost is), people in different regions and countries would still have other priorities which interact in differential ways with those common environmental problems. The difficulty is that environmental protection measures cut directly across so many political and economic policy areas.

Summary of section 5.3

o International and supranational responses to environmental problems have been stimulated by both 'push' and 'pull' factors. On the one hand, the transnational character of many environmental problems has encouraged ('pushed' forward) co-operative activity between states, sometimes resulting in 'intergovernmental' responses. On the other hand, supranational agencies have seized on environmental problems as a way in which to advance their distinctive mission. Such supranational interventions have tended to be of greater significance, especially as some supranational bodies (notably the EU) have legal powers over states and can effectively take over certain aspects of environmental law-making.

o The United Nations has been influential in bringing environmental problems to the attention of governments since the early 1970s. Through UNEP, it has played a key role in advancing agreement on such issues as the abatement of ozone-damaging pollution. The UN has also sponsored developments in the conceptual apparatus (with terms such as 'sustainable development') needed to respond to the world's environmental problems.

o Despite undoubted successes, supranational agencies such as the UN have encountered serious problems in getting states to agree far-reaching environmental reforms. In large part this is because environmental issues are intimately tied to questions of economic development and the distribution of wealth, questions over which countries have strongly competing interests.

5.4   The transnational response

5.4.1   Organized campaign groups

The last section discussed *inter*national responses to environmental problems (that is, responses by governments of two or more nations), but, as noted at the very start of the chapter, other actors besides governments have played an important role. One of these other transnational actors has been environmental campaign groups. Since environmental problems often have a cross-national character, these groups have seen opportunities for international co-operation, opportunities which they have generally seized with greater alacrity than governments. Cynically expressed, governments have an interest in getting other nations' leaders to do as much as possible about remedying a problem so that they themselves have to undertake a minimum amount of work. Social movement organizations do not obey this logic. By and large they are free to press for optimal action on environmental reform. Furthermore, they can use the green performance of the leading reforming country in any particular area of policy to berate their own governments. European campaigners have pointed to US legislation on car exhausts and on freedom of information to support the argument that, 'if the US government can insist on catalytic converters and still retain a car industry, surely European governments can do the same'. This line was adopted in the Greenpeace poster campaign in Britain at the end of the 1980s which employed Ford's own slogan ('Ford gives you more') to point out that a British Ford gave you much more toxic pollution than an American Ford. Ford were indignant because many other manufacturers were in the same position, but the company slogan offered an easy target.

The importance of these international issues has also fed a virtuous circle as far as environmentalists are concerned. As McCormick (1991, pp. 151–2) points out, those British groups which have the most international outlook are precisely the ones which experienced the most rapid growth in the decade to 1990. Furthermore, international co-operation by campaign groups

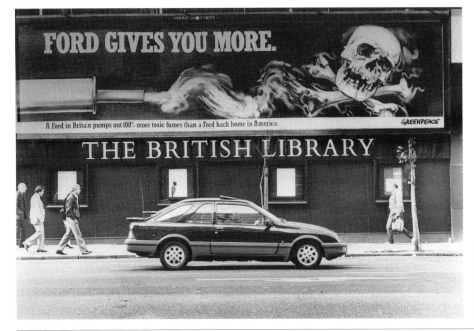

Greenpeace's poster campaign which vividly drew attention to discrepancies between car pollution controls in the USA and the UK

is also stimulated by the fact that it is less susceptible to intra-movement competition than national campaigns since international 'partners' are not often fishing in the same pools for support. If two campaign organizations in Britain co-operate, this lessens their distinctiveness and they may risk losing some members to the other organization. This is not a danger in liaisons between, say, Swedish and British groups.

Activity 6 Now turn to Reading E, 'Think globally, act locally?' by Dieter Rucht.

In the reading Rucht sets out systematic reasons for non-government organizations (NGOs) to co-operate at the transnational level. Briefly, make a list of these reasons in note form. Using your own list, consider whether there are any factors working against co-operation. Would these factors be likely to run counter to the tendencies identified by Rucht?

Some practical features do militate against such transnationalism. Environmental campaign organizations develop a deep familiarity with their own countries' laws, politicians, civil servants and media. It may be easier and appear more promising to continue to plough this furrow. Environmental organizations are often small with a tiny staff; they are often so busy addressing domestic issues that the practical scope for internationalism is limited. Thus we are not claiming that the green movement has transcended national barriers. But there are sociological and political reasons for believing that it stands a better chance of doing so than governments or other would-be universal social movements such as the Peace Movement.

A further factor promoting the significance of environmental issues for globalization is that green campaigners have often focused on aspects of the 'commons'. The two most striking examples of this are the Antarctic and the oceans. All the time that negotiations proceed over various nations' exact

Monitoring the dumping of toxic waste at Koko, Nigeria

*Greenpeace confronts
the whalers*

entitlements to Antarctica, it is possible to argue that it is a common
inheritance for the whole planet and ought to be specially safeguarded
(witness the fifty-year moratorium signed in 1991). Similarly, the seas beyond
territorial waters have long been accepted as a form of commons; countries
which dump into them, over-fish them, or contaminate them with radioactive
dust or incinerator waste can be represented as fouling the joint nest. In
short, it is possible to identify campaign themes which embody and symbolize
the notion of 'common wealth'. These are areas whose special status has
already been internationally acknowledged in one form or another. And
many nations' environmentalists are ready to subscribe to such causes. These
initiatives may be difficult to administer but they are a ready opportunity for
international solidarity and the promotion of a sense of global community.

Again, this status as part of the 'commons' should not be seen as arising
solely from the physical characteristics of, say, the oceans. As already
mentioned, the atmosphere is also in many respects a common holding.
Emissions of greenhouse gases or of ozone depletors can travel more or less
anywhere in the atmosphere and thus, in geographical terms, present a
common threat. The status of the oceans as a common good was established
first in relation to trade and the rights of free passage and, secondarily, in
relation to fishing. The sense that the oceans are an 'environmental
commons' is largely parasitical on these already established meanings. All the
same, it is still a powerful way of engendering a sense of international
environmental solidarity.

Lastly, it should be noted that there are specific occasions when pressure
groups can take advantage of uncertainties and delay in international
environmental policy-setting to advance their own agendas.

Activity 7 Read the story from Fred Pearce in Reading F on how CO_2 reduction
targets were influenced by the behind-the-scenes manoeuvres of determined US
pressure groups.

5.4.2 Transnational companies

In general, it is safe to claim that the vast bulk of environmental problems result from economic activity and that there are strong market pressures on companies to cut costs by exploiting the environment (see **Yearley**, **1995** for a fuller account). In some sectors, firms have moved dirty production to underdeveloped country locations where pollution control laws are more lax. Companies have been willing to cut costs by dumping their wastes in poor countries who are willing to 'sell' their unpolluted land and rivers to waste traders. However, large companies are not exclusively a negative force in environmental policy. For example, once it is clear that environmental regulations are going to come into play, companies' outlooks begin to change. Within the EU, for example, companies have been very active in pressing for uniform standards, not necessarily because they value the environment highly, but so that they can sell straightforwardly into the markets of all the member states. Furthermore, high environmental standards effectively reduce the competition from cheaper but less 'green' producers outside the EU; they act as a palatable alternative to trade sanctions. Even within the EU, industry spokespersons in the less economically advanced states have complained that the Commission's preference for high environmental standards tends to favour 'northern' states such as Germany, Denmark and The Netherlands (Aguilar-Fernández, 1994).

Firms can also have a commercial reason for wishing to see the introduction of tougher environmental standards if they are strong in the areas of research and development. Increasingly, firms commission research to anticipate future regulatory trends and, naturally enough, once the research is completed they are keen to receive the 'pay-off' in market terms. Under special circumstances therefore, firms can have a vested interest in rising environmental standards.

In these ways, through their transnational spread, firms can place strong pressure on governments to shape their environmental and regulatory policies in ways which suit the firms. Depending on the economic and market conditions, firms can exercise pressure for stricter as well as for looser environmental policies.

It should also be remembered that while Greenpeace and Friends of the Earth are known as 'pressure groups', firms and industrial associations are formidable exercisers of pressure. At the Rio Earth Summit some industrial associations even managed to attend as non-governmental organizations, a term usually reserved for non-commercial, public-interest groups (Middleton *et al.*, 1993, p. 27). Some firms aim to shape not only national regulatory policies, but also the way in which the 'global' environmental agenda gets put together.

European level, but can his optimism necessarily be extended to the underdeveloped world? What, in your view, are the key differences between the countries of the EU and the countries of the underdeveloped world in this regard?

5.4.3 Local initiatives

On the face of it, it might seem unlikely that there should be significant local initiatives in response to transnational environmental problems. One might have thought that nation-states and cross-national lobby groups would be the lowest level at which significant action could be anticipated. Yet, particularly since the Earth Summit in 1992, there has been a number of locally based responses addressing both small- and large-scale environmental issues.

One of the products of the Earth Summit was the document *Agenda 21* (United Nations, 1992) which was mentioned in Reading B. *Agenda 21* is a long document, listing the activities which governments have agreed should follow from the Rio Earth Summit. For each item (for example the conservation of biological diversity) it lists overall objectives, specific recommended activities and a costing estimate. One chapter in particular (Chapter 28) is devoted to 'Local authorities' initiatives in support of Agenda 21'.

While the response across the globe has been far from overwhelming, local authorities in a number of countries have taken up the opportunity offered by *Agenda 21*. For example, local environmentalists and city planners have pioneered a scheme in Brisbane to reduce its contribution to global warming through recycling (reducing emissions from manufacturing and methane emissions from waste dumps) and energy efficiency schemes. Related city programmes have appeared in Austria, Germany and The Netherlands. In Britain in 1994 Friends of the Earth launched its 'climate resolution scheme' which calls on local authorities to sign up to a pledge to cut carbon dioxide emissions from their area by 30 per cent by the year 2005.

The organization signed up three authorities (Cardiff, Leicester and Newcastle upon Tyne) for the launch in February 1994. Friends of the Earth published a detailed guide showing authorities what they could achieve by using, for example, energy audits, combined heat and power schemes, a switch to diesel for certain vehicles and so on. One factor encouraging participation by some local authorities in Britain is that they feel they have been stripped of power and influence by successive centralizing Conservative administrations. The Friends of the Earth scheme is calculated to appeal by giving local authorities the chance to participate in solving 'global' problems, while also improving local environmental quality *and* yielding the opportunity to be seen to be out-performing central government, which has adopted much less ambitious abatement targets.

Finally on this point, it should be noted that such local authority action is also popular with sections of the EU which are keen to establish links with regional and city authorities as a means of bypassing recalcitrant national governments. As noted in Chapter 2, section 2.4, some regions in the EU have established offices in Brussels which allows them to deal directly with the Commission.

Summary of section 5.4

o Although transnational environmental problems might seem to require action by governments and supranational authorities, they have prompted and provided opportunities for transnational responses from a variety of non-governmental actors. These include NGOs (such as pressure groups), business interests and local authorities.

o Many environmental pressure groups have shown themselves to be effective actors at the transnational level, pioneering new forms of cross-national co-operation and playing one state's environmental policy performance off against another.

o Industrial and commercial interests have also generated a transnational response. Although (as shown in **Yearley, 1995**) industries have often taken advantage of lax pollution control laws to produce goods in a cheap and dirty manner, there are also some conditions under which firms can have a commercial interest in seeing environmental quality standards rise. For example, German and Danish manufacturers often wish to see high environmental standards adopted in the European Union because these tend to favour their factories over those in the (cheaper but dirtier) 'south' of the EU and those on the fringes of the EU (such as in Hungary and Poland). Because of the competitive relationships between firms, industrial and commercial interests have not always found it as easy to co-operate as have NGOs. However, this disadvantage is compensated by the greater wealth and resources available to the industrial sector.

o Although it might initially seem unlikely, many local authorities have been keen to take up transnational/global environmental issues, particularly in response to the United Nations' *Agenda 21*. Aside from the inherent importance of these issues, they appeal to local authorities as ways of enhancing their political significance and as a means for adopting the moral high ground over national governments. Such local-scale responses have also been encouraged by the EU and by the States in Australia, bodies which are keen to promote regional political authorities and to limit the power of national governments.

5.5 Conclusion

The aim of this chapter has been to demonstrate how the response to transnational environmental problems has generated political action and, sometimes, co-operation at a variety of levels and offered practical and ideological challenges to the sovereignty of the nation-state. At the same time, the opportunity has been taken to question the ideology of global unity commonly associated with environmentalism and thus to offer a critical assessment of assumptions associated with globalization.

Overall, we have seen that there is a strong sense in which environmental problems are coming to be seen as global. This is partly to do with the nature of the problems themselves, but it also reflects the globalizing of production, trade and communication. Partly in response to this (and also partly promoting awareness of it), there has been increased international collaboration and action on environmental themes. Many policies have had to be formulated cross-nationally; campaign organizations have had to take a more international outlook; new UN bodies have been established in the environmental field; and there have been innovations in international science.

But the appeal to common interest in global environmental management actually appears rather fragile. Differences of interest keep reappearing through the talk of universal values and common objectives. This is despite the fact that many officials and some commentators propose that there are common human interests in environmental protection, an idea encapsulated in the title of the 1987 UN report, *Our Common Future* (World Commission on Environment and Development, 1987).

The unevenness of development and the inequalities of power and wealth associated with globalization indicate how idealistic the notion of a 'common future' still is. The majority of transnational environmental problems are easier to read as displays of conflicting interest than as instances of people shaping a future in common. The transnational politics of the environment provide us with a good insight into the diversity of the political actors in a globalizing world. Sadly, it also provides a less than optimistic outlook on the likely future management of the world's environmental and development problems.

References

AGARWAL, A. and NARAIN, S. (1992) *Global Warming in an Unequal World: a Case of Environmental Colonialism*, Delhi, Centre for Science and Environment.

AGUILAR-FERNÁNDEZ, S. (1994) 'Spanish pollution control policy and the challenge of the European Union', in Baker, S., Milton, K. and Yearley, S. (eds) *Protecting the Periphery: Environmental Policy in Peripheral Regions of the European Union*, London, Frank Cass, pp. 102–17.

ALLEN, J. and HAMNETT, C. (EDS) (1995) *A Shrinking World? Global Unevenness and Inequality*, Oxford, Oxford University Press in association with The Open University (Volume 2 in this series).

BLUNDEN. J. (1995) 'Sustainable resources?', in Sarre and Blunden (eds) (1995).

DOBSON, A. (1990) *Green Political Thought: an Introduction*, London, Unwin Hyman.

FRIENDS OF THE EARTH (1994) *The Climate Resolution: a Guide to Local Authority Action to Taking the Heat Off the Planet*, London, Friends of the Earth Limited.

GRANT, W. (1993) 'Transnational companies and environmental policy making: the trend of globalisation', in Leifferink, J.D., Lowe, P.D. and Mol, A.P.J. (eds) *European Integration and Environmental Policy*, London, Belhaven Press.

HURRELL, A. and KINGSBURY, B. (EDS) (1992) *The International Politics of the Environment*, Oxford, Clarendon Press.

LEAN, G. (1993) 'Troubled waters', *The Observer Magazine*, 4 July, pp. 16–25.

MCCORMICK, J. (1991) *British Politics and the Environment*, London, Earthscan.

MCCULLY, P. (1991) 'The case against climate aid', *The Ecologist*, Vol. 21, No. 6, pp. 244–51.

MIDDLETON, N., O'KEEFE, P. and MOYO, S. (1993) *The Tears of the Crocodile: From Rio to Reality in the Developing World*, London, Pluto.

PEARCE, F. (1991) *Green Warriors: the People and the Politics Behind the Environmental Revolution*, London, Bodley Head.

PORRITT, J. and WINNER, D. (1988) *The Coming of the Greens*, London, Fontana.

REDDISH, A. (1991) 'Energy resources', in Blunden, J. and Reddish, A. (eds) *Energy, Resources and Environment*, London, Hodder and Stoughton in association with The Open University.

RUCHT, D. (1993) 'Think globally, act locally?' in Leifferink, J.D., Lowe, P.D. and Mol, A.P.J. (eds) *European Integration and Environmental Policy*, London, Belhaven Press.

SARRE, P. (1995) 'Uneven development and sustainability', in Sarre and Blunden (eds) (1995).

SARRE, P. and BLUNDEN, J. (EDS) (1995) *An Overcrowded World? Population, Resources and the Environment*, Oxford, Oxford University Press in association with The Open University (Volume 3 in this series).

SILVERTOWN, J. (1990) 'Earth as an environment for life', in Silvertown, J. and Sarre, P. (eds) *Environment and Society*, London, Hodder and Stoughton in association with The Open University.

TICKELL, O. and HILDYARD, N. (1992) 'Green dollars, green menace', *The Ecologist*, Vol. 25, No. 3, pp. 82–3.

THACHER P.S. (1992) 'The role of the United Nations', in Hurrell, A. and Kingsbury, B. (eds) *The International Politics of the Environment*, Oxford, Clarendon Press.

UNITED NATIONS (1992) *Agenda 21: Programme of Action for Sustainable Development*, Geneva, United Nations.

WORLD COMMISSION ON ENVIRONMENT AND DEVELOPMENT (1987) *Our Common Future* (The Brundtland Report), Oxford and New York, Oxford University Press.

YEARLEY, S. (1995) 'Dirty connections: transnational pollution', in Allen and Hamnett (eds) (1995).

Reading A: Andrew Dobson, 'Green political thought'

[Greens have often called for a] simple 'change of consciousness' […] and in the following quotation from Arnold Tonybee, cited approvingly by Jonathon Porritt, this is made explicit: 'The present threat to mankind's survival can be removed only by a revolutionary change of heart in individual human beings. This change of heart must be inspired by religion in order to generate the will power needed for putting arduous new ideals into practice' ([Toynbee, in Porritt] 1986, p. 211). Generally speaking this kind of sentiment is accompanied by an exhortation to education as a necessary preface to conversion. However, as David Pepper has rightly observed, 'people will not change their values just through being "taught" different ones' ([Pepper] 1984, p. 224). Pepper goes on: 'What, then, is the real way forward, if it is not to be solely or even largely through education? It must be through seeking *reform at the material base of society, concurrent with educational change*' (ibid., emphasis in the original). Quite – but how?

The answer to this question might just turn on initially sidestepping it and asking instead: *who* is best placed to bring about social change? A central characteristic of Green political theory is that it has never consistently asked that question, principally because the answer is held to be obvious: everyone. The general political-ecological position that the environmental crisis will eventually be suffered by everybody on the planet, and that therefore the ideology's appeal is universal, has been perceived as a source of strength for the Green movement. What could be better, from the point of view of advertising an idea, than to be able to claim that failure to embrace it might result in a global catastrophe that would leave no one untouched? From the present point of view this may be the movement's basic strategic political error because the universalist appeal is, properly speaking, Utopian. It is simply untrue to say that, given present conditions, it is in everybody's interest to bring about a sustainable and egalitarian society. A significant and influential proportion of society, for example, has a material interest in prolonging the environmental crisis because there is money to be made from administering it. It is Utopian to consider these people to be a part of the engine for profound social change.

References

PEPPER, D. (1984) *The Roots of Modern Environmentalism*, Beckenham, Croom Helm.

PORRITT, J. (1986) *Seeing Green*, Oxford, Blackwell.

Source: Dobson, 1990, pp. 152–3

In 1972 another element had been injected into [debates on the state of the planet] by the United Nations Conference on the Human Environment. Usually known as the Stockholm Conference, or simply as 'Stockholm '72', it was presided over by Olaf Palme, then prime minister of Sweden and a man widely recognized for his liberal humanitarian views. This conference focused concern about the ever-increasing number of environmental problems and pointed up the close links between poverty and the destruction of the environment. It did this so effectively that it is now rare for either issue to be discussed without reference to the other – this is progress of a sort. Stockholm '72 also led to the foundation of the United Nations Environment Programme (UNEP), an organization designed to keep a close watch on all major environmental problems and to produce schemes for safeguarding the future of the environment. Up until recently UNEP has been hamstrung by under-funding and the need not to upset the governments that provide such funds as it has. *Agenda 21* [see section 5.4.3] calls for its greater funding and organization strengthening and it is possible that, as the threats to the environment grow and as public concern about them increases, UNEP will be able to work more effectively in the ways envisaged at Stockholm.

The very idea of environmental degradation became common currency in a different way which was, once more, marked by an important conference. It, too, was held in Stockholm in 1982 and was convened by the Swedish government, who invited the signatories of Stockholm '72 to attend. This conference, on the acidification of the environment, did a huge amount to publicize the origins of and the problems caused by acid rain. It was also in the 1980s that disturbing stories of holes in the ozone layer became widespread.

So the stage was set for the most recent international study – that of the World Commission on Environment and Development, named in short the 'Brundtland Commission' after its president, the prime minister of Norway, Gro Harlem Brundtland. The secretary-general of the United Nations called this commission into being towards the end of 1983; its purpose was to look into the alarming rate at which environmental resources were being consumed, at the levels of their waste, particularly in the cause of 'development', and at the ways in which 'developing' countries were falling further and further behind the industrialized world in their standards of living. Three years later, in the spring of 1987, the Commission published its report under the title of *Our Common Future.* It is perhaps worth noting that the three most important environmental-cum-political documents in modern times, *Silent Spring* by Rachel Carson, *Only One Earth* by Barbara Ward and this report were all written by or under the aegis of women.

In a sense the report was all-embracing. It tackled population and human resources, food security, urbanization, industry and energy, biological diversity, oceans, war, Antarctica and space. One of its key concepts was that of 'sustainable development', and its formulation by the Commission has had a profound and largely beneficial effect on thinking about the state of the world. But the concept is one which the Brundtland Report both failed sufficiently to clarify and which it finally fudged. This is scarcely surprising since the twenty-two (including the chair and the vice-chair) commissioners, who were politicians, academics, lawyers and bureaucrats of widely differing persuasions, could not be expected to agree on a tough, radical position. Nonetheless, the Commission's own short definition will do: 'Sustainable development is development that meets the needs of the present without compromising the ability of future generations to meet their own needs'.

Source: Middleton *et al.,* 1993, pp. 14–16

Reading C: Andrew Hurrell and Benedict Kingsbury, 'The international politics of the environment: an introduction'

The problem of distributing the costs of environmental management and the seriousness of conflict will depend on the character of the issue and the structure of state interests. In some cases the costs of tackling environmental problems are relatively modest and the benefits clearly large, in which case distributional problems are unlikely to be insuperable. Nor do such problems necessarily prevent agreement even on global issues, as demonstrated by the successful negotiation of the Ozone Convention and its amended and extended Protocol. In this instance the scientific evidence established the nature and general consequences of the danger beyond any reasonable doubt. The costs within the industrialized world of abandoning CFC production could be accurately assessed and were low relative to the expected benefits. Similarly, the costs of assisting developing countries to move away from CFCs were moderate and involved the creation of a fund of only $160–240 million over three years. Finally, the number of relevant technologies was limited and controlled by a very small group of companies, for whom the shift to CFC substitutes and the transfer of technologies to developing countries did not entail reduced earnings. Indeed, restrictions on CFCs would create a new market for substitutes in which the major companies had a strong lead. Yet the ozone precedent is a narrow one. On an increasing number of environmental issues a discussion of the costs of international action is inseparable from broader debates about the character of economic development and about the need to promote more sustainable forms of development.

Source: Hurrell and Kingsbury, 1992, p. 38

Reading D: Peter Thacher, 'The role of the United Nations'

The Montreal Fund. Barely visible in 1972, the threat posed by CFCs to stratospheric ozone has come into focus largely as a result of UNEP's successful assessment activities, notably the international assessment work that revealed the threat and identified the steps necessary to reduce that threat, as well as the costs. Agreement on a new fund to reduce this global risk was reached in London in June 1990 when contracting parties agreed to accelerate the phase-out of CFCs and other harmful compounds and to set up a fund of at least $160 million over three years to help developing countries switch to less harmful compounds. The precedent is very narrow; the scientific case is beyond any serious question; CFCs really do strip stratospheric ozone and boost incoming harmful radiation – nobody argues otherwise and industry no longer objects; the costs of reducing CFC production and use can be quantified and compared to quantifiable benefits; a strong case can be made that tropical countries are especially dependent on cheap CFCs, such as for refrigeration (chiefly to reduce food spoilage and protect medical supplies), yet lack the means to adapt to CFC substitutes. So as to avoid creating new mechanisms, the World Bank has been asked to administer and manage this fund.

Source: Thacher, 1992, p. 199

The need for cross-national co-operation may be obvious from the previously described nature of environmental problems. Given the transnational nature of many environmental problems, an approach which moves from their symptoms to the causes must inevitably shift its attention to a supranational level. Thus, international co-operation may emerge from the inner nature of the problem. However, one can list additional arguments for such co-operation:

o *Learning from each other.* Although strategic and tactical know-how is often context specific, many lessons such as successful mobilization and tactics provide inspiration and encouragement and help other groups anticipate the future. Even failures can be instructive.

o *Sharing common resources.* Compared with industry and government, environmental groups are typically limited in resources of money, staff and expertise. Since some groups have better resources, leaders, access to mass media and decision making than others, or have more active constituencies, the pooling of organizational resources could enable all to benefit.

o *Advocacy and support for foreign sister groups.* In some regions concerned people lack the knowledge, material resources, access to media and decision makers to defend their interests. They would benefit greatly from those abroad who are better equipped and able to lend a helping hand or even act on their behalf.

o *Preventing the shift of problems from one place to another.* Both within and between national entities we can observe a tendency to 'solve' environmental problems by shifting them to the responsibility of other agencies (a tendency also found among citizen's groups) [...] If watchful and well-prepared groups were active in many places, however, problem-shifting would become more difficult.

o *Overviewing the nature and scope of the problem.* As mentioned, apprehending the technical complexity, and geographic and temporal extent of environmental problems requires sophisticated observation and analysis. At any given point in time or place we often see only the most immediate manifestation of a problem. Closer co-operation between environmental groups could contribute to a more complete and coherent analysis. Short-run improvements may ultimately result in a deterioration of conditions. In the Third World, for example, external interventions in family life or local economies have often proved disastrous ecologically. With a comprehensive view of the natural and social environment we would be assured of a better understanding of possible consequences.

o *Enlarging the environmental consciousness of the broader public.* The exchange of information and close co-operation among environmental groups could serve the broader public's education concerning the interrelatedness of many environmental problems. Publicity and education could lead those who are otherwise not involved in time-consuming and at times risky protest actions to change their voting and consumer behaviour, donate money to environmental groups, etc., and thus exert a certain influence on both domestic and foreign environmental policies.

o *Standardizing regulations.* The variation in environmental conditions and standards among nations can function so as to impede change. For example, indicating a place or country where conditions are worse or standards less restrictive, administrative bodies may attempt to downplay a problem and resist political pressure. Sometimes it has been falsely argued that technical solutions are unavailable, as was the case in the debate about catalytic converters [...] Close co-operation between environmental groups could be helpful towards exposing such tactics as well as putting pressure on countries which lag behind.

o *Challenging political decision makers directly.* Increasing nation-state centralization and the shift of competencies to international and supranational agencies contribute to decision makers' distance from the objects (including the victims) of their policies. Decision makers sometimes simply lack the personal experience to take concerned people seriously. Psychological experiments have demonstrated that social responsibility is strongly influenced by face-to-face contacts [...] Therefore, direct confrontations – including participation in hearings, negotiating and lobbying, or being physically present in disruptive actions at the place where decisions are made – may be an effective means of influencing policy decisions. In that respect, environmental groups could learn from farmer mobilization processes in the European Community. Farmers defend their interests by conducting direct actions in their home country capitals and in Brussels.

Most of these arguments are by no means specific to environmental action. In the history of political protest and social movements there are many examples of cross-border co-operation. The early 19th century European journeymen defended their interests by forming cross-national alliances. More explicitly, internationalist labour movements sought to overcome nation-state idiosyncrasies. Probably the most convincing example is the long tradition of international co-operation, networking and supranational organization among peace and disarmament movements.

With the growing internationalization of economies and capital, new technologies and their spill-over effects, the emergence of transnational mass media, and the partial shift of political decision making to international and supranational bodies, those affected have more reasons than ever before to respond in forms extending beyond national boundaries.

Source: Rucht, 1993, pp. 77–8

Reading F: Fred Pearce, *'Throwing stones in the greenhouse'* _____

The conversation over dinner in Toronto before the big conference went something like this. Rafe Pomerance, lobbyist for the World Resources Institute in Washington, put the opening question to Michael Oppenheimer, a fellow lobbyist at the Environmental Defence Fund: 'OK, this week we have a chance to set the agenda for international discussion about the greenhouse effect. The US drought has turned the issue into a big story and there's a media circus in town to hear what the scientists think the world should do. But the scientists don't know. Environmental groups have left themselves out of the greenhouse debate so far. But we can make up for lost time. Let's get the scientists to tell it our way.'

'Well,' said Oppenheimer, 'we should

offer a target. To stabilize greenhouse warming would require a 50 per cent cut in emissions of carbon dioxide from burning fossil fuel. That number has scientific credibility, so let's propose that.'

Pomerance frowned, 'You may be right but it sounds too much. They'll never buy it. How about 20 per cent by the end of the century and 50 per cent eventually?'

The deal was done. The two men pushed through their proposal at the meeting of environmentalists running in parallel to the main conference of scientists and politicians. And, with a slight modification allowing an extra five years to reach the 20 per cent target, they got it adopted by the main meeting. The conclusion of the Toronto conference on 'Our Changing Atmosphere' made headlines around the world. A cut of 20 per cent by the year 2005 became the benchmark for the debate on how the world should go about tackling the greenhouse effect. It has had world leaders like Margaret Thatcher and George Bush on the defensive ever since, working hard to justify the delay and their own refusal to endorse any target to reduce the pollution that is warming the planet.

Source: Pearce, 1991, p. 283

Reading G: Wyn Grant, 'Transnational business organizations in the European Community' _____

There is a considerable divergence between the resources available to business and environmental organizations at the EC level, even when account is taken of the assistance that has been given by the EC to organizations such as the European Environmental Bureau. Multinational firms operating in EC markets increasingly have their own public affairs or government relations managers in Brussels ... [S]tateless firms are particularly likely to view a global government relations policy as an integral feature of their corporate strategy. Government relations managers in such firms are actively engaged in scanning developments in Community policy, and lobbying to influence policy outcomes as the tortuous and lengthy process of Community decision making proceeds. Often their objective is to stop or delay something happening, and Community structures and processes provide multiple access points and opportunities at which that objective can be achieved. Interviews conducted by the author in Brussels in April 1992 produced evidence of the extent to which government relations divisions in multinational firms are paying attention to environmental issue management. For example, one conglomerate had recently established a high level environmental steering group, and each constituent company was thought likely to establish its own environmental group.

Both in terms of the multiplicity of access points, and the openness and informality of access to decision makers, the lobbying context in Brussels is more like Washington than many European capitals. This is helpful to government relations representatives of individual firms who can pursue their particular objectives in private, informal conversations, often in a social setting [...] Public arenas, such as parliaments, may be more permeable to environmentalists, but less central to the decision-making process.

Drawing on research in which the author has been involved [...] a number of generalizations can be made about organized business interests operating at the European Community level. In the first place, there are large numbers of Community level business associations. A precise count is difficult, but in the chemical sector alone (excluding pharmaceuticals) the writer's own database, which is certainly incomplete, identifies nine major European sectoral or subsectoral associations, and 65 product level associations. There is an increasing tendency towards the formation of direct membership associations operating at the EC level (as in motor vehicles and petrochemicals) as distinct from the more common model of federations of federations which sometimes have difficulty in arriving at coherent policy positions. Secondly, the associations are well resourced relative to other organizations operating at a Community level. They would claim that they are not well resourced in relation to the range of tasks which they have to undertake. Even so, when one considers that, for example, the chemical industry federation, CEFIC, has a permanent staff of 70, and has four thousand persons from its member companies and associations involved in its expert committees, it can be seen that leading business associations are well placed to defend the interests of their members.

Finally, the associations have good access to the Commission. Although the Commission is a relatively open body, business interests generally have well-established contacts at a high level within the Commission. For example, the steering committee of the European [Business] Round Table meets twice a year with the President of the Commission and five or six other commissioners to discuss a current policy problem. Such contacts are important from the Commission's point of view because a good working relationship with large-scale business is important in such key policy areas as the completion of the internal market and high technology policy.

The business associations are making a number of responses to the emergence of new issues related to the politics of collective consumption, notably environmental issues, on the Community's policy agenda. CEFIC has recently completed a major internal reorganization which in part is intended to help it cope with what it sees as the priority issue of the environment. CEFIC is particularly concerned about the issue of environmental auditing. Its president has commented: 'CEFIC is very pleased that the stand adopted by DG XI seems to evolve in the right direction, as a management tool, rather than the imposition of bureaucratic control' (*European Chemicals News*, 1 July 1991).

Federations of federations such as CEFIC, however, experience limitations in their ability to unite their memberships behind a coherent policy. CEFIC has tackled this problem by allowing companies to become direct members alongside associations. As noted above, another approach is the formation of direct membership associations of business firms at the European Community level. Such organizations usually have the senior executives of firms on their key committees, and are able to respond more quickly to changing events.

[...]

[Overall] there seems to be an irreversible trend towards the creation of a more integrated and interdependent global economy. One consequence (but also a catalyst of the process) is the emergence of the stateless firm which is a sophisticated economic and political actor that approaches problem solving from a global perspective rather than the interests of a particular nation-state. There is an interesting tension between the stateless firm and the emergence of transnational forms of political organization such as the EC. Both phenomena represent a move beyond the nation-state; one in the economic, the other in the political sphere. The newness and relative fragility of both make their future development difficult to predict. The stateless firm has an interest in transnational forms of authoritative decision making which reduce regulatory divergence between nation-states, yet the existence of the stateless firm gives a further impetus to the extension of the regulatory role of transnational political structures. Organizations such as the EC may sweep away at least some national regulatory structures, but they may also create new structures at the transnational level. They are at one and the same time a potential ally and foe of the stateless firm. In assessing the balance of political power between them, it should be remembered that the EC is a regional political organization controlled by its member states, whereas the true stateless firm is a global entity with no geographical loyalties.

All this does not, however, lead to pessimistic consequences in terms of progress in protecting the environment. Stateless firms may want more uniformity in environmental standards, particularly if they have environmental control businesses. An international regulatory agenda has begun to develop. Such an agenda is reinforced by the increased public concern with environmental issues. Despite some fluctuations in the level of public interest, the underlying shift from a politics of production towards a politics of collective consumption seems likely to be a permanent one.

Source: Grant, 1993, pp. 69–71, 72–3

Global worlds and worlds of difference

by Allan Cochrane

6.1 Globalization and localization

There is widespread agreement that the world around us is changing fast – and possibly changing faster than ever before. The increased speed of communication, the interpenetration of cultures and economies, the *globalization* of environmental problems, the growth of international migration and the power of global financial markets are all among the factors that have transformed our everyday lives over the past few decades. The question remains, however, how are these changes to be interpreted and understood?

globalization

Two main analytical responses have tended to dominate discussion, each an apparently polar opposite of the other. The first, and perhaps most obvious, interpretation stresses the global aspects of change, emphasizing the extent to which no particular experience – of individual, social group or place – can be understood without first looking at the global dynamics which shape it. At its simplest, such an approach suggests that it is possible to identify a process of social and cultural *homogenization*, dominated by the USA and most easily summed up in words such as 'Coca-Colaization' or 'Hollywoodization', or in the powerful image of McDonalds' golden arches striding purposefully across the world. Such visions clearly have a significant political resonance with many people. They help to explain why the sticking point in the GATT (General Agreement on Tariffs and Trade) negotiations in 1993, over international trade, seemed to centre on a disagreement between the USA and the European Union (EU) (and France in particular) over the extent to which it was legitimate to protect cultural industries – such as the film industry – from the threat of Hollywood (see, for example, **Allen, 1995a**; and Chris Brook's comments in Chapter 3).

homogenization

More complex and compelling versions of this thesis (as expressed, for example, by Sassen, 1991) stress the importance of global processes (in Sassen's case that of social polarization in global cities – see also **Hamnett, 1995**), but acknowledge that the precise way in which these work themselves out will vary from place to place, depending on historical context and other local factors. Such approaches, therefore, avoid suggesting that globalization means that everything everywhere is inexorably becoming the same. Even so, the direction of argument is clear enough, with the stress on the similarities generated by the operation of global forces, rather than on the residual differences which are legacies of the past. The underlying assumption seems to be that global factors are dynamic, while local ones are necessarily 'conservative', sources of ultimately fruitless resistance, rather than bases for change (see also Harvey, 1989; **Massey, 1995a**).

If an emphasis on globalization provides the basis of one attempt to grasp the nature of change, paradoxically, a stress on the *fragmentation* and *localization* of lived experience seems to represent a second. In this case the argument is that the extent of globalization is such that it is no longer possible to sustain the old hierarchical and clear-cut sets of political and economic power relations. Instead of homogenization, stress is placed on the diversity of culture, on the ways in which even dominant worldwide cultural icons (such as Coca-Cola, Hollywood or McDonalds) are reinterpreted locally so that they take on different meanings in different places (see, for example, **Allen, 1995a**).

fragmentation
localization

One consequence of such an analysis is to highlight the ways in which the centralized arrangements of the past are now under threat. In the field of economic and industrial organization, emphasis is placed not on the global corporations themselves, but rather on the ways in which they are increasingly challenged by smaller and more dynamic companies, and on the ways in which the larger corporations have themselves been forced to reorganize through decentralization, franchising, devolution and fragmentation. (One of the most popular examples is that of IBM, in the field of personal computing, having to accept the role of companies such as Microsoft – now itself a corporate monolith – as suppliers of software, as well as direct competition from hardware producers such as Apple, Sun and a multitude of so-called 'clones'.) McDonalds may be a powerful expression of globalization, but its very ubiquity relies on a system of franchising, utilizing 'local' businesses to deliver its services.

In the cultural field, stress is placed on the vitality of local cultures, with, for example, a contrast being drawn between the failure of the major record companies – despite the satellite music television station MTV – to produce a 'global' music which dominates everywhere, and the growth instead of what has been called 'world' music, which celebrates difference rather than homogenization. Not only are the major corporations apparently unable to determine the direction of popular music, but they tend to lag behind in identifying the new directions being taken, even if they generally succeed in incorporating them eventually – the case of rap music is a powerful recent example of the initial difficulty the corporations faced in responding to the rise of a new (popular) musical form (see, for example, George, 1992, part 1). In politics, attention is focused on the breaking up of the old arrangements of 'nation'-states, under threat from regionalism and sub-state nationalism, and on the rise of more complex networks of locally based politics which tend to bypass traditional hierarchies (see, for example, Chapter 2 in this volume; Cooke, 1990). Instead of the emergence of a global political order dominated by one or other hegemonic world power, it has become fashionable to suggest that we are moving towards a more fragmented politics (sometimes called a 'new medievalism') without a dominant world power (or even a dominant political ideology) (see Chapters 1 and 2).

There are, however, serious problems in starting from either of these models. The implicit polarization is a false one, which makes it more difficult to grasp and interpret the main directions of change. The one-sidedness of each overemphasizes one aspect of developments at the risk of downplaying the significance of other aspects. Globalization does not mean the end of difference, nor does recognizing the importance of differentiation and *uneven development* mean that global forces are irrelevant. On the contrary, it   uneven development
is precisely the interconnectedness of these processes that helps to define the contemporary condition. But that does not mean that the answer is somehow to combine the two polar opposites, as if the 'truth' lay somewhere in the middle, modifying each global claim with a counterposing local or regional claim and vice versa (even if it may sometimes feel as if we have constantly to balance such oppositions in our daily lives). One feature of the 'new world', with its increasing *interdependence* between places and between activities, is –   interdependence
as **Massey and Jess (1995)** argue – that geographical scales themselves become increasingly difficult to separate into neat hierarchies. In a

'shrinking world' characterized by inequality and uneven development, old hierarchies may even be inverted since the speed of electronic interaction through global financial markets may be faster than talking to a neighbour over the garden fence (**Allen and Hamnett, 1995**). In other words, some transnational linkages may even be tighter than some of those within nations and localities. The earlier chapters of this volume explore the complex and overlapping relationships between local and global processes. They confirm the extent to which each process actively constitutes the other in a contested and continuing process of interaction, helping to define the space of political action – both geographically and in terms of power relations.

In Chapter 1, Anthony McGrew highlights some of the ways in which new relationships within the international arena have begun to be institutionalized. He questions traditional (or 'realist') views of international relations which start by identifying the key actors as self-contained states defined in terms of territorial sovereignty. He draws on the arguments of critical geopolitics which stress the importance of the connections and flows that intersect with, and cut across, the political boundaries as they are generally drawn on maps. By using this approach it becomes possible to move beyond the hopeless search for some sort of global government, to the analysis of emergent systems of global governance,

international regimes constituted through increasingly complex forms of *international regimes*. These not only involve national governments and international (quasi-autonomous) agencies, but also other interests – particularly major business organizations, including transnational companies. It is through these regimes that regulatory frameworks are constructed and help to shape the ways in which economic, social and political life operate on a day-to-day basis.

James Anderson's arguments in Chapter 2 focus on the changing roles and

nation-states definitions of *nation-states* in a changing world. Traditional interpretations

macro-regions are increasingly brought into question by the emergence of *macro- (or global) regions* (with their own political and economic institutional expressions)

micro-regions alongside a renewed emphasis on *micro- (or sub-state) regions*. The linkages between them help to undermine the significance of existing boundaries, while at the same time allowing them to be used for political purposes as part of the global bargaining process. The chapter title directly poses the question of whether we are seeing the end of the nation-state. In some ways the answer given is ambivalent, suggesting that, despite the apparent threats to their existence, nation-states stubbornly survive and retain their power to mobilize popular support. But the argument goes beyond that. Like Anthony McGrew, James Anderson stresses the ways in which our understandings of nation-states are being defined and redefined in terms of networks of connections and flows. These networks challenge dominant geographical models which construct a straightforward hierarchy of scales, with each succeeding level relating unproblematically to the one below (from world to macro-region, macro-region to nation, nation to region, micro-region to locality, locality to neighbourhood). Instead of heralding the 'death' of the nation-state, however, this implies its resurrection in a different form – not as something static and timeless, but as a contested expression of political and economic mobilization.

In Chapter 3, Chris Brook takes the arguments of the previous two chapters further by exploring the development of economic and political arrangements at the level of global, or macro-, regions, drawing particularly, but not only, on evidence from the European Union. His conclusions, too, are equivocal. There is some evidence that macro-regional political structures are becoming more important, but it is less clear quite how they are likely to develop – that is, whether they remain trapped within intergovernmentalism or whether they will be able to move towards becoming genuinely transnational. Even in the case of the EU, the most politically developed of the existing macro-regions, the gap between institutional pretensions and independent – Europe-wide – political power remains marked. Meanwhile, instead of removing borders as a step towards a seamlessly global political space – a 'borderless world' – the politicization of global regions seems more effective at defining sharper divisions and creating new boundaries. These may be at a larger scale than before, but they also help to define with still greater clarity those who gain and those who lose out from uneven development.

The space within which the economic and political institutions, discussed in the first three chapters, are able to operate is in large part an expression of complex networks of social relations which connect, or 'stretch', across the world. The extent to which such social and cultural relations are connected is a reflection of *time–space compression* as it helps to define new spaces of political interaction. Brian Beeley's discussion in Chapter 4 not only highlights Islam's importance as a global cultural and political movement, but also confirms the importance of acknowledging its local roots in different cultures. Islam is a rich and multifaceted tradition which is not reducible to the stereotypical form of a monolithic global cultural force, particularly one which can be characterized by popular terms such as 'fundamentalism'. In a sense, indeed, Islam is not just one (singular) global movement but comprises several such movements, each of which is, in turn, the product of local movements developing in the context of shared but contested global traditions. Islam offers an inherent or immanent critique of (and implicit alternative to) existing international regimes, but at the same time its followers have to operate in a global space within which the rules are laid down by others.

time–space
compression

The arena of environmental politics is, perhaps, the one in which it is easiest to make claims for globalization, with the need to campaign for global solutions and to develop global strategies often apparently taken as read. In Chapter 5, Steven Yearley questions some of these easy assumptions and sets out some of the difficulties and tensions involved in attempting to construct new forms of global politics. Although often assumed to be unproblematic in 'green' thinking, uneven development and the associated inequalities of economic and political power help to undermine 'green' claims to be able to move beyond the self-interest of particular groups towards a general, or global, interest. Yearley questions the role of agencies such as the World Bank and even the apparently rational universalism of scientific language or discourse which, in practice, tends to reinforce the position of the powerful (developed) at the expense of the weak (less developed). The emergence of international environmental regimes does not represent the victory of global rationality over the irrational particularism of local interests, but is itself the product of political processes in a world shaped by inequality and uneven development. Even the emergence of transnational political movements needs to be assessed carefully. Such movements may offer the possibility of developing global responses to global problems, but they may also provide a means of defining those problems in ways which tend to reflect the interests of one group at the expense of others.

All the earlier chapters, therefore, in their different ways, point to the complexity of the issues with which we are concerned in this volume, and, indeed, to the necessary complexity of the concepts which must be used to analyse them. It is important to recognize that we cannot operate as if there were some easily definable sets of global processes which just happen to work themselves out in particular places. Similarly, it is unhelpful to believe that each different place starts out with some clear-cut identity of its own, only later interacting with others which are also fully formed expressions of their societies (see **Massey, 1995a**). Agnew makes this point forcefully in discussing the geographical assumptions of international relations theory. While he recognizes the importance of territorial (nation) states (and the importance of their territorial self-definitions), he stresses that: 'even when rule is territorial and fixed, territory does not necessarily entail the practices of total mutual exclusion which the dominant understanding of the territorial state attributes to it' (Agnew, 1994, p. 54). This may already be apparent from the discussion in earlier chapters (particularly Chapters 1, 2 and 3), but it bears restating. 'The critical theoretical issue', says Agnew, 'is the historical relationship between territorial states and the broader social and economic structures and geographical order (or form of spatial practice) in which these states must operate' (Agnew, 1994, p. 77). This point is just as important if the territorial units under discussion are labelled as nation-states, regions, towns, cities, localities or neighbourhoods.

This chapter began by asking how we should interpret and understand the ways in which the world was changing. There is no simple answer to this question. But that does not mean that it is impossible to answer it, and the arguments put forward in this volume so far should help to do so. In the rest of this chapter attention will be focused on considering the ways in which different analyses of globalization and fragmentation may be combined to produce a coherent approach to understanding the changes taking place, yet one which also succeeds in acknowledging the complexity of the emerging future. In particular, emphasis will be placed on the relationships between uneven development and globalization, recognizing that both are important in assessing the changes and neither makes sense without the other. Regional and local experiences are shaped and influenced by processes of global change, but those processes are themselves, in turn, not only influenced and shaped, but, in a sense, also constituted by those regional and local experiences. Recognizing the continuous interrelationship of these processes helps to explain both the ways in which new political arrangements are emerging and the limits to them.

Although terms like 'global' and 'local' are often taken for granted in everyday (and academic) discourse, it is important to recognize that we use them to help us make sense of the world in which we live – they are social constructs or representations whose meaning and implications vary depending on the contexts in which they are used. Sometimes concepts such as these seem to take on a life of their own – to attain a status of unchallenged 'truth' – which in turn helps to shape what is possible or acceptable. Here, we believe that it is necessary to explore the ways in which they are shaped and reshaped, defined and redefined, in order to understand the relations of which they are a part (and sometimes an expression). In the rest of this chapter, therefore, these issues will be considered further by returning to two key aspects of the debates. Section 6.2 focuses on transnational movements, their nature and significance. If the potential of developing democratic political structures and systems capable of responding effectively to global issues is to be taken seriously, then it is these movements which will provide the base on which to build. Section 6.3 considers the other end of the political scale – the changing role of local politics, both in responding to and in influencing global change. In principle, one might expect an increased porosity or fuzziness of boundaries and the blurring of territoriality to lead to significant changes in the operation of local politics. Finally, in section 6.4, the argument returns to broader concerns to focus on the relationship between uneven development and globalization.

6.2   Looking for transnational movements

In this context, *transnational movements* (analogously with transnational corporations – see **Allen, 1995b**) may be defined as comprising social, cultural and political networks which cross the territorial boundaries of existing states, without having a dominant base expressing the interests of any single country or groups within it. They can be expected to make claims to having (or may be more generally seen to have) a wider set of concerns than those constructed by the boundaries of national politics. In any discussion of transnational movements, particularly political movements, however, it is difficult to disentangle arguments which focus on what commentators think *ought* to happen from those which focus on trying to identify what *actually* is taking place. Clearly, the two aspects of the discussion are (or should be) closely related: unless what people think ought to happen relates to the opportunities which are available, there is little chance of them realizing their hopes. A difficulty arises, however, when the direction of argument is reversed, with the wish (in this case that some global response will meet an identified global challenge) becoming the parent to the thought – here the belief that, because a global response is necessary for the problem to be overcome, such a response will necessarily emerge. There is a danger that the search for evidence of emergent political arrangements will come to substitute for their existence in practice. It is, therefore, important to be able to distinguish between the 'ought' and 'is' aspects of political change, as well as to recognize the consequences of failing to maintain such a distinction.

Some of the problems associated with this will already be apparent from earlier chapters. As Steven Yearley notes, they bedevil discussions of environmental politics: since the environment is a global issue there really *ought* to be a global political response and it is therefore tempting to exaggerate the significance and influence of global political actors and campaign groups.

Such problems are not restricted to the political arena of the environment, however. The experience of the socialist and communist movements provides another powerful example. Since at least the middle of the nineteenth century, many of those involved in socialist or left-wing politics have been

transnational movements

eager to argue that, since capitalism is a global system (and the working class is said to share interests which cross national boundaries), a global political organization is needed to challenge it. Karl Marx was an active participant in the First International Workingmen's (*sic*) Association (known as the 'First International'). After its acrimonious collapse, Marxist and social-democratic organizations set out to create a Second International (which survives today, although it has little international authority over its constituent members), while, after the Bolshevik Revolution in Russia in 1917, an attempt was made to split the International. The Communist parties set up a Communist (or Third) International which had an international leadership based in Moscow. The Third International was dissolved after the Second World War, when the international political strategy of the Soviet Union changed (and emphasis was placed instead on military and political 'alliances' such as the Warsaw Pact and Comecon), but a Fourth had already been created by Trotskyists who broke with the Communist Party in the 1930s. The Trotskyists felt that the global (and globally centralized) nature of capitalism was already so apparent that it was necessary to have an international revolutionary organization, even before there were strong national parties: the national parties would be created as branches of the international organization.

Whether the political activists involved in these projects were, in principle, right or wrong – in thinking that some sort of international association was required if ever capitalism was to be effectively challenged by the political organizations of the working class – it is clear that the wish to create powerful political movements whose interests transcend national boundaries is not enough in itself to ensure that they are brought into existence. The temptation is a strong one, however, and is not just restricted to environmentalists or Marxists. Nor is it restricted only to radicals (whether 'green' or 'red') intent on challenging existing power structures. The dangers of identifying 'objective' forces in history and then assuming that they have worked out in practice, are perhaps nowhere so clear as in the field of international politics, as organizations with grand-sounding titles are invented to give an appearance that 'progress' really is being made, even where it is not. The founders of the original European Economic Community (EEC) in 1957, for example, can by no stretch of the imagination be described as radicals – one of their main inspirations was to construct a bulwark against communism – but they did have a belief in the necessary and inexorable progress of history towards European unity. As Chris Brook shows in Chapter 3, however, their high hopes are still some distance from realization, and this has been highlighted by the process of institutional renaming, first in 1967 to the European Community and then again (rather painfully) in 1993 when the European Community was somehow supposed to have been transformed into something called a European *Union*.

Yet it is also important not to be mesmerized by these criticisms of the over-enthusiasm of others. There is sometimes a danger of reducing complex processes to simple theoretical models (for example, of globalization or even time–space compression) which then attempt (and fail) to explain everything. But that does not mean that we should be afraid of looking for wider explanations and theorizations of social processes. There may be no necessary connection between the form of globalization taken in one area of activity and its expression in another. And the rise of multinational and transnational corporations may not mean that there must be an equivalent move in terms of political institutions or cultural developments. But it does not follow that we should dismiss the idea that changes are taking place, or fail to acknowledge that there is an important relationship between different aspects of change: economic, cultural and political. On the contrary, it emphasizes the necessity of exploring the connections rather more carefully and charting directions of change rather more systematically.

Activity 1 'Think globally, act locally' is a slogan which has been widely utilized both by environmental groups and by campaigners against world poverty (see Figure 6.1 overleaf). Like many effective slogans, when we first come across this one it is easy to accept it without really thinking about it too much. It also has the advantage of helping us feel that we are making a wider contribution to global well-being every time we plant a tree, buy a car with a catalytic convertor or go into our local charity shop. Even The Open University in the UK has used this slogan to underpin its international strategy (see Figure 6.2 overleaf). The slogan helps to define those who adopt it inclusively as part of a global movement, however minor a role they (and by implication thousands or even millions of others) might be playing within it. It seems to promise the globalization of citizenship and of welfare discussed by **Sarre (1995)**. But it is worth giving a bit more thought to the meaning and implications of the slogan. What do you think it implies as a guide to political action?

In considering this question, you may find it helpful to focus on some particular global or local issue and try to follow through the consequences of developing a response along the lines suggested by the slogan. You may find the following examples helpful in doing this:

o   The problem of global warming (local responses might include, for example, imposing carbon taxes, and the insulation of homes; but it might also be important to ask about the ways in which the global political economy and the international environmental regimes discussed by Steven Yearley in Chapter 5 help to shape what is possible locally and globally).

o   The problems of famine and natural disaster (local responses might be based around the collection of aid to be sent to the country or countries affected, and in those countries the distribution of that aid is likely to be locally focused and there may sometimes be tension between using it for immediate relief and using it for development projects; but it may also be important to ask how or why the problems exist in the first place and whether it is necessary to challenge the more global economic and political circumstances which allow them to develop).

o   Campaigns to defend local amenities against development (in this case local interests may at first sight seem to be fairly clear, but it may also be worth considering whether local divisions between groups are masked by the notion of a unified 'local' interest; it is often taken for granted that any defence of green space is of global benefit, but perhaps more careful attention should be paid to looking at who benefits and who loses from particular campaigns).

In some ways the meaning of the slogan is probably reasonably clear: it is important to understand that we are facing global problems, but that does not mean we have to wait for a global programme of change to be implemented. We, as individuals and groups, can take actions which may in themselves help to alleviate particular *local* problems, but which may, more importantly, also contribute to cumulative change in the *global* context and challenge dominant attitudes. The slogan highlights the interdependence of the world, while implicitly acknowledging the importance of uneven

Figure 6.1   Thinking globally and acting locally for a fairer world (Source: OXFAM)

Figure 6.2   Thinking globally and acting locally as a marketing strategy (Source: The Open University)

development and suggesting that it provides a valuable basis for political mobilization which may have global implications.

In a sense, the slogan assumes that there is just one 'global', of which everyone is a part, and on some issues, of course, this is a persuasive argument. If the ozone layer disappears, we will all suffer, whether we are rich or poor, women or men, live in Africa, Asia, America, Europe or Australasia. But the argument fails to recognize the different (and overlapping) global worlds of which people are a part (see **Allen, 1995a**). Although they use similar slogans, Figures 6.1 and 6.2 highlight quite different notions of the globe: for Oxfam, the key is to bring the attention of people living in richer countries of the world to the plight of those living in poorer parts; for The Open University, the key is to find new marketing opportunities outside the UK. As **Massey (1995b)** argues more generally, our conceptions of the world, even as expressed in cartography, are themselves representations, with the imaging or imagining of the world changing over time (in Figure 6.1, for example, the map projection emphasizes the importance of Africa). Dominant representations or understandings help to shape what is and is not possible, but they are also likely to be contested, with different interpretations sometimes existing more or less uneasily alongside each other. So, for example, the world of Islam is not the same as the world of high finance, although the decisions of the Islamic rulers of some oil-rich states may have significant impacts on the world of high finance, and the decisions taken in the global stock markets may dramatically affect the lives of people living in Islamic countries. As Steven Yearley notes, even in debates over environmental 'degradation' the world may be conceived quite differently from different standpoints: for Western campaigners, any development which leads to the destruction of forests or to increased air or water pollution is likely to be seen as a threat to the world as a whole; for some of those in poorer countries the world may look like a rather different place in which the richer and more powerful countries keep finding reasons to stop the development of competitors anywhere else, with the arguments of the environmentalists simply being the latest in a long line of excuses.

The linkages between the local and the global remain problematic. The slogan implies an easy solution to a problem that still has to be overcome, because it assumes that the global strategy is already clear enough, just waiting for local activists to carry it through. Though this may be the case in some areas – for example, in moving away from the use of harmful or toxic materials – it is less likely to be so in others. An emphasis on the local might also encourage a fragmented approach in practice, fitting uneasily into wider strategies or even discouraging their development. In the UK, for example, resistance to wind farm development may be justified in terms which stress resistance to environmental degradation (in this instance, the use of otherwise green space, unsightliness and intrusive noise from the turbines), while others argue that in global terms wind farms are important as a means of reducing polluting emissions from other forms of energy production. Which is to be the 'global' priority: the defence of green space or the defence of the atmosphere? As this example illustrates, the aggregation of locally based 'green' campaigns may not always come together to produce a coherent 'green' agenda for the world as a whole.

6.2.1 Transnational movements and uneven development

As a starting-point in our analysis, it is important to understand – as **Allen (1995a)** argues – that the world is 'global' in both unequal and uneven ways. Within a global system some countries, some groups and some corporations are in more powerful positions than others. Indeed, the existence of a global system with a few nodes of power may make it easier for inequalities to be sustained and increased because of the ways in which those in powerful positions set the rules and determine developments. The notion of unevenness implies something rather more than inequality. In principle, at least, it would be possible to conceive of a highly centralized world system in which forms of inequality (including spatial inequality) were endemic and unchanging, largely imposed from above. Uneven development, by contrast, necessarily implies flexibility and fluidity, based on *difference*. It suggests that   difference existing hierarchies of geography, society, politics and economics cannot be sustained over time, because it highlights the possibilities of challenge and supercession – as one global region develops at the expense of another, or as one hegemonic political power is replaced by another, or by a more uncertain process of global bargaining.

The importance of this in the analysis of transnational movements is difficult to exaggerate. The recognition that it is possible to identify transnational movements is only the beginning of the process, since their nature and dynamics will vary from case to case even if each may also be understood as a particular expression of globalization. In practice, some movements may focus individual campaigns on the governments of particular countries, but will do so in terms which justify such campaigns in terms of some wider (probably more 'global') strategy. For other transnational movements the issues may be rather different, not so much focusing on campaigns or pressure-group activity as traditionally understood in the language of political science, but, rather, setting out to construct alternative political worlds outside those defined by states and cutting across their boundaries by accident as much as by design.

Some of these issues are made clear in earlier chapters. In the case of the environmental movements discussed by Steven Yearley in Chapter 5, for example, the context is provided by the widespread realization that the activities of individuals, organizations and nation-states can have global implications, literally threatening the life of the planet or, at any rate, affecting what have come to be called the global 'commons' (the shared aspects of our lives on earth, from oceans to atmosphere). The attempts to construct transnational movements on environmental issues have had mixed success. Campaign groups have been able to utilize a global perspective to point to best practice in some countries in order to influence others, while some international agencies have used the environment as an issue around which to focus their own initiatives, and environmental issues have also provided a convenient focus around which scientific and 'expert' groups have been able to mobilize professional interests at international level, even if, as Yearley notes, they have often done so under the banner of a universal rationality.

Meanwhile, however, the globally unequal distribution of economic power, which reflects and reinforces particular uneven patterns of development, has often made it difficult to challenge powerful economic interests. At the same time there has frequently been national resistance to environmental pressures from the weaker as well as the stronger states. Governments of some poorer countries complain that they are being faced with stricter environmental controls as a means of reducing their ability to compete, and not out of any concern for environmental issues. The globally uneven distribution of political power has helped to determine how 'global' and 'local' political agendas are constructed, defining which issues are legitimate from time to time (through international conferences such as the 1992 Rio Earth Summit, for example, and the formation of international agencies of one sort or another). As Yearley points out, not all environmental issues are global, even if local political campaigns are generally justified in rhetorical terms which claim a more global and universal significance.

As well as often being undermined by the consequences of uneven development, transnational movements are themselves often the products of it: initially often of political processes located in Western/Northern countries (where affluence has been taken for granted, at least by some sections of the population), but which have then set out to build links with groups in other parts of the world. Global environmental campaigns have generally been led by groups based in the more prosperous countries of the world, sometimes conflicting with the priorities of the governments of less prosperous countries (for whom economic growth is often a high priority), but attempting to cut across official channels by making links with non-governmental organizations in those countries. The tensions underlying these relationships are apparent, for example, in the complex and changing patterns of argument which have underpinned debates about the Brazilian rainforest, as first one group and then another has claimed to speak for the native peoples of the area, and those peoples have themselves attempted to clarify their position in the context of substantial development pressure, while sustaining their position as the champions of Western environmentalists.

Meanwhile, the emergence of (Western) European-wide transnational politics has been more apparent at the institutional and formal level than at the level of activism and interaction. Indeed, the way in which the EU has been built through negotiations between nation-states has, in practice, tended to militate against more active citizen participation and the construction of European political movements. As Chris Brook notes in Chapter 3, the development of the EU has been state-based, initially drawing its legitimacy from its member states, and then setting out to develop its own legitimacy by largely bureaucratic methods, in some ways copied from those states (see, for example, Sbragia, 1992). European social policy, for example, has been developed in a largely piecemeal fashion through regulatory frameworks and court decisions (see, for example, Cochrane, 1993; Cram, 1993). The process of global economic competition has encouraged the development of the EU as a trade bloc and alongside this there has been a gradual extension of different political arrangements, including the creation of an advisory committee of the regions and localities.

Institutional change in Europe, encouraged by economic globalization, might have been expected to generate new opportunities for transnational political movements. To some extent it has done so, but, as Brook shows, the form which these movements have taken has been a predominantly bureaucratic one, rather than one rooted in popular politics. Local and regional authorities have opened offices in Brussels, or formed cross-national pressure groups, while trade union groupings have been set up at European level alongside similar groupings of employers' organizations (see, for example, Benington, 1994). Cross-boundary Euro-regions have even been created from alliances between local and regional authorities (the largest of these brings together Kent, Nord-Pas de Calais in France and all the Belgian regions). Where the politics underlying the initiatives has not been concerned with underpinning the political claims of the European Commission, they have generally been rooted in national, rather than international, political debates, using 'Europe' to shift local balances of power, or to outflank national governments.

6.2.2 Politics and culture: the case of Islam

The role of Islam as a transnational movement is a markedly different one, not least because its origins lie outside the boundaries of the core global regions. Islam is both a powerful cultural and political movement, which finds a direct expression in transnational political organizations and institutions as well as in the structure and politics of particular states. The dominant historical interpretation of Islam in the West has been one of a global (and monolithic) cultural, religious and political (almost elemental) force whose ambition is to take over the world (see, for example, Said, 1978). From this perspective, Islam might be seen as a very powerful and unified transnational movement, inexorably sweeping the globe, although, as Brian Beeley shows in Chapter 4, this is not an interpretation which would be easily accepted in the rather more beleaguered communities of Islam, which see themselves facing increasing pressures towards secularization under the influence of Western corporations and their governments.

The world's Islamic communities are products of processes of uneven development which have found complex (secular as well as religious) expressions across the 'Islamic world'. In part, Islamic 'fundamentalism' is a construction of Western intervention and interpretation in a global context, as much as it is a product of Islamic communities themselves. The 'fundamentalist' label is not one used by those who are so labelled (and is a term transferred unaltered from debates within Christianity). It carries with it a meaning which makes little sense in the new context, since – as Beeley argues – the basis of Islam as a whole is indeed 'fundamentalist' in the sense that it stems from the word of God as revealed to His Prophet. As a result, while 'fundamentalism' may imply criticism when in the mouths of Western commentators, it has no such meaning within Islam itself. Of course, this does not mean that there have been no significant religious (and political) movements within Islam which have set out to challenge forms of secularism and Western influence as incompatible with Islamic culture. But it is important to consider them, as far as possible, as movements on their own terms, and not through the lens of 'fundamentalism'.

The countries of Islam have been shaped by their position within a wider global system. Islam as a transnational movement has been forced to operate from a position of global exclusion or marginalization, while nominally holding political power in particular states. Most Islamic countries are not part of the three core economic regions of the world (based around North America, Europe and Japan), but either relate to them as oil producers or agricultural suppliers, or are effectively marginalized and excluded. Even the exceptions, such as Malaysia and Indonesia, have distinctive and secondary roles within a regional economy dominated by others. In many cases (from Iran to Kuwait, Pakistan to Algeria, Sudan to Palestine, Syria to Indonesia), their borders have been drawn by the hands of the practical geographers and map-makers employed by Western empires in an attempt to impose the dominant (European) discourse of territorially defined nation-states even in those places where definitions of nationality are hard to find (and may make little sense). To a large extent, therefore, the basis for the expression of Islam as a political force in a range of state forms was given neither by Islam itself, nor by the followers of Islam.

The range of political regimes within Islamic countries is extensive: from variants of secular nationalism (in Turkey, Egypt and Algeria) to religious monarchies (in Saudi Arabia, Kuwait and the Gulf states), and from revolutionary religious republicanism (in Iran) to forms of dictatorship which often call on religion for support (in Iraq and Sudan). Some regimes are more or less democratic (such as Turkey, Pakistan and Malaysia), even while others call on the teachings of Islam to support monarchical and dictatorial regimes. Because of the way Islam links its religious, social and political teachings, these differences do not have a clear legitimation, as they do within Western political theories. The Islamic state should, in principle at least, be a unified one. This means that approaches adopted in any one state – such as Iran – may be presented as ones of universal applicability, and decisions made – for example, the *fatwa* issued against the writer Salman Rushdie – may be seen as having universal enforceability, in ways which leave legal state boundaries as practical obstacles, but without any particularly strong moral status. The movement for Palestinian independence combines a powerful secular message – about statehood and national independence – with an equally powerful religious message – about the oppression of Muslims. It is one which has linked the existing states of Islam (whatever their political regime), but which has also gone beyond them to build a broader movement campaigning on a global scale (sometimes through 'terrorism' and sometimes through more open forms of political action) and particularly appealing to those within the Islamic diaspora around the globe, in Berlin and Paris as well as Bradford and Birmingham, within the countries of the West.

The transnational linkages associated with Islam are tied into sets of a religious understanding which are – in principle at least – shared by those who are involved. In a sense the overall agenda is set by readings of the Qur'an and Hadith. Islam also straddles two notions of politics: the more familiar one (in the West) which is orientated towards particular states and groups of states, and a second one, in which political movements may go beyond and even operate outside state regimes, since even legal authority exists beyond the state. The claim to global legitimacy of the pronouncements of Islamic political leaders is not made on the basis of the legitimacy of the regimes in the countries in which they are based, but, rather (as Beeley shows), on the basis of their consistency with the laws and norms of Islam.

6.2.3   Beyond traditional politics: moving beyond the state

Transnational movements are increasingly difficult to explain in terms of traditional definitions of politics. Although one element in their political agendas is frequently the desire to influence states and their policies – to engage in traditional pressure-group politics of one sort or another – they rarely restrict themselves to this. Indeed, it could be argued that one of the reasons for the EU's relative weakness in terms of political support is precisely that it is so institutionally, or state, based (although, as Brook notes, a vast network of lobbying organizations has developed around it). As we have seen, Islam transcends such notions by offering its own transnational – and literally transcendental – political alternative, based on a (more or less) shared community of understanding, not only cutting across the boundaries of Islamic countries, but also finding an expression in the secular (nominally Christian) countries of the West. Green politics, too, makes similar claims: so that, for example, campaigns to boycott (or, more positively, to purchase) particular goods, or attempts to live in a more environmentally conscious way, represent alternative political possibilities (and may even suggest less hierarchical and more co-operative ways of organizing social and political life), without necessarily being directly orientated towards the changing of government policies nationally or internationally.

Similar points can be made about other transnational movements. The international women's movement, for example, frequently concerns itself with the policies of particular states (for example, in campaigns over abortion rights, or in debates about equal opportunity policies), but its members also see themselves as acting outside state networks, providing support for women wherever possible, in practical as well as campaigning terms. Global women's networks are not just about campaigning to influence government policies, but are also about bringing women together to develop their own initiatives in more supportive contexts than are otherwise available to them. Similarly, the international campaigns for gay rights and in response to the spread of AIDS are clearly concerned, in large part, to influence the policies of individual states and collections of states, but they also offer crucial support to those who are suffering or under threat. The construction of a massive patchwork quilt from individual panels in memory of people who have died from AIDS was undertaken as a global initiative, with the quilt itself travelling the world to have new panels added to it. This quilt is a powerful image which reclaims the humanity of its subjects in the face of those who seek to marginalize and denigrate them, or even simply to define them as 'victims'.

A less familiar claim can be made for transnational forms of politics which are still less campaign orientated (as well as being particular forms of and responses to uneven development). A Chinese transnational network, for instance, a diasporic economy of 55 million people spread across the globe, works within the political frameworks of a multitude of countries. Yet the network largely sidesteps national governments through its decentralized, family-orientated structure. In this transnational economy, business is often conducted across vast distances on the basis of trust inscribed in family, kinship or clan relationships (see **Allen, 1995a**). A starker example is offered by Gilroy (1993a,b) who argues that it is possible to see the emergence of a 'black Atlantic' political culture – linking black people in the USA, the UK and the Caribbean – which incorporates a dynamic and changing vision of

New forms of transnational politics: the Names Project commemorating those who have died of AIDS comes to London's Hyde Park

new possibilities (see also **Hall, 1995**). As one aspect of this (alongside consideration of literary and intellectual traditions), Gilroy carefully charts the cross-cutting linkages between different musical forms across the Atlantic – soul, funk, reggae and rap – and between cultures, providing links back to the period of slavery, while at the same time incorporating the possibility of generating alternative (and shared) political identities. The 'expressive culture' of the songs and music, he says, 'is dominated by the need to construct them as narratives of redemption and emancipation', producing 'a potent historical memory and an authoritative analytical and historical account of racial capitalism and its overcoming' (Gilroy, 1993b, p. 42).

Gilroy argues that the black Atlantic has to be understood as 'a non-traditional tradition', and stresses that:

Even when the network used to communicate its volatile contents has been an adjunct to the sale of black popular music, there is a direct relationship between the community of listeners constructed in the course of using that musical culture and the constitution of a tradition that is redefined here as the living memory of the changing same.

(Gilroy, 1993a, p. 198)

In a sense, Gilroy's claim for the (inevitably transnational) black Atlantic culture is much more fundamental than any concern with state-directed political campaigns: it represents, he says, a counterculture of modernity (Gilroy, 1993a, chapter 2). It may be seen, in other words, as a continuing (immanent) critique of the way in which the whole political project which found its expression in nation-states, industrial revolution, capitalism and slavery came to be formed. Gilroy sees it as a 'social movement which is the contemporary heir to a non-European radical tradition [which] has a more total critique [of capitalism, industrialization and their political counterparts] than that currently spoken in furtherance of the struggle to emancipate labour from capital' (Gilroy, 1993b, p. 44).

Even if one does not fully accept Gilroy's thesis about black Atlantic culture and its role, for our purposes it highlights the possibility of a transnational politics which goes beyond formal political organizations and pressure groups (based around forms of consumption, rather than production or 'political' issues). It suggests ways in which strategies and understandings may be shared across space, without it always being clear to those involved that they are engaged in a political process. In other words, it offers us the possibility of identifying global political movements which may be able to bypass the territorial boundaries of 'nation'-states, to the extent that they may not even be recognized as 'political', although they may also offer the promise of more extensive change than that generally offered by conventional politicians.

Activity 2 Transnational movements are generally analysed as if they were *products* of some impersonal (and objective) process of globalization. Because a problem is a *global* problem, because markets are *global*, or because electronic communications networks are *global*, it is concluded that some global or transnational response is required (even if only at the macro-regional scale through institutions such as the EU or NAFTA). Yet it could equally reasonably be argued that transnational movements themselves help to define what is global. The example of the black Atlantic is instructive here, since the movement has been made possible by the black diaspora, but is not reducible to it. The emerging relationships expressed in the black Atlantic have helped to shape the ways in which the world itself has been identified and understood.

Try to think of other examples from earlier chapters of the volume which illustrate this point. For example:

o   How has the world been defined and redefined through the development of the European Union? (Chapter 3.)

o   What is the world as defined by Islam? (Chapter 4.)

o   What image of the world is implied by the campaigns of transnational environmental movements? (Chapter 5.)

Hopefully, it will be clear from your answers to these questions that definitions of the 'global' are themselves shaped by our political and cultural starting-points: in other words, the notion of the 'global' is itself a representation, albeit one whose meaning is also defined by changing economic, technological and political relationships over which we may have little control.

Summary of section 6.2

o   Transnational movements consist of social, cultural and political networks which cross the territorial boundaries of existing states, generally with concerns wider than those specified by the boundaries of national politics.

o   Transnational movements are of increasing importance because of the ways in which they are opening up new forms of (and spaces for) global politics.

o   Within transnational political movements there is often a danger of confusing what activists think ought to be the case with what is the case (a belief in the need for a global movement is sometimes translated into the conviction that one already exists).

o   There are complex sets of linkages and interconnections between overlapping 'global' and 'local' political and social movements, with each helping to constitute the other.

o   Despite the rhetoric of some of them (in claiming a worldwide legitimacy), transnational movements often reflect the impact of uneven development, building from bases in one or other set of countries, interests or cultures, and reflecting (and even reinforcing) existing relations of economic and political power.

o   Some transnational movements have the potential to move beyond traditional forms of pressure group politics focused on particular states or policies, to suggest the possibility of new political understandings and forms of engagement.

o   Although in a sense all transnational movements are concerned with 'global' issues, the ways in which each defines those issues and the 'globe' to which they relate are significantly different (in other words, each is likely to draw on and develop a different geographical imagination in developing its political agenda).

6.3   Looking for local politics

The argument so far has tended to concentrate on the ways in which – and the extent to which – global political processes are the outcomes of complex (and partial) relationships of power, space and place. They are the products of uneven development and have an uneven expression in practice, which means that the search for global and homogeneous transnational political movements is ultimately likely to be a fruitless one.

A second aspect of the changes frequently associated with economic globalization has been the suggestion that there may be increased scope for local politics, and, in particular, for initiatives at the micro-regional and sub-regional level. If not exactly a consequence of globalization, political fragmentation is, at least, frequently seen to be consistent with it.

In this debate it is sometimes easy to forget the points we have just been making about the search for global politics. It is easy to slip into a view of the local as if it had some basic essence which was relatively easy to define – in other words, the 'local' might be seen as the neighbourhood, community or even local government area at the 'bottom', overarched by the 'global', or the wider world, at the 'top'. But just as stress has been placed on understanding global politics through the connections and flows which help to constitute it, so local politics has to be approached in a similar way by focusing on connections and flows which stretch beyond any narrow boundary imposed by locality or individual places (see also **Massey, 1995a**). Representations and interpretations of what is local will vary according to the issues under discussion. In debates about world trade, for example, macro-regional blocs, such as the European Union, might even be seen as the appropriate 'local' nodal point for political action, while individual member nation-states could be seen as performing the same role (within Europe) in debates about intra-European trade.

It has been strongly argued that new spaces of local politics have begun to open up in the process of economic restructuring, reflecting the increased globalization of production, since, as firms move beyond the national scale, competition becomes important not only between *countries* (and global regions), but also (and possibly more importantly) between *places or localities*, where production (of profits as well as of services and manufacturing) is actually based. Allen and Hamnett note that, as the 'barriers of physical distance have been lowered', so the 'distinctiveness of places has become all the more important' (**Allen and Hamnett, 1995, p. 242**). Local politics – the politics of localities, not only as expressed in elected local government – is increasingly about economic development and place marketing as much as, or more than, the delivery of welfare services.

The growing importance of supranational forms of political bargaining (for example, through the EU), which lay down the ground rules of localized competition, is paralleled by the growing importance of activity at the local and regional scales. The European Commission has itself explicitly set out to develop this, partly perhaps in an attempt to strengthen its own political position, but also partly because it is at these scales that effective initiative is likely to develop and working partnerships between different interests (particularly across levels of government and between the public and private sectors) are most likely to emerge (see Benington, 1994, particularly section 4). A condition for the distribution of some forms of regional aid is that there are regional partnerships through which it can be delivered (in countries such as the UK where there are no formal regional governments, *ad hoc* partnerships have to be constructed to meet this requirement). *Europe 2000*, a publication of the European Commission's Directorate General for Regional Policy (1991), sets out to construct a planning vision of the future for Europe, based around the identification of a series of cross-national regions, and attempts to catalogue the priorities for development in each. It also suggests that the urban areas of Europe need to develop their own initiatives to take account of wider changes and points to the need for them to work together to achieve this, with the help of the EU.

6.3.1 'Place marketing' and localities

Some (such as Cooke, 1990, chapter 5) argue that new opportunities for

place   political proactivity are being generated for localities or *places*, particularly in the developed world. Above all, it is suggested that localities are both increasingly able and increasingly required to operate in an entrepreneurial fashion, to market themselves in ways which will enable them to provide economic growth and employment opportunities to their residents. This

place marketing   '*place marketing*' (see, for example, Kearns and Philo, 1993) goes beyond simple 'boosterism' or the attempt to attract development through promotional activity or the provision of serviced land and premises. It implies an active process of geographical shaping and reshaping in which places are refashioned and redefined to reflect the images which are associated (particularly by developers and managerial groups) with prosperity and attractive lifestyles. This is consistent with the arguments developed by **Massey (1995b)** who highlights some of the ways in which places may be reinterpreted and reimagined, but the question of who does the reimagining, and on whose terms, is one which becomes central in this context (see also the discussion of the selling of Liverpool in **Meegan, 1995**). Cooke's approach stresses the extent to which localities themselves, or key groups within them, may play an active part in this, ensuring that the competitive redefinition of place is undertaken in ways which express locally defined priorities. Without such a basis, it might be argued, the possibility of success is limited since advertising hype on its own will ultimately be unconvincing. Others, however, are more sceptical (for example, Cox and Mair, 1991; Harvey, 1989) and emphasize that local politicians have limited room for manoeuvre. Because localities have to please the businesses they wish to attract or retain, it is argued that their political agendas are largely determined by others, whether directly or indirectly.

It is difficult to draw any definite conclusions from this debate because it tends to rely on assertion from both sides. It is not easy to provide evidence which shows that proactivity has increased or decreased, since the same evidence (of successful economic development in a particular locality, for instance) might equally well be used as an example of successful initiative, or as proof that the locality is in the pocket of this or that industrial conglomerate. Are the examples of Nissan moving to Sunderland or of Toyota relocating to Derbyshire proof of the vibrancy of local politics or signs of the overwhelming economic power of Japanese capital in the last quarter of the twentieth century? Perhaps it is a mistake to see the two possible answers as alternatives. Instead, it may be important to recognize their dependence on each other, so that competition between places is, in large part, seen as a reflection of economic globalization and the ability of major corporations to choose between locations. However, it may also be important to recognize (as Cox and Mair, 1991, suggest) that it is easier to construct effective political/economic alliances in some places rather than others in the processes of bargaining. The more effective local alliances may also be less dependent on their formal positions within existing state hierarchies, tending to bypass national agencies in the processes of negotiation, or at least leaving them with the role of supporting player rather than lead. If, as Jessop (1994) argues, welfare is being redefined in terms which stress the linkages between local economic competitiveness and ability to innovate, then, whatever the constraints, local and regional political initiatives are likely to be of greater importance in the future than they have been in the past.

Clearly, not all localities will be able to play the same dynamic and successful role. Just as uneven development creates the possibility of some being actively defined and redefined as those where development will take place, so it creates the likelihood (indeed the certainty) that others will be the places bypassed by growth. The notion of 'place marketing' suggests that all places will be forced to play the same game, but it does not imply that all places will be equally successful. On the contrary, the success of some will imply the failure or stagnation of others (see, for example, **Meegan, 1995,** on Liverpool). Some visions of the future imply the existence of a few islands of growth and economic security (based around core economic activities) within a wider sea of places whose economies are dominated by low-paid, casualized employment and whose local politicians are relegated to the desperate struggle to attract investment and contracts from the (relatively wealthy) places which have effective local politico-economic networks and sunrise industries. On a world scale, the gaps between rich and poor are, of course, particularly clear, even if some aspects of uneven development may be quite surprising – for example, as India comes to provide a substantial amount of (low-cost) software development down the lines of computer technology on the information superhighway.

If it is hard to make judgements about the importance of local politics, the argument that power is shifting away from nation-states is one which is equally difficult to assess. Some commentators – as Anthony McGrew notes in Chapter 1 – suggest that the power of nation-states is being dissolved into wider (state-like) international arrangements, while others – as Chris Brook notes in Chapter 3 – point to the emergence of political institutions based on global regions. James Anderson has shown, in Chapter 2, some of the ways in which these territorially defined nation-states have retained (and in some cases even increased) their importance. Within a global system it is important to acknowledge that such states may themselves often have an important 'local' role to play since they, too, may be seen as operating as 'local' actors in some respects within that system. So, for instance, particular national strategies may influence the way in which individual states fit into a global economic and political system – the most obvious recent examples of such strategies have been in East Asia, where countries such as Taiwan, South Korea, Singapore and Hong Kong have helped to reposition their economies through export-orientated industrialization (although it might be argued that the size of some of these states makes them look rather more like city-states than nation-states).

It has also been argued that one consequence of globalization has been that nation-states are increasingly being threatened from below. It will be clear from the arguments in Chapter 2 that, despite some evidence of new pressures arising from regionalism – and what might be called sub-state nationalism – nation-states seem to be adapting to a more global political environment with some success. Where the existing state system has been under most pressure (and former states such as Yugoslavia, the USSR and Czechoslovakia have been dismembered), the appeal of the challengers has been to nationalist politics and alternative nation-states, rather than to the vision of a world without nations. Despite managing to set up an advisory Committee including representatives from the local and regional governments of its member states, the European Commission's attempts to build a Europe of the Regions (as an alternative to a Europe of the Nations) have so far remained a bureaucratic vision rather than a political reality.

6.3.2   Global spaces and local places

Places, regions and even nations define themselves, and are defined within, global networks of interrelationships, but they also help to shape those relationships in ways which cannot be comprehended without looking at 'local' sets of relationships and understandings – what Geertz (1983) calls 'local knowledge'. These sometimes appear to co-exist uneasily alongside the apparently more powerful globalizing forces, but often retain a dynamism which is not so easily dismissed. As Brian Beeley shows in Chapter 4, one of the underlying reasons for the strength of Islam as a global movement is precisely the way in which it interacts with specific cultures and understandings to produce locally embedded sets of social and political relations. It is here that people interact most clearly to produce their own interpretations of the world and the rules by which they operate within it. They play a key part in the operationalization and definition of power relations.

What these networks of 'local' interrelationships do, however, cannot simply be understood as some sort of locally specific superstructural growth on top of a more or less uniform set of global processes, not least because each redefinition always turns out to be rather different from the next, whatever the shared origins to which attention may be drawn (and whatever the historical battles that are fought and refought in distorted ways in new settings). What, for example, is one to make of Davis' description of the complex ethnic 'fault lines' emerging in Los Angeles? There, he suggests, the 'neighbourhood geography of Los Angeles has redrawn the map of the world to place El Salvador next to Korea, Armenia next to Thailand, Samoa next to Belize, and Louisiana next to Jalisco' (Davis, 1993, p. 41). More generally, it has been argued that:

Old-fashioned attempts to map the globe as a set of cultural regions or homelands are bewildered by a dazzling array of post-colonial simulacra, couplings and recouplings, as India and Pakistan apparently reappear in post-colonial simulation in London, pre-revolution Iran rises from the ashes in Los Angeles, and a thousand similar cultural dramas are played out in urban and rural settings all across the globe.

(Gupta and Ferguson, 1992, p. 13, quoted in Agnew, 1994, p. 75)

stretching social relations across space

The increasingly active sets of interrelationships between those living in places apparently at opposite ends of the globe – the *stretching of relationships across space* – makes this particularly clear, so that, for example, daily life for many of those living in Bradford (in the UK) cannot be understood without linking it to the rather different experiences of daily life in Mirpur (in Pakistan) (see also **Rose, 1995**). Side by side in the same place, not only is it clear that local experiences are constructed differently, but – equally important – local experiences of globalization are constructed differently, too, and largely through the prism of interrelationships between places across the globe, rather than through any abstract understanding of the ways in which the global economic system works or of the direction of global migration patterns (see also **Massey and Jess, 1995**). As we have seen in section 6.2.3, Gilroy (1993a) discusses the ways in which the experiences of black people in the UK are necessarily linked into a wider context through their relationships with the black Atlantic. For him, this does not undermine the importance of local relationships, but emphasizes their global nature – both in helping to define the lived meaning of the black Atlantic, and as a basis for political action, defined in the broader cultural terms which he favours. In this context, Gilroy even discusses the importance of record shops (and the record sleeves displayed in them) as a basis for the development of local political understandings in the 1970s, through interaction and debate between those using them and with the wider culture distributed through them (Gilroy, 1993b, chapter 16). Images from the inner cities of the USA or the streets of Jamaica took on different meanings in the record shops of Harlesden in west London.

Local politics is the product of complex processes of interdependence, interconnectedness and uneven development which cut across a range of spatial scales (between which it is increasingly difficult to differentiate convincingly). One starting-point for the analysis of local politics might be to recognize that different rounds of economic development, social change and political formation leave legacies that continue to interact over time, helping to construct continuing traditions which shape local political possibilities. The strength of such an approach is that it captures key aspects of continuity of local identities and representations (reflecting the local dependence of some businesses and residents: see Cox and Mair, 1991). Conversely, its weakness may be that it underestimates the extent to which understandings of localities are contested both within their own boundaries and through linkages, connections and flows which stretch beyond them (see, for example, **Massey and Jess, 1995**). It is increasingly important to take both of these aspects into account in developing an analysis of local politics. They come together to give local politics both a relative stability over time (what Duncan and Goodwin, 1988, p. 110, following Harvey, 1989, call a 'spatial fix') and a fluidity which reflects the changing contexts in which they develop.

The case of Berlin offers a particularly powerful illustration of the relationships which help to determine the space of local politics and the difficulty of trying to distinguish sharply between different spatial scales. Berlin's role within Germany, within Europe and within the global system has changed dramatically across the twentieth century: it was capital of Germany under the Kaiser, under Hitler and within the German Democratic Republic until 1989; it is set to become capital of a unified Germany in 2000; it was a centre of culture and radicalism in the 1920s with a Europe-wide reputation (which stretched as far as the west coast of the USA); West Berlin was an island of capitalism in a sea of communism between 1948 and 1989; Berlin

BERLIN

1920s: European capital
of decadence and culture

1930s: capital of Nazi
power

After the war: front-line
against Stalin in the
Cold War

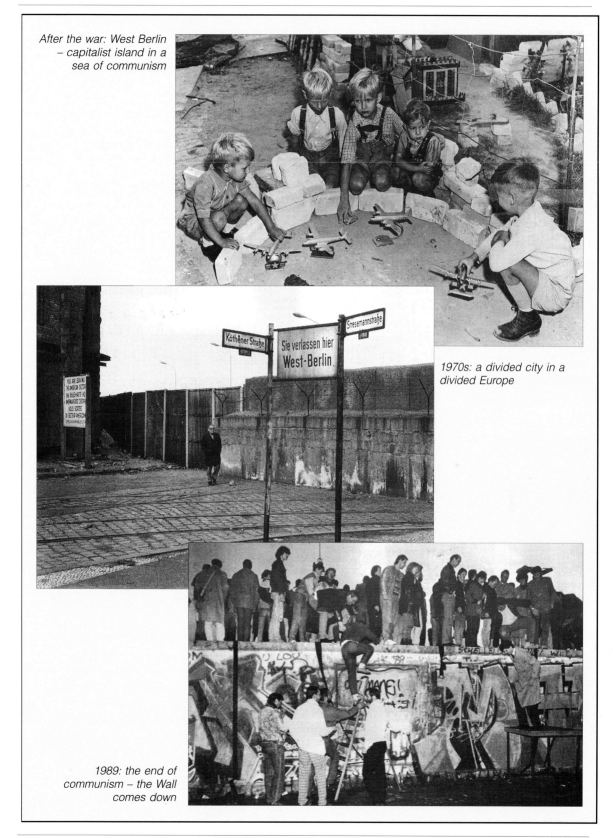

After the war: West Berlin – capitalist island in a sea of communism

1970s: a divided city in a divided Europe

1989: the end of communism – the Wall comes down

was first a symbol of the Cold War and then a symbol of its ending, finally sealed with the collapse of the Wall. The local politics of Berlin was also the global politics of the Cold War. The unification of Germany in 1989 brought the unification of Berlin, breaking some of the old connections and opening up possibilities of new ones. For some residents of West Berlin (particularly Turkish people and those attracted to the city because its residents did not have to participate in military service), the new arrangements represented changes which were not always welcome – with increased racism, higher rents and property prices and a more conservative cultural environment – as the city redefined its role in the new world. And for some of those in East Berlin, the promised changes did not bring unalloyed benefits, since in practice they included increased unemployment, reduced facilities for child care and what feels like a secondary status in a world whose rules are defined by the West. For others (particularly those in the property development industry) new opportunities are emerging as the city is developed and redeveloped, not only to become a capital once again, but also in the belief that it will become the EU's bridge to the East and the countries of the former Soviet bloc, rather than a marginal Eastern outpost of Western culture and Western capitalism.

At the end of the twentieth and the start of the twenty-first centuries, the new Berlin is being shaped by the interaction of a complex series of economic and political processes which cut across various spatial scales, from local to global. Local politicians are seeking to market the city in ways which will encourage foreign investment at the same time as putting pressure on the federal government to transfer its functions and employees as quickly as possible. At the same time, some local residents are campaigning against major development schemes threatening to change the character of the city.

Activity 3 In earlier sections of this chapter, and in other chapters of this volume, we have focused on the ways in which the spaces of global politics are shaped and defined by networks of connections and flows. Here the focus is on the spaces of local politics, but the same arguments are important. Think again about the case of Berlin discussed above. How have connections and flows across the globe helped to shape the context of local politics there?

As mentioned earlier, Berlin's position has changed dramatically over the twentieth century, and the space of local politics has changed equally dramatically: in the 1920s Berlin was the site of major conflicts between left and right, in which the social-democratic left generally tended to have the upper hand; in the 1930s and early 1940s it was the capital of a centralized Nazism, which had ambitions to rule a wider Europe, was committed to removing all the local symbols of opposition, and planned to build a new city – Germania – on the site of the old; from the late 1940s local politics was redefined in terms which reflected the divisions of the Cold War (although, paradoxically, at least in West Berlin, this allowed and even encouraged the growth of a strong alternative politics, based around both younger 'radicals' and the local Turkish community); and since 1989 the city has been forced to look for a new role in the 'new' world emerging after the end of the Cold War – whether as world city, capital city or bridge between East and West.

A second question flows from this: how has Berlin's local politics influenced the direction of global change?

Historically, Berlin's role as a cultural centre in the 1920s clearly had wider resonances, which continue to find significant cultural echoes throughout Europe today, helping to provide symbols of Bohemianism and decadence, if only as expressed through images and representations like those supplied by the film of *Cabaret*. After 1945, the population helped to provide many of the symbols of resistance to communism which were so important in constructing the discourses of the Cold War (not just by being the inhabitants of a divided city, but by being a population whose survival first depended on an airlift and which went on regularly to provide martyrs seeking to escape from East to West, particularly after the building of the Berlin Wall – 'Checkpoint Charlie', spy swaps over the Glienicke Bridge and President Kennedy's claim to be a 'Berliner' were all part of this symbolism). More recently, the most powerful symbols of the *end* of the Cold War were provided in 1989 by the population of East and West Berlin coming together across the Wall and setting out to pull it down almost with their bare hands.

Berlin may seem to provide an extreme example of the ways in which local and global political spaces are related to each other, but a similar analysis could be constructed for most large cities – and, in principle, for much smaller towns and districts. You might usefully try to ask the same questions of places with which you are familiar: how have connections and flows across the globe helped to shape the context of local politics? How has local politics influenced the direction of global change? The second question is, perhaps, a little more difficult to answer than the first, but it is worth trying to pursue it – particularly with bigger cities.

Summary of section 6.3

o   One consequence of economic globalization seems to be that new or more developed forms of locally and regionally based political initiative are emerging, particularly in the arena of economic development and place marketing.

o   This implies an active process of reimagining particular places within a wider global marketplace and economic hierarchy of places, although the scope for this will vary significantly between places, and the rules according to which the process takes place may effectively be set by global corporations as much as by locally based political initiative.

o   Local social and political relations are not just the product of the ways in which global processes work themselves out in practice. On the contrary, they may help to shape and influence the global context.

o   'Local' interrelationships are not restricted to the boundaries of artificially constructed localities, but reflect an extensive set of overlapping interconnections which often stretch far across space, whether to the other end of the world or within particular countries, through powerful cultural as well as economic linkages.

o   The social meanings of places are contested and questioned directly and indirectly both within their own boundaries and through linkages, connections and flows which stretch far beyond them.

6.4   Uneven world: uneven response

The notion of globalization is one which lends itself to misleading characterizations which emphasize the extent of homogenization and the power of monolithic 'global' forces to shape everything else. It is easy to slip into a discussion in which what happens in particular places is simply the end result of the working through of these forces. Instead, it is necessary to locate them within a broader notion of uneven development – a more complex set of processes within which relationships help both to construct global frameworks and allow for the generation of activity, locally and regionally. This also makes it easier to question interpretations which predict the inevitable fragmentation or breaking up of an existing (or past) world order. A focus on uneven development both undermines the possibility of a world order being imposed from above and highlights the ways in which order is nevertheless maintained through networks of interdependence, interrelationship and interconnections.

In attempting to understand the present, it is necessary both to be able to identify the main trajectories of change, while at the same time holding onto its details at different spatial scales. It is important to do this not only because it helps us to gain a fuller picture of what is going on, but also – and more importantly – because the interconnections across and through these scales make it difficult to distinguish between them analytically. Globalization and localization are not the polar opposites which one might expect them to be. On the contrary, each is dependent on the other. Processes of globalization should not be read as necessarily implying homogenization, not least because there are many different contested and overlapping 'global worlds', as they are interpreted by different people, different groups and in different places through a range of geographical imaginations (see **Allen, 1995a**). Similarly, localization should not be taken necessarily to imply a fragmentation of social processes, not least because it is an important aspect of the redefining of the global context and the building of networks of linkages and connections which stretch across the world.

There is a danger that too sharp a focus on globalization and localization will leave one stuck with two extremes – the world at one end and the neighbourhood at the other – with nothing in between. Such a conclusion would be highly misleading. As the chapters of this volume suggest, the world is a much more complex place, with cross-cutting linkages, different forms of social and political institutions and different sets of social relations being important at different times. The chapters have discussed emergent global (worldwide) political arrangements, but it should also be apparent that the politics of macro-regional political groupings, of nation-states and of sub-state regions and 'nations' are also important. It is not the case that we all choose to live our lives either at the global or the local scale: on the contrary, cultural and political identifications are often focused on national or regional concerns. In the UK, for example, if voting in elections is any guide, then only Europe has a lower priority for the British electorate than local elections, while national elections continue to attract much greater involvement – more than twice as many people vote in national elections than in local elections.

It is, therefore, important not to be distracted by the arguments of globalization in ways which encourage us to ignore important continuities, nor to be seduced by the arguments of localization in ways which make it difficult to acknowledge the continued and, in some cases, emergent significance of regional and national political formations. But focusing on the global and local, as we have done in this chapter, is nevertheless helpful because it highlights in a sharp (and admittedly exaggerated) form some of the main directions of change which are likely to dominate our lives over the next decades. The extent to which traditional boundaries and borders are being undermined is apparent both in movements which celebrate the changes and, perhaps even more clearly, in movements which search for some way of returning to the old certainties. In the UK this is apparent in the disputes over Europe (and representations of Europe) which seem to divide first one and then another major political party. Elsewhere in Europe it is reflected in the rise of parties of the nationalist right and in the fragmentation of the former Yugoslavia and the former Soviet Union into uncertain components seeking to develop their own national definitions. At the same time, the growing importance of place-based competitive and entrepreneurial initiatives linking national, regional and local agencies is difficult to ignore. Every city wishes to become a global player, with the ritual of Olympic bids – from Berlin, Manchester, Beijing and Sydney for the year 2000 – being given an increasingly high profile as just one aspect of this. National governments are mobilized in support of their local candidates for prestigious projects, as the success of each country is increasingly defined in terms of the success of its national urban champions.

Globalization is underpinned by the realities of uneven development. Uneven global processes work themselves out in uneven ways and in turn are themselves shaped by local forms of unevenness. This is a continuing process of interaction which contains within it the promise that those processes will constantly be challenged and questioned. The predominant fear associated with globalization is that every aspect of difference is permanently under the threat of some great homogenizing force determined to bury all difference beneath a coating of bland similarity (which would also help to protect the powerful from scrutiny or challenge). Uneven development in an age of globalization, however, opens up different possibilities. It offers the promise of continually generating and regenerating oppositional cultures and alternative visions, locally and globally – not the end of geography, nor of history as Fukuyama (1992) predicted – but, as **Allen and Hamnett (1995, p. 253)** suggest, the promise of its continuation through the power of 'unevenness, diversity and difference reproduced through global relationships'.

References

AGNEW, J. (1994) 'The territorial trap: the geographical assumptions of international relations theory', *Review of International Political Economy*, Vol. 1, No. 1, pp. 53–80.

ALLEN, J. (1995a) 'Global worlds', in Allen and Massey (eds) (1995).

ALLEN, J. (1995b) 'Crossing borders: footloose multinationals?', in Allen and Hamnett (eds) (1995).

ALLEN, J. and HAMNETT, C. (1995) 'Uneven worlds', in Allen and Hamnett (eds) (1995).

ALLEN, J. and HAMNETT, C. (EDS) (1995) *A Shrinking World? Global Unevenness and Inequality*, Oxford, Oxford University Press in association with The Open University (Volume 2 in this series).

ALLEN, J. and MASSEY, D. (EDS) (1995) *Geographical Worlds*, Oxford, Oxford University Press in association with The Open University (Volume 1 in this series).

BENINGTON, J. (1994) *Local Democracy and the European Unions: the Impact of Europeanisations on Local Government*, London, Commission for Local Democracy.

COCHRANE, A. (1993) 'Looking for a European social policy', in Cochrane, A. and Clarke, J. (eds) *Comparing Welfare States: Britain in International Context*, London, Sage/The Open University.

COOKE, P. (1990) *Back to the Future*, London, Unwin Hyman.

COX, K. and MAIR, A. (1991) 'From localized social structures to localities as agents', *Environment and Planning A*, Vol. 23, No. 2, pp. 155–208.

CRAM, L. (1993) 'Calling the tune without paying the piper? Social policy regulation: the role of the Commission in European Community social policy', *Policy and Politics*, Vol. 21, No. 2, pp. 135–46.

DAVIS, M. (1993) 'Who killed Los Angeles? Part two: the verdict is given', *New Left Review*, Vol. 199, pp. 29–54.

DIRECTORATE GENERAL FOR REGIONAL POLICY (1991) *Europe 2000*, Luxembourg, Commission of the European Communities.

DUNCAN, S. and GOODWIN, M. (1988) *The Local State and Uneven Development*, Cambridge, Polity.

FUKUYAMA, F. (1992) *The End of History and the Last Man*, London, Hamish Hamilton.

GEERTZ, C. (1983) *Local Knowledge: Further Essays in Interpretive Anthropology*, New York, Basic Books.

GEORGE, N. (1992) *Buppies, B-Boys, Baps and Bohos: Notes on Post-Soul Black Culture*, New York, HarperCollins.

GILROY, P. (1993a) *The Black Atlantic: Modernity and Double Consciousness*, London, Verso.

GILROY, P. (1993b) *Small Acts: Thoughts on the Politics of Black Cultures*, London, Serpent's Tail.

GUPTA, A. and FERGUSON, J. (1992) 'Beyond "culture": space, identity, and the politics of difference', *Cultural Anthropology*, Vol. 7, pp. 6–23.

HALL, S. (1995) 'New cultures for old', in Massey and Jess (eds) (1995).

HAMNETT, C. (1995) 'Controlling space: global cities', in Allen and Hamnett (eds) (1995).

HARVEY, D. (1989) *The Condition of Postmodernity: An Enquiry into the Origins of Cultural Change*, Oxford, Blackwell.

JESSOP, B. (1994) 'From Keynesian welfare state to Schumpeterian workfare state', in Burrows, R. and Loader, B. (eds) *Towards a Post-Fordist Welfare State?*, London, Routledge.

KEARNS, G. and PHILO, C. (EDS) (1993) *Selling Places: The City as Cultural Capital, Past and Present*, Oxford, Pergamon.

MASSEY, D. (1995a) 'The conceptualization of place', in Massey and Jess (eds) (1995).

MASSEY, D. (1995b) 'Imagining the world', in Allen and Massey (eds) (1995).

MASSEY, D. and JESS, P. (1995) 'Places and cultures in an uneven world', in Massey and Jess (eds) (1995).

MASSEY, D. and JESS, P. (EDS) (1995) *A Place in the World? Places, Cultures and Globalization*, Oxford, Oxford University Press in association with The Open University (Volume 4 in this series).

MEEGAN, R. (1995) 'Local worlds', in Allen and Massey (eds) (1995).

ROSE, G. (1995) 'Place and identity: a sense of place', in Massey and Jess (eds) (1995).

SAID, E. (1978) *Orientalism. Western Conceptions of the Orient*, London, Routledge and Kegan Paul.

SARRE, P. (1995) 'Uneven development and sustainability', in Sarre, P. and Blunden, J. (eds) *An Overcrowded World? Population, Resources and the Environment*, Oxford, Oxford University Press in association with The Open University (Volume 3 in this series).

SASSEN, S. (1991) *The Global City*, Princeton, NJ, Princeton University Press.

SBRAGIA, A. (1992) *Euro-politics*, Washington, DC, Brookings Institute.

Acknowledgements

We have made every attempt to obtain permission to reproduce material in this book. Copyright holders of material which has not been acknowledged should contact the Rights Department at The Open University.

Grateful acknowledgement is made to the following sources for permission to reproduce material in this volume:

Text

Chapter 1: Boxes 1.1 and 1.2: *World Telecommunication Development Report 1994*, © 1994 International Telecommunication Union; *Reading C:* Agnew, J. (1994) 'The territorial trap: the geographical assumptions of international relations theory', in *Review of International Political Economy*, Vol. 1, No. 1, © Routledge 1994; *Reading D:* Camilleri, J.A. and Falk, J. (1992) *The End of Sovereignty?: The Politics of a Shrinking and Fragmenting World*, Edward Elgar Publishing Ltd, © Joseph A. Camilleri, Jim Falk 1992; *Reading E:* Camilleri, J.A. (1990) 'Rethinking sovereignty in a shrinking, fragmented world', from *Contending Sovereignties: Redefining Political Community*, edited by R.B.J. Walker and Saul Mendlovitz. Copyright © 1990 by Lynne Rienner Publishers, Inc. Reprinted with permission of the Publisher; *Chapter 2:* Gray, J. (1994) 'Against the world', *The Guardian*, 4 January 1994; *Readings A and B:* reprinted from *International Organization*, Vol. 47, No. 1, Ruggie, J.G. 'Territoriality and beyond: problematizing modernity in international relations', by permission of The MIT Press, Cambridge, Massachusetts and the World Peace Foundation, copyright © 1993 by the World Peace Foundation and the Massachusetts Institute of Technology; *Reading C:* 'Nation-states in Europe and other continents: diversifying, developing, not dying', reprinted by permission of *Daedalus*, Journal of the American Academy of Arts and Sciences, from the issue entitled, 'Reconstructing Nations and States', Summer 1993, Vol. 122, No. 3; *Chapter 3: Box 3.2:* Watts, D. (1993) 'Lobbying Europe', *Talking Politics*, Vol. 5, No. 2, The Politics Association; *Reading A:* Gibb, R. and Michalak, W. (1993) 'The European Community and Central Europe: prospects for integration', *Geography*, Vol. 78, Part 1, No. 338, The Geographical Association; *Reading B:* Ford, R.E. and Hudson, V.M. (1992) 'The USA and Latin America at the end of the Columbian age: how America "cut the Atlantic apron strings" in 1992', *Third World Quarterly*, Vol. 13, No. 3; *Reading C:* Crone, D. (1992) 'The politics of emerging Pacific co-operation', *Pacific Affairs*, Vol. 65, No. 1, copyright © 1992, University of British Columbia; *Chapter 4: Reading A:* from *Orientalism* by Edward W. Said. Copyright © 1978 by Edward W. Said. Reprinted by permission of Pantheon Books, a division of Random House, Inc. Also by permission of Routledge; *Reading B:* Halliday, F. (1992) *Arabs In Exile*, I.B. Tauris & Co. Ltd, © 1992 by Fred

Halliday; *Reading C:* Castles, S. and Miller, M.J. (1993) *The Age of Migration*, Macmillan Press Ltd, © Stephen Castles and Mark J. Miller 1993. Also by permission of Guilford Publications, Inc; *Reading D:* Williams, J.A. (1994) *The World of Islam*, Thames and Hudson Ltd. Copyright © 1994 by the University of Texas Press; *Reading E:* Beyer, P. (1994) *Religion and Globalization*, © Peter Beyer 1994, by permission of Sage Publications Ltd; *Reading F:* Esposito, J.L. (1992) *The Islamic Threat: Myth or Reality?* Copyright © 1992 by John L. Esposito. Reprinted by permission of Oxford University Press, Inc; *Chapter 5: Box 5.1:* Lean, G. (1993) 'Troubled waters', *The Observer Magazine*, 4 July 1993, © 1993 The Observer; *Reading B:* Middleton, N., O'Keefe, P. and Moyo, S. (1993) *Tears of the Crocodile: From Rio to Reality in the Developing World*, Pluto Press; *Reading E:* Rucht, D. (1993) 'Think globally, act locally? Needs, forms and problems of cross-national cooperation among environmental groups', in Liefferink, J.D., Lowe, P. and Mol, A.P.J. (eds) *European Integration and Environmental Policy*, © The editors and contributors 1993. Reprinted by permission of John Wiley & Sons, Ltd; *Reading G:* Grant, W. (1993) 'Transnational companies and environmental policy making: the trend of globalisation', in Liefferink, J.D., Lowe, P. and Mol, A.P.J. (eds) *European Integration and Environmental Policy*, © The editors and contributors 1993. Reprinted by permission of John Wiley & Sons, Ltd.

Figures

Figure 1.1: Kidron, M. and Smith, D. (1983) *The War Atlas: Armed Conflict–Armed Peace: A Pluto Press Project*, Pan Books Ltd, © Pluto Press Limited 1983; *Figure 1.2:* McGrew, A. (1992) 'Conceptualizing global politics', in McGrew, A. and Lewis, P. (eds) *Global Politics*, Polity Press; *Figure 1.3*: Short, J.R. (1993) *An Introduction to Political Geography*, 2nd edition, Routledge, © 1993 John Rennie Short; *Figure 1.5*: Nierop, T. (1994) *Systems and Regions in Global Politics*, John Wiley & Sons Ltd. Reprinted by permission of John Wiley & Sons Ltd; *Figure 2.2:* Aitchison, J. and Carter, H. (1994) *A Geography of the Welsh Language 1961–1991*, University of Wales Press, © John Aitchison and Harold Carter, 1994; *Figure 3.1:* Evans, R. (1995) 'Brave new world order', *Geographical*, Vol. LXVII, No. 1, illustration © Michael Roscoe; *Figure 3.2:* adapted from Dicken, P. (1986) *Global Shift*, Paul Chapman Publishing Ltd, ©

Index